GEORGE IV

Also in the Yale English Monarchs series

Edward the Confessor by Frank Barlow*
William the Conqueror by David C. Douglas*
William Rufus by Frank Barlow
Henry II by W.L. Warren
Richard I by John Gillingham
King John by W.L. Warren*
Richard II by Nigel Saul
Edward I by Michael Prestwich
Henry V by Christopher Allmand*
Edward IV by Charles Ross
Richard III by Charles Ross*
Henry VII by S.B. Chrimes
Henry VIII by J.J. Scarisbrick*
Edward VI by Jennifer Loach
James II by John Miller

*Available in the U.S. from University of California Press

GEORGE IV

E.A. Smith

YALE UNIVERSITY PRESS
NEW HAVEN AND LONDON

For Virginia

Set in New Baskerville by Best-set Typesetter Ltd, Hong Kong
Printed in Great Britain by St Edmundsbury Press

Library of Congress Cataloging-in-Publication Data
Smith, E.A.
George IV/E.A. Smith.
(Yale English monarchs)
Includes bibliographical references and index.
ISBN 0–300–07685–1 (hbk.)
ISBN 0–300–08802–7 (pbk.)
1. George IV, King of Great Britain, 1762–1830. 2. Great Britain – History – George III. 1760–1820. 3. Great Britain – History – George IV. 1820–1830. 4. Great Britain – Kings and rulers – Biography. 5. Regency – Great Britain. I. Title. II. Title: George the 4th. III. Title: George the Fourth. IV. Series.
DA538.A1S6 1999
941.07′4′092 – dc21
[b]
98–46868
CIP

A catalogue record for this book is available from the British Library.

10 9 8 7 6 5 4 3 2

CONTENTS

ILLUSTRATIONS

PREFACE

There have been several biographies of King George IV. The fullest and most detailed is the two-volume work of Christopher Hibbert, published in 1972–3. This is an attractively written and thoroughly researched book, but it is a personal biography rather than a work of political analysis and it does not fully evaluate its subject's role and importance in the political world of his time, and his place in the evolution of monarchical government. Joanna Richardson's *George IV, a Portrait* (1966) is also attractively written, and on the artistic achievements and interests of its subject it is unsurpassed, but it too neglects the political dimension. Roger Fulford's biography (rev. edn 1949) is more balanced but it is relatively short and selective in its treatment, especially on the political side. The earliest writer was Robert Huish in 1831, who set the tone for the prevailing nineteenth-century view of George IV as a libertine unworthy of serious political study. This view was confirmed by Thackeray whose biased and censorious essay in *The Four Georges* (1855) created a monster of profligacy and incompetence. More serious and scholarly authors included Shane Leslie (1926), P.W. Sergeant (1935) who concentrated on the years before 1820, J.H. Plumb in *The First Four Georges* (1956) and J.B. Priestley (on the Regency) (1969). All have merits but all are to some degree superficial, and most follow the view that George IV was a dissolute, pleasure-loving dilettante and a feeble, ineffective monarch who dissipated the popularity of the throne created by his father, allowed the constitutional power of the crown to be eroded by unscrupulous politicians, and brought the royal family into a disrepute from which it was rescued only by the virtuous reign of his niece Victoria and her husband Prince Albert. Even the late Arthur Aspinall, whose impeccable and scholarly editions of the correspondence of George III and IV are among the indispensable printed sources for the political history of the later eighteenth and early nineteenth centuries, took an equally censorious view of George IV as Prince, Regent and King, stressing his weaknesses of character, his self-indulgence and neglect of the duties of his position, and his supposed incompetence in affairs of state. George IV has come to be the traditional scapegoat for the decline of the power and reputation of the crown in the last years of the old, unreformed constitution of Great Britain before it was reinvigorated by the Great Reform Act and its consequences.

There were contemporary precedents for this judgement. George and his ministers after 1810 were accused of indifference towards the sufferings of the country in time of war and financial stringency and of supporting the repressive regimes of European despots abroad in opposition to Napoleon and the cause of 'liberty all over the world' – the favourite whig toast of Fox's day. George was pilloried in the radical press, which grew more outspoken than ever during and after the wartime years as its favourite panacea for all ills, parliamentary reform, was blocked by the resistance of the old élite, who were alleged to maintain themselves in power by a system of corruption in which the crown was a willing partner. Their identification with the monarch was completed by the alleged treatment of George's wife, Queen Caroline, who was perceived as the victim of George's personal vendetta and the symbol of the injustices inherent in the whole system of privilege. She became the short-lived but intensely damaging focal point for criticism of the political establishment as a whole. The increasingly wealthy and influential commercial and professional classes were attracted to radical politics as an affirmation of the growing importance of trade and industry against agriculture and the landed sector of society, and they regarded George IV as a symbol of the age of aristocratic decadence which they sought to end. For all these reasons George grew more unpopular with his subjects, especially in London, the commercial capital of the nation and the centre of political radicalism. Added to this was the resentment felt by his former friends, the self-styled 'Whigs', at his supposed desertion of them and his apostasy from the old connection with Fox and his companions. His support of their rivals, now coming to be called 'Tories', was attributed to the influence of his new mistress, Lady Hertford, and her family, who were alleged to have drawn him away in particular from the cause of Catholic emancipation, which was now the cornerstone of whig political identity. Radical attacks were now supplemented by the spiteful personal criticisms of such whig partisans as Thomas Creevey, the diarist, and poets and literary men including Shelley, notorious for the phrase 'Swellfoot the tyrant', Byron, who condemned George's treatment of his daughter Princess Charlotte, and Leigh Hunt, who was imprisoned for libelling him in a famous passage as a reprobate, libertine and adulterer. In such hands George was portrayed as the most despised monarch in modern British history.

This study attempts to take a more balanced view. George's faults were many, but his good points were rarely appreciated. His youthful escapades were chiefly embarked upon in order to spite his father, in reaction against the discipline with which George III sought to model his heir as a worthy successor in the self-imposed battle against the vice and immorality of the times. These adventures laid the foundation of George's lifelong reputation as a libertine who cared only for worldly pleasures rather than duty towards his country, and this was confirmed by the association with Charles James Fox, one of the most dissolute men of his age and, in the eyes of George III, a traitor to his country as well as a despiser of all moral principle. George by association with the Foxite party appeared to support their programme of political reform and the cause of 'liberty all over the world', but when in his middle years he came to political responsibility as Regent, and later as King, he abandoned these ideals and attempted to behave responsibly, to support ministers with experience in government and commitment to the national interest in the war against France. His former allies gave him no credit for it but it cannot seriously be contended that he acted otherwise than from a sense of patriotic duty. After the war was over, George did show sympathy for the plight of the poor and unemployed, but in accordance with the prevailing theories of the time he believed that governments could do little to relieve distress in face of the natural order of things. Governments were not entirely heartless – poor relief expenditure rose to unprecedented heights in the post-war years – but solutions to the problem were not easy to come by.

In private life – in so far as a monarch was allowed to have one – George could be selfish and inconsiderate but he was also often kind and generous to his friends and towards those who served him well, and he even tried to relieve his estranged wife Caroline from her debts, despite his own financial difficulties. His relationship with Maria Fitzherbert showed him for a time in the best light, although it was always precarious and in the end it broke up in circumstances which did him little credit. His legal marriage to Princess Caroline was a disaster from the start, but she bore some responsibility for their failure to agree and her later history showed what an unsuitable partner she was for such a fastidious husband. Though George became notorious for his mistresses, he was seeking companionship which his marriage could not give him rather than gratifying a sexual appetite which seems to have declined as his life went on. Towards children too he was fond and affectionate, though he was like his father in his inability to construct a close relationship with his own offspring. Above all, George IV was a knowledgeable and discriminating patron of the arts, interested in literature, poetry, painting and above all in architecture. His sense of style in all these spheres marks him out as the most distinguished of all modern monarchs in aesthetic matters and it is in this respect that he has left the most permanent memorials of his life.

That is not the end of George IV's achievements. This study attempts to show that previous critics of his political role as king have given him less than his due. Far from being the most disastrous monarch of modern times, he appears as an important figure in the preservation of the status and constitutional importance of the Crown in British politics. It is true that during his reign the 'influence of the crown' in terms of its ability to dominate the executive and to control the actions and composition of parliament was steadily declining, but that was less the result of royal deficiencies than of external circumstances. George III could not have stemmed this tide any more than his son was able to. What George IV did achieve was to preserve for the crown a role in the political governance of the nation at a time when that role could easily have been reduced to a cipher. Victoria and Albert may well have accepted the diminution of the royal function to a purely advisory one, as Walter Bagehot famously suggested: George IV however deserves credit for its survival, and for its enduring relevance to British politics.

NOTE ON PARTY NAMES

'Party' was a controversial term in the later eighteenth century, when politics was regarded as an activity restricted to the King's ministers and their supporters on the one hand, and to the ordinary Members of Parliament on the other, who were elected to represent the people in general and their own constituents in particular, but not to contest for power, which was in the sole gift of the sovereign. It was the patriotic duty of MPs to support the King's ministers unless their actions contravened the national interest. This view was now becoming outdated. Since the Revolution of 1688–9, which greatly increased the importance of Parliament, politicians who served the Crown had to build up a party of supporters in both Houses, and those who were excluded tended to form groups of their own, usually under the leadership of political figures who sought by means of this pressure to force the King to give them office, either as replacements for the current ministers or in association with them. These groups, often disparaged as 'factions', usually took the names of their leaders, being called 'Chathamites' or 'Rockinghamites', for example. By the second half of the century, however, and especially after George III attempted to enforce the older view that all honest men ought to support the King's chosen servants, and refused to employ men of whom he disapproved on either political or moral grounds, those excluded from power increasingly sought to justify their opposition by appealing to a political principle. They argued that the King and his ministers were seeking a monopoly of power for their own ends, and neglecting the true interests of the country. Furthermore, they claimed that only they themselves were to be trusted with those interests and that in serving them they looked back to the 'Glorious Revolution' and its label of 'Whig'. Thus arose the self-styled 'Whig party' of the later years of the century.

In this work, the adjective 'whig' with a small 'w' is taken to signify a general set of political principles; 'Whig' with a capital letter refers to the party, principally associated with Charles Fox and his successors in opposition to George III. The terms 'tory' and 'Tory' came into use much later, to refer to those who supported the King's government, and after 1810 especially those who supported the royal refusal to concede religious equality to Roman Catholics. Not until the 1820s can politicians normally be designated 'Tories' whereas 'Whigs' may be used to label those who saw themselves as a party in opposition to the King's ministers from at least 1782.

ACKNOWLEDGEMENTS

I have to acknowledge the gracious permission of Her Majesty the Queen to consult and to work in the Royal Archives at Windsor, and to quote from both the original records relating to George IV and other members of the Royal Family, and from those printed by the late Professor Aspinall in his editions of the later correspondence of George III, the correspondence of George IV as Prince of Wales, Regent, and King, and the letters of Princess Charlotte. I am most grateful to Lady de Bellaigue, the Registrar of the Royal Archives, and her staff for much advice and unstinting assistance in my research, and not least for the uniformly pleasant coffee breaks in their common room every morning. I am also grateful to Sir Geoffrey de Bellaigue, formerly Director of the Royal Collection and Surveyor of the Queen's Works of Art, for advice on George IV's artistic activities and for reading my chapter on that subject. Lady de Bellaigue and Mr Oliver Everett, the Deputy Keeper of the Royal Archives, kindly read through my typescript and corrected many mistakes and misunderstandings: any that remain are my own. Finally, I thank Dr Robert Baldock and Miss Candida Brazil of the Yale University Press for the efficiency and good humour with which they turned my manuscript into a book.

My principal academic debt must be to the late Arthur Aspinall, whose department at Reading University I joined in 1951 and who gave me endless encouragement in my various research projects. He drew me in a small way into his own work on the royal correspondence and first introduced me to the Royal Archives, to which I returned after his death. Doubtless he would have disapproved of some of my ideas about George IV but, such as it is, I offer my present work as a small tribute to his memory.

I am grateful to the owners and keepers of the MS sources named in the bibliography to this book, and I owe a debt to several previous writers on the subject for the enlightenment and stimulus which their works have provided. Lastly but by no means least, I am beholden to my severest critic, my wife, for her constant watchfulness and perceptive interest which have guided me through many problems in the writing of this book, which I dedicate to her.

NOTE ON ABBREVIATIONS AND REFERENCES

The following abbreviations are used to refer to sources in the footnotes:

Arbuthnot	F. Bamford and the Duke of Wellington (eds), *The Journal of Mrs Arbuthnot, 1820–1832*. 2 vols. 1950
CGPW	A. Aspinall (ed.), *The Correspondence of George, Prince of Wales, 1770–1812*. 8 vols. 1963–71
DCM	Duke of Wellington (ed.), *Despatches, Correspondence and Memoranda of... the Duke of Wellington, 1819–32*. 8 vols. 1867–80
LCG3	A. Aspinall (ed.), *The Later Correspondence of George III, 1783–1810*. 5 vols. Cambridge 1962–70
LG4	A. Aspinall (ed.), *The Letters of King George IV, 1812–1830*. 3 vols. Cambridge 1938
RA	Royal Archives, Windsor Castle

References to material in these volumes are by page numbers, not document numbers.

Full bibliographical details of printed sources are given in the bibliography on pp. 293–300. For greater ease of reference, documents which have been published in print are referred to in their published versions rather than by their location in MS archives. After the first reference to printed works their titles may be abbreviated, or they may be referred to simply by their authors' or editors' names.

In the case of material in the Royal Archives which has not been published, the documents are referred to by their archive classes and numbers, preceded by 'RA'.

Chapter 1

A PRINCE AND HIS EDUCATION

At 7.30 in the evening of 12 August 1762, in the royal apartments in St James's Palace, the young Queen Charlotte, wife of King George III since the previous September and aged only eighteen, was delivered of a son. He was the first of what were to be fifteen children in twenty-one years, and the first to be born to a reigning monarch since the unfortunate example of James 'III', the Old Pretender, in 1688, whose parentage was alleged to be spurious in order to justify his exclusion from the royal succession after the 'Glorious Revolution'. Since that event it had been laid down that the birth of any child to a reigning queen was to be witnessed and authenticated by a number of high officers of state and members of the royal household, and as this was the first such occasion when a reigning consort had given birth to a child in England it was the first in which the procedure was adopted. To spare the embarrassment of all concerned, the numerous group of 'witnesses', which included the Archbishop of Canterbury, the Princess Dowager of Wales (the child's grandmother), two dukes, seven lords, and all the ladies of the royal bedchamber and maids of honour, were stationed in an adjoining room with the door into the Queen's bedchamber left open. The royal husband and father, as was the custom in those days, was not required to be present and he awaited the news elsewhere in the palace, having arranged for a messenger to be sent immediately after the birth to bring him the details, with the promise of a reward of £1,000 if the child was a boy, or £500 if it was female. The confusion which seems typically to have pervaded the royal court at this period was in full operation: the Earl of Huntingdon, the chosen messenger, must have been short-sighted, for he told the King that the child was a daughter. The King declared his indifference to the sex of the child so long as the Queen was well, though possibly his parsimonious soul was well enough pleased to have saved £500. It is not recorded whether he paid the difference when he went to see for himself and discovered a male heir to his throne.

Five days later the baby Prince, to be named George Augustus Frederick, was given the titles of Prince of Wales and Earl of Chester, and a week later he was exhibited to the public view at St James's for periods of two hours on the next six drawing-room days. The facility was so much appreciated that fashionable people in successive groups of up to forty in number crowded the room to see the baby in his cot behind a screen or on the lap of his wet-nurse, and the consumption of the refreshments provided, in the traditional shape of cake and caudle, a mixture of eggs and wine, was prodigious. It was said that 500 lb. of cake and 8 gallons of caudle were consumed every day. The daily expense for cake alone amounted to £40.[1]

The Queen too was delighted with her first child, and she had a life-size model made of him in wax lying naked on a cushion which she kept under a bell-glass in her apartments at Buckingham House, known at this period as the Queen's House because her husband had bought it for her the previous year. The young Prince was also provided with a governess, Lady Charlotte Finch, who was to preside over the nursery of all the royal children for thirty years and who was affectionately known to them as 'Lady Cha'. A more constant presence than their parents in an age when aristocratic children saw them only on special occasions, she provided much of the adult company the royal children enjoyed. There was also a sub-governess, and wet- and dry-nurses and other necessary attendants. Both parents were devoted to their children when they were young, but as they grew up the strains of parenthood were to become too great and they found that high-spirited youngsters were much more taxing than docile babies. George III had been an affectionate and obedient child, dominated by his parents: he was to discover that his own offspring were less amenable.[2]

The royal infant was christened on 18 September by the Archbishop of Canterbury, Thomas Secker, and he was later inoculated against the smallpox, a proceeding still considered a novelty, especially at so young an age and, before Jenner's discovery of vaccination over thirty years later, not without its dangers. In this respect at least the King and Queen showed themselves to be 'modern' parents, patronizing the latest ideas in bringing up children. Their ambition also to be model parents was less easy to achieve, and soon became a source of frustration rather than delight.

The royal court at this period was indeed intended to be a predominantly domestic place, rather than the busy, highly ritualized courts of continental Europe which were thronged by courtiers, politicians and supplicants. Both George III and Charlotte disliked elaborate ceremo-

[1] Accounts of the prince's birth are given in earlier biographies such as R. Huish, *Memoirs of George IV* (2 vols., 1831); Shane Leslie, *George the Fourth* (1926); P.W. Sergeant, *George, Prince and Regent* (1935); R. Fulford, *George the Fourth* (rev. edn. 1949); Joanna Richardson. *George IV, a Portrait* (1966); C. Hibbert, *George IV* (2 vols. 1972–3) and others. The principal contemporary account is that of Charlotte Papendiek in V. Delves Broughton (ed.), *Court and Private Life in the Time of Queen Charlotte, being the Journals of Mrs Papendiek* (2 vols. 1887).

[2] Lives of *King George III* by John Brooke and by Stanley Ayling.

nial and preferred a quiet and homely existence, more like that of the wealthy commercial classes than the great aristocracies of Europe, or even of Britain. By temperament as well as inclination they chose to retreat from public show into a private family environment. Both feared contamination from what they considered the immorality and irresponsibility of high society, and saw it as their duty to uphold and disseminate moral and religious standards of behaviour – even more so than did their later grandchild, Victoria. The term 'Victorian values' is a misnomer: they derived chiefly from King George III and Queen Charlotte. The King too had a strong distaste for extravagance and luxury in any form, although he did spend considerable sums in building up his collection of some 63,000 books, now the King's Library in the British Library, in adding to the Royal Collection of old master drawings and watercolours, and on the purchase, alteration and furnishing of the Queen's House (later renamed Buckingham Palace by George IV) as a town residence, where his library was housed. The decoration of the Queen's House was in the latest style, witnessing the fact that in their younger days the King and Queen were among the leaders of fashion as well as forward-looking parents. Their eldest son was to far surpass his father as a patron of the arts and scholarship, and certainly in extravagance in the role, but the interest at any rate was a legacy from his father. George III, however, set himself strict limits on his expenditure and this restricted his activities on this account, no doubt adding a keen edge to his censure of his son's excesses. He considered it his duty, and that of his children (who were to prove less conscious of it), to avoid placing financial burdens on his subjects and to live as cheaply as possible. He dressed simply, as a country gentleman rather than a royal personage, ate and drank abstemiously (partly from fear of the corpulency which afflicted some of the Hanoverian family) and took his pleasures – in music and literature – as a private individual.

To the habitués of the great aristocratic houses and salons in the town and the country, the court seemed a dull and inexpressibly boring institution at which attendance, so essential to the nobility of other states, was to be avoided unless absolutely necessary. In any case, Parliament was the centre of political life and power, and since the 'Glorious Revolution' prominence there was the key to public eminence and the focus of ambition for the political class. The court had become little more than the private preserve of the royal family in the narrower sense of that word, and apart from the politically and socially necessary regular weekly drawing rooms and levees – and those less brilliant than in the past – it provided a domestic setting for a king who preferred to meet his ordinary subjects rather than shine amongst his nobility as a model of fashion and ostentation. George III was in any case nervous in society so his conversation tended to be staccato and rather banal, and the Queen, whose English was still a trifle hesitant, did not enjoy formal occasions. Etiquette remained stiff, partly as a consequence of fear of informality, and although attendance by the leading politicians and office-holders was *de rigueur*, in full court dress or, later, in what George III himself designed, the 'Windsor uniform' of blue coat with red facings and cuffs, conversation was usually concerned with private matters and personal gossip rather than affairs of state.

The social side of the court diminished in importance after 1770 with the rise of the new society hostesses. The salons of Devonshire House and other leading London noble palaces became the resort of the fashionable *ton*, whose luxurious tastes, dissolute habits and free language could not commend themselves to a puritanical King and Queen. The rage for gambling in particular was anathema to George and Charlotte. Fortunes were won and lost at faro banks, whist, and other card games in private houses as well as on the racetrack and in the betting books at the principal gentlemen's clubs. The dashing young blades of London society scoffed at the piety and dullness of the court, preferring the theatres, gambling clubs, brothels and other places of fashionable resort. The young princes of the Royal Family as they grew up were attracted to these more exciting pleasures and came to resent the boredom of the court and the strictness of their parents. They looked enviously and rebelliously at the glittering world outside, and courted the temptations they discovered there.[3]

The royal parents did indeed take a heavy-handed attitude towards religion, morality and education, all of which were provided in quantity for their children. Both King and Queen were devoted to their genuinely pious religious faith and constantly exhorted their offspring to obey its precepts. The King's prayer on the eve of his marriage, that God would 'make her fruitful', was certainly answered in full measure, to the embarrassment of his belief in household economy: he constantly reminded his children, who perhaps inevitably tended to extravagance, that his means were limited and that they must live within strict bounds of expenditure. Failure to do so was a moral as well as an economic defect. A tribe of young saints would have been tried by this parental insistence, and the royal princes and princesses were far from that. It was indeed counterproductive, for if any characteristic appeared dominant in the natures of at least the elder sons it was a tendency to rebellion against parental authority and a determined pursuit of self-gratification at almost all costs. What Horace Walpole called 'the palace of piety' had little appeal to George Augustus and his nearest brother

[3] Marjorie Villiers, *The Grand Whiggery*, 13–14. The chief London salons were those of the Duchess of Devonshire, Mrs Crewe, and Mrs Bouverie on the whig side, and the Duchesses of Gordon and Rutland and Lady Salisbury for the tories: W. Sichel, *Sheridan*, 163.

Prince Frederick, who soon became bosom companions in league against parental repression.[4]

From his earliest years the young Prince of Wales was the target of moral lectures from both his parents. Oppressed by his belief that the times were vicious and unprincipled, as exemplified by the corrupt politicians he had to employ to govern, George III possessed an almost pathological sense of duty and responsibility toward his subjects. In his anxiety to instil these virtues into the heir to his throne, the King went some way towards suppressing them in his son. From his early childhood, the Prince experienced contradictory treatment by his father. The King loved his children with an affection that was possessive, overprotective and no doubt stifling to a high-spirited boy. George complained that he was kept in baby-clothes long after his contemporaries were more suitably dressed. He was made to wear a cambric frock with lace collar and cuffs, and later in his childhood he and his brother Frederick were often dressed up in exotic costumes, sometimes as Roman soldiers, at the whim of their young mother who had been introduced to the theatre by her husband and had become enraptured by this, to her, new entertainment. She announced her determination to go once a week, and sometimes went even more often. Her eldest son inherited something of this fascination with the theatrical. Lady Sarah Lennox remarked when he was five years old that he had become 'the proudest little imp you ever saw'.[5] He loved to poke fun at the formality and artificiality of court life and etiquette, and developed a considerable talent for mimicry of those around him. On one occasion he is said to have crept up to the door of his father's study and bellowed 'Wilkes and Liberty!' through the keyhole.

The King's response to these high spirits was to modern eyes at variance with the love he repeatedly professed for his children. Any signs of laziness or misconduct were visited with severe physical punishment in order to inculcate industry, good manners, truthfulness and punctuality, all of which he considered to be lacking in his eldest son. Punishment was even administered in the presence of his sisters. The King's affection was heavy-handed and conditional on good behaviour: all too often his son felt that it was repressive rather than affectionate. The Queen too found it difficult to understand and relate to her sons, and over-compensated by lavishing her attention on her daughters, who were to feel throughout their mother's life dominated and repressed by her. In later life they showed greater love for their father, accusing her of lack of maternal feeling. Just as her overbearing attitude alienated her daughters and made them favour their father, so the

[4] Horace Walpole, *Last Journals*, ii, 405.
[5] Claire Tomalin, *Mrs Jordan's Profession*, 12–15.

King's repressive conduct towards his sons turned their affection towards their mother. She and her eldest son in particular were drawn together by a lifelong if not always consistent bond. She was supportive in his later marital troubles and when she died in 1818 he was holding her hand.

From their earliest days, the royal children were taught the duty they owed to their parents and the necessity of keeping up the ceremonial at court. When George was barely two years old he and his brother were brought into the drawing room at St James's to receive company on the anniversaries of their father's succession, dressed in 'Jammers [drawers] of White and Gold Brocade, with Gold Sashes', and on the Queen's birthday in January 1765 they appeared at the drawing room and at the court ball in the evening in 'rich blue and silver jammers, with new point lace tuckers and cuffs, diamonds round their tuckers and diamond belts and the Prince of Wales had diamond buttons down his petticoat'. On St David's Day that year the young Prince received a deputation from the (Welsh) Society of Ancient Britons, each of the three delegates wearing three ostrich feathers in his hat, with the Prince's motto. He 'spoke a short answer' to them and handed over, through Lady Charlotte Finch, a purse containing 100 guineas for the Welsh charity school on Clerkenwell Green. A month later George was put into breeches and on the King's birthday in June appeared in a suit of 'silver stuff with small purple and green flowers, a diamond button in his hat and point lace ruffles'. The following day he attended a fête at Northumberland House, where the garden was illuminated and several bands played. In the middle was a temple of painted canvas with a light inside, in honour of his parents' marriage and his birth. A year later he was allowed to let off fireworks, and on his birthday he 'danced a Hornpipe in Sailor's Dress', Frederick appearing as Harlequin.[6]

These frivolities did not survive long into George's schooldays. On his eighth birthday the curtain descended. The Queen sent him a letter of good advice, to be read aloud to him by Lady Charlotte Finch, so that he could not pretend not to have taken it in. The Prince was about to be introduced to the second stage of his education: he would leave the nursery and be placed under the tutelage of his first governor, to study what his mother called 'more manly learning than what you have done hitherto'. He was abjured to fear God as his first and supreme duty, to abhor all vice, disdain all flattery, avoid partiality, love and esteem all about him, treat nobody with contempt, be charitable to all, even his 'meaner servants', and finally to treat his father with 'the highest love, affection and duty' and regard him as 'the greatest, the best, and the most deserving of all friends you can possibly find'. He was also to love

[6] Diary of Lady Charlotte Finch: RA Add. Geo. 21.

his brothers and sisters. This comprehensive if somewhat conventional advice was acknowledged by a brief assurance written 'in a very childish hand' that 'I will always endeavour to follow the good advice you give me'.[7] Time was to tell.

The Prince's education began in earnest in 1771 when Lord Holdernesse, a former Lord of the Bedchamber to George II and Secretary of State in the 1750s, was appointed as his governor, with Leonard Smelt as sub-governor, Dr Markham, the Bishop of Chester, as Preceptor and the Revd Cyril Jackson as sub-Preceptor. The regime, strictly supervised by the King, was designed to ensure that the devil would never find idle hands to do his work. George and Frederick, who were now constant companions, rose at six and began lessons at 7 a.m. Two hours in the schoolroom were followed by breakfast with their parents promptly at nine. Refreshed by tea and dry toast, they returned to lessons for a further two or three hours, after which they took exercise by walking in the gardens, in preparation for dinner at three o'clock. The main meal of the day was nourishing without being lavish: soup 'when not very strong or heavy', followed by 'plain meat without fat, clear gravy and greens', or fish 'without butter'. Dessert was 'the fruit of a tart without crust' and on Thursdays and Saturdays the special treat of an ice of whatever flavour they preferred. A glass of wine was allowed to end the meal, with coffee twice a week. The contrast with the rich, gargantuan meals in which the adult Prince was to indulge could not be more extreme: here again George III only succeeded in creating the appetites he strove to suppress.

Dinner was followed by more outdoor activities – games, particularly cricket and football, or work on a model farm where the elder princes were expected to cultivate a strip of land in imitation of, but without the royal enthusiasm for, the King's agricultural hobby. The King sometimes supervised with a watering-can in hand. At five the family met in their parents' apartments for reading, writing or 'improving conversation' until bedtime at 6.30 after a light supper.

This family routine continued after 1772 at Kew, the King and Queen's favourite residence, where they lived a remarkably ordinary life. The White House was the royal residence, and after 1773 young George and Frederick were given their own establishment at the Dutch House opposite their parents. The other sons in turn were boarded out at houses round the Green. The public were not kept away from the area and large numbers often gathered on Sundays to watch the royal family in crocodile, the King striding at their head, taking their exercise on the lawns, providing a spectacle of 'Royalty living among their subjects to give pleasure and to do good', as Mrs Papendiek, daughter

[7] Queen to George, 12 Aug. 1770: *CGPW*, i, 5–6.

of one of the courtiers, remembered fifty years later. Kew became 'quite gay', she recollected, and the Green was often covered with the carriages of parties come to see the family; others arrived by water, complete with bands of music.[8] The impression made by the young princes was a favourable one. Miss Planta who was their 'tutoress and teacher of English' under Lady Cha, remarked that George was 'a fine boy, has an open countenance, a manly air, & you may read his high birth in his looks; he possesses the most obliging politeness, such as can only spring from goodness of heart, & by the accounts I hear, he is most amiable and good'.[9]

Occasionally the family moved up to Buckingham House or to St James's Palace, where the King performed his public duties. The princes were required to attend the weekly drawing rooms on Thursdays during the 'season', when the leading families and officers of state were in town for the Parliamentary sessions, and after they were ten years old to be present at the evening card and music parties which were their parents' chief diversions at Kew and Windsor. These were so boring that, despite not being allowed to sit down, they sometimes fell asleep standing behind the Queen's chair. At other times, Mrs Papendiek disapprovingly recorded, 'Some of those about the young Princes . . . introduced improper company when their Majesties supposed them to be at rest, and after the divines had closed their day with prayer'.[10] This was to be a more agreeable precedent for the future than the usual life of the royal family.

The educational syllabus devised for the elder princes was extensive on paper but probably not very deep, and not wholly successful, though George was an intelligent and perceptive pupil. Languages – French, German and Italian, with Greek and Latin authors as a foundation for classical studies – were supplemented by mathematics, history and government, religion and morals, 'natural philosophy', or elementary science, and a limited diet of approved English authors – Shakespeare, Milton and Pope being those considered worthy of attention. Music, drawing and fencing were added as necessary 'polite accomplishments'. The Court in those days was a place of some culture. The King was especially fond of Handel and throughout his life the royal couple regularly attended the concerts of 'Ancient Music' – which meant chiefly in the classical Handelian mode. His eldest son not only inherited his father's musical taste, but showed considerable talent as a performer on the keyboard under the tuition of Johann Christian, 'the

[8] Delves Broughton, Papendiek, i, 61, 77–8, 94.
[9] RA, Queen Victoria papers Y.171/81, n.d.
[10] Delves Broughton, Papendiek, i, 91–2.

English Bach', son of the great Johann Sebastian, and Sir William Parsons, the master of the King's Band. George took lessons on the cello from John Crosdill and played with skill and feeling. He developed a fine baritone voice and was always fond of singing rounds and other songs at musical parties.

The chief purpose of his education in his father's eyes, however, was to inculcate a sense of Christian duty and personal morality and piety. At the age of thirteen he was copying into his writing book lines from Thomson's 'Address to the Deity', exhorting the Almighty to 'Save me from folly, vanity, and vice / From every low pursuit! And feed my soul / With knowledge, conscious peace and virtue poor.' He copied the passage four times, either to perfect his handwriting or, more likely, to make sure that he did not forget the sentiments. There followed extracts of an improving nature from Fénelon's *Télémaque*, Seed's sermons, and other sources, and a passage praising history as 'a School of morality for all men', demonstrating 'that there is nothing great and commendable, but honour and probity'.[11] These exercises in the conventional thinking of the time probably did little to form his character but in later life he showed a remarkable breadth and depth of intellectual understanding which enabled him to converse knowledgeably and effectively with men of distinction in many separate spheres.

These future talents were not so obvious at the time of his education. Holdernesse assured his royal charges at the outset that 'the pride of my heart and the wish of my heart is your Royal Highnesses' welfare and happiness' and that 'the path of virtue is the road to both'. Clearly, however, he soon came to recognize the limitations which his own deficiencies and the princes' characters were to place on his success. In May 1772, on the first anniversary of his appointment, he wrote to say that while he saw 'a fair year's improvement' in their progress, yet 'still much is to be done' and 'if you do not turn out those amiable Princes nature intended you to be, I shall and perhaps I ought to be blamed'.[12] This appeal to his pupils' co-operation seems to have been ineffective, bearing out the criticism of some observers that Holdernesse was not entirely adequate to his duties. Horace Walpole, waspish as ever, called him 'that formal piece of dulness' and alleged that at ten years old George was 'very ungovernable'.[13] Two years later Holdernesse declared that though his charges were improving, there were 'some little faults arising from want of thought' which made him liable to be misunderstood. He later added that he did not wish to seem merely 'a

[11] RA Add. Geo. 3/1.
[12] Holdernesse to George, 15 Sept. 1771 and 3 May 1772: *CGPW*, i, 7–8.
[13] Walpole, *Last Journals*, i, 125–6.

censor of small blemishes' and while no doubt he gave the princes much good advice, they hardly suffered from a shortage of that commodity from their parents.[14]

George seems to have been fond of Holdernesse as an individual, but he was largely ineffective as a governor and when he fell ill in 1774 and had to go abroad his regime soon collapsed. His subordinates were said to have taken the opportunity of his absence to prejudice the princes against him. Rumours must have reached Holdernesse at Montpellier, whence he wrote to warn them to be on guard against 'that most deadly of all [poison], which is poured in at the ear'.[15] Walpole asserted that when he returned to England in the autumn of 1775 they 'treated his authority with contempt, and often ridiculed him to his face.' Holdernesse blamed Jackson for turning the princes against him and resigned his post in May 1776. Smelt and Jackson also left their posts, to be succeeded by Lieutenant-Colonel George Hotham and the Revd William Arnold respectively. All the Prince of Wales's household was changed, one of his French tutors reportedly blaming his 'ungovernable temper'. Thomas Bruce-Brudenell, Earl of Ailesbury, was now appointed the Princes' governor but almost immediately threw up the office without any explanation and was replaced by his eldest brother, George, Duke of Montagu, a man renowned for his 'formal coldness of character' in contrast to the rather gushing manner of Holdernesse, though Walpole declared that he was 'one of the weakest and most ignorant men living'. Richard Hurd, Bishop of Lichfield and Coventry, became Preceptor in succession to Markham. True to form, Walpole described him as 'a servile pedant, ignorant of mankind'.[16]

The change of regime does not seem to have had much effect on the progress of the older princes towards the state of virtue wished for by their father. When the King and Queen visited Portsmouth in May 1778 the former wrote to his eldest son with an account of their journey, concluding with the now familiar exhortation to 'place ever your chief care on obeying the commands of your Creator' and assuring him that he would ever be 'not only an affectionate father but a sincere friend'. The Prince in reply assured his father that 'by the pains I shall take in imbibing your Majesty's admirable principles of virtue and religion' he would be worthy of that affection. The King was so touched that the Queen wrote to assure the prince that he had been prompted to declare his pride in his two eldest sons.[17] Behind this façade of polite assurances, however, the royal parents were becoming increasingly worried at their sons' conduct and the princes increasingly careless of

[14] Holdernesse to George, 18 March 1774 and 10 Nov. 1774: *CGPW*, i, 9, 17–18.
[15] 9 Dec. 1774: ibid., 18.
[16] Walpole, *Last Journals*, i, 556–8, ii, 350.
[17] 3–6 May: *CGPW*, i, 25–30.

their good opinion. George and Frederick, now in their mid-teens, were launching into a world of dissipation of which the King could not be kept unaware as it became public knowledge through the newspapers.

Two days after George's eighteenth birthday the King wrote to express his anxiety.[18] It was not only that 'you have not made that progress in your studies which, from the ability and assiduity of those placed for that purpose about you, I might have had reason to expect', but 'your love of dissipation has for some months been . . . trumpeted in the public papers'. He urged him to consider the position in life he held and was to fulfil in the future, and the effect that his bad example would have on the moral tone of the country. He warned George about his neglect of religion and the need constantly to examine his own conduct and check his propensity to vice; and he expressed his disappointment that his son had not made better use of his educational opportunities in order to understand his future responsibilities. In particular he deplored his lack of progress in learning German, pointing out that 'in Germany you will have possessions that will place you in one of the superior stations in that Great Empire' and that he must 'acquire a knowledge of its Constitution and more particularly that of your future dominions, whose prosperity must chiefly depend on the fatherly hand of its Sovereign'. This heavy-handed fatherly advice was supplemented by the warning that George lacked as yet 'any comprehensive knowledge of the Constitution, laws, finances, commerce, etc, of these Kingdoms' which was essential if he was to govern with success.

George's rather curt reply, expressing 'how extremely sensible I am of the parental attachment & kindness you profess towards me' and promising that 'it will be my principal object thro' life to merit them', betrayed more irritation at the extent of the good advice he was constantly being given than gratitude for it. The King had believed for twenty years since he came to the throne that no one but he by his good example could save the country from moral collapse, and he now declared to his eldest son that it was 'by the co-operation of my children only that I can effect it'. 'Princes must serve as examples to others', he wrote, which might have been George III's motto throughout his reign. He was now aware that in his eldest son the example might be the opposite to what he had wished, and in framing and appointing the new Household for him in December 1780 he endeavoured to surround him with individuals who would counter his deficiencies.[19]

In the same letter the King announced the limitations which his finances, encumbered by the need to bring up all his children, would set to his son's activities. His personal expenses were to be no more than

[18] King to George, 14 Aug. 1780 and reply 15th: ibid., 33–6.
[19] 22 Dec. 1780; ibid., 36–8.

George III had been allowed when he was Prince of Wales thirty years ago, though he might keep sixteen 'road horses and hunters' where his father had never had more than three. He was to be allowed to dine with his household and friends no more than twice a week when the King was in town, 'but I cannot afford it oftener'. The Prince 'may very naturally chuse to go oftener to Plays and operas than I may', but only after giving his parents prior notice and only in his own box and with his regular attendants. If he desired dancing he must also give notice before holding a ball, 'but I shall not permit the going to Balls or Assemblies at private houses, which never has been the custom for Princes of Wales', and masquerades (being notorious as opportunities for assignations) were absolutely forbidden. He was 'of course' to go to church every Sunday and to the drawing room when the King attended, to ride out with his father in the mornings and at other times by himself, 'provided it is for exercise, not lounging about Hyde Park', and always with an attendant. The King also assured him that on evenings when he did not go to the theatre or the opera suitable company would be invited to play cards or to converse. In this manner the Prince's social life would be regulated to protect him from temptation or at least to make it as difficult as possible to give way to it. 'Be but open with me', the King concluded, 'and you will ever find me desirous of making you as happy as I can, but I must not forget, nor must you, that in the exalted station you are placed in, every step is of consequence, and that your future character will greatly depend in the world on the propriety of your conduct'. At eighteen years old, George was to have the semblance of an independent establishment but to remain subject to the control and authority of a father who believed in his mission to regulate his son's life in the interests of moral purity and public reputation – for neither of which the Prince of Wales showed much concern. It was not a happy augury.

Chapter 2

THE PURSUIT OF PLEASURE

By the time of his eighteenth birthday, George had become the senior member of a family of thirteen children: two more, Alfred and Amelia, born in September 1780 and August 1783, were to follow, but Alfred died in 1782. Octavius, the last brother to be born before 1780, also died young, at the age of four in 1783, and Amelia lived only until 1810. Otherwise, for the greater part of his life George was surrounded by a group of seven brothers and five sisters, with all of whom he was for most of the time on close and affectionate terms. Elizabeth, the second of his sisters, said after his death that he was '*all heart*', but was spoilt by flatterers and the temptations of the world.[1] In the family circle at any rate he showed himself to be a fond companion to whom they all at various times turned for sympathy and understanding and were rarely denied. The sisters found him a staunch ally in their troubles with their mother, and the brothers, with rare exceptions, looked up to him for support in their difficult relationships with their father.

In their younger days, George was especially close to his next brother, Frederick, who became Duke of York. They were only a year apart in age, and they shared the schoolroom, pursued the same educational programme, received joint parental admonitions as to their behaviour, and as young men embarked together on a life of dissipation which alarmed and angered their pious father. The King however always regarded Frederick as his favourite and when Frederick got into scrapes it was always George whom the King blamed, although it is altogether possible that it was sometimes the other way round. When in 1781 he sent Frederick to Hanover to study languages and to complete his military education it was largely in order to keep them apart and protect Frederick from his brother's supposed bad influence.

The parting of the brothers was an emotional one. The *Annual Register* reported that George 'was so much affected . . . that he stood in a state of entire insensibility, totally unable to speak'.[2] They did not meet again for over six years. All the other brothers except Augustus, who was a lifelong sufferer from asthma, were sent into military or naval

[1] D.M. Stuart, *Daughters of George III*, 193.
[2] *Annual Register*, 1781 (Chronicle), 161.

service away from England. The third son, William, who was in some respects the weakest in character of all, and in his youth the most disreputable of the princes, was sent into the navy at the age of thirteen, and after eighteen months with the Channel fleet was posted to North America to avoid the temptations of home. His and Frederick's loss at about the same time deprived George of his two closest companions and left him open to the temptations of the debauchees who clustered around him in their stead. When the King deplored the company his eldest son kept it never occurred to him to think that he bore much of the responsibility. Even the younger brothers were sent in their teens to Germany, Edward to join Frederick in Hanover and to train for the army, while Ernest, Augustus and Adolphus were dispatched to Göttingen to finish their education and perfect their German. The King frowned upon their pleas to be allowed to visit England even for brief holidays. Despite these precautions, the younger princes found little difficulty in pursuing their amorous inclinations but their activities did not come so closely to their father's notice as did George's.

Left in England with only his sisters for company, and as the sole remaining target for his father's moral admonitions, George not surprisingly continued to show his rebellious streak, if only for lack of constructive occupation to fill his time. Unlike Princes of Wales in later reigns, he had no constitutional role, no duties, ceremonial or charitable, to perform, and no purpose to his existence other than to wait for the King to die. Nor were princes educated to perform their future duties. The Hanoverian monarchs, like their successor Queen Victoria, refused to share any of their political or constitutional duties or experience, to allow their heirs access to state papers or other confidential information, or to discuss with them or encourage them to take an interest in public affairs. This excessive constitutional propriety was perhaps encouraged by politicians who had no desire to deal with knowledgeable or strong-minded monarchs; but even when Gladstone tried to persuade Victoria to allow her eldest son to play a role in Ireland, to show favour to the Irish as well as to keep him out of harm's way, the Queen indignantly refused.[3] George III showed the same reluctance to allow his son to play any prominent part in the government of Ireland in 1797 or in defence of his country in the French wars, or to hold any high military rank. George IV was not the only monarch who was left in ignorance of the details of his role in government until he was actually called upon to do the job as Prince Regent: he then had to be told by his ministers and officials how to carry out such elementary tasks as putting his signature in the right place when approving papers.

[3] Roy Jenkins, *Gladstone*, 350–1.

He did at least correct one anomaly when one of his first acts as Regent was to promote himself to Field Marshal.

In these circumstances the pursuit of pleasure became the only outlet for his energies and talents. He was not entirely without sensible guidance as to his conduct. Lieutenant-Colonel Gerard Lake, one of his earliest and closest friends, who was appointed his first equerry in his new household, might have been a restraining influence, but he was posted to fight in the American war in 1781. 'Our parting, as you may suppose, was a very severe trial to us both,' George wrote to Frederick. 'You know how much I love him & therefore will easily conceive what a loss he is to me at the present moment, more especially as I have not you, my dear brother, with me, from whom I could always meet with disinterested advice'.[4] Lake perceptively wrote on his departure to warn him that 'your great good nature is liable to be impos'd upon by people who have not the smallest pretensions to your civility or attention, & who will presume upon that goodness', and that 'too many there are in this world who, to gain your favor, will acquiesce & encourage you in doing things that they themselves would perhaps be the first to condemn'. As Lake pointed out, George had not been educated with others of his age at a public school and had not had the opportunity to form judgements of men and the world. A wider circle of both male and female companions might have set him a better example or at least given him a more rounded experience of human nature.[5]

As Lake understood, the Prince was easily susceptible to bad company and they were equally drawn to his charm and friendliness of manner. Sheridan was dazzled by him at their first meeting and remained captivated for the rest of his life, though he fell out of favour towards the end. Himself something of an expert on the matter, Sheridan noted frankly that George was frequently drunk throughout the 1780s. Among those with bad reputations who were drawn to exploit his friendship were Lord Barrymore and his two brothers (known respectively as Hellgate, Newgate and Cripplegate), as well as their foul-mouthed sister 'Billingsgate', and Sir John Lade, who was a famous driver and encouraged the Prince to attempt daredevil exploits with his phaeton. He could reputedly drive to Brighton and back in ten hours. In 1781 he boasted to Frederick that he drove Frederick's phaeton four in hand for 22 miles in under two hours. 'I am become a tolerable good whip', he had announced in March and in October he declared he had become 'an exceeding good shot'. Lady Lade, formerly known as Mrs Smith, who may have been for a time one of the Prince's mistresses, was equally rackety. Her first husband had been a

[4] George to Frederick, 31 Jan. 1781: *CGPW*, i, 43 (misdated 20th).
[5] Lake to George, 23 Jan. 1781: ibid., 44–6.

highwayman and was hanged for it. George later granted her a pension of £300. The Prince was taught fencing by the Angelos in their fashionable Soho studio, and boxing with others of his set. He dabbled in the 'sporting life' of the day, and attended the racetracks and the prize-fights – the latter came to an end when he witnessed the death in the ring at Brighton of one pugilist and swore never to watch boxing again. He showed his sensitivity when he settled an annuity on the widow.[6]

George's susceptible character was never more in evidence than in his relations with women. He was not unattractive to them. Writing in 1782, Georgiana, Duchess of Devonshire, who reigned over aristocratic London society, described him as 'rather tall' with a 'striking' but not perfect figure, being

> inclined to be too fat and looks too much like a woman in men's cloaths, but the gracefulness of his manner and his height certainly make him a pleasing figure. His face is very handsome and he is fond of dress. . . . His person, his dress & the admiration he has met, & thinks still more that he meets, from women take up his thoughts chiefly. He is good natur'd and rather extravagant.

Georgiana read his character shrewdly: he was 'more inclined to extravagance than generosity', though he was capable of the latter quality, and he 'does not want for understanding, & his jokes sometimes have an appearance of wit'. However, 'to judge of the sense and abilities of a young man of twenty, occupied by the pleasures & [the] noisy, gay & lively, is impossible'. He was not so 'capricious in his tastes & inclinations' as was commonly supposed, but 'he loves being of consequence, whether it is in intrigues of state or of gallantry, he often thinks more is intended than really is'. He had a quick intelligence and, like his father, 'has a wonderful knack at knowing all that is going forward'.

As regards his social life, 'He had long felt an inclination to break thro' the strict confinement he was kept [in]', but 'As he only went out in secret, or with the King & Queen, he form'd very few connections with any other woman than women of the town', though he was 'considerably ogled' when he rode in the Park every morning or in his box at the play or the opera. All this gave him the impression that he was much sought after by the female sex and naturally encouraged him to respond to their temptation.[7]

[6] Villiers, 33; Sichel, i, 110, 141, 34; George to Frederick, 11 May, 30 March, 22 Oct. 1781: *CGPW*, i, 326n, 62, 55, 75; Shane Leslie, *George the Fourth*, 23.

[7] Anecdotes concerning HRH the Prince of Wales (1782): Bessborough, *Georgiana*, 289–92.

George's first attachment at the age of sixteen was to Mary Hamilton, niece of Sir William, one of his sisters' attendants, who was six years older than he was. He wrote her a series of sentimental letters and offered her gifts, but she was too sensible and virtuous to encourage such a youthful infatuation and he turned his attention elsewhere. He met considerably more encouragement from Mary Robinson, an actress whom he saw playing Perdita in *The Winter's Tale*, and who was married with an infant daughter. Her life was a precarious one – she and her husband had seen the inside of a debtors' prison – and she saw in the prince's attentions a prospect of financial security for the future. He gave her a locket with his portrait, wrote her a series of passionate letters, signing himself 'Florizel' after the prince in the same play, and promised her in writing a sum of £20,000 when he should come of age. She carefully kept all his letters and when after a year or so George tired of the affair their existence was brought to his father's notice. The King was furious but he bought them back for £5,000, and after further prolonged negotiation she agreed to give up the Prince's bond in return for life annuities of £600 for herself and £200 for her daughter.[8] The episode not only confirmed the King's low opinion of his son's self-discipline but further offended his sense of economy.

Worse was to follow. In his brothers' absence George continued to live a rakish life, often in the company of his dissolute uncles the Dukes of Cumberland and of Gloucester, defying the King's attempts to forbid him their society. George was particularly attached to Cumberland and his father's prohibition merely stoked the flames. He was forbidden to attend a ball proposed in his honour by the Duke in February 1781 and even his servants were not allowed to go to one of Cumberland's dinners.[9] The Duke and Duchess were well matched: she was said to be addicted to coarse language and behaviour. A major reason why the King forbade his son their company was his anger at the Duke's marriage, for she was a commoner. This was one of the principal

[8] Richardson, 13. 'Perdita' Robinson was a fashionable beauty and an acclaimed actress at Drury Lane. She was painted by Romney, Reynolds and Gainsborough. She became a celebrated authoress, published a volume of sentimental verses in 1775, and went on to produce seven novels and a tract on women's rights. A further volume of poems was published in 1791, the Prince of Wales heading the list of subscribers. Despite the notice of celebrities such as Fox, Sheridan and the Duchess of Devonshire, she was always in financial straits, through her extravagance and the gambling debts of her wastrel lover, Banastre Tarleton. She developed a painful rheumatic or arthritic condition and died in poverty in 1800. Among her patronesses was Lady Hertford, who later became George's mistress. Three of her portraits still hang in the Wallace Collection at Hertford House in Manchester Square: J. Ingamells, *Mrs Robinson and her Portraits*, The Wallace Collection (1978).

[9] Walpole, *Last Journals*, ii, 347. Both Cumberland and Gloucester had married commoners, to the disgust of George III.

circumstances which led the King to introduce the Royal Marriages Act of 1772, to forbid the marriage of any descendant of George II under the age of twenty-five without royal permission. Unfortunately, it was this Act, strictly enforced by George III, which lay at the root of most of the marital and extramarital troubles of his own family.

In Cumberland's company, George fell into even more rakishness. Horace Walpole alleged that the Duke 'carried the Prince to the lowest places of debauchery where they got dead drunk, and were often carried home in that condition'. 'Dissipation is at high-water mark', Walpole wrote in the summer of 1781, hinting that the Prince of Wales was at the centre of it. 'He drunk hard, swore, and passed every night in [brothels]'. The Cumberlands also introduced him to gambling. They set up a faro bank in their own house for his benefit and to the King's even greater disgust. This particular vice, however, did not establish a permanent hold on him and in later life he showed little enthusiasm for it, except on the racetrack. The Duke and Duchess also encouraged him to adopt bad language which shocked even some of his companions. However, the intimacy with the Cumberlands was not long-lasting. The Prince resented the Duke's familiarity – he began to call him 'Toffy' – and after a year or so the association weakened.[10]

George sustained one of his vices for a much longer period than his association with the Cumberlands. All his life he was susceptible to women and his numerous liaisons became and have remained notorious, though he was hardly more profligate than most young men of his age and social position. Among those who became his mistresses, mostly for short periods of time, were Grace Dalrymple Elliot, Perdita's immediate successor, Lady Melbourne, who was one of the most immoral women of the time and whose children – including the later Prime Minister – were of a variety of fathers[11] – and a number of actresses who, then as always, had a peculiar fascination for young men of royal birth and who, at that time, were generally regarded as willingly available. Nevertheless, the scandalous stories propagated after George's death by Robert Huish in his so-called *Memoirs of George IV*, which painted him as a totally unscrupulous womanizer who chased every attractive female in sight, are certainly exaggerated.

George's reputation has always been tarnished by allegations of debauchery, gluttony and drunkenness, as if he were a monster of depravity from whom no female was safe. His brothers acquired similar

[10] Ibid., 349–50, 353, 384, 405–6; Walpole to Lord Harcourt, 18 May 1781: *Letters of Horace Walpole*, ed. Cunningham, viii, 41–2; Sichel, ii, 32.

[11] Lady Sarah Napier wrote in March 1783 that George 'is desperately in love with Lady Melbourne & when she don't sit next to him at supper he is not commonly civil to his neighbours': Countess of Ilchester and Lord Stavordale (eds), *Life & Letters of Lady Sarah Lennox*, ii. 36.

reputations. It was a licentious age, when young and adolescent sprigs of nobility sowed wild oats with reckless abandon. Drunkenness was the vice of the age among all classes. The Younger Pitt was no more of a drunkard than most members of the fashionable world and he was accustomed to drink two or more bottles of wine at a meal. He once entered the House of Commons for an important debate leaning on his drinking companion Henry Dundas and seeing double: he retired behind the Speaker's chair to be sick. Sheridan, Grey and Fox were renowned for their excessive drinking and the Duke of Norfolk who was averse to soap and water was said to be washed and have a change of linen only when he was so dead drunk that his servants could remove his clothes without his knowledge.

Sexually too, men of the upper classes since the time of Charles II, when the repressive Puritanism of the mid-seventeenth century was swept away, expected to behave promiscuously, and wives were expected to tolerate their husbands' amours with indifference. The keeping of mistresses, or casual sexual affairs, was seen as normal behaviour. As the historian of sexual behaviour in early modern England has remarked, 'during the middle years of the eighteenth century attitudes towards sex in England, especially in London, were unusually relaxed'. This applied to both sexes. Women were frequently as free in their social and sexual behaviour as men: an author of 1739 remarked that female adultery in high circles was considered 'a fashionable vice rather than a crime'. Lady Oxford's large brood was nicknamed 'the Harleian miscellany' after the fifth Earl's manuscript collection. Lady Elizabeth Foster bore two children by the Duke of Devonshire while being the close friend of his wife, Georgiana, who in turn had a daughter by Charles Grey. Extramarital affairs, discreetly conducted, could be ignored at least in public among the fashionable set.[12] While aristocratic marriages were arranged for dynastic reasons, to preserve property and estates or to promote political alliances, women might have to seek sexual gratification elsewhere than in the marriage bed, and their husbands were by convention free to keep mistresses or seduce their housemaids and servants or other men's wives. Young aristocratic women were carefully kept in seclusion until they were suitably married and had produced a son and heir of unblemished legitimacy to inherit the title and estate. Until then they were not available to young men of their own social level who had to look elsewhere. After they had performed their dynastic duty they might consider themselves, as Lady Melbourne advised the Duchess of Devonshire, free to seek pleasure where they wished.[13]

[12] Stone, *Family, Sex and Marriage*, 328–31; Jane Aiken Hodge, *Passion and Principle*, 5.

[13] A. Calder Marshall, *The Two Duchesses*, 25.

George's pursuit of pleasure was no more remarkable: his opportunities were greater because he was a royal prince and a liaison with him, however brief, might lead to social and financial benefits, while the easy availability of all but the most virtuous women accustomed him to being able to take his pleasures as and when he could. When in 1785 he was admitted to the exclusive Beef-steak Club, its numbers being enlarged by one to accommodate him, *The Times* sardonically commented that he was known to be remarkably fond of rump steaks. At least he was handsome and well-mannered, and capable of giving pleasure in return. In the Vanity Fair of late eighteenth- and early nineteenth-century society pleasure was king, and for a time George was its prince.

One of his earliest escapades, with overtones of comedy if not farce, was his seduction (or possibly hers of him) in the early summer of 1781 of Madame Hardenburg, wife of the Hanoverian Minister in England. He described in detail to Frederick how after meeting her at a card party in the Queen's apartments he was struck by a 'fatal tho' delightful passion . . . in my bosom . . . for her. . . . O did you but know how I adore her, how I love her, how I would sacrifice every earthly thing to her; by Heavens I shall go distracted: my brain will split.' She resisted his advances at first but probably only to increase his ardour. When he made himself ill with his longing for her – 'I have spit blood & am so much emaciated you would hardly know me again' – she, as he put it, completed his happiness. 'O my beloved brother,' he wrote, 'I enjoyed beforehand the pleasures of Elyssium'. Unfortunately the press got hold of rumours about the affair and the lady's husband faced her with the accusation that she had cuckolded him. She was forced to admit that the Prince had 'made proposals' to her and Hardenburg wrote an angry letter to him. George 'almost fell into fits' on receiving it, thinking that she must have confessed, and therefore was guilty of 'ye blackest ingratitude & cruelty'. Nevertheless he wrote to assure Hardenburg that he was the only person to blame for the affair and that she had treated him 'with ye utmost coolness' – at the same time writing her 'ye most passionate of letters'.

She responded by pleading with him to elope with her that night. This put rather a different complexion on the matter. The thought of 'Ye noise my flight would cause in ye world' and the likely reaction of his father with his 'severe disposition' were enough to make him pause: he at first consented to her demand but rapidly changed his mind when he considered that the consequence might be a life of poverty. He decided to make a full confession to his mother, and fainted or affected to do so in the course of it: his mother wept and consented to his going, but his father was quicker off the mark. He sent Hardenburg immediately to Brussels 'with my little angel', leaving George to 'all ye agonies of misery & despair'. He wrote to his brother to beseech him not to make love to her himself '(supposing her to [be] capable of allowing it, wh. I believe impossible . . .)'. Frederick unkindly, or perhaps with the best intentions, replied that he had already been invited to do so. On his arrival in Hanover he had attended a masquerade at which he had danced with Madame Hardenburg and she offered to go alone into another room with him. 'I desired no better fun', he wrote, 'but unluckily the room was full . . . I know also other stories of her still worse than this'. Two months later Frederick assured him that 'she has abused you so terribly by all accounts here that I am thoroughly persuaded she is completely cured of her love for you, if she ever had any . . . [and] if one may judge by her behaviour here, she cannot have had much. . . .You ought to rejoice at having got rid of her'.[14]

George's ardour rapidly cooled. He confessed to always having had doubts about her, but he had been carried away by his passion: 'In short it was a very miserable and unhappy affair alltogether'. Nevertheless, six months later he was still asking for news of her: no one had yet replaced her in his affections. As for the King, not surprisingly he was 'excessively cross & ill-tempered & uncommonly grumpy, snubbing everybody, in everything. We are not upon ye very best terms.' George had requested leave to go abroad when the Hardenburgs left in order to recover his composure, but had received in reply a lecture on his conduct.

> It is now allmost certain that some unpleasant mention of you is daily to be found in the papers. . . . Examine yourself . . . and then draw your conclusion whether you must not give me many an uneasy moment. I wish to live with you as a friend, but then by your behaviour you must deserve it. If I did not state these things I should not fulfill my duty either to my God or to my country.

The King subscribed himself 'an affectionate father trying to save his son from perdition' so that he might 'become worthy of the situation that Divine Providence probably intends for you'.[15]

Frederick from the safe distance of Hanover begged his brother to try to set matters right, 'as it only plagues both of you without answering the least end in the world', but George assured him that the King and Queen abused them both and that he had had a blazing quarrel with his mother, none of which did any good. In March 1782 the King reprimanded him for being absent from the levee and threatened to take 'disagreeable' steps if he did not obey the rules set out for him in 1780. George rudely and defiantly replied that he had 'inconsiderately acquiesced' in that plan because of his 'youth and inexperience' and claimed

[14] George to Frederick, 17 July 1781; Frederick to George, 28 Aug. and 8 Nov. 1781: *CGPW*, i, 66–9, 72, 76.

[15] Same to same, 25 March 1782; King to George, 6 May: ibid., 84, 60–2.

that his present conduct did not reflect 'the smallest discredit either upon yourself or upon me'. He signed himself 'your Majesty's most dutiful son and subject'.[16]

George's defiance of his father reflected his resentment at Frederick's enforced absence. His departure, George assured him at Christmas in 1781, was 'ye longest twelvemonth I ever passed' without his 'best & dearest friend'.[17] His dissipations and adventures might not have been much lessened if his brother had been there, but the way he threw himself into the vain pursuit of pleasure at all costs suggests that his separation from the brother he loved most left an emotional blank in his life that no pleasure could ever fill, and left him even more vulnerable to sycophants and adventurers who exploited his loneliness for their own purposes.

Among the women with whom the Prince enjoyed sexual associations was Elizabeth Armistead, a noted courtesan, who later settled into a permanent relationship with Charles Fox and eventually became his wife, to the astonishment of his friends when, several years after the wedding, he made the fact public. George's involvement with Charles Fox went beyond sharing a mistress, and its repercussions were profound. Fox's habits exceeded the Prince's in licence, extravagance and depravity. From his early youth, even at Eton, Fox had been indulged in every whim by his doting father, Lord Holland, and had sampled most of the available vices, becoming addicted to gambling, drink and women. His reckless conduct and his powerful personality attracted a circle of devoted friends and admirers who shared or adopted his tastes, and George became one of his foremost companions. Through Fox the Prince was introduced to Whig society, led by Georgiana, the Duchess of Devonshire, whose town house became the centre of a fashionable and glittering if shallow circle, both social and political. George was introduced to its delights in 1779 and was immediately captivated.[18] Georgiana resisted his importunities to become his mistress, but they struck up a close relationship, calling each other brother and sister. Georgiana was to become his ally in the pursuit of Mrs Fitzherbert, while the Prince in later years was her constant resource for funds to help finance her enormous gambling debts, or at any rate to stave off the bailiffs.

[16] Frederick to George, 12 Oct. 1781; King to George, 30 March 1782 and reply: ibid., 74, 86–7.

[17] George to Frederick, 24 Dec.: 1781 ibid., 78. The pain of separation was mutual. In the twelve months after their parting Frederick wrote him twenty-three letters, but George managed only eight in reply. On 30 Dec. 1781 Frederick begged him 'Pray write often; it is near two months that I have not received the least line from you': ibid., 79.

[18] Villiers, 32.

The King could hardly approve of these associations, and not only for moral reasons. The later 1770s and early 1780s were a period of crisis for the Empire, with the American War of Independence, and of consequent political extremism at home. The American cause was espoused by the Rockingham Whigs, an opposition party closely associated with the Devonshires and led in the House of Commons by Fox himself. George III believed that they were abetters of treason in America and disloyalty at home. In their turn the Rockingham Whigs stood for the reduction of the royal influence in politics and the supremacy of Parliament over the King. Knowing that they could never attain office under George III with his consent, they sought to achieve it through Parliamentary pressure and to subject George III to their control. The Prince of Wales had no interest in the political doctrines of whiggery or their 'Revolution principles' – a reference to England's 'Glorious Revolution' of 1689, to which the Americans in the 1770s also appealed. His association with the Whigs was social and selfish. Like previous Hanoverian princes of Wales, he sought to increase his political weight by association with politicans opposed to his father's ministers, and they in turn hoped for future favours in the next reign to compensate for exclusion in the present. This 'reversionary interest', as it was called, was a recurrent feature of eighteenth-century political life, and disappeared from the political scene only with the death of Princess Charlotte in 1817.

The Prince's involvement with Whig politics was therefore personal rather than politically motivated, but it added another dimension to his quarrels with his father. The King suspected that if his eldest son was provided with a generous income he would contribute to the Whigs' electoral and other political expenses, in opposition to his own ministers and government, as well as using his funds for immoral and extravagant expenditure. It made him all the more determined to resist George's request for a large settlement when he came of age in 1783, at which point, by coincidence, the government had fallen into the hands of the Whigs because of the collapse of Lord North's ministry after the loss of the American war. The King was conscious of the burdens of taxation and economic dislocation under which his subjects suffered because of war expenditure, and was determined to enforce economy in every possible way. When the Whigs proposed that the Prince should have an annual income of £100,000 – double what George III had had when he was heir to the throne – the King blankly refused to condone what he termed 'a shameful squandering of public money . . . to the wishes of an ill-advised young man'. He offered instead an annual income of £50,000 from the existing Civil List, to avoid any new taxes, which together with the proceeds of the Duchy of Cornwall which would go to the Prince at the age of twenty-one, would give him £62,000. The furthest he would go was to ask Parliament for a capital sum of £30,000 to pay the Prince's debts and a similar sum to pay for his outfit, and this on condition that George would promise to incur no more debts. The Prince was angry, but was forced to submit when even Fox admitted that the government could go no further than the King would allow. He got something of his own back when he made his first appearance in the Lords at the end of the year to speak and vote in favour of Fox's India Bill, which George III saw as a blatant attempt to place India and its vast patronage under the control of 'Charles Fox, in or out of office'.[19] Fox's schemes however came to nothing when the King dismissed his Whig ministers and Pitt came to his King's rescue. George unrepentantly flaunted his political sympathies by allowing Fox to use Carlton House as his election headquarters in 1784 and adopting the Whig colours of 'blue and buff' for his uniform – which enraged the King still further because they were the colours of George Washington's rebel Americans.

George III's intentions were public spirited as well as those of a parent wishing to instil sensible habits into a wayward son, but without co-operation from the Prince the result was to be financial disaster. The main cause was the Prince's favourite project to refurbish Carlton House as a fit palace for the heir to the British dominions and in accordance with all the latest styles and fashions in architecture, furniture and decorations. The enormous expenses already incurred were only a foretaste of what was to come: George's refusal to modify his plans and his total indifference to money opened the path to ruin again.

[19] Corresp. between Portland and King, 15–17 June, King and North, 16–17 June, Fox to George 16, 18 and 20 June, Portland to George 16, 17, 18 June 1783: *CGPW*, i, 114–24, 126–8; E.A. Smith, *Whig Principles*, 42–5.

Chapter 3

A PALACE FOR A PRINCE

Carlton House on Pall Mall belonged to the Crown. It had been a royal residence in the middle of the eighteenth century, when it was occupied by George III's widowed mother, the Princess Dowager of Wales. It was a compact and not particularly grand or attractive building and after her death in 1772 it fell into a state of dilapidation. When the King granted it to his eldest son as his first independent residence in 1783 it was in need of considerable repair and restoration. However, George was not to be satisfied with his father's expectation that he would limit himself to 'only painting it and putting [in] handsome furniture where necessary'.[1] He had much more grandiose ideas. He had set himself up as a leader of fashion and as patron of the latest styles and he aimed to make his house a new Versailles, though on a smaller scale, to glorify his position and the British monarchy. It was an age of aristocratic display, and he was determined not to be outshone by any subject. Millions, in today's monetary values, were being spent in building, tearing down and rebuilding the great town and country houses where an immensely rich governing class indulged its fancies in imitation of the arts and lifestyle of ancient Rome. The grand tour, the study of Palladian architecture and the paintings of Claude and Poussin, and, in the second half of the century, of the recently discovered lavish interior decorations of Herculaneum and Pompeii, provided models for imitation by a patrician élite which was becoming more and more cut off from the lives of ordinary people and living in a fantasy world of luxury.

George's enthusiasm for this new movement contrasted vividly with the habits and values of quiet domesticity and household economy upheld by his father, and the Prince's extravagance increased in consequence as his parents expressed their mounting disapproval of his activities. Carlton House became not merely a vehicle for the expression of the latest aesthetic taste, but a public testimony to the Prince's political defiance of his father. As in all his activities, he carried everything to excess. In his teenage years he and Frederick had indulged their love of finery: George assured his brother in March 1781, for

[1] King to George, 27 Aug. 1784: *CGPW*, i, 156.

example, that he was sending over to him in Hanover 'two new uniforms . . . with ye dress and undress of my hunting uniform . . . [which] is universally admired thro'out London, tout ce qui s'appelle ton', and he gave him serious advice on how to wear the 'vandyke dress', which he had had made for him by the tailor, to Covent Garden theatre.[2] The extravagance resulting from this insistence on the best of everything was equally characteristic of his designs for his new house.

George chose as his architect Henry Holland, a fashionable whig practitioner who was thoroughly versed in the classical tradition. As can be the way of architects, his enthusiasm outweighed any consideration of expense to his client, and with the Prince as a willing partner rather than as a check on his activities his expenditure exceeded all bounds. Nothing mattered to either except the attainment of perfection. There seems to have been no attempt to control the profusion of money spent, or more commonly owed. The ends took precedence over the availability of the Prince's means. To stint resources for the task was to settle for the second rate and to forgo the purpose of the enterprise; and the Prince's character always had a touch of the Micawber in it. Something was sure to turn up.

First he hoped that his father would give way over his income and allow him the £100,000 a year which his Whig friends had promised him and which he considered the absolute minimum with which to support a Prince's lifestyle. When this hope was dashed, he agitated to be paid, on coming of age, the whole arrears of the Duchy of Cornwall, whose proceeds had been received by the Exchequer during his minority. That too was refused, and he was restricted to the £12,000 a year which was the average annual yield of the Duchy after 1783, in addition to his allowance of £50,000 from the Civil List. It was clear to the Prince that this would never be sufficient, but rather than try to bring his expenses within the limits of his actual income he continued to spend without restraint, on the principle that if his father did not allow him enough then his father would have to pay the debts which he was driven to incur. The one unthinkable solution was to stop the work on Carlton House and settle for something less. 'Would your Lordship,' he demanded of the King's emissary Lord Southampton, his Groom of the Stole, in 1784, 'with your ideas of propriety, have the Prince of Wales the Heir of Apparent [*sic*] to the Crown of Great Britain, dismiss his servants, sell his horses, and part, in short, with every magnificence annexed to his situation in life? A moment's reflection will I am sure convince yr Lordship of ye absurdity as well as impossibility of adopting so ridiculous as well as indecent a measure . . . it wd be improper for me to live with a less degree of magnificence than I hitherto have done.'[3]

[2] George to Frederick, 30 March and 10 April: ibid., i, 55, 57.
[3] George to Southampton, 1 Sept. 1784: ibid., i, 159.

Holland's estimate for the first stage of the work on Carlton House in 1784 amounted to £30,250 – the equivalent possibly of £1.5–£2 million in today's money.[4] The work was partly rebuilding: the east wing was to be raised to correspond with a new west wing, and was to be extended by the addition of a bathroom, dressing room and staircase in the basement, and an oval dressing room, powdering room, closet and WC on the principal storey – these works to cost £2,500. In the centre, a new hall, 45 feet long by 28 feet wide and 37 feet high, an octagonal tribune 24 feet in diameter, a staircase 35 by 20 feet, and servants' rooms, kitchen and offices were to be added. The rather plain and dull front of the house on Pall Mall was to be faced with Portland stone with a grand portico of Corinthian columns, 'richly detailed', and a balustrade the length of the building, 'probably the most refined specimen of the Corinthian order ever built in London', as one architectural authority has pronounced.[5] Additional expenses were to be incurred for purchasing and demolishing some old houses adjoining the site and altering walls and drains. A further sum of £6,500 was allowed for fitting up and furnishing the hall, staircase and tribune, £1,500 for building another lodge in the Great Court, building walls and gates and making a carriageway, with other minor works, and no less than £9,000 for building a *manège* 270 by 55 feet with stalls for seventy-three horses and standings for twenty carriages and accommodation for the stable staff and services. Interior decorations were extra: William Gaubert, who was the Prince's interior designer and upholsterer (he had been recommended by Georgiana), sent in a bill for £38,021 17s 4d for work carried out over three years to 1786.[6] By that time, Holland estimated that a further £69,700 would be required to complete the building work 'on an extended plan', including taking down more old houses, finishing the new buildings, adding a circular music room 40 feet in diameter, throwing together the exising two dining rooms, building stables and a riding house, a gallery and portico on the south front, and four new wings: all of which would 'render the Palace completely magnificent'.[7]

The decoration and furnishing of the interior was lavish. Carving, gilding, marble and ormolu decorations, glasses, windows and furniture

[4] Prince of Wales accounts: RA 35014.

[5] Summerson, *Georgian London*, 131–2; Summerson, *Life and Work of John Nash*, 97.

[6] RA 25075.

[7] Ibid., 35048–9. Not everyone shared this opinion. About 1815 Captain Gronow condemned the house as 'one of the meanest and most ugly edifices that ever disfigured London'. Behind the screen of columns in front of the house the building was ill-proportioned and disfigured by the capital's smoke and layers of soot: J. Grego (ed.), *Reminiscences and Recollections of Captain Gronow*, ii, 255. Dorothy Stroud, *Henry Holland*, 69, mistranscribed Holland's estimate as £49,700.

'for the 2 Seasons' were estimated in 1784 to cost £35,000 plus extra for crystal chandeliers and girandoles.[8] The upholstery was to be of the finest materials and quality: nothing was to be spared in the search for perfection. Nor was this the end. In 1789 the furnishing and decoration of more rooms, including 'a new rich magnificent throne' and a state bed, 'hangings and furniture trimmed with rich gold lace, gilt bronze chandeliers, Girandoles [and] tables' in the state apartments together with the replacement of some articles furnished in the earlier years, was estimated to cost a further £110,500. The sum included the fitting up of the music room with two chimneypieces (with two pairs of ornamental dogs), two large looking-glasses in frames, two tables and eight girandoles, four large and four small armchairs, eighteen other chairs, and a large sofa. The room was 'hung with rich silk Damask manufactured in Spitalfields' and the floor covered by 'a rich Moorfields carpet'. In 1790 a bill came in for upholstery materials in green, white and yellow lustring, rose-coloured Italian mantua, and rich crimson satin ground tissue for the backs and seats of twenty-three chairs. The mercer's bill for the Chinese room amounted to over £1,083.[9]

These operations created an interior of decorative brilliance on a grand scale, and provided a sumptuous setting for the Prince's entertainments. Horace Walpole was vastly impressed by the results: 'In all the fairy tales you have been [*sic*], you never was in so pretty a scene'. There was, he wrote, an 'august simplicity' about the whole; 'You cannot call it magnificent; it is the taste and propriety that strike'. Sheridan's biographer remarked that the gardens at Carlton House 'resounded with Italian music', a fit setting for a Prince who was not only handsome and athletic in appearance but loved music and dancing. Georgiana, attending a ball in February 1785 when the state rooms were first displayed in their new magnificence, described how 'The Palace will be one of the finest in the world when finish'd . . . the dancing room white and gold, the outward room laycock and jonquil scagliola, highly polish'd and gilt. The supper rooms, the library and a small music room, beautiful white and gold and light blue furniture'. The company, *The Times* reported, was 'noble and splendid' and after supper dancing went on until 4 a.m.[10] George loved entertaining and shining in the company of his fashionable friends, and his lavish arrangements outshone everyone.

[8] Prince of Wales accounts, RA 35014. The final account submitted by the prince's upholsterer and interior designer, William Gaubert, in May 1786 came to £38,021 17s 4d: ibid., 25075.

[9] Ibid., 25078–82, 25086, 25091, 25094. George always tried to encourage British manufacturers with his patronage.

[10] Walpole, *Letters*, ed. Toynbee, xiii, 321; Richardson, 21; Bessborough, 96; *The Times*, 18 Feb. 1785.

Carlton House underwent many changes in decoration, in the use of the rooms and in furnishings, and further additions were made during the rest of its life as George's London residence. Throughout this period it sparkled with life as his chief centre for entertainments both of private friends and of large gatherings of society. A description of 1811 may be taken as typical of its middle period: at the foot of the stairs, visitors to Carlton House entered a large green-panelled hall, hung with some of the Prince's collection of Dutch pictures and housing busts of Whig statesmen. This led into the library, adorned with buhl cabinets and miniature sculptures of triumphal arches among oak bookcases in 'gothick' style. From the library one entered the golden drawing room 'gay with crystal, crimson and gold' on the east side, or on the west a small sitting room leading to the dining room whose ceiling was painted to represent the summer sky and where the furniture was upholstered in scarlet. After the dining room came 'the principal architectural glory of Carlton House', a 'Gothic conservatory' with columns of green scagliola marble and a ceiling of fan tracery filled with coloured glass, and in the vertical windows the arms of all the sovereigns of England from William the Conqueror to George III and all the princes of Wales (excepting the son of James II) and electoral princes of the House of Brunswick. Hexagonal Gothic lanterns hung from the points of the arches. In the garden were long walks, which were covered over for parties and decorated with flowers and mirrors.[11]

Lavish meals were served at banquets. In June 1785 *The Times* reported that five rooms were laid out for supper, with 'all the first [Whig] families in the kingdom' present among a total company of 450. There were 'eight removes, and the most choice dishes, and a grand display of confectionery, with the most curious fruits that could be procured'. Twenty-six years later a guest described 'Tureens, dishes, plates, even soup plates . . . everywhere of silver . . . there were hot soups and roasts, all besides cold but of excellent and fresh cookery' and all the fruits in season, iced champagne and excellent wines were provided.[12] Whatever else may be said of George, no one knew better how to entertain and no one took more pains to see that everything was done to perfection. Sarah Lyttelton came to see over the House in 1810 and remarked:

> Carlton House is very beautiful, very magnificent, and we were well amused. . . . The beauties of old china vases, gold fringes, damask draperies, cut-glass lustres, and all the other fine things we saw there. I can only tell you the lustre in one of the rooms, of glass and

[11] Fulford, *George the Fourth*, 112–13; D.M. Stuart, *Portrait of the Prince Regent*, 23–4.
[12] *The Times*, 14 June 1785.

> ormoulu [*sic*], looking like a shower of diamonds, cost between *two and three thousand pounds.*[13]

Many other guests were equally impressed. One declared 'Carlton House finer than anything in England and not inferior to Versailles or Saint Cloud' and in the Hanoverian minister's view even the royal palace at St Petersburg was 'not equal to this in elegance and richness'. To more restrained tastes it was overdone: 'not a spot without some finery upon it, gold upon gold – a bad taste', one critic remarked.[14]

Furnishing, entertaining and building at Carlton House were not the Prince's only extravagances. He was obsessed by riding, driving, and equestrian pursuits in general. Huge sums were spent on stables, horses and carriages, which were magnificently turned out, and repeated attempts by his treasurers to bring these expenses within reasonable bounds were always mysteriously frustrated. The Prince also began to lavish funds on rebuilding and decorating his newly acquired house at Brighton: these activities became an obsession which had to be indulged at whatever cost to his resources, his creditors or the public. No doubt, like others who fell into these habits, his tradesmen and agents compensated for the likelihood that their bills would never be paid in full by inflating them as much as they could get away with; even so, the scale of the Prince's financial recklessness was astounding. By 1786 his debts had risen to over £269,000. Arrears in building and furnishing amounted to £52,637, in the stables £32,399, and provision for finishing Carlton House £79,700. In today's values, this was a total debt of around £15 million.[15]

Already in 1784 the King had become alarmed by his son's improvidence. He considered that the settlement of his income arrived at and reluctantly accepted in the summer of 1783 was quite sufficient for all legitimate needs. He feared that any larger sum would be used to help finance the political and probably the scandalous and immoral activities of the Prince's Whig friends. George had indeed thrown himself wholeheartedly into supporting Fox's election campaign in Westminster in the spring of 1784, when Georgiana and her sister Harriet Duncannon had thrown propriety to the winds by openly canvassing their social inferiors, supposedly promising kisses for votes from tradesmen. Fox displayed the Prince of Wales's feathers as his election badge and the Prince wore the Whig cockade of the fox's brush with the blue and buff Whig colours. The election was seen as more than a contest for a single seat in Parliament. Rather it was a national demon-

[13] Sarah Lyttelton to R. Spencer, 11 May 1810: Mrs Hugh Wyndham (ed.), *Corresp. of Sarah Spencer, Lady Lyttelton*, 104.

[14] Quoted in J.B. Priestley, *The Prince of Pleasure*, 36.

[15] RA 41854; list of debts in George to King, 15 June 1784: *CGPW*, i, 228–9.

stration of popular support for either Pitt's new government, or Fox and the Whigs whom he had replaced in December 1783, and the King and the Prince were seen as the leaders on each side. George even made Carlton House the headquarters of Fox's election campaign and when Fox won a narrow victory he was carried there in triumph after the close of the poll. There was a grand ball at Devonshire House at which the Prince was, as one spectator observed, 'so far overcome by the wine he had drunk' that in the middle of dancing a quadrille he fell flat on his face on the floor and on being picked up, threw 'the load from his stomach into the midst of the circle'.[16]

After the rejoicing came the reckoning. It is unlikely that George had contributed to Fox's election fund, which soaked up subscriptions from the whig nobility for the rest of the decade, but his debts were in any case so enormous that there was nothing for it but to appeal to his father for assistance. He did not endear himself by the means he took to do so. In August 1784 he baldly announced to his father that he intended to go abroad, since 'nothing but my absenting myself from this country for a certain time' could enable him to reduce his expenses. Temporary retreat to the continent was a well-established method among the impoverished aristocracy to enable them both to economize, by shutting up their houses and dismissing their servants, and to avoid arrest for debt on the initiative of their creditors. For a Prince of Wales to take this course however was another matter. It would have declared to the public the disgrace which he brought on the throne by reckless profusion and callous disregard of creditors and honest tradesmen. The King unhesitatingly and brusquely refused to give him permission to leave the country, and threw in a lengthy sermon on his iniquities. His 'reprehensible conduct' had grown 'worse every year, and in a more glaring manner since his removal to Carlton House'. He had aligned himself with the King's political enemies – opponents would have been too mild a description – despite his promise not to do so, and despite the King's hope that he would not be 'such a fool as not to know his interest was inseparable with mine'. His extravagance at Carlton House was unforgivable – in defiance of his father's admonitions he had carried out extensive building works and as if this was not enough, 'the most expensive Fêtes' had been given and still more were projected. 'Every frivolous and irregular passion' had been indulged. Instead of running away, his only 'manly' course was to retrench his expenses and set up a sinking fund into which to pay part of his annual income to clear his debts. Otherwise 'his character would be for ever blasted in this country, & also in all Europe'. If however he would put his mind to forming a plan to pay off his

[16] Sichel, ii, 60–4.

debts, 'I will see whether I can contribute towards getting it sooner effected'.[17]

George ignored the proffered carrot and declared that he meant to set out at the beginning of September, to be faced by a stern prohibition on leaving without his father's permission. He had no alternative but to submit and order his Treasurer, the long-suffering Colonel Hotham, to draw up an account of all his debts to present to the King. Hotham could not forbear to point out that debts were arising 'from hour to hour' over which he had no control and which were entirely unexpected: he remonstrated against 'the amazing expense of your stables' which was still increasing, and he pointed out that the Prince was 'totally in the hands, and at the mercy of your builder, your upholsterer, your jeweller & your tailor'. The two first act 'without a single care or enquiry from whence money was to arise . . . ; neither my advice, my expostulations, nor my representation of there being no fund whatever for this purpose, has been regarded'. His total estimate of what was owed amounted to £147,293, of which £15,000 was a debt about which there was no information. When the Prince refused to specify how and to whom it had been incurred his father, suspecting it had been used for political purposes, refused to help unless there was a full disclosure.[18] The negotiations were deadlocked, and had the King realized what other scrape the Prince had now become involved in and the true reason for his wanting to go abroad his anger would have exceeded anything so far expressed.

[17] George to King, 24 Aug. 1784 and reply, 27th: *CGPW*, i, 155–7.

[18] George to King, 30 Aug.; to Southampton, 1 Sept.; King to Southampton and enclosure, 2 Sept.; George to King, 5 Sept.; Southampton to George, 6 Sept. and reply 17th: ibid., i, 158–62.

Chapter 4

MARIA FITZHERBERT

In 1783 George fell genuinely in love, for the only time in his life. He is said to have first noticed Maria Fitzherbert in 1780 when she was driving in Hyde Park with her second husband. Her golden hair, hazel eyes and fresh complexion attracted him, and though she was no conventional beauty, with an aquiline nose and a determined chin, her face was full of character. She showed her spirit when the Prince turned to look at her and she took no notice of him, an unusual experience for him which no doubt aroused his curiosity, but the encounter did not lead to any consequences until three years later. In the meantime Maria became a widow for the second time. Her first husband, Edward Weld, a rich Catholic landowner from Dorset, died after a fall from his horse after only one year of marriage, when she was nineteen, and she was equally unfortunate with her second husband, Thomas Fitzherbert of Swynnerton in Staffordshire, also a wealthy Catholic squire, with a London house in Park Street, Mayfair and a wide social acquaintanceship. He died of a pulmonary infection in the south of France, where he had gone to try to recover his health, when Maria was still only twenty-six. She inherited the house in Park Street and a jointure of £1,000 a year, a comfortable income which enabled her to go out in society. However, she stayed for a further year at Nice before returning to England in 1781. She set up house in Park Street but she could not face living constantly in London and took lodgings in newly fashionable Brighton. During the winter of 1783–4 her uncles, Lord Sefton and Henry Errington, persuaded her to return to town and set about bringing her out of her seclusion and back into society, where she was soon a popular figure. She agreed to go with them to the opera, heavily veiled to preserve her privacy, and was seen by the Prince as she was waiting for her carriage. Whether or not he remembered their first encounter, he came up and demanded to be introduced.[1]

He was immediately fascinated by her and determined to bring her into his circle. He gave a number of balls and parties at Carlton House especially for her, but she, no doubt aware of his reputation and her danger, tried to avoid him. He let it be known that he would attend no

[1] Anita Leslie, *Mrs Fitzherbert*, 21–6.

parties unless she was present and on one occasion he went to her house at night and battered on the door, but was refused admittance. Maria was a virtuous and deeply religious woman and would never consent to be his mistress, with all the shame and gossip that would follow. Clearly, too, she could never be his legal wife, for the Prince of Wales could not marry a commoner. Far worse, she was a Roman Catholic and marriage to her would cost him his title to the throne under the Act of Settlement of 1701. Such a marriage would in any case be impossible until the Prince became twenty-five because the Royal Marriages Act made it illegal without his father's consent. Maria wished only to be left in peace without having to fend off his embarrassing attentions.

Nevertheless, the Prince was handsome, impeccably mannered and charming, a superb dancer, a showy driver and a fine horseman. And he had made up his mind. She was the centre of his life, the obsession of his thoughts, for her he would gladly give up his rackety existence and if need be the throne itself, and settle down to a life of domestic bliss. He would never take no for an answer and he was not accustomed to being denied what he set his heart upon. 'He hungered, he thirsted, he cried to heaven, he was the most infernal bore', wrote Maria's biographer.[2] With all the resources of a demanding nature he plagued her and all his friends with assurances of his devotion and passion. Georgiana Devonshire bore the brunt. She had befriended Maria and become her protectress, but George tried to use his own friendship with her to win her support and collusion.

Georgiana had been through it all before. She too had been the target of the Prince's amorous advances and, though attracted to him, was strong-minded and sensible enough to know that it could only lead to ruin and disgrace. George had settled for a close but platonic relationship which enabled him to use her as his confidante. 'He would not rest till he told me his passion for Mrs. F. and his design to marry her', she noted, 'and any remonstrance from me was always followed by threats of killing himself &c. &c'. Georgiana knew well enough that the cemeteries were not full of suicidal rejected lovers, and she understood and shared Maria's reluctance to become involved in a scandalous affair. Yet even she hesitated when the Prince seemed to be ready to carry out his threat.

On 8 July 1784, Georgiana was giving a supper party when she received a message that he had stabbed himself with his sword at Carlton House, and was determined to bleed to death unless Maria went to him. Maria would go only if Georgiana accompanied her. They drove in Maria's chariot to Carlton House, where George played the

[2] Ibid., 33–4.

deathbed scene to such effect that to save his life she agreed to marry him, using a ring from Georgiana's finger as a token. Both ladies immediately afterwards agreed that a promise extorted by such blackmail was null and void, and signed a paper to that effect. Maria assured the duchess again that she had never had any intention of agreeing to a marriage and that she had always made it plain to the Prince and to his friends that this was so. Georgiana wrote in turn to the Prince that the scheme was 'madness', that she could not be present at any pretended marriage since it could not be a legal one, and that she had been 'quite wild with the horror of it ever since'. She begged him to consult Charles Fox at once before taking any further step.

A few days later, the Duchess wrote to the Prince's friend George Onslow, suggesting that he might persuade him to be examined by a surgeon to prove whether the suicide attempt had been genuine or whether, as she suspected, he had merely scratched himself. The Prince's reaction was one of hurt indignation: he declared that his conduct towards Maria had always been perfectly honourable and towards Georgiana herself guided by the sentiments of 'the tenderest of Brothers' towards a sister. Nevertheless he persisted in wild scenes designed to persuade Maria to keep her promise to him.[3] As Lord Holland memorably recorded, 'He cried by the hour . . . he testified to the sincerity and violence of his passion and his despair by the most extravagant expressions and actions, rolling on the floor, striking his forehead, tearing his hair, falling into hysterics, and swearing that he would abandon the country, forego the Crown, sell his jewels and plate, and scrape together a competence to fly with the object of his affections to America.'[4]

The object of his affections had already fled to the continent on the morning after the scene at Carlton House to escape his attentions. This explained George's sudden decision in July 1784 to go abroad to economize. His true object was to follow Maria and persuade her to marry him, even if it meant giving up the throne. He declared his willingness to give up his right and that of any children he might have to Frederick, whose intended marriage to the daughter of the King of Prussia would settle the succession to both the British and the Hanoverian possessions. He would give up everything for his beloved Maria.[5] Whether the king knew anything of what had happened is not known, but he certainly suspected that his eldest son's sudden desire

[3] 'Statement by the Dss. of D.', 29 Jan. 1794; 'Statement by the Dss. of D. and Mrs Fitzherbert', 9 July 1784; Maria to Georgiana [n.d.]; Georgiana to George [n.d.]: Bessborough, 85–90; George to Georgiana, 19 July [1784]: *CGPW*, i, 150–2.

[4] Holland, *Memoirs of the Whig Party*, ii, 126.

[5] J. Harris, First Earl of Malmesbury, *Diaries*, ii, 128–30; Anita Leslie, *Mrs Fitzherbert*, 46.

for economy must have some ulterior cause. His blunt refusal to allow him to leave the country was accompanied by further demands that he should retrench his expenditure and change his way of life.

So matters rested for over a year. The Prince, unable to pursue his beloved in person, dispatched a series of passionate letters by his own courier beseeching Maria to return. Fox and his political friends joined in, urging her to comply and become the Prince's mistress to save his life, and with it their own prospects. George visited Georgiana daily to pour out his feelings, even pursuing her to the Devonshires' villa at Wimbledon so regularly that gossips began to wonder if there was an affair between them. Maria meanwhile set off to travel to Holland, France and Switzerland, vainly hoping to elude couriers and expostulations and find peace. Yet in the end her resolution weakened, whether because of the intolerable pressure or because she became convinced of George's sincerity, or perhaps she realized that she loved him after all. In the autumn of 1785 she indicated that she might return but insisted that a valid, if secret, marriage should be arranged if she was to submit.[6]

George was overjoyed. On 3 November he wrote a letter of forty-two pages addressed to 'my dearest & only beloved Maria' and concluding 'Come then, oh! come, dearest of wives, best & most adored of women'; he promised to be 'ye best of husbands & . . . *unalterably thine*'. Hugh Elliot, a diplomat, was trying on behalf of the King and Pitt to discover whether the Prince was, or was about to be, married to Mrs Fitzherbert, and was authorized to hint about the possible payment of his debts if he would consent to be betrothed to the Princess of Orange. George assured Maria that he would never consent to such a plan, that she was 'my life, my soul, my all, my everything' and asserted: 'I have look'd upon myself as married for above this year & a half, ever since I made to thee & thou madest to me in the face of Heaven, a vow mutually to regard one another as man & wife . . . wh. vow [he pointedly reminded her] thou hast so lately confirmed by ye consent thou hast given to *become mine*'. He urged her to set out at once for England where they could be married that same night in a 'happy tho' secret union'. He promised to meet her within ten minutes of her arrival in Park Street, where he would 'fly upon ye wings of love' as soon as he heard she was there. He could not desist from repeating his threat to do away with himself if she deceived him: between professions of eternal love and warnings of instant death he left her no room for denial.[7]

George's arrangements for the wedding, which was to be at Maria's

[6] Anita Leslie, *Mrs Fitzherbert*, 37–47; Villiers, 75; *CGPW*, i, 173–4.

[7] George to Maria, 3 Nov.: *CGPW*, i, 189–201. On Elliot's mission, see Elliot to Pitt, 17 Oct. 1785: RA 50201–2.

house, encountered some difficulty, since any clergyman officiating in defiance of the Royal Marriages Act was liable to heavy penalties and no respectable one would risk it. Eventually in desperation George found the Revd John Burt, a prisoner in the Fleet prison for debtors, paid £500 to settle his debts, and promised him a bishopric when he came to the throne. The ceremony was set for Thursday, 15 December, a week after Maria's arrival.[8]

The news of her coming set alarm bells ringing in the mind of Charles Fox, who was well aware of the dangers the Prince was putting himself into, as well as of the consequences for his political friends. If he excluded himself from the succession he blasted their hopes of his calling them into office. On the 10th, Fox wrote a long and urgent plea to him to reconsider what he described as 'the very desperate step . . . of marrying her at this moment', when the King 'not feeling for you as a father ought' favoured his brother Frederick, who was likely to marry as his father wished, and when anti-Catholic prejudices were prevalent in the nation – it was only five years since the Gordon Riots against 'popery' had set London ablaze. Furthermore, the marriage would not be a real one 'according to the present laws of the country' and if there were doubts as to its legality, particularly if there should be children, there would be 'perpetual agitation' and the prospect of future disputes over the legitimacy of heirs to the throne. It was all too distressing to think of. 'The sum of my humble advice, nay, of my earnest entreaties', he wrote, '. . . is this, that you would not think of marrying till you can marry legally' (that is, after his twenty-fifth birthday), and that 'In the meanwhile, a mock marriage, for it can be no other, is neither honourable for any of the parties, nor, with respect to your Royal Highness, even safe'.[9]

Strong words from a subject to the Prince of Wales, and especially from one who was in effect his political adviser: but the Prince ignored the warning. A few hours later, at 2 a.m., he wrote a letter of reassurance: 'Make yourself easy, my dear friend; believe me the world will now soon be convinced [how, he did not specify] yt there not only is [not], but never was, any ground for these reports, wh. of late have been so malevolently circulated'.[10]

Four days later the marriage took place. It was melodramatic enough. George was accompanied to Maria's house only by his friend Orlando Bridgeman, who stood at the door with a drawn sword while the vows were exchanged in the presence as witnesses of Henry Errington and Maria's brother, John Smythe – both Roman Catholics, and both putting themselves in peril of punishment for a capital felony for

[8] Anita Leslie, *Mrs Fitzherbert*, 48–50.

[9] C.J. Fox, *Memorials and Corresp.*, ii, 278–83.

[10] George to Fox, 11 Dec. 1785: ibid., 283–5.

Maria's sake. The marriage was valid in the eyes of both the Anglican and the Roman churches, but as there could be no official record or certificate George himself wrote out a statement for Maria to keep as proof declaring that the marriage had taken place, which he, Maria, and the two witnesses signed. She later cut out the witnesses' signatures to protect them in case of disclosure. Burt was rewarded but he never got his bishopric. He was given the Rectory of Hoo St Mary's Rochester and became Vicar of Twickenham, no doubt by the Prince's patronage, but he died in October 1791, aged only thirty-five, before he could claim his promised elevation.[11]

The Prince's conduct could hardly be defended as prudent or even honourable. It put both himself and his wife in great jeopardy – to himself, of losing his right of succession, to her and her relatives of the severest penalties of the law. If Maria had consented to be his mistress all these perils would have been avoided and they could have lived together openly for as long as they wished to do so, for royal liaisons of this kind were so common as to be almost universal in George III's family. Yet Maria's religious scruples overrode all matters of convenience. She would not degrade herself to the position of a kept woman, which would lower her standing in society, and she would not give herself to any man without the blessing of her church, as this would imperil her immortal soul. She had done as much as she could to dissuade the Prince, and had given way only under extreme pressure amounting to moral blackmail.

The Prince's detractors (and there have been many) have universally condemned his conduct, ascribing it to mere selfishness and to weakness of character. Yet he was under an enormous emotional stress. After twenty-three years during which he had never experienced the affections of his parents and searched fruitlessly for a permanent and stable emotional attachment, he had at last found someone on whom he could lavish his deepest feelings. He could bear no obstacles to the fulfilment of his needs: nothing mattered save the happiness he believed he had found. He could, like a later monarch, have given up his throne and gone into a life of exile to be with the woman he loved, but his father was unlikely to condone such a step or to allow him any but the smallest income. George could not contemplate such a fate, despite his declarations that he would suffer anything for Maria. In any case, in his state of emotional turmoil he was incapable of rational decisions.

Maria's behaviour has been less openly condemned because of the coercion to which he subjected her, but it was she, after all, who insisted

[11] Villiers, 76–85; the marriage 'certificate' is reproduced in *CGPW*, i, frontispiece. On Burt, ibid., 174 and memorial tablet, Hoo St Mary's, Rochester: *The Times*, 10 June 1839; Burt to George, 25 Feb. 1791: RA, Fitzherbert papers.

upon a valid, if secret, marriage in full knowledge of what the consequences might be. She too was suffering deep emotional stress. She undoubtedly loved him, for it is impossible to suppose that she would take such a step otherwise: the future was to prove the truth of her affections, and to show that they were deeper and more constant than his. Her sincerity impressed not only George himself but most of the Royal Family, including, perhaps surprisingly, the King and Queen. They all behaved towards her with genuine affection even if they did not know the whole truth. After George's death she told William IV and showed him the marriage 'certificate'. The King, who had always been kind towards her, burst into tears and begged her to accept the title of Duchess, but she refused, asking only permission to wear widow's weeds and to dress her servants in royal livery. She remained faithful to George throughout the rest of her life.[12] He eventually proved incapable of the same devotion, but despite his later attachments to other women he never found anyone whom he loved as he had loved her.

The newly married couple still had troubles to contend with. The marriage ceremony removed Maria's scruples, but as it was secret she could not live openly with the Prince without appearing to be his mistress. After a brief honeymoon at Richmond they maintained separate houses, George at Carlton House or Brighton, Maria at Park Street and then, for greater convenience, in Pall Mall near to Carlton House, or in a rented house near the Brighton Pavilion. Every night they had to separate, George returning home in his carriage. Even an appearance in public together was liable to create gossip and endanger Maria's reputation. The change in her conduct and their being constantly together and obviously lovers itself raised questions: had they secretly married, or had she sacrificed her virtue and her reputation? Tongues began to wag. Possibly Bridgeman, or Maria's brother, may have dropped hints about the marriage, and Georgiana and her sister guessed it, but a curtain of discretion hid the truth, though the caricaturists were doing their best to provoke a disclosure or a denial by depicting the happy couple in surroundings of domestic bliss.

Even more significant to many observers was the change in the Prince's way of life. He no longer appeared alone at fashionable amusements, gave up excessive drinking and gambling, was seen no more at brothels and clubs, but spent his time with Maria in London or at Brighton where they gave select parties to a few close friends. The two years after the marriage – together with the few years after their reconciliation in 1800 – were probably the happiest of his life. Only the

[12] Shane Leslie, 'The Truth about Mrs Fitzherbert': *Everybody's Weekly*, 1 July 1950 (copy in RA, ibid.).

shadow of his still mounting debts, despite his reduced expenditure, lay across his path; and these were to bring the subject of his marital state more ominously into public discussion in 1786.

The Prince could never live cheaply. The simpler but still grand lifestyle at Carlton House, the Brighton Pavilion, now being fitted up in classical elegance and at considerable expense by Holland, or Maria's house in Pall Mall which he decorated lavishly for her at a cost of £50,000, hardly reduced his expenses. Mary Frampton described an assembly at Maria's as 'the most splendid I was ever at', with servants in green and gold lining the staircase to announce the guests and carry refreshments. One room was hung with puckered blue satin which was the model for wallpapers in all the fashionable drawing rooms. Maria was an unobtrusive hostess, who charmed the company with her serenity and quiet conversation, a contrast to the boisterous parties at other great houses, but everything was lavish, the Prince as usual taking no thought for the cost.[13]

As a result, by the summer of 1786 his debts were once again at crisis point. He was threatened with legal actions and inundated by pleas from creditors, tradesmen and suppliers to his household as well as builders, jewellers and sellers of paintings and decorative objects. His weary and besieged Treasurer calculated that by Lady Day in 1786 he owed more than £269,878, of which over £160,000 was on account of arrears in various household departments, and nearly £80,000 was still needed for completing and furnishing Carlton House.[14] He had no option but to appeal yet again to his father, who once more demanded a full account and explanation, a plan for setting aside a part of his income as a sinking fund, and an assurance of future economy. When the Prince submitted details of his debts, the King pointed out that some £60,000 of private debts were 'wholly unexplained' – not surprisingly as most of it had gone on Maria's house – and that a total of over £100,000 was estimated as necessary 'to support farther extravagance'. He demanded full disclosure. The Prince brusquely replied that if his father was not satisfied, he would trouble him no further as 'I have no reason to expect either at present or in future the smallest assistance from your Majesty'. Two days later he wrote to Lord Southampton that he had no alternative but to dismiss all the gentlemen of his household, promising to reinstate them only 'whenever it is in my power to reassume yt splendid situation my birth has placed me in'. He told Lord Parker, one of his lords of the bedchamber, that he had determined not to appear again in public 'till I can do it again with that dignity and splendour which my rank in life entitles me to'. Work on Carlton House

[13] H.G. Mundy (ed.), *Journal* of Mary Frampton, 14–15.
[14] *Supra*, Chapter 3, n.15.

was stopped, the state apartments were shut up, and his racing stud, horses and carriages were sold by public auction for 7,000 guineas. The Prince set off for Brighton in a hired post-chaise to live as a private gentleman. Mrs Fitzherbert shut up her house in London and rented one adjacent to the Pavilion.[15]

As a gesture, George's action had some impact. Fox wrote that 'it had united the universal opinion of all descriptions of men in your favour' and that if he carried it through it would 'render [him] . . . popular in the extreme' and dispose Parliament in the next session or two to come to his relief. The Duke of Cumberland too assured him: 'your manly conduct is universally approved of' and 'will make you rise superior against the cruel calumny of the world'.[16] However, it had no effect on the King, who was prepared to wait for the Prince to come to heel. It was now too late to bring the matter before Parliament before the end of the current session, but George's political friends laid plans to do so in the next.

Towards the end of April 1787 Gilbert Elliot, a recent recruit to the ranks of the Whigs, told his wife that 'the Prince's affairs are coming on'. There was a growing volume of newspaper comment and speculation, much of it concerning Mrs Fitzherbert. Elliot was worried that

> the constitutional dangers and doubts belonging to this most equivocal condition of things, will force itself into the [parliamentary] discussion . . . I have always thought that part of his conduct, so far as it is known to me, a most heavy offence against duties and interests too sacred and too important to eight or ten millions of us to be excused even by the levity or the *passions* of youth.

He feared that '*our country gentlemen*', the backbench MPs, were against him and a meeting of Whig leaders showed reluctance to back an appeal to Parliament.[17] Fox, Sheridan and a few others were in favour, but the Duke of Portland, the party leader, who had forbidden his wife to receive Mrs Fitzherbert, and the other grandees were opposed. On 30 April, however, after some preliminary negotiations with Pitt, Alderman Newnham, a City MP and friend of the Prince, submitted a motion to the Commons calling for consideration of his financial affairs. John

[15] King to George, 3 July 1786; George to Ernest, 4 July; George to King, 5 July; Hugh Elliot to George, 6 July; George to Southampton, 7 July; letters from various members of George's household after their dismissal: *CGPW*, i, 231–6; George to King, 11 July: ibid., 239–40.

[16] Fox to George, 16 July; Ernest to George, 31 July 1786: ibid., 247–9, 254–5.

[17] Sir Gilbert Elliot to Lady Elliot, 20 April 1787: *Life and Letters of Sir Gilbert Elliot* (henceforward *Elliot*) i, 155.

Rolle, a Devonshire tory, took the opportunity to hint at possible constitutional difficulties in the way of a settlement, meaning of course the implications of the marriage. Fox, who must have had his suspicions about the matter, received assurances from the Prince that there was no truth whatever in the insinuation. He chose to believe him and decided to deny the rumours categorically, in the hope of fending off a crisis and protecting the Whigs' political interests. He rose to speak:

> He denied it *in toto*, in point of fact, as well as law. The fact not only never could have happened legally, but never did happen in any way whatsoever, and had from the beginning been a base and malicious falsehood.

On being asked by Rolle whether he spoke from direct authority, he replied that he did.[18]

The relief in the House was palpable. Fox's explicit statement reassured all sides and Pitt now persuaded the King to agree to a settlement and to grant a further £10,000 per annum from the Civil List and a capital sum towards the payment of George's debts and the completion of Carlton House. It was, wrote Gilbert Elliot, 'a good day for the Prince', though he admitted that it left Mrs Fitzherbert 'in an awkward way'.[19]

Maria considered her situation more than awkward. She was publicly branded as the Prince's mistress, and by his own authority. Furthermore, George's method of breaking the news was hardly well judged. He took her by both hands and said, 'Only conceive, Maria, what Fox did yesterday. He went down to the House and denied that you and I were man and wife. Did you ever hear of such a thing?'[20] She was naturally furious and declared that she would have nothing more to do with him. In truth, George was at his wits' end. Whether or not he had always intended to deceive her, the full recklessness of his conduct now came home to him. He still hoped to avoid a public admission of his marriage while reassuring Maria that it was genuine and that he was committed to her for ever. To achieve this masterpiece of casuistry was however beyond his or anyone else's ingenuity. He decided to call in help from his Whig friends, and chose for the task the young Charles Grey, who had taken his seat in the Commons only three months before but who had already become a companion and admirer of Fox and a habitué of Devonshire House. Grey later recollected the scene:[21] he

[18] *Cobbett's Parliamentary History*, [henceforward *Parl. Hist.*], xxii, 225–31; Anita Leslie, *Mrs Fitzherbert*, 68–70.

[19] Sir Gilbert to Lady Elliot, 7 May 1787: *Elliot*, i, 157.

[20] Anita Leslie, *Mrs Fitzherbert*, 71.

[21] E.A. Smith, *Lord Grey*, 18 quoting 'Memorandum of conversation between

found the Prince 'in such disorder and agony of mind as he scarcely ever saw any other person in . . . he was in tears walking about the room and beating his head against the walls'. He confessed the marriage and declared that it was '*absolutely necessary*' that Fox's denial should be contradicted, but without actually admitting the truth. Even Grey, headstrong young man as he then was, could see no way of constructing such an extraordinary statement, and he had the courage to say so. He also told Fox what the Prince had said.

Fox had in any case found out the truth. He met Henry Errington on the steps of Brooks's Club shortly after his statement to the House; Errington told him that he had actually been present at the ceremony. Fox was shocked and dismayed that he had been deceived into lying to the House of Commons and he and his leading Whig colleagues promptly withdrew from Carlton House society. Grey later alleged that the Prince never forgave him for refusing to protect him: it was the first stage in the process that led the Prince eventually to deny Grey the political favour he had given to Fox, and to draw him as Regent into the arms of the Tories.

Grey having refused to oblige, the Prince turned to a less scrupulous spokesman. 'Then Sheridan must do it', he muttered. But even Sheridan shrank from an outright denial of Fox's statement and George and Maria had to make do with a highly ambiguous statement in the House which muddied the waters still further. Sheridan, who was fond of Maria – as most people were – did however pay her a graceful tribute in his speech. She was 'a character upon which truth could fix no just reproach, and which was in reality entitled to the truest and most general respect'. It placated Maria's feelings to some degree, though it transferred some of the obloquy to the Prince, and it attracted the sympathy of many leading society figures for her. Lady Gideon gave a party called 'The Feast of Reconciliation', attended by George's two uncles and their wives and many other notables, at which Maria presided wearing white roses – the symbol of her marriage.[22]

Politically, the episode had significant consequences. Many of the Prince's old friends never completely trusted him thereafter, though out of self-interest they sought his favour again in 1788 when the prospect of his becoming Regent during his father's first serious illness opened the possibility of office once more. In the interim, there was a breach with his old friends, including the Duke of Portland and other leaders of the Whig party. George was left with only a few second-rank members of the opposition, like Sheridan, who always retained

Lords Grey and Grenville', 28 April 1814: BL Add. MS 58949, ff. 116–21; Sichel, ii, 118.

[22] Lord Stourton's Narrative, Fitzherbert papers, quoted in Anita Leslie, *Mrs Fitzherbert*, 71–2; *Parl. Hist.*, 4 May, xxii, 255–6; Sichel, ii, 118.

affection for him, and Jack Payne, a naval captain and ADC, a long-standing crony and a leading figure in his restored household. In politics, they and a few others formed a separate political group, which became known as the Prince's party and complicated the future political scene from time to time.

Despite these complications, the affair turned out well for the Prince. Those who chose to turn a blind eye to Sheridan's equivocation were prepared to accept that the marriage was only a rumour. The Prince's income was increased, the House voted £161,000 to pay part of his debts and £60,000 to finish Carlton House, and a scheme to set aside a part of his income every year towards payment of the rest pleased his father, who genuinely wished to live on more affectionate terms with his eldest son. His household was now restored, and life returned to its agreeable tenor, with Maria again acting as his hostess and companion and no one wishing to upset the social peace by raising awkward questions. Long residences at Brighton, bathing and playing cricket, visits to the races at Newmarket and Windsor, parties, dinners and balls made up a glittering yet comfortable existence.

George had established himself at Brighton, using it as a summer seaside residence before his marriage. In his boyhood it was still a small fishing port, but it was becoming known as a health resort. Dr Richard Russell was one of those far-sighted medical men who realized the potential benefit to himself as well as to his fashionable patients of fresh air and sea bathing as a cure for most of the ills they suffered as a result of over-indulgence at the table and lack of exercise. By 1783, when George first visited the town in the company of his raffish uncle Cumberland, seeking relief in sea bathing for swollen glands in his neck, it was buzzing with life, not yet on the scale or with the established facilities of Bath, but beginning to provide a rival attraction much nearer to London than the highly regulated and expensive society of that west country resort. It also provided easy access to the popular Lewes races and the facilities for cricket and for shooting, hunting and coursing on the Downs.

Its informality appealed to the Prince: he could be found, as the poet Samuel Rogers remarked, 'drinking tea in a public room' of an inn, 'just as other people did'.[23] He determined to buy a house there, and commissioned his German cook and companion Louis Weltje to find a suitable residence. Weltje, who had prospered from his obscure beginnings as a gingerbread baker to become rich and celebrated, owned a

[23] C. Musgrave, *Royal Pavilion*; H.D. Roberts, *A History of the Royal Pavilion*; Richardson, 19. The Prince's first visit was greeted with ringing church bells and a salute of guns, one of which unfortunately exploded, killing one of the gunners who was blown off the battery.

number of houses in Brighton. He fixed on a 'respectable farmhouse' for sale at £20,000. It had a view of the sea on the west side of the Steine, the fashionable centre of the town. Once in possession, first as Weltje's tenant at £150 a year, then as owner, George as usual sent in his architect, Henry Holland, to plan the house's transformation into a pleasant classical bow-fronted villa with balconies and verandas from which he could preside over the society of the town. It was completed in five months, to be ready for the summer of 1787, at a total cost of some £22,000.[24]

Brighton quickly became fashionable, began to grow rapidly, and attracted to the Sussex coast the *ton* of society and above all George's sporting and drinking companions. His favourites, like the dashing horseman and driver Sir John Lade, Beau Brummell, the dandy of dandies, or George Hanger, roistering and barely literate, were the types of Regency buck who might be found racing their chariots through the narrow Lanes of the town to the danger of the public in the daytime, and gambling, drinking and carousing into the small hours of the morning. One of his cronies, Onslow, won a bet by driving four horses in his phaeton galloping twenty times through the gateways of Cumberland's house at full speed without touching the pillars. George's time was filled by hunting, racing, attending balls at Shergold's and Hick's, shooting partridges, bathing, and going to the theatre.[25] Above all, however, it was to Brighton and the Pavilion, as the house came to be called, that he brought Maria Fitzherbert after their marriage. They were celebrated by Gainsborough, who painted them in a boat with Sheridan and Lord Radnor, and George commissioned him, at a time when landscapes were out of fashion, to paint two for Maria. He also patronized his portraits and bought the *Blue Boy*. The Prince possessed seven of Reynolds's portraits and in 1789 he commissioned Romney to paint Maria. In 1792 he was painted by Hoppner and in 1805 by Mme Vigée-Lebrun, another portrait destined for Maria at Brighton.

Since for the sake of propriety the Prince and Maria could not live under the same roof, she was provided with her own house on the Steine. It too was elegantly fitted up and furnished, and she gave parties there as well as acting as hostess at the Pavilion. Their life in Brighton was, however, a quietly domestic one – rising late, bathing from their machines, George under the care of the well-known character 'Smoaker' Miles, riding or driving in the afternoons, with dinners and supper parties in the evenings. During the Revolutionary Wars his

[24] H.D. Roberts, 24–5.
[25] Ibid., 10.

regiment was stationed there, providing an occasional diversion in the form of exercises and manoeuvres at which he displayed his 'truly martial' figure. For a time at least, it was an idyllic existence.

However, George was unable to resist occasional bouts of drunken revelry with his friends, and Maria's patience began to grow thin. The episode of 1787 had burnt deeply into her mind. She began to mistrust him, and her temper – never far below the surface – began to flare up so that he started to feel that his idyll was passing. By the summer of 1788 the relationship was beginning to wear thin. Never one to stay faithful to one woman for long, the Prince's eye began to wander and Fox, who was now alienated from Maria, and saw her separation from the Prince as the Whigs' only hope, sought to encourage him. He introduced George to an opera singer named Anna Maria Crouch, the mistress of Michael Kelly who was also an opera singer and friend of Mozart. The affair lasted only a few days, but it was ominous for the future.[26] Maria never lost her hold on his affections, but it now appeared that his deeper feelings were always liable to be overriden by momentary temptations. A quiet domestic existence with the woman he loved was ill-suited to his temperament and could not satisfy him for long. Maria was the victim of his inconstant character, but she still could not help loving him and she put up with his moods despite occasional bouts of nerves and low spirits.

So matters continued for another six years. In the summer of 1794 Maria, needing to get away from George's unpredictable moods, rented Marble Hill House at Richmond, once the residence of George II's mistress, Lady Suffolk, and while the Prince dallied at Brighton she passed quiet days in the gardens or on the river, followed by dinner parties either at her house or in the nearby residences of George's brothers Frederick and William, who were always fond of her. The Prince was now falling under a new spell. One day in late June Maria received an affectionate note from him announcing that he intended to dine at Windsor on the following day. She was invited to the Duke of Clarence's that evening and George was half expected to join them, but as she was sitting down to dinner she was handed a note from him. It announced that he intended never to see her again. White and shaken, she refused her host's offer to take her home, and drove back alone. When she entered her bedroom she picked up the note she had received that morning and had left on her dressing-table, and wrote on it:

> This letter I received the morning of the day the Prince sent me word he would never enter my house. Lady Jersey.[27]

[26] Anita Leslie, *Mrs Fitzherbert*, 76–7.
[27] Ibid., 90–2.

Maria was right to suspect that Lady Jersey was behind the Prince's unforgivable conduct. She was in truth to be his *éminence grise.* A grandmother at forty-one and married to the fourth Earl of Jersey, who was a prominent courtier and complaisant husband, she was an attractive, vivacious and seductive woman of considerable charm, with 'thick dark hair, doe eyes and creamy bosom',[28] and her husband's position at court provided many opportunities for her to meet the Prince. She intrigued to get him to herself, away from Maria, and in order to do so permanently she conceived the idea of persuading him to offer to his father to marry legitimately a German princess who, she assured herself, would be a wife only in name while *she* would remain his mistress and be the power behind the throne. She worked on George's growing dissatisfaction with his relationship with Maria: he complained to his brother Frederick in August 1794 of 'the very uncomfortable situation I have been in for some months, & indeed for some years' over 'various disagreements & misunderstandings'. His new way of life was beginning to seem a drag on the amusements and dissipations that still attracted him, and Maria's disapproval of his old lifestyle irritated him. As he drifted away from her, Maria became, as Prince Ernest noticed, 'very low-spirited'. She was not deceived by George's request to his friends to show her 'the same attention as before', which Georgiana also thought strange. It was obvious that he was about to leave her, though he did try to ensure that she should have a suitable settlement. She was eventually granted an income of £3,000 a year, gave up her house in Pall Mall and bought number 6 Tilney Street, Park Lane, where she lived and entertained her friends until their next reconciliation six years later.[29] Meanwhile, the reign of Lady Jersey began.

[28] Flora Fraser, *The Unruly Queen*, 41.

[29] George to Frederick, 29 Aug., 26 and 29 Oct.: 1794 *CGPW*, ii, 453–4, 472n., 473.

Chapter 5

HOPES DISAPPOINTED

Since the beginning of his friendship with Charles Fox, George had been identified with Foxite whig politics as well as society and had come to be regarded as the potential leader of Whig governments, should they ever be formed. After the defeat of the Coalition's India Bill in December 1783, and even more after the disastrous outcome of the 1784 general election, that possibility had seemed more remote than ever. Pitt's administration was graced wholeheartedly by the favour of George III who regarded Fox as a personal enemy, and was buttressed by the approval of the large number of independent MPs who deplored 'faction' as prejudicial to the true interests of the country and regarded Pitt as the ablest and most patriotic of the available political leaders, deserving of support as the King's Minister. Pitt also had the enthusiastic endorsement of the public at large who were benefiting from the revival of prosperity after the American War. This was ascribed to his economic management and diplomatic skill, especially in negotiating the advantageous commercial treaty with France in 1785. In contrast, the Prince of Wales and his political allies were seen as selfish, extravagant and immoral and therefore unfit to be trusted with the nation's interests. Yet the fundamental reality of eighteenth-century government remained unaltered: power and office were at the disposal of the monarch, who had sufficient political influence to dismiss the ministers and appoint others of his own choosing – as indeed George III had done as recently as 1783 – and to provide them with the necessary majority in Parliament to carry on the government. If George III were to be removed from the political scene, his eldest son would acquire those powers, and that could mean only one thing in the penultimate decade of the century – the construction of a government under the dominant authority of Charles James Fox. It was no coincidence that in the autumn of 1788 the sudden illness of George III threw the political world into confusion and aroused the eager hopes of Pitt's opponents.

Starting in the summer with a series of apparently digestive and rheumatic disorders, the illness began to show alarming symptoms of feverish agitation. The King's normally hurried and abrupt speech began to become incoherent and there were signs that his mind was wandering. The Queen and her family moved into a remote wing of the

Queen's Lodge at Windsor, while the King's attendants were organized into a shift system for constant surveillance. Gilbert Elliot reported – from what source it is not clear, but perhaps from Dr Warren, one of the royal physicians and a partisan of Fox, who was disclosing details of the illness to his political friends – that the King was 'extremely impatient under this separation, and was indeed violent and outrageous in his attempts to get to her [the Queen's] apartments'. He had to be restrained from approaching her, while she shrank from his company, fearing his violence. Rumours began to circulate and at the end of October the Prince of Wales was summoned from Brighton. His father's eccentricity became more marked and his physical symptoms more painful and alarming. On 5 November, by strange coincidence the centenary of William III's landing at Torbay to rescue the Protestant succession, it became evident that the King's mind was totally deranged: he had seized his eldest son by the throat and thrust him against the wall, demanding who it was that forbade him to whisper. The Prince nearly fainted and had to be revived by rubbing Hungary water on his temples and by bleeding.[1]

The Prince sent for Dr Warren, who was also his physician and who foretold that the King was unlikely to live long, which, in view of Warren's brutal treatment of his patient by applying hot blisters to the King's shaven head to draw off the 'humours' believed to be responsible for his condition, seemed likely to be a self-fulfilling prophecy. Jack Payne, now Comptroller of the Prince's Household, let out the news at Brooks's and Devonshire House. On the 7th, according to Payne, the King 'awoke with all the gestures and ravings of the most confirmed maniac', howling like a dog and chattering ceaselessly on religious subjects, 'from which his physicians draw the worst consequences'.[2]

The true nature of the 'Royal malady' puzzled his doctors, which, in the then rudimentary state of medical knowledge of both physical and mental disease, was not surprising. Until a few years ago the general opinion of historians was that it was a form of manic depressive psychosis,[3] brought on perhaps by the frustration felt by a man naturally highly sexed but married to a woman he had never wanted to marry and, despite their numerous offspring, never able to satisfy his sexual appetites. There seemed to be no obvious cause in political affairs, which were proceeding calmly enough, nor in the King's relations with

[1] Ayling, 329–32; Charles Chenevix-Trench, *The Royal Malady*, 13–23; Fanny Burney, *Diary and Letters of Mme D'Arblay*, iv, 131.

[2] Ayling, 333, 335; Sir Gilbert to Lady Elliot, 8 and 20 Nov. 1788: *Elliot*, i, 230–1, 234; T. Moore, *Sheridan*, ii, 19–25.

[3] For example, L.B. Namier, *Crossroads of Power*, 133–40, J.H. Plumb, *The First Four Georges*, 139–44, Chenevix-Trench, 9–12, J. Derry, *The Regency Crisis*, 4–10.

his sons, the Prince of Wales's affairs having not yet relapsed into the worry and chaos of two years previously.

Later researchers, led by two psychiatrists, Ida Macalpine and her son Richard Hunter, have put forward the alternative hypothesis that the King suffered from a rare hereditary disease of the metabolism known as acute intermittent porphyria, in which the mental symptoms are the product not of any disease of the brain, nor of mental stress, but of a physical disorder during which toxins in the nervous system make their way to the brain and produce delusions, giving the appearance of insanity.[4] The matter is of some importance for a biographer of his eldest son, because the disease is a hereditary one and the Prince was a lifelong sufferer from conditions which, while never so acute as his father's, were said to bear some resemblance to them. Whether porphyria is in fact the correct diagnosis cannot however be conclusively proved and although it has come to be generally regarded as the true one there is always a possibility that some other condition, possibly as yet unrecognized as porphyria was until quite recently, may have been responsible. More recently, two molecular geneticists who have investigated the genetic make-up of some of Queen Victoria's descendants have claimed that traces of porphyria have been found in one or two such cases, but there is no new evidence that the disease, if present, was inherited from George III, or that this is the correct diagnosis of his illnesses, much less those of his eldest son. George IV, so far as is discernible, did not suffer from mental derangement like his father and many of his physical symptoms may well be ascribed to rheumatic complaints and the consequences of his over-indulgence in wine and food – something of which his father was never guilty. The fashionable claim that George III suffered from porphyria and passed it on to several of his descendants is supposition, not proven fact.[5] Historians must be cautious when leaving their area of professional competence, as must medical practitioners in venturing into territories where modern diagnostic techniques were unavailable. The present writer prefers to reserve judgement and believes that certainty on the point may never be achieved.

There is no doubt about the political implications of the King's illness. The immediate threat, that he would quickly die, soon passed over. The possibility of the Prince's succeeding to the throne in a short time therefore vanished. No one however could know when, or whether, the King would be capable of resuming his official functions

[4] I. Macalpine and R. Hunter, *George III and the Mad Business.*

[5] For criticism of the Macalpine–Hunter thesis, see Professor Geoffrey Dean in *British Medical Journal,* 17 Feb. 1968, 443. The recent research by Professor J.C.G. Rohl, Martin Warren and David Hunt is incorporated in *Purple Secret: Genes, 'Madness' and the Royal Houses of Europe* (1998).

and until he could do so some provision had to be made to supply them. The constitution could not function without a head of government, as the King still was in reality, to supervise and control the executive, making appointments and approving policy, to assent to parliamentary legislation, and to fulfil the ceremonial duties of the monarch. Few seriously questioned the need for a regent to do so, nor did anyone seriously envisage that anyone other than the heir to the throne should be the person appointed. There were some suggestions that the Queen might be chosen, but this was no more than a piece of hopeful speculation on the part of a few of Pitt's supporters – the Queen being committed to him and hostile to Fox. The questions were, on what authority was that appointment to be made, and what extent of royal power and prerogative should be placed in his hands? These were political rather than constitutional questions, for there was no modern precedent and no ready-made procedure for the appointment of a regent on which to rely. The rules would have to be made up as the politicians went along, and they would be fashioned according to political expediency.

The crucial fact was that the Prince of Wales was regarded as a supporter of the Foxites and that if he was given the authority to choose and dismiss ministers and to make appointments he would transfer the power of government into their hands. It was accepted that even under a restricted system a regent must have the right to change and appoint his own ministers. The mood in the Prince's circle at the beginning of what came to be known as the regency crisis was therefore optimistic, and jostling for offices soon began. George found himself courted on all sides, and the heady excitement of Cabinet-making almost drove other pleasures from his mind. His chief ally and adviser was Sheridan, for Fox as luck would have it was taking a holiday in Italy: no one knew at first where he was, and it took until 24 November for him to reach England. Even then he was so exhausted by his hectic journey that he was too unwell to assert his control for several days. Until that time Sheridan, Payne and their cronies filled the role of the Prince's advisers and led him into situations which wiser and more cautious heads would have avoided.

At first, in the early days of the King's illness, the Prince had shown filial distress and affection for his father, weeping copiously and showing such emotion that his physicians thought it necessary to bleed him.[6] He and Maria left Brighton immediately to go to Windsor and on 6 November he sent for the Chancellor, Lord Thurlow, ostensibly to ask

[6] R. Neville to Buckingham, 7 Nov. 1788: Duke of Buckinghan and Chandos (ed.) *Court and Cabinets of George III*, i, 437; Sheridan to Payne, [Oct.–Nov. 1788]; 'I really write in an agitation of mind yt. is easier to be conceived than described': George to P. Goldsworthy [Oct.–Nov. 1788]: *CGPW*, i, 360–2.

his advice on the proper custody of the King, but probably also on the recommendation of Sheridan and Payne, who were hatching a scheme to win Thurlow over to their cause. As Payne wrote to his fellow-conspirator, Thurlow's 'law authority would have great weight' and his support in the House of Lords would be a great advantage. Thurlow on his part was willing to bargain on condition that in any new regency administration he would retain the great seal. His relations with Pitt were far from amicable. He disapproved of what he considered the Prime Minister's youthful naivety and his 'haughty impracticable spirit' and they had come into conflict over such measures as Pitt's support for Warren Hastings's impeachment and the Slave Trade Abolition Bill. At the same time, Thurlow was unwilling to commit himself decisively until he could see how matters would turn out, so he tried to keep the Foxites in hopeful suspense while not openly deserting his current colleages.[7]

The Prince's interview with Thurlow on 6 November was followed by a summons to Pitt to come to Windsor on the 8th, when they had a long conversation. Although Pitt was treated with civility, neither gave anything away as to their intentions. Further interviews on the 10th and 12th were similarly unrevealing, both parties waiting for more positive news from the physicians.[8] By the 13th Pitt had decided to proceed by a Parliamentary Bill to appoint the Prince as regent, but no decision had been taken as to the extent of his future powers. The Ministers were well aware that it would hardly be practicable to prevent the Prince from changing his government, but they hoped to limit his power to make any irreversible decisions. It was finally decided to restrain him from granting peerages or offices or pensions for life, and if possible from dissolving Parliament in order to provide the Foxites with a majority in the Commons through the Prince's use of the royal influence in elections. They still hoped that George, faced with limitations on his powers as regent, would offer to negotiate a compromise, perhaps a joint administration with both Pitt and Fox in office. George himself was equally undecided, awaiting Fox's return from Italy, but as the days passed and the King's condition seemed to deteriorate he became more impatient and less inclined to have anything to do with Pitt. Payne and Sheridan were trying to persuade him to make up his mind to abandon the minister, and hoping that Thurlow would disclose the secret discussions in Cabinet to convince him that there was no intention of a compromise on their side. 'Everything depends so entirely on the Prince's steadiness', wrote Elliot on the 26th.[9]

[7] Derry, 40–3.
[8] Pitt's memorandum of the conversation, *c.* 8 Nov. 1788: *CGPW*, i, 366–7.
[9] Sir Gilbert to Lady Elliot, 25 Nov. 1788: *Elliot*, i, 239.

When Fox returned to the fray, he found the Whigs still not united. The breach between the Prince and the Duke of Portland, their nominal leader, over the Prince's debts and the marriage to Mrs Fitzherbert was not healed until the end of November, when George sent a message to Portland 'cancelling all former discontents' and asked Fox to assure the Duke that he hoped 'everything that is past may be forgot between us'. They met and shook hands at Burlington House, Portland's residence, on 30 November.[10]

George had so far managed to behave with propriety, at least in public, but the strain was becoming too much. Elliot thought that he was 'pretty sick of his long confinement at Windsor, and it is very natural he should be so, for . . . he has been under greater restraint in his behaviour and way of life than he has ever known since he was his own master'. He broke out in the last weeks of November, when he drove his sisters and Lady Charlotte Finch through Windsor recklessly enough to break several lamps, and after the King was moved to Kew at the end of the month he began to throw wild parties at Carlton House and returned to his old dissipated habits at Brooks's. Sir William Young wrote that 'Drinking and singing were the order of the day in his company'.[11]

George after all was only twenty-six years of age, and had so far lived a life devoted to pleasure. He had received no training in political affairs or the duties of a monarch and his character was still to some extent unformed. His political attachment was not founded on study or knowledge of political ideas, but solely on the friendships he had made with Fox, Sheridan and a few others, and on a dislike and resentment of Pitt, whom he blamed for his father's refusal to pay his debts and allow him a larger income on which to afford his amusements. He was suddenly cast into a world of political intrigue for which he was ill-prepared and at the mercy of men who were seeking to use him for their own advantage. He was flattered and excited by the attentions he received: like a child with a new toy, he took delight in his new position and could hardly think of anything else. Admittedly, Sheridan urged him to be cautious in his conduct and to give the public 'no possible ground . . . to misrepresent [his] best actions'.[12] The mood amongst the Prince's friends however was becoming frenetic, as they began to anticipate the benefits that they would receive when he became regent: their celebrations as it turned out were premature, but they enjoyed the

[10] Georgiana's diary, 26 and 30 Nov. 1788: Sichel, ii, 408; *Elliot*, 26 Nov, i. 241–2; George to Portland, 28 Nov.: *CGPW*, i, 390.

[11] Buckingham and Chandos, *Court and Cabinets*, ii, 25.

[12] Sheridan to George [?23 Nov. 1788]: *CGPW*, i, 378–9. Sheridan and his wife had recently taken refuge from the bailiffs and were staying with Mrs Fitzherbert. The Archbishop of Canterbury described him as 'the prime favourite': 16 Jan. 1789: Bishop of Bath and Wells (ed.), *Auckland . . . Journal and Corresp.*, ii, 267.

fruits of office and influence in anticipation and the Prince himself responded to their mood to escape his apprehensions about the responsibility he would have to assume.

However, Pitt, the supreme political realist, had now recovered his confidence. When the House of Commons met to receive particulars of the proposed Regency Bill it was immediately clear that he retained the full support of his majority and of many of the numerous independent members, while Fox and the opposition threw away their chances by ill-advised tactics. The Prince assembled the ex-ministers who had served in the coalition Cabinet of 1783 to advise him, and counselled by Edmund Burke and Lord Loughborough, their candidate for the Lord Chancellorship before the scheme to draw Thurlow over to their camp, Fox put forward the notorious 'claim of right' – declaring that Parliament had no constitutional power to interfere but that the Prince assumed the regency automatically by hereditary right, as if the King were dead. Pitt's immediate response, that this was contrary to the Constitution and a betrayal of the spirit of the 1688–9 Revolution, won many potential waverers to his side and was influential with the public; it reinforced the view that Fox and his friends were merely a gang of rapacious politicans willing to ride roughshod over the Constitution in pursuit of power. The outcome was never in doubt from that moment: Pitt had won the initiative and the Regency Bill with its restrictions on the Prince's prerogative was never in danger of defeat or even of amendment.

It was unfortunate for the Foxites, who claimed to be the true heirs of Whiggism, that their self-interest was in direct conflict with their constitutional doctrine that the power of the Crown was limited by Parliament, just as Pitt, apparently the defender of the prerogative of the Crown, but also acting from self-interest, now relied upon the right of Parliament to determine the conditions on which royal authority should be exercised. In fact Pitt's position was logically and constitutionally defensible: Parliament had done just that in 1689, in the Bill of Rights, and again in 1701 in the Act of Settlement. Both had limited the power of the crown in certain important respects and had adjusted the succession to the throne accordingly. When Fox rose in the House of Commons to declare the Prince's hereditary *right* to the regency, Pitt is said to have slapped his thigh and declared, 'I'll unwhig the gentleman for the rest of his life!'[13]

The contest in Parliament lay therefore between Pitt's proposal that Parliament should decide how much of the royal power the regent should have, for how long and on what conditions, and Fox's contention that the Prince of Wales was automatically invested with the full

[13] *Parl. Hist.*, xxv, 187–96; Derry, 65–70.

royal power from the moment of his father's incapacity. The decision, in favour of Pitt's 'restricted regency', was inevitable: as long as the King could be expected to recover in a foreseeable time, politicians in office would hesitate to change sides, and on grounds of principle Pitt's contention that the constitution was a parliamentary and not an absolute monarchical one was irresistible to eighteenth-century freedom-loving Englishmen. The point was effectively decided in December 1788 when a series of resolutions moved by Pitt was accepted by both houses. The situation was not lost on Thurlow, and on Christmas Day there was, Elliot reported, 'a final explanation with the Chancellor, which terminated in a decided separation between him and our party, to the great joy of . . . every one of us except the Prince himself'. George, declared Elliot, 'has always had a partiality for the Chancellor, probably on account of his *table* qualities', and had been 'holding long conversations with him', by which means Thurlow had been able to learn of the opposition's designs and betray them to Pitt. It was not a happy augury for the Prince's political skills, and from that point the Whigs were on the defensive. It only remained to work out the details and embody them in legislation.[14]

Pitt notified the Prince of the proposed terms and restrictions on the regent's power on 31 December. As expected, they comprised a veto on making peers and granting places for life and placed the control of the Royal Household and of the King's real and personal property in the Queen's hands. The opposition was furious and in his letters Elliot accused the Queen of setting herself up as the leader of Pitt's party.[15] It was certainly the crucial victory for the Minister. Pitt took his time: the longer the passing of the Act could be delayed, the greater the hope that the King would recover and remove the necessity for it. The government therefore insisted on putting to the vote Fox's 'claim of right', and then introduced a series of resolutions embodying the principal proposals for the Regency before bringing forward the Bill itself. The opposition unwisely chose to fight each clause to a division, wasting time, since Pitt's majority never wavered. In the end the King's recovery was announced on 20 February and the Bill was abandoned in the House of Lords a few days before it would have been finally passed.

The Prince and his friends had protested about several of the features of Pitt's Bill, none more so than the provision that the care of the King's person and control of his household were to be in the hands of the Queen and not the Regent. Not only did George protest that this was a slur on his character: it was clear that, as the Queen was a firm

[14] *Parl. Hist.*, xxv, 334–5; Sir Gilbert to Lady Elliot, 27 Dec. 1788: *Elliot*, i, 249–50.
[15] Same to same, 20 Jan. and 18 Feb. 1789: ibid., i, 266–7, 272–3.

supporter of Pitt, the Prince would be unable to tap the considerable patronage resources of the household and so the ability of his ministers to control the House of Lords, where nearly all household appointees sat, would be in doubt. It was a double insult that Thurlow was to be one of a Council to assist the Queen. The House of Lords itself added further powers over the Royal Family to the Queen, which, Gilbert Elliot wrote, 'hurt the Prince of Wales more than all the rest [of the restrictions]'. Elliot alleged that it was 'the prevailing principle, not only with ministers but with all the party, and quite to a degree of passion and fury', to consider the Prince and all his supporters 'as a prey to be hunted down and destroyed without mercy', and he voiced suspicions that the King had not yet fully recovered and that his true state was being concealed so that the regency would not come into operation.[16] It was in pursuit of this suspicion that the Prince of Wales and the Duke of York attempted several times during this week to be admitted to see the King, only to be refused on one pretext or another. They were finally allowed to do so on 22 February.

Elliot described the scene:

> The King, when he came to the door of the room where they were, stopped and said he was not yet able to go in, and cried very much, but after a little pause he said he found himself better, and came in. He embraced them both with the greatest tenderness, and shed tears on their faces, and both the Princes were much touched with the scene. . . . The Queen was present, and walking to and fro in the room with a countenance and manner of great dissatisfaction . . . for she has acquired the same sort of authority over him that Willis [his doctor] and his men have, and the King's mind is totally subdued and in a state of the greatest weakness and subjection.[17]

In the eyes of the Prince and his supporters, the Queen was responsible for turning the King's mind against his two eldest sons and for the breach in the Royal Family that was a major consequence of the regency crisis. The Queen was anxious to protect her husband from any stress that might retard his recovery and she continued to obstruct attempts by the brothers to see him. George and Frederick on their part, ignoring their own blatant partisanship, blamed their mother for allying with Pitt and his followers. The opposition accused her of attempting to disgrace her sons in the hope of herself becoming regent in case of further attacks of the King's insanity. Relations remained frosty for some time and access to the King at Windsor continued to be barred.

[16] Same to same, 20 Feb. 1789: ibid., 274.
[17] Same to same, 23 Feb. 1789: ibid., 275.

An immature young man, surrounded by flatterers and politicians 'on the make', and now once again condemned to political impotence, George understandably reacted selfishly. The Princes returned to their old habits of dissipation. At the beginning of March deputies from the Irish Parliament in Dublin, where the Irish Whigs had gained the upper hand, arrived to present addresses offering the Prince the unrestricted regency in Ireland. They were entertained to a lavish dinner at the Duke of York's and the Prince, reported Elliot, was 'uncommonly agreeable and captivating . . . the whole time. . . . Amongst other agreeablenesses he sang an excellent sea-song extremely well. . . . All very excellent for giving a favourable impression'. The King's recovery of course nullified the addresses but a good time was had by all.[18]

Popular celebrations of the King's restoration to health followed and the princes had to demonstrate their filial affection by joining in. A 'most prodigious illumination' was displayed in the West End on the 10th, with, Elliot reported, 'devices of different sorts executed in coloured lamps and transparent paintings, and the blaze or masses of light in some of the squares was fine enough', including loyal devices such as 'G.R.' with a crown, or 'God Save the King'. The Foxites were forced to join in to avoid having their windows broken by the patriotic mob, though Elliot's servant 'not being expeditious enough, had a pane of glass broke in the library windows'. George and his brother spent the evening at the opera, but on the way their coach was held up in a traffic jam and the crowd called on them to join in shouting 'God Save the King!' which they did willingly enough, but when one man demanded that they should shout 'Pitt for ever' and 'God bless Pitt!' the Prince refused and the man pulled the coach door open and threatened to assault him. George made to get out and fight, but Frederick pulled him back into the coach, struck the stranger on the head, and ordered the coachman to drive on, the still-open door flapping about as they went. After the opera the Prince and his friends decided to walk home to see the illuminations, and several of the crowd cheered him as he joined in their loyal shouts. He called at Brooks's to share the celebrations and then ordered his coach to go home, 'just a little elevated with his dinner and claret', observed Elliot, 'but not drunk'. The episode showed that he had what Elliot called 'popular qualities' when he was willing to show them.[19]

However, the breach with the King and Queen was not over. At the beginning of April the King gave a concert at Windsor to which the princes were not at first invited, on the ground that, as the Queen

[18] Same to same, 4 March 1789: ibid., 277–8.
[19] Same to same, 28 March 1789: ibid., 288–9.

informed them, it was intended only for those 'who have *supported us* through the late business, and *therefore* you may possibly not choose to be present'. The princes were furious at the insult but were persuaded by the Duke of Portland and Elliot to send a conciliatory answer accepting the belated invitation as a means of 'testifying our warmest and most dutiful affection' to the King. At the concert, Elliot reported, the King was 'remarkably attentive and kind to the Princes; the Queen quite the contrary, and it is said appeared dowdy and glum at the King's behaviour to them'.[20] The culminating celebration of the royal recovery was a five-hour service of thanksgiving at St Paul's on 23 April, St George's Day, attended by vast crowds including the members of the Lords and Commons and 6,000 children from the various charity schools in the City, who 'set up their little voices and sang part of the hundredth psalm' as the King passed them. It was a moment which, Elliot confessed, 'I found most affecting; and . . . I found my *eyes running over,* and the bone in my throat, which was the case with many other people'. It was a magnificent occasion, George's three older sisters appeared splendid in purple silk gowns, gold Indian muslin petticoats over white satin, and white satin scarves and a bandeau embroidered 'God Save the King' in gold embroidery. George and Frederick naturally attended but attracted unfavourable notice by chatting together during the service, laughing at each other's jokes and, according to one hostile observer, eating biscuits during the sermon.[21]

In the mood of patriotic enthusiasm engendered by the King's illness and recovery, the royal brothers suffered from popular disgust at their conduct during and after the crisis. 'Gluttony, drunkenness and gambling', *The Times* wrote, were their habitual occupations, and the cartoonists had a field day in depicting them 'in the unbuttoned enjoyment of their favourite sports and weaknesses'. *The Times* even alleged that the Prince spent his time drinking, wenching and swearing, behaving as one who 'at all times would prefer a girl and a bottle to politics and a sermon'.[22] It was not an inaccurate description of his habits but it contrasted markedly with the demonstrations of popular affection and even adoration which were lavished on his father. The regency crisis had done nothing but damage to the Prince; his relations with his mother and father had sunk to their lowest level, his public image was confirmed as selfish, dissolute and uncaring, and his political supporters had been divided more than ever by the strains which the events of

[20] Same to same, 9 April 1789: ibid., 300.

[21] Same to same, 25 April 1789: ibid., 303–4; Ayling, 347–8; Stuart, *Daughters of George III*, 78.

[22] Ayling, 349–50. *The Times* was a ministerial hireling at this time.

the winter had placed upon them. As the first rumblings of revolution in France were heard across the Channel in the summer of 1789 the Prince and his partisans were ill-placed to recover the popularity or public regard which their conduct had done much to alienate.

Chapter 6

CLOUDS OF WAR

The regency crisis past, the Prince's life resumed its normal course. The unpopularity he suffered because of his conduct during the King's illness soon diminished, and was partially dissipated by the success of a tour to the north of England in August. He attended the York races, where his horse won – *The Times* unkindly suggested that the race was 'fixed' – and he was presented with the Freedom of the City in a gold box. He stayed at Wentworth House, the magnificent palace of Earl Fitzwilliam, one of the richest men in England, and the headquarters of the Whig interest in Yorkshire since the days of Fitzwilliam's uncle, the Marquess of Rockingham. Fitzwilliam put on a lavish entertainment, including a grand ball in the Prince's honour, 'the most brilliant ever seen beyond the Humber' said the *Annual Register*, and a dinner for 247 guests at which he received the leading figures of consequence in the county on the Whig side. The common people were not excluded. There was a festival in the grounds for an estimated 40,000 persons, at which 55 hogsheads of ale were provided 'in the true style of ancient English hospitality', accompanied by 'all the rural sports in use in that part of the kingdom', lasting the whole day. The Prince drew loud applause by holding up his host's infant son, Lord Milton, before the crowd, which 'charmed the people'. He showed attention to all those present, not only the 'whigs', and on travelling on to York and Castle Howard, left behind him an impression of friendly condescension which did something to take the edge off the fervent displays of loyalty to the King organized by Pitt's partisans in the county. Though *The Times* alleged that scenes of 'gluttony, drunkenness and gambling' characterized the royal visit, it admitted that the Prince 'gained great affection from all ranks of people'.[1] Across the Channel, the clouds of the French Revolution and of European war began to form, heralding popular repudiation of 'the cause of Kings'; it was a telling moment for the popularity of the British monarchy to reassert itself.

Whatever the effect on the Yorkshire public, the Prince's tour did not change the attitude of the King and Queen towards him, but worsened

[1] *Annual Register*, 1789, 221; *The Oracle*, 8 Sept. 1789; Smith, *Whig Principles*, 107–8; *CGPW*, ii, 31n.

relations with his parents scarcely touched his private life which had long been independent of their regard or opinions. At Brighton, where Henry Holland was beginning to remodel the Prince's home as a graceful classical pavilion, or at Kempshott near Basingstoke which George leased in 1788 as a shooting box, he lived as a country gentleman surrounded by his friends and in the company of Maria Fitzherbert. Her influence had at first moderated his reckless behaviour, but by the end of the decade the Prince was slipping back into his old ways, encouraged by disreputable intimates who played on his weakness for drunken revels and riotous behaviour. Kempshott in particular became notorious for carousing until the early hours after days of shooting and hunting. Jane Austen, whose family home at Steventon was not far away, heard the house spoken of as 'the Royal Lion's Den' and recounted the occasion when the father of her dancing partner, Stephen Terry, was lured into the company and became the victim of their practical jokes, returning home with his clothes in tatters and covered in tar.[2]

The Prince's chief obsession was now horses and horse-racing. His household treasurer remonstrated many times against the inordinate expense of the stables at Carlton House: his racing establishment alone now cost over £30,000 a year. It was said 'Horses, & everything connected with them, were his idols & no man had a finer eye for them' and that 'the one character, in which he pre-eminently shone, [was] that of an English sportsman'.[3] He rented a farm near Newmarket in the 1780s and kept a string of racehorses which appeared on the course in scarlet livery for seven seasons from 1784 to 1791. His first Newmarket winner, Anvil, won a £60 plate in his first season and by 1790 he had a stud of forty-one. The Prince's leading horses were Selim and Escape, the latter regarded for a time as the finest racehorse in England, and his racing manager and leading jockey was Sam Chifney, who rode several winners for him. In 1791 however he became involved in a scandal when Chifney was accused of improper riding.[4]

At the Ascot meeting Chifney, on Escape, won easily a trial against three other horses, but he switched in a subsequent race by his own request to Baronet, a well-beaten second. Baronet won, and it was alleged that Escape had been given a bucket of water before the race to 'stop' him. On the next day Escape ran again at longer odds, and heavy bets were laid against him, but with Chifney again in the saddle he won easily. It was believed that Chifney and the Prince had won large sums on the race, though Chifney protested that he had bet only 20 guineas.

[2] Review of G.H. Tucker, *Jane Austen the Woman: Sunday Telegraph*, 8 Jan. 1995.
[3] 'The Druid', *The Post and the Paddock*, 100, 107–8.
[4] Ibid., 77, 81–4, 101.

The incident nevertheless harmed the Prince's reputation and Sir Charles Bunbury, a steward of the Jockey Club, warned him that if he allowed Chifney to ride his horses again no gentleman would start against him. George responded indignantly. He attributed the scandal to the jealousy of rivals on the turf and declared that he would never set foot at Newmarket again. He withdrew his horses, gave up his stables, and ordered the sale of his entire stud. It was nine years before he returned to racing as an owner. Chifney was given an annuity of 200 guineas, as an earnest of the Prince's confidence, and he published a pamphlet defending his innocence, but suspicion was never completely allayed.[5]

In later years George returned to the turf, though he never ran a horse again at Newmarket. Ascot was his favourite course, but he also patronized the races at Brighton. He adopted what are still the royal colours of purple jacket, scarlet sleeves, gold braid buttons and black cap with gold tassel. Brighton and Lewes races became 'the gayest scene of the year in England', crowded with the fashionable London set, the Prince standing out in green jacket with a white hat and tight nankeen pantaloons and accompanied by such raffish figures as the Duke of Bedford, Lord Jersey, Sir John Shelley and Beau Brummell. Sir John Lade acted as coachman of his barouche drawn by six dark bay horses in which he drove from the Pavilion to the grandstand. In the evenings after the races there was a fashionable parade along the Steine, the ladies in high head-dresses and 'peacock tails', and at night the Pavilion was 'resplendent with lights'.[6]

This luxurious lifestyle did not help the Prince's finances, which were deteriorating rapidly again. Carlton House continued to be a drain on his purse. In November 1789 an estimate of a further £110,500 was produced for furniture and decorations. Though Holland declared that this sum had been reduced from the original of £120,500, at the cost of making the furniture 'ill-suited to the general magnificence of the building',[7] the scale of this expenditure went far beyond what had originally been proposed. Lord Southampton, the head of the Prince's household, confessed to Pitt that the furnishing of Carlton House had 'fallen into a state of embarrassment and delay', and that there was 'a most pressing necessity' for the sum concerned: he had done everything possible to reduce the estimates consistent with the need to

[5] The Duke of York supervised the sale of George's horses in 1792. Escape fetched 2,500 guineas. Sixty-five horses were sold at Tattersall's in March for sums from 25 to 270 guineas: letters from Frederick to George, 9 Feb., 9, 12 April, 11, 16 July 1792; George to Frederick, 29 July 1792. *CGPW*, ii, 237, 246–7, 259–60, 261–2.

[6] 'The Druid', 88–90, 92, 106–7.

[7] Accounts: RA 25078–84.

provide 'a residence suitable to his situation'.[8] Pitt was unimpressed and the Treasury refused the application as exceeding the intentions of the House of Commons grant of 1787. Over £55,000 had already been provided for Carlton House and no more would be provided from the Civil List. George and his two brothers, York and Clarence, who were also deeply in debt, turned to Dutch moneylenders. They borrowed 350,000 guilders from bankers at the Hague at 5 per cent interest, to be repaid in four annual instalments from December 1801. This proved beyond their means, and neither interest nor repayment was ever received. The lenders went bankrupt and it was alleged they committed suicide. A further Dutch loan of £300,000 was negotiated through the good offices of the Duke of Orleans at the end of 1790 when the princes' other creditors called in the same amount: this was agreed under stricter conditions and the burden of interest and repayment added to their difficulties in the future.[9]

Further measures were resorted to in May 1791 when the Prince pawned his jewels, including his diamond George and Garter and diamond-hilted sword for £25,000 to avert an execution for £14,000 on account of furniture for Carlton House. He appealed again in vain to his father for money to complete the furnishing, 'which, in consequence of several unfortunate misapprehensions, remains imperfect & unfinish'd' while work already done had not been paid for, but to no avail. He then appealed for permission to go abroad, the Queen interceding with his father on his behalf, but the King still refused to allow it. Possibly the Prince still hoped to raise more money abroad, or possibly, as he was said to have told his father, he intended to look among the German princesses for a wife in the hope that marriage would gain him an enlarged income. His brother Frederick was about to marry the King of Prussia's daughter, and although George assured him that *he* had no such intention at present, or indeed at any time unless 'I thought I preferr'd the woman I was going to marry to every creature existing in the world, and knew enough of the disposition of my wife to think it would form the happiness and not the misery of my future days', these praiseworthy sentiments were to be forgotten four years later when he agreed in desperation for an increased allowance to marry a totally unsuitable princess whom he had never seen.[10]

The Queen's intercession on her eldest son's behalf did show that the breach between George and his parents was healing. She disliked their

[8] Southampton to Pitt, 24 Nov. 1789: *CGPW*, ii, 48–9; RA 31997.

[9] RA 32012–15; on the Dutch loan, Portland to George, 26 Sept. 1790: *CGPW*, ii, 95–7.

[10] Southampton to George, 25 May 1791: RA 32017; assignment of jewels, and George to King, 5 June 1791: *CGPW*, ii, 151–3, 158–9; *Elliot*, i, 391–2, 8 Aug. 1791.

being on bad terms and tried to persuade the King to look more kindly on him. He was invited to keep his birthday at Windsor in 1791, which he interpreted as a sign that 'the whole family are better together than they have been for some time'. On Frederick's wedding day, 29 September, George was unwell and could not be with his parents and sisters, but the Queen assured him of their affectionate feelings. Had it not been for the King's continued disapproval of his way of life and his extravagance a full reconciliation might have taken place, to the benefit of George's future position. However, the lure of pleasure, of bad company and of luxury was too strong and the Prince continued to go his own way.[11]

Nevertheless, the world was beginning to change around him. The attack on the fortress prison of the Bastille in Paris in July 1789 set off a popular movement in France against absolutist government. At first, it seemed that it would produce a reformed constitutional monarchy on the English model, and on the British side of the Channel people responded favourably and optimistically: 'How much the greatest Event it is that ever happened in the World! & how much the best!' exulted Fox, who saw a parallel with his own attempts to subject George III's rule to parliamentary control. The parallel soon began to break down. As the French quickly moved from constitutional reform to egalitarian revolution, they seemed to threaten the very foundations of traditional society. A few liberal intellectuals in Britain responded enthusiastically to the ideology of freedom and equality, and Thomas Paine's pamphlet *The Rights of Man* (1791–2) spread the sentiments among the more educated working men. The political establishment and the propertied classes in general however recoiled from these 'levelling' ideas and, influenced by Edmund Burke's counterattack on French doctrines of equality, sought to reassert the traditional social order of rank and deference. Though Pitt's government did not at first join the attempt of the reactionary powers of central Europe to put down the revolution by force, it took urgent measures to wage a propaganda war and what the English 'Jacobins' – so called in imitation of the French revolutionaries – called a 'reign of terror' to suppress radicalism in Britain. The consequence was an awakening of conservatism as a defence of existing society. In this respect, George III's illness and recovery proved providential. The swing in the public mood, begun as a thanksgiving for the King's safe recovery on the eve of the storming of the Bastille, turned into patriotic enthusiasm for the Monarchy and the Constitution as the guarantors of British liberty against French democratic subversion. Whatever the Prince's personal relationship with his father, he could hardly support or even

[11] George to Frederick, 29 July 1791 and Queen to George, 29 Sept. 1791: *CGPW*, ii, 178–9, 201–2.

tolerate a movement designed to destroy the monarchy and undermine his own social position.

This had important consequences for George's political associations. Fox quarrelled with Burke in the House of Commons and provocatively expressed his admiration for the principles of the French Revolution, though his real motivation lay in his determination to support everything that Pitt's administration opposed. Suffering intense frustration since the regency crisis had dashed his party's prospects, he became more and more extreme in his sentiments. A royal prince, even one so much under Fox's spell, could not approve of such opinions. Indeed, Fox's extremism had begun to worry his own party leaders and by 1792 the Whig party was splitting into two groups, defined by Burke as the 'new Whigs' who admired the French Revolution and the 'old Whigs' who looked to the more moderate English revolution of a century ago. The latter clustered round the aristocratic leadership of the Duke of Portland and Earl Fitzwilliam.[12] The Prince's political stance was bound to be closer to the Portland Whigs than to the Foxites, and on 31 May 1792 he spoke in the House of Lords in order to denounce 'seditious' literature and to support the royal proclamation against seditious writings which Pitt and the loyalists sought to use as a test to identify those for or against the established constitution and to tar the Foxites with the unpatriotic brush. The Prince's short speech praised 'those principles of attachment to our present happy Constitution wh. I very early in life imbibed & shall glory in professing to the latest hour of my existance [*sic*]' and which it was the duty of every loyal subject to support to the utmost.[13] The speech made a strong impression favourable to the Prince. Jack Payne declared, 'the moment[um] lost at the Regency is recover'd & may easily be maintain'd by consistent perseverance'.[14] That was not a quality which George often showed, but he did not change his view in this case, and by the time of Fox's death in 1806 only the links of personal friendship remained to bind them together. After Fox's death he became a thorough conservative like his father.

If the French Revolution drew the Prince more towards his father's politics, it did not change the King's attitude to his son's extravagance. Indeed, as the approach and eventual outbreak of war with France greatly increased the burden of taxes on his subjects, George III became even more censorious. When in 1792 the question of the Prince's debts arose again his father was no more inclined to go to his aid than before. Lord Loughborough, the Portland whig lawyer who was

[12] Smith, *Whig Principles*, 117–40; F. O'Gorman, *The Whig Party*, *passim.*
[13] Speech in House of Lords, 31 May 1792: *CGPW*, ii, 250–1.
[14] Payne to Hugh Seymour [?16 June 1792]: ibid., ii, 251n.

to become Lord Chancellor in Pitt's wartime cabinet, had advised George in January 1792 that the reduction of his debts by his own efforts was essential if he was to win the respect of the public, which was 'particularly requisite at this moment to secure and maintain the affections of the people' towards the existing form of government. He advised that application to Parliament would have a worse effect even than continuation of the debts, but that a loan, with strict provision for repayment out of existing income, would create a good impression. He suggested that £300,000 might be raised on the security of an annual payment of £20,000 out of the three princes' incomes, of which £12,000 would be borne by George.[15] Nothing tangible seems to have come of the proposal, and in the summer of 1792 a memorandum on his financial affairs was submitted, possibly by Lord Thurlow on the Prince's behalf. It was admitted that he had incurred debts amounting to £400,000 in five years since the inadequate settlement of 1787, which had not taken account of certain additional debts arising from works at Carlton House and which had given him £72,000 per annum instead of the £79,000 which he claimed he needed. Things were constantly going from bad to worse, his servants were unpaid, and an execution on Carlton House was imminent. Only two possibilities seemed available: either Parliament should make a grant of £20,000 per annum for ten years, or the Prince should close up his establishment, surrender Carlton House to the Crown, and retire into a 'private situation'.[16]

There was no response from the King before the autumn. The Prince's friend Lord Rawdon (later Earl of Moira) expressed the opinion that ministers were deliberately keeping him in a state of embarrassment to have a hold over him. He suggested that the Prince should make a direct application to the King rather than go through Pitt, who was his enemy, and enlist his mother's support. George wrote to assure her of his loyalty to his father and to the throne by disclosing information he had received from a trusted confidant about French Jacobin agents who were reputedly haunting alehouses in the capital in an attempt to spread revolutionary sentiments among the people. He also sent her a copy of a new pamphlet entitled *The Jockey Club* which he described as 'the most infamous & shocking libellous production yt ever disgrac'd the pen of man'. Designed, according to its author, a radical journalist, 'To hold the mirror up to nature, to show vice its own image', the pamphlet focused on the racing circle round the Prince and his brothers, cronies described as 'creatures with whom a man of morality or even common decency could not associate', and repeated the allegations about his behaviour at Newmarket in 1791. The writer

[15] Loughborough to George, 20 Jan. 1792: ibid., ii, 230–1.
[16] Memorandum respecting the Prince of Wales's debts: ibid., 254–8.

also attacked the Prince's extravagance: 'decency was set at defiance, public opinion scorned, the turf establishment revived in a more ruinous style than ever, the wide field of dissipation and extravagance enlarged, fresh debts contracted to an enormous amount . . .'. George asserted that these accusations were designed to discredit the royal family in order to promote revolution – they arose out of 'those *damnable doctrines* of the *hell-begotten Jacobines*' (*sic*). As he declared in April 1793, it was 'all owing to the fanaticism & shallow brain'd philosophy of the Deists, Religionists, Pedants & Politicians wch *we are cursed* with'. The Queen suggested that the Prince should send a copy to Pitt, who would be a better person to draw the King's attention to it. Henry Dundas, the Home Secretary, assured him a week later that steps were being taken to prosecute the author.[17] George now also drafted a direct appeal to his father, admitting a lack of prudence and of economy in his expenditure, throwing himself on his 'paternal affection' for relief, and declaring that if it were to be refused he would have 'to live in complete retirement' from his public situation, a step which he suggested might be unfortunate at a time when a 'levelling spirit' was spreading throughout Europe. Before the letter could be sent, Lord Thurlow appeared with the long-awaited reply from the King to the Prince's memorandum in the summer. It was distinctly unhelpful: the King regretted that he could not go beyond what he had done in 1787 and repeated that the Prince must regularly set aside a large part of his own income to pay off his debts, even if as a consequence he had to carry out his threat to retire from public life. The Prince of course had no wish to do any such thing: his threats were merely intended to force his father to help him, and the King was calling his bluff.[18]

George responded with a long letter, drafted for him by Lord Thurlow, justifying his failure to provide the full and accurate estimates of costs at Carlton House required by his father, and declaring that he had never asked for money from Parliament to pay his debts. He even admitted that the 'narrowness' of his income was no excuse for his getting into debt, and the justice of his father's demand that he should take steps to pay them from his own income. He therefore announced that he would live only on the income from the Duchy and apply all the rest to that purpose.[19] In this he at least recognized that persistence in running up debts which he had no expectation of being able to pay would destroy his own popularity, and prejudice that of the monarchy

[17] George to Queen, 24 Sept. 1792; Queen to George, 27 Sept. 1792: *CGPW*, ii, 284–8, 291–2; George to Frederick, 22 April 1793: RA 44048–9; Dundas to George, 5 Oct. 1792: *CGPW*, ii, 298.

[18] George to King, [5 Oct. 1792], Thurlow to George, 8 Oct.: ibid., 298–301, 301–3.

[19] George to King [*c.* 1 Nov. 1792]: ibid., ii, 310–14.

itself at this sensitive time. As war against revolutionary France drew nearer at the beginning of 1793, the Prince of Wales attempted, in public at least, to show a united front with his father and brothers in pursuit of the patriotic cause.

This meant that he had to break his association with the Foxite Whigs who were becoming more extreme in their opposition to the war and who advocated political reforms which to the loyalists appeared to reflect contamination by French republican ideas. In late January he wrote to the Duke of Portland, still the titular leader of the Whigs, to declare his support for 'our happy Constitution' and his resolution to support with all his power the King's government. He professed to retain personal affection for Fox and his friends but declared the impossibility of a political 'rejunction' with them.[20] Portland was not yet ready to break his connection with Fox, but the Prince's letter added to the agony of mind which he suffered for another eighteen months before the inevitable separation of the Whigs took place.

George nevertheless professed no reservations. He wrote to his father assuring him that 'there is no one existing who, both in heart & mind, can be more truly or more sincerely devoted & attached to your sacred person than myself' and told his mother that he was 'truly overpowered' by 'a species of sentiment towards *my father* which *surpasses all description*' so that the depth of his emotions prevented him even from coming to the Queen's House in person.[21]

However, George's ambition to serve in a military capacity was thwarted. His brothers, all but the sickly Augustus, were serving officers of high rank in the army or navy, and Frederick was Commander-in-Chief. All were destined for active service in the field, and George longed to emulate their achievements, but the King refused to contemplate allowing the Prince of Wales to endanger his safety and insisted that he remain in England. The most he was prepared to do was to give him a colonelcy in the Light Dragoons, which offered little more than the opportunity to parade in a lavish specially designed uniform. That this was highly congenial to George, who loved showing off in elaborate uniforms and spent some of his time designing them, was little consolation for the lack of an active role in the defence of his country, though his figure, now swollen to greater bulk, was hardly military. He nevertheless devoted part of the summer of 1793 to parading and exercising his Light Dragoons along the Sussex coast and the South Downs, though he was hardly subjected to the privations of a military campaign on the battlefield: his headquarters was a large marquee containing a huge divan in lilac and green chintz and other elegant furniture.

[20] George to Portland [Jan. 1793]: ibid., ii, 329–31.
[21] George to King, 24 Jan., to Queen [*c.* 24 Jan. 1793]: ibid., ii, 333–5.

George professed a devotion to the military profession and longed to be made a general, but his lack of training and experience as well as his father's scepticism about his fitness for the role brought that ambition to nothing.[22] It added to his frustration as the country mobilized for what was to be the longest war of modern times, to discover that all he could do was to await news of the military campaigns on the continent and to emulate in his imagination the contribution of his brothers to British arms. Despite his outburst of patriotic zeal, the King's unresponsiveness did nothing to repair the relations between father and son or relieve George's financial worries. Further steps were needed to achieve reconciliation.

[22] Cf. George to Lord Amherst, 10 Oct. 1793: ibid., ii, 394–5.

Chapter 7

CAROLINE

As 1793 moved into 1794, George's financial problems remained unresolved and even worsened, as he failed to translate his good resolutions to economize into practical effect. His personal life was also falling into disarray again. Relations with Maria Fitzherbert were fading, and it was clear that the way to the King's pocket lay through a marriage to a suitable German princess and the birth of a legitimate future heir to the throne. The Prince's debts would then be paid and he would be provided with an increased income. The choice of a bride was a restricted one, for few suitable candidates could be found, and, whether or not by Lady Jersey's choice, it had fallen on Caroline, daughter of the Duke and Duchess of Brunswick-Wolfenbüttel, the latter being George III's sister. The King was pleased with the match and wrote joyfully to Pitt that 'the Prince of Wales . . . has . . . broken off all connection with Mrs Fitzherbert, and [expressed] . . . his desire to entering [*sic*] into a more creditable line by marrying; expressing at the same time that my niece, the Princess of Brunswick, may be the person'. He told his son that he had 'made him quite happy' and that he could have wished for such an alliance himself.[1] All the rest of the family approved, with the significant exception of the Queen, who favoured her own niece Louise of Mecklenburg and whose dislike of her future daughter-in-law was to remain evident for the rest of her life. She told her brother, the Duke of Mecklenburg-Strelitz, that, according to a relative of the Brunswick family, Caroline was so badly behaved and untrustworthy with men that a governess was detailed to accompany her at all times and especially at dances, to check her 'indecent conversations'. Frederick however wrote to declare that Caroline was 'a very fine girl and in every respect in my opinion a very proper match for you'. So the Prince was led towards disaster.[2]

Caroline Amelia Elizabeth of Brunswick-Wolfenbüttel was born in 1768, nearly six years later than her future husband. She grew up 'a lively, pretty child with light-coloured hair hanging in curls on her

[1] King to Pitt, Sept. 1794: Lord Stanhope, *Pitt*, ii, app.; George to Frederick, 29 Aug. 1794: *CGPW*, ii, 453–4.

[2] Frederick to George, 2 Sept. 1794: ibid., 454: Queen to Duke of Mecklenburg-Strelitz, n.d. [Aug. 1794], quoted ibid., iii, 9; Fraser, 27–8.

neck, with rosebud lips . . . and always simply and modestly dressed'.[3] The Brunswick court lacked the stiff formality of most petty German princely courts and Caroline was something of a tomboy, loving parties and frivolous gossip with her lady companions. At the age of twenty-six she was still unmarried, with no likely suitor in sight until she was chosen as the future Princess of Wales. George himself had nothing to do with the choice. He was prepared to marry anyone considered suitable, only to escape the mountain of debts that now threatened to overwhelm him: 'Any damn'd German frau would do', he is said to have uttered. Portraits were exchanged so that the young couple would have some idea of each other's appearance, but as is often the way with royal portraits the images turned out to be somewhat idealized. George's concealed the fact of his increasing stoutness, and Caroline's provided little clue as to her boisterous and uneducated personality. They were not to meet until three days before their wedding day, when the shock of reality struck them both.

Lord Malmesbury, formerly Sir James Harris, a Whig politician turned diplomat and an old acquaintance of the Prince, was sent to Brunswick in the autumn of 1794, partly to co-ordinate future operations in northern Germany against the French, but chiefly to bring Caroline back to England – a slightly hazardous expedition while the campaigns in the Netherlands were still going on. As might have been expected, the return journey was delayed over the winter in Hanover for reasons of bad weather and Caroline's safety and during that time Malmesbury had ample opportunity to get to know her.[4] He was apprehensive at what he saw. His first impression was that she had a pretty face, but 'not expressive of softness', a figure 'not graceful' but with 'fine eyes – good hand – tolerable teeth, but going – fair hair and eyebrows, good bust . . .'. This cautious estimate soon gave way to dismay at her skittish behaviour, gossipy manner, and a certain lack of hygiene in person and dress. Three weeks later he noted that she 'has no *fond*, no fixed character, a light and flighty mind, but meaning well, and well-disposed'. She was anxious to find out what would be expected of her at the English court, but she seemed to lack the steadiness and self-discipline to adjust her behaviour accordingly. Whatever the Prince's lack of consideration for others and his bad habits and self-indulgence, he was, as Malmesbury was well aware, a fastidious and cultivated individual with a high sense of social proprieties and etiquette. Caroline was bound to fail these tests and Malmesbury feared the worst.

He set himself to try to remedy the most obvious of her defects before

[3] Fraser, 19.
[4] Harris, Malmesbury *Diaries*, iii, 148, 160–205, *passim.*

she met the Prince, for there was no hope of cancelling the marriage contract and he must do what he could to make her acceptable. He lectured her on her dress and her neglect of her toilette, with the assistance of a German and an English lady at court to deal with the more delicate aspects of the task, hoping at least that she would present herself 'well washed *all over*'. He feared however that these matters made only a temporary impression on a mind naturally flighty and lacking depth. He admitted her quick intelligence and warm feelings but he saw her as essentially a trivial and impressionable woman lacking judgement or discretion. With the Prince this was a recipe for disaster, and so it turned out. When she eventually arrived in London and was presented to him by Malmesbury there occurred the famous scene when she attempted to kneel before him but the Prince turned aside after a perfunctory embrace, retired to a far corner of the room, demanded a glass of brandy, and fled 'with an oath' to the Queen, leaving his bride astonished at both his corpulence and his brusqueness. Since she was not entirely unattractive in appearance, his disgust may have arisen from what Malmesbury had feared, her failure to wash 'all over'.

At dinner that evening Caroline, now thoroughly flustered, made matters worse with conversation which Malmesbury described as 'flippant, rattling, affecting raillery and wit, and throwing out coarse vulgar hints about Lady [Jersey], who was present'. Caroline had been warned in an anonymous letter before leaving Brunswick about the Prince's affair with Lady Jersey and though both he and she naturally denied that she was his mistress Caroline had no doubt that she was – and had therefore been scandalized when George had sent Lady Jersey to meet her from the boat, to order her to change her dress, and to be her lady-in-waiting. As Malmesbury noted, 'this unfortunate dinner fixed his dislike'. It was downhill all the way from then. As George declared on the way to the wedding, to his friend Lord Moira, 'It's no use, Moira, I shall never love any woman but Fitzherbert.'

It was far too late to change anything now, and on 8 April 1795 in the evening the marriage ceremony took place at St James's, with the King, Queen, princesses and courtiers present. The bride, in white silver tissue, lined with ermine and richly ornamented with jewels, a coronet and robe of crimson velvet with ermine border, seemed happy and animated, chatting to her bridesmaids and attendants. The groom, however, was strangely detached, and seemed more interested in Lady Jersey than in following the ceremony. The King, optimistically as it turned out, had written to his son that morning to wish that his bride's character 'may . . . prove so pleasing to you that your mind may be engrossed with domestic felicity . . . and that a numerous progeny may be the result of this union'. Perhaps to emphasize the point, the Archbishop of Canterbury, who officiated, was seen to pause meaningfully at the passage concerning 'any lawful impediment' and twice repeated the injunction to 'live from that time in nuptial fidelity'. The Prince was observed to be unsteady on his feet and had to be supported by his two groomsmen. Lady Maria Stuart thought he 'looked like death'. It was not emotion that was affecting him, but alcohol. Further consumption at the subsequent dinner rendered him incapable and according to his new wife he collapsed on the floor of their bridal chamber and spent the wedding night lying insensible by the fireplace. When he recovered consciousness in the morning he summoned her into bed and apparently managed to perfom his duty to his country. Three days later he actually called his carriage to go to Maria Fitzherbert and had to be physically restrained by his equerry.[5]

The honeymoon was equally disastrous. After two days at Windsor they drove off to Kempshott where a party of the Prince's male cronies gathered, with Lady Jersey the only female guest, and, again according to Caroline's later account, the men spent the time drinking, gambling and carousing, lying about in their dirty boots, 'sleeping & snoring in bouts on the sofas . . . the whole resembled a bad brothel much more than a palace'.[6]

Nevertheless, for a few months the Prince and Princess managed to live together in reasonable harmony and appeared in public on friendly if not affectionate terms, though it seems likely that after two or three weeks they ceased to sleep together and Lady Jersey's constant presence was a major irritant. Yet Caroline was pregnant, and on 7 January, nine months to the day after her wedding, her daughter Charlotte, 'an immense girl', was born after twelve hours' difficult labour. The Prince was sufficiently concerned for his wife to stay up two whole nights before the birth, and sufficiently relieved to write to his mother that 'notwithstanding we might have wish'd for a boy, I receive her with all the affection possible'. Yet two days afterwards he sat down to write out a will, a long, rambling document evidently composed in a state of nervous excitement bordering on hysteria, leaving all his personal property to '*my Maria Fitzherbert, my wife, the wife of my heart & soul*, & though by the laws of this country she *could not avail herself publicly of that name, still such she is in the eyes of Heaven* . . .'. To 'her who is call'd the Princess of Wales' he left one shilling, while the care and education of his daughter he entrusted to the King and Queen and after them to his

[5] Ibid., 210–13, 220; Fraser, 59–62; King to George, 8 April 1795: *CGPW*, iii, 50–1n; N.M. Wraxall, *Memoirs*, v, 391; Lady Charlotte Bury, *Diary*, i, 21; Queen Victoria's Journal, Jan. 1839 and 13 Nov. 1838, and Leopold to Victoria, 17 May 1845: RA Y71/63; RA Geo. 12/39.

[6] Sir Gilbert to Lady Elliot, 14 July 1798: *Elliot*, iii, 14.

brothers and sisters, insisting that 'the mother of this child' was to be 'in *no way*' concerned in her care or education.[7]

Why the Prince should act in this manner it is difficult to know. He was not suffering from any physical illness, though the stress of the last few days evidently affected him and he was copiously bled by his doctors. Yet unless he had some fear or premonition of approaching death it is almost inconceivable that he would so suddenly dredge up his deepest emotions and feelings for Maria. What it does show is that despite the superficial appearance of contentment in his marriage he was seething with hidden resentment against his wife.

This came out into the open in the middle of March 1796, when after a quarrel with her he admitted to Lord Malmesbury that he was considering a separation. Malmesbury warned him that his private feelings must not be allowed to override his public duty, and that such a step would have dangerous consequences for the country in the present time of discontent and disaffection. George reminded the Earl that immediately after his marriage Malmesbury had told him his opinion of the Princess's character and regretted that he had gone through with the marriage: those forebodings had been justified, and despite an attempt a few months before to discuss and resolve their differences he and Caroline remained incompatible.[8]

Caroline now took the offensive and towards the end of April wrote a letter to her husband, since, she declared, she never had the opportunity to speak to him alone, and objected to being made to dine tête-à-tête with Lady Jersey 'qui est votre maitresse', and to have to spend all day in her company. The Prince was outraged at this outspokenness and indignantly, but hardly truthfully, denied that Lady Jersey was any other than 'a friend to whom I am attached by the strong ties of habitude, esteem and respect'. He concluded a long letter of stinging reproof by writing that 'we have unfortunately been oblig'd to acknowledge to each other that we cannot find happiness in our union' and in a further letter asserted that it was court etiquette, and not his behaviour, that 'prevents your mode of life from being more gay and amusing'. If she wished for more of his company 'the natural mode of obtaining it is to make my own house not obnoxious to me'. He was willing to live on terms of 'tranquil and comfortable society' and to accept her stipulation that there should be no further intimacy between them, but no more.[9]

Caroline appealed to the King, who had always been kind to her, and

[7] George to Queen, 7 Jan. 1796 and reply [7th]: Elizabeth to George, 7 Jan. 1796: *CGPW*, iii, 126–8; George's will, 10 Jan. 1796: ibid., 132–40; Fraser, 74–7.

[8] Malmesbury to George, 24 March 1796 and reply, 26th: *CGPW*, iii, 159–62.

[9] Corresp. between George and Caroline, and with Lady Cholmondeley, 21–30 April 1796: ibid., 168–9.

laid the whole matter before him. At the same time she demanded that the Prince should dismiss Lady Jersey from her household, which he flatly refused to do on the grounds that it would 'confirm every slander' about her relationship with him. However, she persisted, declaring that it was intolerable that a woman she regarded as the cause of their inability to live as man and wife should remain under her roof.

The Prince now determined to end the matter for good and wrote at length to his father, laying all the blame on his wife and 'a party' who he alleged were using her to 'strike at the whole Royal Family', and asking for a 'final separation'.[10] It was true that Caroline's case had become public knowledge – *The Times* disclosed on 24 May that a 'separation in high life' was imminent and on 10 June wrote bluntly of 'high personages' who 'stoop to the most disgraceful connexions' and whose 'vices, disorders and imprudence raise just apprehensions for the welfare of the State, if through some unfortunate event they should be placed on the highest point of the political and social State'. If there was any doubt where public sympathy lay it was quelled when Caroline attended the opera at the end of May and the audience reacted with cheers, rising to their feet 'as if electrified by her presence'. The Prince attributed the demonstration to the work of close friends of Mrs Fitzherbert, chiefly Lord Hugh Seymour, Lord Hertford, Jack Payne, Lady Stafford and others 'whose views have been disappointed'. He urged his mother to persuade the King to 'throw some stigma, & one very strong mark of disapprobation upon the Princess, [or] this worthless wretch will prove the ruin of him, of you, of me, of every one of us'. Otherwise, he compared the likely outcome with the results of the weakness of Louis XVI. George's almost hysterical denunciation of Caroline's 'personal nastiness' and 'entire want of all principle' and descriptions of her as 'a very monster of iniquity' showed that he had lost all control of his temper: and never in all these letters was there the slightest hint that he himself might bear any of the blame.[11]

The press continued to provoke his fury. On 2 June the *True Briton*, normally a pro-government paper, deplored the 'unmerited ill-treatment' suffered by an 'amiable and accomplished personage' and the '*total disregard* to the opinions of the world' shown by 'the *gentleman* principally concerned' who was '*incorrigible*' and who was doing more to promote Jacobinism than all the labours of the radicals. It ended by asserting that Lord Jersey had sought an audience of the King 'to assure HIS MAJESTY that Lady JERSEY was the most pure and virtuous woman living!!!' It was a portent of the future, for throughout Caroline's life a

[10] Caroline to King, 7 May, to George, 26 and 30 May; George to Caroline, 27 May, to King, 31 May and reply, 2 June 1796: ibid., 182–3, 187–95.
[11] George to Queen (two letters) 2 June 1796: ibid., 195–8.

large section of the press and the public was eager to take up her cause and to use her to discredit her husband. In this respect at least the Prince must be regarded as one of the chief authors of his own misfortunes and of his long-lasting if not wholly justified reputation, even beyond the grave, as a heartless, unfeeling, disreputable liar and cheat.

His father too was inclined to blame George for what was happening. He returned the letter which George had written under the stress of the *True Briton* article and begged him to be calmer and reflect on the consequences of his intended course of action. He read him a lesson on his royal duty: his marriage was not a merely private matter and Parliament as well as public opinion would not look favourably on a separation the result of which could only be evil for the country and the throne. He admitted that Caroline's conduct had been ill-judged, but pointed out that George had made no attempt to guide her in her inexperience. Even George's favourite sister Elizabeth wrote to beg him to recollect that he was not a private gentleman and that everything he did was of public consequence.[12]

The Prince had always resented the way he had, as he saw it, been forced into marriage with someone he had never loved or even liked, for reasons of state and as the price of his rescue from bankruptcy and financial ruin. That his predicament had been self-inflicted did not cross his mind, and he seems to have set out from the very moment of his meeting with Caroline with a determination not to allow his marriage to interfere with his established habits, friendships or pleasures. No woman with any spirit would tolerate such conduct, and whatever Caroline's failings, lack of spirit was never one of them.

For the time being the matter was patched up, and Caroline continued to live at Carlton House though no longer on close terms with her husband. Yet he seemed incapable of refraining from provoking her and even the Queen remonstrated with him in September when she discovered from *The Times* that he had ordered the house next door to Carlton House to be fitted up for the residence of Lord and Lady Jersey. His assurance that 'it was done merely to make it more convenient for Lord Jersey to carry out his duties' of supervising the Prince's stables was rather thin but he took the opportunity again to refer to 'the injustice & persecution of the world' and 'the same pack of blood hounds, or hell hounds' around the Princess who were doing all they could to traduce him.[13]

[12] George to King, 2 June; Loughborough to King, 2 June 1796: ibid., 199–200; extract from the *True Briton*, 2 June 1796: ibid., 200n.

[13] Queen to George, 23 and 24 Sept and reply, 26th: ibid., 271–6: RA Queen Caroline papers, 13/7.

A month later he refused to allow Caroline to pay a social visit to the Cholmondeleys at Houghton on the ground that it seemed to be part of a scheme for her to travel round the country to enlist popular support against him and, to rub salt into the wound, furthermore 'at *my expence*'. He also remonstrated against her having disobeyed the rules established for her at Carlton House by inviting guests to dinner and evening parties beyond the list of those approved by him. Caroline submitted to the cancellation of her visit but complained of being denied 'those innocent pleasure[s] consistant with my rank': the Prince replied that those pleasures must be consistent with 'etiquette or precedent'. He wished to keep Caroline out of the public eye as much as possible: he had become almost paranoiac about the possibility of her becoming a popular heroine and the focus of hostility towards him. He even embarked himself on a visit to Bath to receive the freedom of the city, during which at the Duke of York's house he favoured the assembled company with several songs 'in his best manner'.[14]

Nevertheless the Princess remained the recipient of public sympathy. Lady Jersey continued to reign as favourite – Lady Stafford remarked in June that the Prince was entirely under her thumb and that she rode through the courts at Carlton House attended by a servant in his livery. Even her 'reign' however came to an end: Lady Stafford reported her departure in August 1798 and said the Prince had taken up with a Miss Fox, one of the former mistresses of Lord Egremont and mother of several children, who was said to be a rather matronly figure. 'Elderly Dames seem to be his taste', she remarked.[15]

Caroline finally left Carlton House in February 1797 and went to live at Blackheath. In December she demanded an interview with her husband and declared that she would no longer obey him. The King refused to allow a formal separation on the ground that as the Lord Chancellor, Lord Loughborough, advised, 'a separation on mere disagreement of temper' was contrary to law, religion and morality, and that such a step in the royal family would 'gratify the malevolence of those who wish to promote a system of licentiousness' and undermine public confidence in the government and constitution. Nevertheless, the Prince and Princess never lived under the same roof again.[16] Caroline set up her own establishment and embarked on a life of pleasure in the company of a wide assortment of men and women of

[14] Corresp. between George, Lord Cholmondeley, Queen, Caroline, and Lady Euston, 19–24 Oct. 1796: ibid., 280–7.

[15] Lady Stafford to G. Leveson Gower, 29 [June 1796] and 26 [Aug. 1796]: Harriet, Countess Granville (ed.), *Private Corresp. of G. Leveson Gower*, i, 122–3, 220.

[16] George to King, 5 Dec. 1797; King to Caroline, 7 Dec.; George to King, 24 Dec. 1797: *CGPW*, iii, 378–82, 388–91.

distinction or notoriety. Blackheath became a magnet for the frivolous and the socially ambitious and her dinner parties were as uninhibited as her husband's, as she attracted leading politicians of both sides to her table, and sometimes to her bed. She also interested herself in charitable causes, especially those relating to children. Her appearances in public were always welcomed: crowds turned out to see her pass in the streets and applauded her in the theatres, and she became regarded as a woman wronged by a cruel and dissolute husband who had deserted her for a life of debauchery. The popular view was one-sided and unjust, but the Prince had brought it on himself.

There was not even the compensation of the higher income which he had been promised and which had been the chief inducement for his marriage. His debts had mounted to over £400,000 by the end of 1793, but at that time it was argued that application to Parliament would be likely to arouse republican agitation. A royal wedding, and even better the prospect of an heir to the throne, might have the contrary effect and loosen the public purse-strings. Soon after the marriage, in June 1795, a new 'plan of establishment' was drawn up, allocating an increased income of £65,000 made up of £12,253 for the Princess of Wales, an extra £44,000 for George's own establishment and £8,396 for the stables. His total income was thus to rise from £73,000 to £138,000, including the duchy revenue, and additional sums of £27,000 were to be granted to meet the cost of jewels and plate and £25,000 for items connected with the marriage. A further £45,000 was allocated to finish Carlton House.[17]

However, to the astonishment of the House of Commons, it was now disclosed that since the settlement of 1787 George had incurred further debts totalling £630,000. The public was hardly likely to favour the provision of taxpayers' money to finance such unwarranted extravagance and even the Foxites in the Commons rebelled. Grey even proposed a reduction of £25,000 in the additional income, in terms which the Prince considered highly offensive, and which virtually completed the alienation between them:

> It was a duty which they owed to the Prince himself, to teach him, if reflection had not taught him, that as his family were chosen to the throne for the good of the people, so that his situation was created not merely for luxury and indulgence, but in subservience to that great end; and that they were bound in turn to consult his comfort and enjoyment, that the obligation on their part ceased, if these became his sole objects; and that in consequence of the provision

[17] Financial papers, 7 Nov. 1793 and 1795: RA 32043–6, 32063–72, 32089–97.

> made for the support of his rank, thousands ought to bless his munificence and bounty, not to lament his extravagance and folly.[18]

Grey's words were not unjust and undoubtedly echoed what many felt, but his amendment was lost by 99 votes to 260 and the rest of the scheme was accepted. There was a proviso that £65,000 a year rather than £25,000 in the original plan was to be set aside for the payment of debts, so cancelling out the notional increase in income. The Bill now passed comfortably, but at the expense of George's comfort: he had to reduce his establishment and live once more as a private individual, forgoing lavish entertainments and appearing in public without the elaborate trappings of royalty. Furthermore, his financial affairs were to be managed by five commissioners, including the Speaker of the Commons and Pitt as Chancellor of the Exchequer. His scope for further extravagance seemed to have been curbed. After all, the marriage which was to have solved the Prince's financial difficulties left him no better off, while there was no compensation in terms of personal happiness.

The failure of the Prince's marriage had already turned George's thoughts back to Maria Fitzherbert. In the will which he wrote in January 1796 he had declared her to be his only true wife: in May he demanded a formal separation from Caroline, and followed it by sending Maria a letter via his brother Ernest laying himself again at her feet. Ernest reported that Maria was 'frightened to death' by the letter and would say no more than that she had 'a very sincere regard' for him, but she feared that 'if she did make it up, you would not agree a fortnight'.[19] She continued for another three years to hold him at arm's length, never being alone with him but meeting occasionally in society. He continued to send her messages, directly or through friends, but she could not get over her distaste for his conduct towards Caroline or, especially, Princess Charlotte. Maria was fond of children and she thought George's neglect of and lack of open affection for his daughter showed him in a bad light.

George made no secret of his longing to be reunited with Maria and his manner alone made it plain. In the autumn of 1798 his sister Augusta wrote of her 'very great concern' at his '*dejected appearance*', assured him that she was certain that his 'real affection, not to say adoration' was reciprocated, and urged a reconciliation as the only cure for his depression. She declared that all the family would welcome it and that it was the 'only chance of your *really* being happy' again.[20] The

[18] *Parl. Hist.*, xli, 14 May 1795, 297–304 (Pitt) and 304–8 (Grey).
[19] Ernest to George, 17 May 1796: *CGPW*, iii, 185–6.
[20] Augusta to George [?1798]: ibid., 501; Richardson, 71–2.

Prince told his friend the Duchess of Rutland after he and Maria had met by chance at Belvoir that a reunion with her was the only circumstance 'that can *ever* give me *a taste again for life*' and asked the Duchess to assure her that his affair with Lady Jersey '*is finally at an end*'. A few days later he was driven nearly frantic by a report that Maria had died at Bath and told the Duchess that even the news of her recovery left him 'in a dreadful state still'.[21]

He now redoubled his efforts to persuade Maria to come back to him and, as had happened fourteen years before, her resolve began to weaken under the onslaught of his frantic messages and letters. He sensed that she was wavering, and in June 1799 he again sent Ernest to her with a letter with numerous capital letters and underlinings declaring passionately that 'I AM WRAPP'D UP IN YOU ENTIRELY . . . NOTHING CAN ALTER ME, SHAKE ME OR CHANGE ME': if she rejected him he would end his life, or at least disclose to the world the fact of their marriage and the participation in the ceremony of her uncle and brother.[22] This was nothing short of blackmail and it put Maria into a terrible dilemma. She could not bring herself to go through all the frenzy of 1785 again, but she could not imperil her family. She decided on an appeal to the Pope: if he would endorse their marriage and tell her that she was in duty bound to return to her husband she would obey the dictates of her Church.

In the spring of 1800 the Pope's answer arrived: she must regard herself as the only true wife of the Prince and her duty lay at his side.[23] Maria submitted, and London was amazed at their apparent reconciliation. In June she gave a large afternoon 'breakfast' party at which they presided over a gathering of the leading members of society: it set the seal on their renewed relationship. The house was full of white roses, George's favourite flowers, and Maria appeared with a similar bouquet.[24] Unexpectedly even to Maria, there now began a further period which she spoke of as the happiest years of all their connection. Maria told her cousin Lord Stourton that they were 'extremely poor, but as merry as crickets': on one occasion they drove back from Brighton with less than five shillings between them. This did not prevent the Prince from building a house for Maria on the Steine as well as rebuilding the Pavilion, which he kept mainly for entertaining, using Maria's house as his home. The royal family too were reconciled to

[21] George to Duchess of Rutland, 12 and [23] Feb. 1799: *CGPW*, iv, 12–13, 16–17.

[22] George to Maria Fitzherbert, 11–12 June 1799: ibid., iv, 48–50; Anita Leslie, *Mrs Fitzherbert* 112–13.

[23] Anita Leslie, *Mrs Fitzherbert* 114–16; Richardson, 73.

[24] Sergeant, 237–8.

Maria's presence, and they became very fond of her, seeing her as a good influence on her unstable husband.[25]

The Prince's life now ran more smoothly than perhaps at any time. Only the constant spectre of debt disturbed his tranquillity. Politically he was still frustrated by his father's continuing refusal to allow him an active role in support of his country. His requests for military promotion were ignored while his brothers continued to perform duties on land or at sea. In domestic politics his alienation from the Foxite Whigs persisted and was worsened by the hostile attitude of Grey and the more active younger members of the party towards his financial embarrassments. George still felt personal affection for Fox but could not sympathize with his seemingly unpatriotic attitude towards the war and Pitt's policy of repression of radical agitation. Support of Pitt's administration was also impossible while it seemed indifferent to his financial needs. Retreat into private life seemed his only recourse.

[25] G. Langdale, *Memoirs of Mrs Fitzherbert*, 127–30; M. Bence-Jones, *Catholic Families*, 100.

Chapter 8

A POLITICAL PRINCE

Though George was denied an overt political role by his father, he was not indifferent to the development of events arising from the revolutionary tide in Europe and its repercussions in the British Isles, especially as they affected his former friends among the Whigs, as they now called themselves. In 1794 the aristocratic leaders of that party and their followers, under the Duke of Portland, had joined Pitt's government in a new coalition designed to demonstrate the loyalty of all men of property and consolidate the country's efforts against French Jacobinism at home and in Europe. Fox and the more radical Whigs were left as a rump of the party in opposition. In particular the Portland Whigs, who included several of the major Protestant landlords across St George's Channel, regarded the pacification of Ireland and its attachment to the 'cause of Kings' as their especial responsibility. One of the prime conditions they laid down for the coalition was that the administration of Irish affairs be handed over to them. Portland himself became Home Secretary, the member of the Cabinet directly responsible for internal affairs in Ireland as well as Britain, and Lord Fitzwilliam was appointed Lord-Lieutenant of Ireland and sent to Dublin. Fitzwilliam was highly respected and particularly concerned for Ireland, where he owned extensive property. He was also related by marriage to the powerful Irish Ponsonby clan. Unfortunately, he was politically inexperienced, hasty in action and impatient for results. He was convinced by his Irish allies that emancipation of the Catholics, who comprised the greater part of the Irish population outside Ulster, was the key to winning the loyalty of that island. The conferment of the right to vote, to sit in Parliament and to hold political offices would, Fitzwilliam was convinced, secure the loyalty of the Irish and the co-operation of their upper and middle ranks in the war against France. It would also thwart French plans for invasion of Ireland and its conquest with the assistance of the people.

The strategy may have been reasonable, but it ran directly counter to George III's unshakeable determination never to allow any alteration in the religious establishment in his kingdoms, and in particular never to dilute the exclusive privileges of the Anglican Church, which had been strengthened and confirmed by William III's defeat of the Catholic army of James II at the Boyne in 1690. Fitzwilliam was recalled in disgrace and Ireland was returned to a rigidly Protestant and repressive administration.[1] The consequence of Irish disappointment was precisely as Fitzwilliam had foretold – an increase in unrest, and the encouragement of a union of both Catholics and Protestants to obtain freedom from the English yoke, called the Society of United Irishmen. Under its auspices, violence against English property and Protestant magistrates escalated, tying down thousands of troops who might have been available to fight the French. Instead, the threat of French invasion of Ireland increased, and in 1797 an attempted landing by a French force was beaten off by good fortune rather than by superior strength, while a concerted internal uprising was only delayed rather than averted.

At this stage the Prince intervened in Irish affairs. In 1788 the Irish Parliament had offered him the unrestricted regency in Ireland, and George had never forgotten this evidence of regard. He now wrote to the Prime Minister of the danger which a disaffected Ireland presented to the war effort and the stimulus it offered to a French invasion. He declared that the recent foundation of the Society of United Irishmen threatened a movement for a separation of Ireland from Britain. In these circumstances, conciliation towards the Catholics was the only hope of detaching them from the radical cause. He was sure that Irish Catholics were 'naturally loyal and attached' to the British monarchy and that the concession of political equality would bring that loyalty into play. He concluded by offering 'my wish and readiness to undertake the Government of Ireland' for that purpose.

The initiative for this approach seems to have come from Ireland rather than the Prince himself. However, Lord Keith, who was deputed to negotiate on his behalf with ministers, was told bluntly by Pitt that the King had no wish for any change – a possibly disingenuous reply since there is some doubt whether Pitt even showed him the Prince's letter. George wrote urgently to Pitt to declare that he never had any intention to embarrass the King or his ministers and that he acted only from a sense of duty. He asked him to show the King his letter, but Pitt merely returned a formal answer expressing the King's 'satisfaction in the expression of his Royal Highness's affectionate attachment to his Majesty's person and service'.[2]

The Irish crisis did not go away. Pitt's policy of repression was steadfastly, even brutally, followed. In May 1797 the Prince addressed another memorandum to the Cabinet drawing attention to the increasing danger of civil war:[3] again there was no response and the inexorable

[1] Smith, *Whig Principles*, 196–201; J. Ehrman, *Younger Pitt*, ii, 430–4.
[2] George to Pitt, 8 Feb. 1797; T. Connolly and others to George [n.d.]; George to Pitt, 23 Feb: *CGPW*, iii, 313–16, 320–1, 325–6; Colchester, *Diary*, i, 94.
[3] The Prince's memorandum on Ireland, 29 May 1797: *CGPW*, iii, 343–6.

drift to rebellion in 1798 continued. 1797 was indeed the blackest year of the Revolutionary War. A mutiny in the navy, a financial crisis leading to the stoppage of cash payments at the Bank of England, the failure of Malmesbury's attempts to negotiate a peace with the French, and the beginning of a period of harvest failures and food shortages at home eroded confidence in Pitt's government and created a mood of national despondency. The King however had continued to reject his eldest son's approaches and in particular his request to be given a role in the defence of his country, drily remarking that if the French invaded he could show his valour by leading his regiment of dragoons against them.[4]

Nevertheless, after the suppression of the Irish rebellion of '98 and the execution of its leaders, the British government was compelled to give that unhappy country attention, if only for reasons of security. Pitt's strategy was not unlike the proposals put forward by the Prince before the rebellion, though it was not based on his advice. The notion was that the grant of emancipation, carrying the right to hold public office, to vote in Parliamentary elections and to sit in Parliament, might conciliate the Catholics and draw them over to the British side, so splitting the United Irishmen apart and isolating the more radical Protestant minority who favoured co-operation with the French. This, however, could not be done or even avowed while the separate Irish Parliament remained in existence, since it was feared that if the Catholics were given full rights of representation they would form a majority in the Irish House of Commons, take over the government of Ireland, and put an end to the 'Protestant Ascendancy' through which the British government exercised its control of Irish affairs. Pitt's solution was to abolish the separate Parliament at Dublin – or rather persuade it to abolish itself – since if the Catholics were admitted to representation at Westminister they would always be in a minority.[5]

The task of persuading the Irish Parliament to vote its own abolition and accept minority representation at Westminster was not easy. The powerful Protestant Ascendancy – the leading Irish Protestant nobility and their clients – was bound to resist the loss of its power without being paid a substantial price. That price was paid in patronage, bribery and corruption on a scale unheard of even in Ireland. After an unsuccessful attempt in 1799, redoubled exertions by Lord Castlereagh, the Chief Secretary in Ireland, who was responsible for political management, ensured the passage of the Act of Union which came into effect on

[4] George to King, 25 April 1798 and reply [26th]; George to Loughborough, 2 May and reply 9th; opinion by Mansfield and others whether the Prince of Wales may serve as a general on the Staff, 17 May 1798; ibid., iii, 427–8 and n., 431–2, 435, 438.

[5] G.C. Bolton, *Irish Act of Union, passim.*

1 January 1801. The separate kingdoms of Great Britain and Ireland were fused into the single United Kingdom with a single Parliament but, as yet, separate administrative arrangements for Ireland, under the overall authority of the British Cabinet.

At this stage the wider scheme foundered on the rock of George III's religious scruples. He had sworn at his coronation to maintain the Church establishment in both kingdoms, and he conceived that this forbade him to assent to any change in the status of the Anglican Church in England or Ireland. Despite Pitt's reasoned pleas, he flatly refused to contemplate Catholic emancipation and in February 1801 Pitt resigned, on the ground that the king had withdrawn his confidence.[6] Whig joy at this event was premature: not all Pitt's friends and colleagues shared his views and enough of them were willing to remain in office and pledge their support for the King's position. The Speaker of the British Commons, Pitt's friend Henry Addington, the son of a one-time Reading physician and now a fashionable society doctor in London, was offered the premiership and began to patch together an administration drawn mainly from the remnant of Pitt's ministry. It was bound to be a weak one, and it became an object of derision from the press and in the rest of the political world, but though desultory suggestions were made for strengthening it by admitting leading Whigs to office these came to nothing. Fox was still *persona non grata* with King George, and his friends were unwilling to desert him. In any case, Addington's obvious weakness held out the hope of a more promising future for them.

The break-up of Pitt's empire held implications for the Prince's political position. His own small group of followers in both Houses assumed a greater importance as Addington's position was seen to be precarious: and in addition the news that, under the stress of these events, the King was showing signs of renewed insanity reawakened the possibility of a regency which would put the Prince in control of the government.

The new ministry was not yet fully formed and a mixture of both old and new ministers was in office when on 21 February the King developed symptoms like those of November 1788. On the following morning the Prince summoned both Pitt, who had not yet given up his seals of office, and Addington, as Prime Minister designate, to interviews. Pitt was seen first. He might have considered service under the Prince, who was pro-emancipation, and Malmesbury thought that some of Pitt's friends had so advised him. However, the personal hostility that had grown up between him and the Prince, as a consequence of

[6] Ehrman, iii, 506–9; D.G. Barnes, *George III and William Pitt*, 370–85; L.V. Harcourt (ed.), *Diaries . . . of George Rose*, i, 387–95.

Pitt's treatment of George's attempts to offer his services, was much in evidence: 'they did not meet or part like persons likely to think the same', Malmesbury commented, and Pitt appeared 'stiff' and unaccommodating. He also made it a condition that if the Prince sought his advice, he should not also consult members of the Whig opposition, and at a second meeting on 25 February declared that if a regency were to become necessary the Prince would do well to agree to the terms of Pitt's bill of 1789. George demurred at the first condition only in specifying that he should wish to consult his friend Lord Moira, but on the second he expressed reservations and the meeting ended with the Prince requiring time to consider. Addington in his turn was 'very graciously' received, but the meeting was inconclusive. George was cautious, aware that as in 1789 his father might recover before any changes could be carried out, and also less eager now to commit himself entirely to his former Whig friends. During the next few weeks he saw Addington frequently, behaving it was said 'with the greatest civility and propriety', for he wrote on 8 March that he believed Addington to be 'a perfectly honest man'. Rumour had it that he intended to appoint him Prime Minister, rather than turn to Fox who was unpopular in the country because of his pro-French attitude and who was disliked by Maria because of his denial of her marriage. In any case the old Whig party was fragmented by the strains of disagreements over the war and reform, and Fox himself seemed tired and disillusioned. Even Grey, the most ambitious of the party to succeed Fox, said he hoped that there would be no question of a Whig ministry.[7]

The Prince's political movements were therefore more independent of the Whigs than in 1788–9. He consulted his friends Jack Payne and Sheridan as well as Maria Fitzherbert, showing a sense of propriety in keeping clear of any suggestion of intrigue. He seems to have contemplated his own prospective administration, with Moira as Prime Minister designate, Sheridan – to the horror of those who knew of the latter's financial situation – as Chancellor of the Exchequer, Lansdowne as Foreign and Fox as Home Secretary, Thurlow as Lord Chancellor and Grey in the minor office of Secretary at War, among others. He was, Lansdowne wrote, willing to consider a degree of parliamentary reform, though lukewarm about it, and to be considering sending Lord Fitzwilliam back to Ireland as a sign of his goodwill towards the Catholics. He kept the Whigs at a distance, however, and when Carlisle, Lansdowne, Fitzwilliam and Fox offered to form a group to advise him he replied that he was too anxious for the King's health to think of politics, declined the offer, and even informed Addington of it.[8]

[7] Harris, Malmesbury *Diaries*, iv, 5–7, 18–20; memorandum by Addington (Sidmouth MSS): *CGPW*, iv, 200n.

[8] *CGPW*, iv, 185; Harris, Malmesbury *Diaries*, iv, 34, 51.

In any case, as before, the King's illness proved to be a short one and by the end of March he was convalescent. Pitt took the opportunity to declare privately, through one of the King's doctors, that he would never again advise him on Catholic emancipation, which not only reassured the King and hastened his recovery but cleared the way for Pitt's eventual return to office. For the moment, however, Addington's proposed appointment was confirmed and by April his government was in place and the Prince's friends were again left in the cold. George seems in fact not to have been dismayed by this outcome and he refrained from taking any steps to oppose Addington: he had become well aware of the difficulties at home and abroad to be faced by any new administration, and he may have preferred to leave matters in other hands lest their attempted resolution prove impossible or unsatisfactory.

He was also aware that the events of early 1801 had brought discord among his family. The Duke of York was no longer his close supporter, and took pains to prove his loyalty to the King and support of his mother. Only Clarence and Kent, the next-oldest brothers, sided with him, while the Queen and princesses were too distressed by the King's state of mind for him to contemplate alienating them. The Queen in any case was upset by reports of extravagant parties at Carlton House and other signs that suggested the Prince was lacking in concern for his father. According to some observers, George was behaving selfishly and inconsiderately towards his parents and though this may have been the case only superficially it harmed his reputation and his relations with his mother.[9] The King had now become, since 1793, a symbol of the patriotic British cause against the foreign enemy and his popularity, far greater than it had been in 1788, was a warning that the public would not tolerate disloyalty to his person.

The Prince's reserve was not only politically prudent; it proved to be auspicious for his relations with his father. When he saw the King on 15 April, the first time he had been allowed to do so for a month, he was received 'with every mark of love and fondness' and 'was delighted to find that his [father's] mind was not poisoned on his account, but on the contrary did him ample justice for his correct conduct'. The King's mind was not entirely composed, for the same account (Lord Carlisle's) noted that he turned to 'the most violent accusation of Mr Pitt' and 'detailed methodically a variety of instances of his insolent conduct towards him' and 'warned the P. against his ambition'. He took the Prince up to the room where he had been confined and complained of his treatment 'in terms the most moving'; he concluded by making the Prince sit down to dinner with him, remarking that 'once in his life he

[9] Harris, Malmesbury *Diaries*, iv, 32, 34, 39–40, 53.

should have to say he dined *tête-à-tête* with his beloved son'. According to George Rose, the King declared to the Prince his intention to abdicate in his favour and to retire to Hanover or America: whether this was further evidence that he had not yet recovered his full mental faculties is a moot point, but of course it came to nothing. However, the Prince congratulated himself that 'I have had the good fortune to conduct myself so as to carry with me the general approbation of the country'.[10]

He continued to behave circumspectly for the remainder of the period of political adjustment after the King's recovery. He seems to have taken little interest in the rather desultory negotiations which opened up in the autumn of 1801 for a junction of a number of Whigs and Carlton House supporters with Addington. These came to nothing, apart from the single instance of George Tierney who accepted a minor post outside the Cabinet but failed to persuade Grey and others to join him. When Addington succeeded in negotiating the Peace of Amiens with the French, unsatisfactory as its terms were for the British Empire, the mood of public relief helped to confirm his ministry in office, where it was supported by George III's liking for a Prime Minister who was not 'one of those damned men of genius' but a modest country gentleman after the King's own heart.

If the Prince had any political hopes or ambitions at this stage in his life they were hardly visible. He shared his father's liking for Addington, approved of his peace treaty, and through his friends in Parliament gave the government his support, though Moira's hopes that the Prime Minister would invite some of the Carlton House group to take office were never realized. One or two of Pitt's friends suspected that the Prince was attempting to build up a party with the Foxites and force his friends into office, but there was no real ground for such a suspicion at that time. For the moment he was satisfied with his political position, and more concerned to use his good relations with Addington to assist his financial situation, which was again becoming difficult. In January 1802 he wrote to the Prime Minister to say that 'no one can wish you more success than I do in the arduous and noble duty you are discharging by your country'.[11] Whether Addington's courtly reply boded good or ill for the Prince's financial problems remained to be seen.

The Prince's first move was to apply to the new administration early in 1802 for the payment of the arrears of the revenues of the Duchy of Cornwall which had accumulated during his minority. These had been appropriated by the Treasury for the Civil List and never paid over to

[10] Memorandum by Earl of Carlisle: Hist. MSS. Comm., *Carlisle MSS*, 733; George to Arthur Paget, 23 April (Paget papers): *CGPW*, iv, 208–9n., 209–10n.

[11] George to Addington, 22 Jan. 1802: *CGPW*, iv, 254.

him after he came of age. Robert Manners Sutton, the Prince's Solicitor-General, estimated that, with compound interest added, the Prince would have been entitled to a sum of £900,000 by 1783 instead of which he was granted the paltry sum of £60,000 per annum, an amount not much more than half that enjoyed by his grandfather and great-grandfather when they were princes of Wales. It was no surprise that he had never been able to live on his income or that, in spite of the settlement of his debts in 1787 and 1795, he had continued to fall into arrears. By 1802, the arrangement of 1795 had paid off all but £250,000 of his old debts, but since 1795 he had incurred new ones which in November 1802 were estimated at £146,000. These did include many extravagances, such as the £20,000 a year for the regimental band of his Light Dragoons, £17,000 for jewellers' bills and £4,800 to clockmakers, over £9,000 to tailors, £7,500 to lacemen and over £5,000 to hatters, drapers, hosiers, glovemakers and breeches- and bootmakers; £23,000 was owing for building works at Brighton and £14,000 at Carlton House. His domestic affairs were consequently embarrassed: the agent at Kempshott declared that he had not a guinea left in his treasury to pay poor rates and taxes, and that tradesmen were refusing supplies, including feed for the horses and hounds. The servants were being kept on board wages in the hope that money would be forthcoming to pay them.[12]

The Prince's income now totalled £108,000, including £12,000 for the Princess of Wales, £9,000 for the stables, and £14,000 for provisions, wine, beer and coals. 'Exceedings' for building, furniture, plate, jewellery, pictures, prints and books were added as 'uncertain'.[13]

George was not alone in experiencing financial difficulties. Wartime inflation and ever-increasing expenses affected everyone's housekeeping: even the Queen complained to the King in 1796 that she and her daughters were finding it hard to manage on their restricted incomes when their expenses had doubled in a year.[14] Nevertheless, his formidable debts did not prevent the Prince from pressing ahead with the furnishing of the Pavilion. Furniture was bought in Paris, and two 'elegant and light lustres designed in the Chinese style' with a pagoda in the centre and basket ornaments at the bottom, 'the whole richly cut and gilt', cost over £200. A Dr Garrett was even sent to China to buy 'sundry prohibited articles consisting of pictures of their Customs (and particularly the Emperor's Court) – armour of all kinds – Mandarine

[12] Accounts: RA 32249, 32256, 32243–7, 32258. A memorandum in RA32231, 'Allowances to Princes of Wales', stated that George II as Prince of Wales had received £100,000 p.a., and that in 1742 Frederick's income had been raised to that amount, in addition to the Duchy revenues.

[13] Ibid., 32278.

[14] Queen to King [15 April] 1796: *LCG3*, ii. 470–1.

Dresses – flags, Part-poes [*sic*] & wrought metal of every description, Lanterns, &c. &c.' at a cost of £984, which included 'bribing the Hoppos [customs officials] & their underlings in China, for conniving at the bringing out of the country' all these articles. The diligent but unfortunate Dr Garrett's cabin was 'so lumbered, as to allow me scarcely room to lie down, all the way home'. His booty included rolls of wallpaper, tables, lacquered ware, three garden seats, twenty-six musical instruments, three gongs, jars and pots, stone figure ornaments, lanterns, a 64-piece green enamel tea service, eight iron swords, three bows and bundles of arrows and a box of tobacco.[15]

It was no wonder that Robert Gray, the Prince's Treasurer in the Duchy, described the embarrassment of his affairs as 'really alarming'. He focused on the unrestrained expense of the stables, where the estimate of annual expenditure of £11,000 was being regularly exceeded by £9,000. The coachmakers' bills alone for three months amounted to over £2,000, and regularly averaged over £5,000 per annum, while the stable establishment supported two coachmen, a post-chaise man and postilion, six helpers, four curricle and coach horses, a saddle-horse groom and six helpers, twelve saddle-horses, seven footmen and several other servants. Four huntsmen and a helper looked after thirty couple of hounds and five horses. Gray despaired of bringing these expenses under control, and John McMahon, who became George's private secretary, agreed that it was 'certainly a most gloomy picture & affords very melancholy reflexions'. He laid the accounts before the Prince, who he said was deeply affected and promised that once 'the hurry & profusion' of the Brighton races were over he would 'adopt a rigid economy'. McMahon feared, however, that 'the jealousy which pervades every department here' would thwart all attempts at reform, and no real progress seems ever to have been made. George's professions of amendment and economy were no more effective in relation to his domestic arrangements than in any other aspect of his life.[16]

Nevertheless, it seemed as though the new political situation after Addington's appointment as Prime Minister would be more hopeful. It was a period of confusion and uncertainty in politics. Pitt's following had divided into three groups, headed by Addington, Pitt himself, and Grenville, whose passionate disapproval of the peace treaty and, later, his refusal to follow Pitt in giving up the Catholic question in deference to the King, set himself apart from the rest of his former colleagues. The fragmentation of parties was completed by the creation

[15] Dr Garrett's account: RA 25158, 25176–80.
[16] R. Gray to Payne, 3 Jan. 1801, 24 July 1800; McMahon to Gray 7 Aug.: ibid., 32194, 32179, 32182.

of a 'Carlton House party' supporting George's campaign to have his debts paid and his income increased. In March 1802 when Manners-Sutton raised the question in the Commons he won the support of no fewer than 103 members, an unprecedented and impressive number.[17] Nearly forty of these were not regular members of the Foxite opposition: significantly, a large proportion was drawn from the ranks of the newly admitted Irish members under the terms of the Act of Union. As one commentator remarked, they supported the Prince 'some as a result of his alleged sympathy with the cause of Irish patriotism . . . others as a result of his friendship and patronage, and . . . most because he was likely to succeed to the throne'. The Prince thus for the first time became a key independent player on the political scene. In the following March as many as 139 members supported another motion on George's financial affairs, and in 1804, when Pitt was back in office, 42 of the minority against his proposals for a reorganization of the national defence forces were designated as the Prince's following, compared with 79 Foxites, 23 Grenvilles and 68 Addingtonians.[18] George was assured of a regular Parliamentary following and it stuck to him for the period after Pitt's death and into the 'Ministry of all the Talents' which succeeded him.

When, therefore, early in 1802, Moira, the acknowledged leader of the Prince's group, had a conversation with Addington on George's claims on the duchy arrears, the new Prime Minister did not dismiss the matter as his predecessor had done and Sir John Macpherson declared that it had 'the most extensive and most seasonable political effect'. Moira had previously discussed the matter with Lord Eldon, the Chancellor, who showed, he reported, 'a very fair disposition' towards it, though Eldon himself wrote that it would be very difficult to persuade the King.[19] In fact the business dragged on inconclusively until the end of the year, when Lord Pelham, the Home Secretary, suggested, as a compromise, that a full statement of all the Prince's pecuniary embarrassments be drawn up and that the previous arrangement for commissioners to administer his debts be cancelled, the Prince's income be restored to him in full, and his debts discharged.[20] This satisfactory outcome failed to materialize when it became apparent that Pelham did not have the Cabinet's authority to propose it. At a conference with the Prince's lawyers on 28 November, 'after a vast deal of argument & discussion' the Prime Minister, having expressed 'all possible good disposition & duty towards the Prince', declared that the utmost he

[17] R.G. Thorne, *The House of Commons, 1790–1820*, i, 159, 109.
[18] Ibid., 167, 169–70.
[19] The division was 160–103: Moira to McMahon, 6 Feb. 1802.: Eldon to Addington [n.d.]: *CGPW*, iv, 249, 258–9.
[20] For negotiations with Pelham, Nov.–Dec. 1802, ibid., iv, 321–30.

could agree to was to restore the Prince's full income, settling the remaining old debt administered by the commissioners but making no payment towards the subsequent debts.[21] After further delay, the King put forward an alternative proposal that the Prince should receive an annuity of £75,000 in lieu of his claim to the duchy arrears, out of which he should establish a sinking fund of £50,000 per annum to pay off his new debts. The Prince accepted his father's offer with as good a grace as he could muster, but the arrangement finally approved by Parliament in February 1803 fell short even of that. He was granted an additional income of £60,000 per annum for three years, which would pay off the debt up to 1795, but the debts incurred since then were left to him to pay out of his remaining income. As the country was now at war with France again, the Prince accepted the settlement and assured Parliament that he would not increase its financial burdens.[22] So the long-drawn-out battle over his income and debts drew to a close, to no one's entire satisfaction. The only consolation was that the enormous debts he had incurred in his youth were now settled, or would be so by 1806, and the Prince would continue to set aside £50,000 a year to extinguish the post-1795 debts. In the meantime he would continue to live as a private man. The Cabinet approved this proposal as 'highly redounding to his honour & probity', despite the fact that throughout the negotiations they had based the extra grant to the Prince not on the need to pay off his debts but on the wish to allow him again to live in princely state – so avoiding the accusation that public money was being provided in order to pay debts which ought never to have been incurred.[23]

The renewal of the war now thrust the Prince's financial troubles into the background, but it provided a fresh source of conflict with his father. He had protested at the outbreak of the Revolutionary War that he was denied the opportunity to serve his country in the same way as his brothers, by the grant of a military command and a high military rank. The protests had been renewed, to no effect, in 1798 when Britain was menaced by threats of invasion. The King and Pitt asserted publicly that a Prince of Wales had no need of military rank, and considered privately that he would be incompetent, or, the King believed, lacking in the necessary courage, to perform those duties.[24] George considered their denial to be a slur on his character and in 1803, when Napoleon's invasion barges began to cluster across the Channel, he renewed his plea. He admitted to Addington his lack of military experience but asserted that he had 'long made the Service my

[21] McMahon to Northumberland, 29 Nov. 1802: ibid., iv, 327.
[22] Memorandum by Addington [1802]: ibid., iv, 543–4.
[23] McMahon to Northumberland [?19 Jan.] 1803: ibid., 364–5n.
[24] See n.4 *supra*.

particular study' and that his chief contribution would be by setting an example to excite 'the loyal energies of the nation'. Addington promised to consult the King – only to receive the reply that he had nothing to add to his previous answers. George thereupon wrote directly to his father, asking 'to be allowed to display the best energies of my character, to shed the last drop of my blood in support of your Majesty's person, crown & dignity', and not to stand aside while 'Hanover is lost, England is menaced with invasion, Ireland is in rebellion, Europe is at the foot of France'. The King replied that he applauded his son's 'zeal and spirit' but that he wished to hear no more on the subject. A further appeal was met by silence, and when George remonstrated with his brother Frederick, who was Commander-in-Chief of the army, at his being ignored in the list of military promotions in the autumn, he received a reply which only repeated the King's views.[25]

The consequence was a widening of the breach between the two brothers which had begun at the time of the King's last illness. Fox raised the question again in Parliament in November, with the Prince's approval, but to no effect, and the situation was not improved by the publication of his correspondence with his brother – by whom is uncertain, but probably on George's own initiative. George was even angrier when his regiment was ordered early in 1804 to move to Guildford from Brighton, where it would have been in the firing line in case of invasion and, incidentally, where the Prince could remain comfortably in touch with it from the Pavilion. He considered that this was done deliberately to indicate a lack of confidence in him as its commander: the Duke of Northumberland thought it was a riposte to the publication of the Prince's letters.[26] George expressed his feelings in his birthday letter to his mother in January, declaring that he had received from his own family 'a treatment which my proud soul can neither now brook nor hereafter forgive'. However, acting on his brother Edward's advice, he visited his regiment near Guildford to forestall criticism that he stayed with them at Brighton only for his own convenience. The breach with the Duke of York was made up by the end of February after a cold exchange of notes on the 13th. Sheridan claimed the credit, as usual, but it was a precarious reconciliation.[27]

In May 1803 the war had been resumed, and within a short time

[25] George to Addington, 18 and 26 July 1803; Addington to Fitzwilliam, 28 July; same to King and reply, 29 and 30 July; George to same and reply, 6 and 7 Aug.; same to King, 27 Aug. and to Frederick [2 Oct.]; Frederick to George and replies, 6–14 Dct. 1803: *CGPW*, iv, 386–8, 391–2, 394, 395–6, 407–9, 425, 427–34.

[26] Fox to George, 24 Nov.; George to Fox and reply 27 and 29 Nov. 1803; Northumberland to McMahon, 6 Jan. 1804: ibid., 452, 455–7, 481–2.

[27] George to Queen, 17 Jan. and reply 19th; Duke of Kent to George 19 and 28 Jan.; George to Frederick and reply, 13 Feb. 1804: ibid 483–6, 493 and n.

Addington's deficiencies as a war leader were cruelly exposed. A demand arose both in the House of Commons and in the country for the return of Pitt, Canning's 'Pilot who weathered the storm',[28] but responsible men also considered that in this time of national crisis a new ministry should be one of national unity and include all parties and men of political importance. There were already signs that the Carlton House group was drawing closer to Addington, Sheridan especially favouring this alignment. The leading Foxites, however, the Prince's old friends, suspected Sheridan of promoting his own ambitions. Grey distrusted his 'vanity and folly', resenting what he saw as a rival bid for the succession to Fox. Grey's own standing with the Prince had been far from secure ever since his refusal to deny George's marriage to Mrs Fitzherbert in 1787 and his opposition to the proposed increase in the Prince's income in 1795. To this was added an incompatibility of temperament that was growing more marked. Grey's ambition to be the next leader of the Whig party seemed to the Prince to be too overt, and he feared that in such a role Grey would brook no interference from him or his friends. Grey for his part distrusted the Prince's tendency to intrigue and quoted Lord Thurlow's description of him as 'the worst anchoring ground in Europe'. Fox tried to persuade the Prince to regard Grey as his best prospect, and at what Grey called a 'sad drinking dinner' of Whig notables at Norfolk House on 3 May the Prince professed high regard for him – he was always prone to show affection when in his cups, but Grey was not impressed. Fox also proposed, to Grey's horror, that Sheridan should be authorized to go to Addington to discover on what terms a coalition of parties might be arranged, but he assured Grey that this was intended only to expose the impossibility of any such accommodation and to clear the ground for a better arrangement. When Moira visited Howick in the autumn to discuss the proposal for a union with Addington, Grey made his objections clear and the scheme was abandoned.[29]

Grey's own preference was for a link with Lord Grenville and his followers who, having broken away from Pitt after 1801, had committed themselves to Catholic emancipation and had refused to give those assurances to the King not to raise the question again which Pitt had promised. Grey respected Grenville as an honourable man whose word could be relied on. He was prepared to join him in urging Catholic emancipation and a vigorous prosecution of war against Napoleonic aggression and bad faith. In January 1804 there were discussions between the Grenvilles and Grey's section of the Foxites 'for the pur-

[28] The song was first performed at a Merchant Taylors' Hall dinner on 28 May 1802.

[29] Sichel, ii, 301, 304; Smith, *Grey*, 88–9.

pose of removing the [present] ministry and substituting one on the broadest possible basis'.[30]

For the time being the Prince's group remained separate, without a very clear policy. In March they voted with Addington, but in May Moira confessed that he could not decide what to do. The impending collapse of the ministry and the likely recall of Pitt created an atmosphere of crisis, but all depended on the King's attitude to the possible formation of a new, broadly based coalition; and behind that lurked the prospect of another attack of the royal illness with all its complex consequences.

30 Smith, *Grey*, 91.

Chapter 9

THE ROYAL MALADY AGAIN

On 9 February 1804 the Duke of Kent reported to his brother that the King's manner was ominously hurried, with significant 'symptoms of bile'; he thought the case 'very precarious'. A few days later the King's previous 'mad doctors', John and Robert Willis, were called in for examination by the Cabinet, though they were not ordered to attend the King for fear that their appearance would upset him, with 'the worst consequences'. The Cabinet undertook to take the 'care and superintendence' of the royal patient to themselves, relieving the Queen and Royal Family of the responsibility. Daily bulletins on the King's condition were issued, signed by five physicians, excluding the Willises, but the ministers made no move to relieve him of his royal duties.[1]

The Prince was in a dilemma: he himself had just recovered from a bout of illness, in which his life was for a time considered to be in danger, and he was under pressure from Sheridan who was now his closest confidant and a constant attendant at Carlton House, to stand apart from Fox and the Whigs and to co-operate with whatever Addington decided to do if a regency should be envisaged. Grey reported that he was 'in great agitation, and talks all day without ceasing to Mrs Fitzherbert and McMahon', while Sheridan was admitted to his bedroom during the small hours of the night as he talked till 4 a.m. Lord Thurlow too was in favour of co-operation with Addington, and when Pitt's hostile motion on the country's defence was voted in the Commons at 1 a.m. on 16 March, Sheridan and McMahon with a number of the Prince's other friends voted with the government in a majority of seventy-one.[2] This appearance of strength however was deceptive. Addington's majority was leaking away under Pitt's pressure and the public's lack of confidence in his leadership, while the coalition between Grenville and Fox, formally agreed at the end of February, put further strength into the opposition.

[1] *CGPW*, v, 4; Kent to George, 9 Feb. [1804]; George to Kent, 13 Feb and reply 13th; Kent to Addington [13] Feb.: ibid., iv, 492–6; Harcourt (ed.) *Diaries . . . of George Rose*, ii, 148–9.

[2] T. Creevey to Dr Currie, 2 April 1804: *Creevey Papers*, i, 25–6; George to Sheridan, 5 March and Sheridan to Mrs Sheridan, 27 Feb.: W.F. Rae, *Sheridan*, ii, 245, 249; Grey to Mrs Grey, 24 Feb.: *CGPW*, iv, 519n.

Both Pitt and Fox as well as Addington were bidding for the Prince's support in case of a regency, and Fox advised him not to discourage the hopes of any party in opposition, even including Pitt, but to look to the possibility of a new ministry formed from all opposition groups under his (the Prince's) leadership. Pitt, Fox thought, would decide his attitude on the basis of the King's prospects of recovery, but in the meantime he was exploring the possibility of working with Fox, the Prince's party and the Grenvilles under his own leadership. Only Addington was excluded from consideration, for Pitt resented his successful modification of his income tax scheme and the sniping of Addington's lesser colleagues in the House.[3] On 17 April Moira reported from Edinburgh that Pitt was about to strike 'a thundering blow against Addington' and advised the Prince to join in. He assured McMahon that Pitt would 'attend properly to the Prince' and 'spurn any notion of petty vengeance for past transactions'. George told Georgiana that he had no enmity towards Pitt and that if Pitt wished for a reconciliation he had only to ask for a meeting. He asked her to pass on the information so that it would reach Pitt.[4]

At the end of April the thundercloud burst over Addington's ministry and the Prime Minister resigned to avoid the humiliation of defeat in the Commons. All now depended on Pitt. The King – now fully recovered, as the outgoing ministry had asserted at the end of March – sent for him, and the political world waited to hear whether he had agreed to a 'broadly based' ministry, including Fox. The latter had agreed to stand down if the King would not accept him and to encourage his friends to accept office if it was offered. They, however, refused pointblank to do so without him. Pitt made the gesture, asking the King if he would agree to Fox, but that is what it was. On the King's refusal, Pitt gave way, fearing no doubt to provoke a new fit of the royal insanity, or, as Pitt's detractors would aver, being unwilling to share power. At all events, he agreed to form a ministry without Fox, to Grey's contempt. Whigs and Grenvilles refused to serve on those terms, and Pitt's second ministry came into office in May 1804 as a party and not a national administration, dependent on the support of Addington for its security and facing a strong opposition.

The Prince shared the disgust of Fox's other friends and, still sore at his father's refusal to grant him a military role, threw himself again into Fox's arms. The opposition seemed likely to be formidable, for

[3] Melville to Pitt, 6 April 1804: BL Add. MS 40102 fo.133, quoted *CGPW*, 531n.; Darnley to George, 13 March, Fox to same [?20th], Moira to McMahon, 7 and 13 April: ibid., iv, 522–7, 532.

[4] Moira to McMahon, 24 April 1804: ibid., 534; Lady Bessborough to Granville Leveson Gower [n.d.]: Granville (ed.), *Private Corresp. Granville Leveson Gower*, i, 451–2.

Grenville stuck to his coalition with the Foxites, and if Addington's group joined them Pitt would scarcely have a majority. The Prince's role was crucial: several observers thought that if he would be reconciled with his father and support the new administration Pitt would survive, and throughout the crisis in the spring he had repeatedly spoken of the King to his mother and sisters with affection, concern and respect,[5] but George's continued affection for Fox and resentment against his father were still too strong. It was even at a meeting held at Carlton House that the Grenville and Fox parties decided to refuse office. It was Pitt who had to woo Addington back into office with a peerage and seat in the Cabinet: the Prince and the 'new Whigs' as the Fox–Grenville coalition came to be called, constituted the main opposition. George signified his adherence to them by giving a series of lavish dinners at Carlton House for their leading members, Fox and the Marquess of Buckingham, Grenville's elder brother, as one observer remarked, 'carrying about their big bellies together, exactly like Gillray's horses'.[6]

The King's state of mind gave his family cause for anxiety. He was irritable and hurried, and talked irrationally and sometimes with obscene language in his wife's presence. He was still obsessed with Lady Pembroke and pestered her with love letters – she was 'the handsomest woman of seventy I ever saw', wrote Lady Bessborough. The Queen was less tolerant and there was even gossip of a separation. She had refused to sleep with her husband for several years because of his indecent behaviour in his illnesses. The King's health inevitably aroused political speculation, particularly since his ministers seemed determined to conceal the truth from the public and from the Prince and his friends. On 2 June, after consulting his Whig friends, George wrote to the Chancellor to complain that he was not kept informed of his father's condition, and that ministers declared him to be fully capable of exercising his political functions though he was still under the supervision of one of his doctors. He demanded a full statement to the Privy Council and an official account of 'all material circumstances relative to the King's health & treatment'.[7] Eldon came to Carlton House and, as Grey wrote, 'with great agitation, and occasionally with tears', acknowledged that the King 'had been in a very unpleasant way'. The physicians had certified that he was now capable of performing his royal duties but advised that he be kept quiet and avoid discussion of both family and political dissensions. This somewhat equivocal advice was declared by the Prince to be unsatisfactory. His letters from the Duke of Kent

[5] Same to Lady Stafford [n.d.]: Granville (ed.), *Leveson Gower*, 453–5.
[6] List of Carlton House party: *CGPW*, v, 8, 12.
[7] George to Eldon, 2 June 1804 and reply [3rd]: ibid., v, 26–8.

stressed the instability of the King's condition from one day to another – 'hurry, violence and ill humour' alternating with 'unusual calmness, quiet and good nature' – and his physical appearance was lethargic, with trembling limbs, a furred tongue and a pallid complexion. The Prince pointed out that it was now five months since the return of the King's 'former unhappy malady' and that during this time the ministers had acted on their own authority in not disclosing details of his condition but continuing to act as if he was in good health. He declared 'his entire disapprobation of *principles and measures* which he sees to be full of danger to the British Monarchy' and made a 'solemn protest, as the King's son, as the first subject of his Empire, and as Heir Apparent of his throne'. He demanded that all future proceedings be carried on under proper constitutional authority.[8] Eldon's reply a week later was that 'in the judgement of the physicians, his Majesty is [now] well', though their bulletin added that to guard against a relapse his present regime should be continued under their advice. George then summoned the physicians to Carlton House and put a number of questions to them, from their answers to which it appeared that the King was still 'under the control' of physicians while exercising his royal functions. He wrote again to Eldon in protest against 'a procedure so unconstitutional'.[9]

The Prince's political advisers – including Fox, Grey, Sheridan and Moira – were somewhat divided over what should be done, but on the whole it was felt best for him to confine himself to dignified protest rather than raise the matter publicly. It was suggested that he should seek an interview and reconciliation with the King in the hope that this would either calm the King's mind, or at any rate absolve the Prince from any blame if his father's condition did not improve. He accordingly wrote to the Queen offering 'to throw myself at the King's feet, & offer to him the testimony of my ever-unvarying attachment'. The King however declined to see him until he was no longer under supervision by his doctors. In reply to his mother's birthday greetings in August, George referred to 'the continuance of this barbarous proscription' as 'not only more than the affectionate warmth of my nature & my patience can bear, but more than my spirit & pride can tolerate'.[10]

Matters were made worse by the King's evident infatuation with Princess Charlotte and her mother. He expressed a wish to have Charlotte with him, to superintend her upbringing and education, not

[8] Grey to Mrs Grey, 4 June, Kent to George, 3, 9 and 23 June; George to Eldon 7 and 19 June; Eldon to George, 10 June 1804: ibid., 28n., 31–4, 36–9.

[9] Eldon to George, 26 June; George to Eldon 29 June, 2 July and to Cabinet, 1 July 1804: ibid., 39–40, 43–6.

[10] George to Fox, 2 July and reply 3rd.; same to Queen and reply, 4 July; Queen to George, 12 Aug. 1804 and reply 15th: ibid., 46–9, 68–9.

unreasonably perhaps thinking that Carlton House was hardly an ideal environment for a young girl. The Prince hoped that the concession of this desire might soften his father's attitude, and in June he authorized Lord Eldon to tell the King that he was willing to allow Charlotte to be 'taken under his Majesty's special direction', provided that her mother was not to have any say in Charlotte's education. The King demurred at first, writing that he would not infringe on her mother's rights and that Caroline's 'injuries deserve the utmost attention of the King, as her own conduct has proved irreproachable'. The Prince's wish for a reconciliation with his father was limited by his determination that his wife should have nothing to do with his daughter's upbringing. Moira made the latter point clear in an interview with the Lord Chancellor which the Duke of Kent described as '*satisfactory*', but no response came from the King or the Queen.[11]

It seemed that the promised meeting would not now take place before the King, Queen and princesses left for their annual holiday at Weymouth: yet the King wrote to the Princess of Wales on 18 August that 'It is impossible I can set out for Weymouth without wishing to see you and my ever dear grand-daughter' and summoned them both to Kew to see him. Their interview, the King wrote on the 21st, gave him 'the greatest satisfaction'. Lady Elgin, Charlotte's governess, wrote that the King said that 'he was to take Princess Charlotte to himself, as the Prince wish'd it, but he could say nothing yet'. Lady Elgin was anxious about the King's state of mind: he was very attentive and 'eat very well his pudding & dumplings but I am afraid over exerted himself . . . ; *he is still weak*'. She was anxious about Charlotte and hoped that if she did go to live with her grandparents the Queen and not the King would care for her.[12]

The King now notified Lord Eldon that he was prepared to meet the Prince at Kew on the 22nd. George was setting out on his way there when he was told of his father's receiving his wife and daughter on the 20th: he immediately wrote to Eldon that he could not 'believe that the proposed interview could lead to that cordial, affectionate & lasting reconciliation' which he desired. Eldon refused to forward his note to the King on the ground that it was disrespectful, whereupon he substituted one which declared that the invitation and all the circumstances which had come to his knowledge had produced 'a degree of indisposition' which made it impossible for him to come. The King then replied that their interview must be postponed until after his visit to Weymouth.[13]

[11] Eldon to King, 18 July 1804; Kent to McMahon, 20th: ibid., 54–5, 58.

[12] King to Princess of Wales, 18 Aug. and reply; Dowager Countess of Elgin to Princess Elizabeth [21 Aug.]; same to George, 22 Aug. 1804: ibid., 69n, 76–7, 83.

[13] King to Eldon, 20 and 21 Aug., reply 20th; same to George, 20 Aug., George to

This result did nothing to mend relations among the royal family: Lady Spencer wrote that 'All the royal family are at daggers drawn and in open feuds'. McMahon's memorandum of the affair made it clear that George's attitude was entirely due to the King's patronage of Caroline and his continued lack of any apparent affection for his son, and reflected the Prince's conviction that the King's only objective was 'merely to get possession of the child' and to put her more under the direction of her mother. As the King seemed not to be in a state of mind to bear any argument, the Prince thought it best to decline an interview, lest he be held responsible for a deterioration in his father's health. In the meantime, he informed Eldon that he would allow no change in the present arrangements for Charlotte's upbringing and that her visits to the King must be under the same conditions as before.[14]

Eldon considered that it would be dangerous to pass this message on and urged that the matter be set aside until the family's return from Weymouth. According to McMahon, the King, believing he had achieved his objective, in the presence of several of his sons on the 21st began to abuse the Prince, saying that his visit to Kew must be only a short one, he would be civil to him but would never forgive the publication of his letters and would never correspond with him. McMahon continued that the King had become violent, 'manifests the greatest aversion to the Queen & is quite outrageous with her' and declared he would set up house with Lady Pembroke or the Duchess of Rutland. He behaved eccentrically with servants and declared he had 'humbug'd' his doctors and ministers. The Prince, on hearing of all this, was now determined that Charlotte should not go to her grandfather: he was convinced that it had all been a plot engineered by George Tierney to ensnare him and weaken his influence. Fox joined in, urging George to take Charlotte to Carlton House to protect her from any attempt to seize her by force.[15]

The King's mind had clearly not fully recovered since the attack early in the year, and during the stay at Weymouth further evidence of instability became apparent. The good citizens of that seaside resort, which owed much of its new prosperity to the royal visits, were by now accustomed to their monarch's somewhat eccentric manner, but in the summer of 1804 even they regarded his doings with a mixture of concern and amusement. An unsigned memorandum in the Royal

Eldon, 21 and 22 Aug., Eldon to King, 21 and 22 Aug., George to King, 22 Aug. 1804: ibid., 72–4, 78–81.

[14] Lady Spencer to Lord Spencer, 25 Aug. (Althorp MSS, Northampton); McMahon's memorandum [*c.* 22 Aug.]: ibid., 81 n.1, 82–3; Lady Bessborough to G. Leveson Gower [? Aug.]: Granville (ed.), *Leveson Gower*, i, 460–1.

[15] McMahon to Northumberland, 25 Aug., Fox to George [?26 Aug.]; Wilson to McMahon, 28 Aug., Eldon to George, 30 Aug. 1804: *CGPW*, v, 88–95.

Archives details a number of strange episodes, quirks of behaviour and sudden swings of mood, 'sometimes very intelligent & communicative, at other times sullen or childishly trifling', outbursts of temper and incoherent, indecorous or obscene language. He still raved about Lady Pembroke and Lady Yarmouth, and made an obscene suggestion in public to a Mrs Drax on board the yacht during one of his cruises, which convulsed the sailors so much that several had to retire below 'to have their laugh out'.[16]

The Royal Family left Weymouth at the end of October. Some observers thought the King much better for his holiday, though the Duke of Kent believed that he would never be fully recovered. His return to Kew meant that the postponed interview with the Prince must now take place. According to Tierney, still acting as go-between and still hoping for office for himself, Pitt and the Cabinet were anxious about the possible effects on the King's mind, but some of the Prince's friends feared a trap to lure him into co-operation with ministers. An appointment was fixed for 12 November, and the Prince promised that he would keep faith with Fox and avoid any political discussion.[17] The interview was witnessed by the Dukes of Kent, Cumberland and Sussex and all the princesses, and by general agreement it passed off well. The King welcomed his son at the door with a bow, but neither took his hand nor embraced him, merely saying 'You are come, are you?' They talked on trivial matters – the weather and gossip mainly – avoiding all political questions. George told Fox that the King received him 'well, but not cordially', treated him 'much as he would a foreign minister'. The Prince stayed to dinner and for two hours altogether, but as he said to Fox, 'there was no cordiality or pretended affection'. All parties were relieved that the occasion went so well, and the Queen and princesses, who had suffered a great deal from their enforced separation from the Prince, were overjoyed at seeing him again. 'I go to bed tonight with a lighter heart than I had God knows when', wrote Princess Amelia. The King informed Eldon that the interview was 'every way *decent*' and added characteristically that the Prince's future conduct would show whether the reconciliation was sincere. Some observers thought it doubtful in view of his continuing association with the Foxites, but for the moment the family feuds seemed to be resolved.[18]

[16] Memorandum, ibid., 112–18.

[17] Kent to George, 5 Nov.; Eldon to George, 7 Nov. and reply 8th; same to King, 9 and 10 Nov. and reply 11th; same to George, 11 Nov.; Amelia to same, 12 Nov.; Kent to same, 13 Nov. 1804: ibid., 119–20, 122–7; Fox to Grey, 18 Nov.: *Fox Memorials and Corresp.*, iv, 62 and Duchess of Devonshire to Lord Morpeth, 12 Nov. 1804: Castle Howard MSS, quoted *CGPW*, 125 n.2.

[18] Lady Bessborough to G. Leveson Gower, 'Tuesday' [Nov. 1804]: Granville (ed.), *Leveson Gower* i, 477.

The only unsettled business was the matter of Princess Charlotte. The King was insistent that his wish to supervise her education should now be implemented, but the Prince was equally determined that this should not be a device to allow his wife to become involved in it. Barely a week after George's interview with his father the King wrote that since the Prince had agreed to his proposal to take charge of Charlotte's education, it was now time to put it into effect. He proposed that a bishop should take the responsibility for her education, that the sum (of £5,000 per annum) allowed to the Prince to pay for her maintenance and education should be paid into his hands, and that a new set of female governesses be appointed in place of Lady Elgin, who was too old for the task. Pitt approved of the King's suggestions and commented to Moira that if the Prince consented he might get his military command and some appointments for his friends. Moira protested that the reconciliation had taken place without any implied conditions on the Prince's part and that he could never agree to a proposal which would give the Princess of Wales any share in Charlotte's education. He would approve only a plan in which he retained the right of 'direct interference' in his daughter's affairs. The Prince himself wrote to Eldon on the 24th to emphasize the conditional nature of his agreement to the King's wishes, and called in Fox for urgent consultations.[19]

After a series of letters between Moira, Eldon and the Prince it was agreed that Charlotte should remain under her father's care at Warwick House, next door to Carlton House, whenever he was in London, and that she might reside at Windsor for the rest of the year, with her mother allowed only visiting rights. The King would nominate her governess, but subject to the Prince's approval. Sheridan considered that the arrangement gave the Princess of Wales an increased influence and demonstrated her greater favour with the King, while Fox thought the Prince had given way too much but that the arrangement would have no political consequences. The King and the Prince reached 'a pretty tolerable agreement', as Lady Bessborough put it, on the nomination of Charlotte's attendants and for the time being their relationship, though still distant, was amicable enough. At the same time, a 'sincere and cordial reconciliation' took place with the Duke of York. The King's manner and state of mind were now greatly improved, and his relations with the Queen much better. The royal family was once more united: the only cloud in prospect was the beginning of a deterioration in the King's eyesight which was eventually to lead to

[19] King to Pitt, 18 Nov., to Eldon [22 Nov.]; Eldon to George, 23 Nov. and reply 24th: *CGPW*, v, 131–2, 138–40; Lady Bessborough to G. Leveson Gower, Wed. 21 [1804]: Granville (ed.), *Leveson Gower*, i, 479.

blindness, but Princess Elizabeth informed her brother that he was '*placid*, still, quiet, humble, in short, just his own *fine* disposition'. The annual visit to Weymouth in the summer of 1805 passed off without any of the anxieties of the previous year: 'The King's good spirits do not fail him at all', wrote Elizabeth, and on the Prince's birthday his mother wrote of her 'most sincere & affectionate assurances of my *unseizing* [*sic*] LOVE & attachment'. It was to endure until her death thirteen years later.[20]

[20] Corresp. between George and Pitt, Fox, Eldon, Moira, McMahon and Northumberland re. Princess Charlotte, 27 Nov. to 25 Dec. 1804: Eldon to King, 25 Dec. and Eldon's memoranda 26 and 28 Dec.; King to Eldon, 31 Dec.; Eldon to King, 31 Dec. and reply 1 Jan. 1805: *CGPW*, v, 141–61; letters from Kent [15] April and 19 Aug. 1805; Elizabeth 6 July, Eldon to King, 30 Nov. and King's memorandum: ibid., 213–14, 230–1, 247–8, 277–8; 'Outlines of a plan for Regulating the Education of HRH the Princess Charlotte . . .' and other papers re. her proposed establishment, 1805: ibid., 290–4.

Chapter 10

CHANGING ALLEGIANCES

1806 was a year of vicissitudes in the Prince's family life and political circumstances. The conditions of public life were radically affected by Pitt's death in January, followed by the collapse of his second administration, while on the personal level the year saw the beginning of George's association with the Hertfords and, in turn, the final decline of his connection with Maria Fitzherbert. The death of Fox later in the year carried further the process of estrangement from his old allies.

On the national stage, Pitt's administration began to disintegrate in March 1805, when a report of commissioners looking into the conduct of naval affairs during the recent war exposed malversation in the Navy Pay Office for which Lord Melville, formerly Henry Dundas, Pitt's closest friend and partner in politics, was technically responsible, though he was not directly implicated in any financial impropriety.[1] The matter was nevertheless a gift to the opposition, providing both an opportunity to strike a personal blow against Pitt and also a prospect of weakening Melville's hold on Scottish affairs and patronage which he controlled in the government's interests. Samuel Whitbread, a leading radical populist, moved a motion of censure on Melville in the Commons and it was carried by the Speaker's casting vote in a rare moment of high drama, with Pitt virtually in tears. The Prince had thrown his weight behind Whitbread, and attended the debate as a spectator with his brothers to exert further pressure by his visible presence. It was regarded as a purely party contest, since Melville's personal honour was not seriously in doubt, and though the House voted to impeach him, the outcome was acquittal.[2] However, the public significance of the affair was wide-ranging. Country reformers and City radicals as well as Whig politicians now joined together in the beginnings of a new movement against corruption in high places which attracted strong and widespread support in the press and seriously weakened even Pitt's reputation. More directly, the small but important group in both Houses led by Henry Addington, created Viscount Sidmouth in order to attract his support to Pitt, took the opportunity to seek a

[1] A.D. Harvey, *Britain in the Early Nineteenth Century*, 155–6.

[2] Ibid., 159–60; *Hansard, Parliamentary Debates* [hence forward *Parl. Debates*], iii, 385–400, 1147; iv, 255–322.

greater share of influence within the ministry. Pitt's rebuff of this attempt led them to resign from the government and gravely weakened its majority in the Commons. Pitt was saved, however, for the time being when the main opposition failed to attract Sidmouth's adherence because Grenville and the Whigs raised the Catholic question, to which the Sidmouths were resolutely hostile.

The opposition's initiative also weakened their ties with the Prince's following to a significant extent. George had hitherto given general support to Catholic relief in Ireland, and had attempted to harness moderate Catholic opinion by advocating relief as a means of unifying the two countries and winning Irish loyalty for the war and for the Crown.[3] Though his opinions had not yet overtly changed, personal circumstances now intruded. Maria Fitzherbert's Catholic faith had always been an influence on George's attitude, but the arousal of religious controversy complicated matters at both the personal as well as the political level, for England's anti-Catholic prejudices never lay far below the surface.

George's friends Lord Hugh and Lady Horatia Seymour had a daughter, Mary, born in 1798, and known as 'Minny', to whom the Prince had become strongly attached.[4] He called her 'my little favourite' and was so fond of the child that rumours sprang up that he was her real father by Lady Horatia, with whom he had had a brief affair in the past. No proof of his paternity has ever been found, and the opinions of authorities have in general settled against it, but there is no doubt that the Prince was unusually fond and devoted to her. Maria Fitzherbert had been entrusted with the care of the child while both her parents were abroad on diplomatic service, and she had taken her into her household where the Prince could see her often. In 1801 both parents died. In his will, Lord Hugh had appointed his brother, Lord Henry Seymour, and Lady Horatia's brother Lord Euston as Minny's guardians. They refused to agree to Minny's remaining in Maria's household because of the latter's Catholic religion. Maria on her part was eager to adopt the child and willing to guarantee that her Protestant faith would be respected. The Prince supported her wish and in October 1802 he had offered to invest £10,000 in the funds to provide for Minny until she came of age, on condition that she stayed with Maria. He declared it to be 'his ultimate view . . . to raise her up hereafter as a companion and as he hopes, a bosom friend of his own daughter [Charlotte]'. He repeated assurances that her Anglican faith would not be interfered with and that she would remain in full contact with her own family. He proposed that he himself, Lord Thurlow, the Bishop of Winchester, the

[3] *Supra*, p. 83.
[4] Richardson, 87.

Marquess of Hertford (her uncle) and Lord Robert Seymour should be her guardians and trustees. Minny's near relations declined the offer.[5]

In December 1804 the Prince initiated an appeal to Chancery to keep the child with Maria, but Lord Eldon ruled that she should go to her natural family and upheld her father's will. The Prince then appealed to the House of Lords against Eldon's judgment and in May 1806 the House ruled in his favour, after energetic canvassing of the peers and with the assistance of Samuel Romilly, whom the Prince was anxious to recruit as his legal adviser. Lord and Lady Hertford were now appointed as Minny's legal guardians, as the Prince desired, for they had agreed to leave Minny under Maria's protection. Romilly noted how anxious the Prince was for this outcome; he recorded that the Prince 'loved the child with paternal affection' and was as anxious 'as he could have been if the child had been his own'.[6]

The case assumed wider significance than the merely personal issue of Minny's upbringing. The Prince feared that the proposed Catholic petition for relief from their political disabilities would stir up an anti-popery reaction in the country and prejudice the case for Maria's continued guardianship of the child. He therefore tried to persuade his friends to delay raising the question in Parliament until the legal issue was decided. However, Grey suspected that this was not the only reason: he believed that George was falling under the influence of Lady Hertford, who was strongly Protestant, partly as a result of her support of his wishes for Minny. Grey was convinced that as a consequence the Prince would no longer be a friend to Catholic emancipation – a view which proved to be a true prophecy when the Prince became regent. Lady Hertford's personal ascendancy not only led to his final break with Maria in 1809 but also helped to induce him to desert his old Whig allies after 1812.[7]

Meanwhile, the administration limped along, amid rumours of approaches to or from various opposition groups, but sustained by better news of the war. A new continental coalition in the autumn of 1805 raised hopes that the threatened French invasion would be averted, and towards the end of October the glorious news of Trafalgar raised British spirits again, though celebrations were mingled with mourning for the death of Nelson. The Prince broke precedent by attending the late Admiral's funeral at St Paul's, and he subscribed to a fund for a statue.[8] However, the euphoria over Britain's greatest naval

[5] Anita Leslie, *Mrs Fitzherbert*, 131–3; George to Euston, 10 Sept., 15 Oct., 12 Nov. 1802 and reply [n.d.] and to Hertford, 2 Dec. 1802: *CGPW*, iv, 308–9, 314–16, 319–20 and n., 335.

[6] S. Romilly, *Memoirs*, ii, 147, 114–16.

[7] Smith, *Grey*, 96.

[8] Second Baron Nelson to McMahon, 18 Nov. 1805: *CGPW*, v, 276.

triumph was dissipated by Napoleon's victories over Britain's continental allies at Ulm and Austerlitz, which knocked Austria and Prussia out of the war. There was now a stalemate. Britain was safe from invasion because of her naval supremacy but had no means of defeating France by herself on the continent. A long war of attrition and economic blockade on both sides seemed inevitable: 'Our Cabinet are but as children in the hands of Buonaparte', bemoaned the Duke of Northumberland: 'I much suspect all our Naval victories will not save us, from at least, a most disgracefull peace.'[9]

The news of Napoleon's victories crushed Pitt, whose health had given way under the strain of war and political frustration, and he died on 23 January 1806. George III accepted the inevitable, sent for Lord Grenville to form a government, and gave way without demur when Grenville declared that Fox must be in the Cabinet. The business of making the new appointments to the ministry was a long and difficult one, for not only were the long-standing and competing claims of the respective friends of Grenville and Fox to be considered, but the Prince, who was widely (and not least by the King) thought to be the real head of the ministry, also wished to have appointments for his friends. Fox and Grenville did indeed consult him during the negotiations but even so the Prince and his advisers considered that his views were not sufficiently regarded. In particular George was annoyed that he was given only one representative in the Cabinet (Moira, as Master-General of the Ordnance), and that only after he had exerted considerable pressure. Sheridan, despite his closeness to the Prince, was fobbed off with the junior post of Treasurer of the Navy. Moira wrote on 8 February that 'all is still scramble & confusion' particularly in the lower ranks of the administration, and gave his opinion that there had been 'a strange negligence toward the Prince's friends'.[10]

One reason for the shortage of posts to accommodate all the Whig claimants was the decision to incorporate Sidmouth's group into the government, as Fox put it, 'to stop up the earths' and prevent them from joining the remaining Pittites in opposition: Sheridan doubtless had a hand in the matter and the Prince himself took the credit for it. The step did not please all Fox's supporters or the Prince's friends. The testy Duke of Northumberland, who deplored all co-operation with any group previously friendly to Pitt, whether Grenvilles or Sidmouths, was threatening to withhold his 'confidence and support from an Administration so formed' unless he was consulted and courted as he felt his rank entitled him. Fox assured the Duke that it was only his distance from London that had prevented his being fully consulted and the

[9] Northumberland to McMahon, 4 Dec. 1805: ibid., 279.

[10] Moira to Northumberland, 8 Feb. 1806: ibid., 329 n.1 (from Alnwick MSS).

Prince himself wrote to declare that 'every due defference & respect would be as *a matter of course*, testified & shewn to your Grace'. Addressing him without intended irony 'as an old brother soldier', he claimed to have thought up the admission of Sidmouth 'to completely cut off their [the Pittites'] retreat in that quarter' to regroup their forces. Moira too rushed to give the Duke assurances that he had been left without communication only because of the great hurry in which it had all had to be done, and threw in a hint, which he no doubt knew would be agreeable to him, that his son Lord Percy might be called up to the House of Lords when he attained his majority in April. The haughty Duke replied to Moira, in character, that he was sorry that 'in the hurry of business in which you are now engaged, you should have given yourself the trouble to write to me upon such a trivial subject as the disposal of places' and asserted stoutly that he could not disgrace himself by abandoning 'those principles that have been the rule of my Parliamentary conduct for many years'. He would not co-operate with the new ministry unless he received assurances that the policies which had led Pitt's ministries to interfere with civil liberties were abandoned. However, when he received the Prince's letter the Duke backed down, magnanimously agreeing to 'overlook any inattention which some of his Majesty's present minsters may have shown me upon this occasion'; now that he realized that the administration had been formed under the Prince's 'immediate direction' and superintendence, he would overlook the slight.[11]

The Duke of Northumberland's delicate feelings were symptomatic of the difficulties which faced the new government's attempt to build a union of parties. The Prince himself was aggrieved on behalf of Sheridan, to whom he considered Fox and Grenville had given insufficient recognition, and he wrote in much the same spirit as Northumberland had shown. On the 16th he wrote to Sheridan to express his dismay that he was not offered a Cabinet post and he threatened to withdraw himself and his friends from the ministry unless Sheridan was brought in and a seat in the Commons found for him. 'Nothing but rapacity and overbearing appears to be the order of the day', he lamented, referring to the Grenvilles who were notoriously eager for offices; '. . . I never can cease to love Fox to my last breath, but I never will *join* . . . in seeing him lower himself and his *own* consequence'. His remonstrances were ineffective.[12]

The episode was significant. Once the ministry was formed, the

[11] Northumberland to George, 6 Feb.; McMahon to Northumberland, 8 Feb.; Fox to same, 8 Feb.; George to same, 11 Feb. and reply, 14 Feb; Northumberland to Moira, 14 Feb. 1806: *CGPW*, v, 327–34, 338–9.

[12] George to Sheridan, 16 Feb. 1806: ibid., 343–4.

Prince lost neither time nor opportunity in seeking patronage for his friends and followers, to show the strength of his influence. Lord Holland, Fox's nephew, remarked that great attention was paid to his recommendations even though, he alleged, most of those given preferment were not adherents of the Whigs or even of the Prince himself, and many afterwards deserted to the opposing party. Melville even asserted that the 'influence of the crown', that essential commodity in holding together late eighteenth- and early nineteenth-century administrations, had been handed over to the heir apparent and used by him to consolidate his party. Peerages – particularly the grant of British peerages, with seats in the House of Lords, to existing Scots peers without them – were especially noted. The Prince was trying to place Moira in the disgraced Melville's former position of manager of Scottish political influence in both Houses and to transfer it to his party.[13] The Prince also recommended a large number of baronetcies. In the first such list submitted to the King every name had been placed there by the Prince, by Moira or by Fox, and the Prince was not pleased when there was delay in these honours being gazetted. He also sought to influence appointments in Ireland and in the East India Company's civil service, the latter to the annoyance of the Company's directors. 'This is downright rapine', complained Lord Minto, the President of the India Board.[14] George expected the new administration to be in effect his own, though his father was still living and, for the time being at any rate, in perfectly sound mind.

He also interfered in parliamentary elections, seeking to get his friends elected whenever there was an opportunity, though he made no financial contribution to their expenses, and he was active in several constituencies in the general election which Grenville called in the autumn of 1806 in order to strengthen his majority.[15] The Prince even lobbied his own brother the Duke of York to support the government in a debate early in March on the constitutional point of whether the Lord Chief Justice – a friend of Sidmouth's – could properly have a seat in the Cabinet.[16] All this political activity was congenial to a Prince who had for so many years been kept out of government secrets and never allowed any concern with patronage, but it was peripheral at best. His input into government policy was minimal and was not helped by the loss at the general election of several seats held by members of his following.

[13] Holland, *Memoirs*, i, 228–31; *CGPW*, v, 301.

[14] Qu. *CGPW*, v, 300.

[15] Letters to Lady Downshire and Lady Hertford on the Co. Antrim election, 22 and 25 Oct. 1806, to W. Adam, 24 Oct., and between McMahon and Northumberland, 24 and 25 Oct. 1806: *CGPW*, v, 498–502 and vi, 17–23.

[16] George to Frederick, 3 March 1806: ibid., v, 348.

This role was further reduced when Fox became ill and the decline in his mental and physical strength put more responsibility on Grenville as Prime Minister. In the summer of 1806 Fox even considered giving up the Foreign Office despite his anxious wish to arrange peace with Napoleon before he died, and he made some moves towards having his nephew Lord Holland nominated as his successor. After Fox's death in September those moves were frustrated by Grey, who succeeded in claiming the Foreign Office and reversing Fox's policy, in spite of the Prince's support of Holland.[17] This was one of the incidents which accelerated the changing drift of George's political views from Whig to Tory: Fox's death both cleared the way for Grey's succession to the leadership of the Whig party and also set the Prince free to move away from his old connections.

The Prince was away from London on a tour of the north of England when he heard of Fox's approaching death. He was deeply affected, for Fox had been his admired mentor since his youth in political matters, and one of his closest companions in the hectic dissipations in which he had then engaged. The event aroused all his sentiments of attachment and his strongest emotions. 'My feelings are not to be describ'd', he wrote to Holland;

> the loss of such a man, such a friend . . . is so incalculable, & such a stab that I candidly acknowledge to you that I have neither resolution nor spirits sufficient to stand up against it, & the only wish I now feel remaining, is that of retiring entirely from all political career, for in losing Fox, we lose everything.

He wrote again two days later:

> He has not only been the friend of my heart, but with his all-powerful mind he has instructed me, & with his hand from the earliest period of my youth he has led me along the path of true patriotism.

On the news of Fox's death on the 13th, he declared himself 'overwhelmed . . . with grief'. He was staying at Trentham with Lord and Lady Stafford, and was said to be so overcome that he could not eat, sleep or drink. Lord Fitzwilliam wrote of him a few days later at Doncaster races: 'he has lost all appetite, and even taste for wine', and Lady Caroline Stuart-Wortley observed that he looked '*very* ill & very low indeed, looking shockingly & I hear eats nothing & drinks nothing

[17] Howick to George, 15 Sept.; George to Howick 18 and reply 19 Sept.; ibid., v, 432–4, 439–44; Smith, *Grey*, 106–8; Grenville to Windham, 11 Sept., Howick to Grenville, 20 Sept. 1806: Hist. MSS Comm., *Fortescue MSS*, viii, 319–20, 345–7.

but water, glass after glass'. When he visited the Stuart-Wortleys later in September he did not touch the 'beautiful collation' prepared in his honour, and conversation flagged awkwardly until he went to bed at eleven. Though he was accompanied by his usual crowd of racing cronies, he did '*not* mix in their riotous and *blackguard* conversation'. Lady Caroline remarked that 'his present passion is Lady Hertford', and Lord Holland suspected that his low condition was due to the onset of passion for that lady: it was 'his usual system of love-making' to impress the object of his desire with 'commiserations for his sufferings and . . . apprehensions for his health'.[18]

This was ungenerous. Holland was writing some years later when the Prince's relations with the Whigs were no longer so friendly and the memory of Fox's death had faded. There is no doubt that George was genuinely and deeply grief-stricken, and though when he returned to town he did not attend Fox's funeral, this was in deference to his father, who declared that it was unprecedented for a senior member of the royal family to attend the funeral of a subject unless, as in Nelson's case, it was a national event. The Prince appealed to Grenville against his father's wishes but submitted to them. He wrote to Lord Holland an affecting and sincere tribute to Fox on the eve of the funeral. He lamented his 'not having it in my power . . . to give my personal attendance at the funeral, & thereby to testify . . . the steady & inviolable attachment & love I felt for your uncle through a long series of years . . . & the veneration & reverence for his memory which will ever live in my breast to my last moments'. For months afterwards he wore nothing but black.[19]

The political consequences of Fox's death had now to be faced. The Prince's desire that, as Fox had wished, Holland should succeed his uncle at the Foreign Office was circumvented by Grey, who had set his heart on being Fox's successor, and Grenville, who supported Grey (now Lord Howick) on the grounds that there was no other way in which the complicated and necessary exchange of offices could be satisfactorily arranged. The Prince made the best of it and assured Grey of his satisfaction, with the odd remark: 'My dear friend, this is a strange world we live in, and nothing can be done in it without a little temper and a little policy.' He consoled himself by urging Grey to maintain

[18] George to Holland, 10, 12 and 14 Sept. 1806 & reply [13th]: *CGPW,* v, 426–9; Fitzwilliam to Grenville, 24 Sept. 1806: *Fortescue MSS*, viii, 356; C. Grosvenor and Lord Stuart of Wortley (eds), *First Lady Wharncliffe*, i, 124–8; Holland, *Memoirs*, ii, 69. He was also greatly upset by Georgiana Devonshire's death in March.

[19] Moira to George, 1 Oct.; George to Grenville, 7 and 8 Oct.; to Holland, 9 Oct. 1806: *CGPW,* v, 465–6, 468–9, 472. On 11 Oct. 1806 Fitzwilliam told Adam that George had contributed £500 towards Fox's funeral expenses: ibid., v, 499.

Fox's aims and policy, a line of conduct from which Grey soon departed under the conviction that Napoleon had no sincere desire for peace without further conquests.[20]

There were other signs that all was not well in the Prince's relations with his former allies. In the autumn of 1805 allegations against the Princess of Wales were made by Lady Douglas, who had been Caroline's friend and companion at Blackheath for a time. Lady Douglas suspected that the Princess had written anonymous letters to her husband Sir John accusing her of a sexual relationship with Sir Sidney Smith. In retaliation the Douglases declared that Caroline had confessed to them in 1802 to being pregnant, and that she had given birth to a child whom she kept with her and named William Austin.[21] It seems that Caroline had indeed pretended to a pregnancy but it is clear that the child was the son of a poor woman, wife of a shipyard worker at Deptford, and that Caroline had taken a fancy to the child and informally adopted him as a focus for her thwarted maternal instincts.[22] Lady Douglas's accusations did not stop there: she alleged that Caroline had had other lovers, including Thomas Lawrence, George Canning, Admiral Sir Sidney Smith and a naval captain, Thomas Manby. Several of these had incontestably been frequent visitors at Blackheath and servants later were to testify that some had stayed overnight in circumstances that strongly suggested sexual relations. The Princess for her part was prepared to assert that the Prince was the father of her alleged child, a threat which would menace Charlotte's succession to the throne.[23]

The Prince determined upon action, in the hope both of proving Austin's illegitimacy and of securing evidence for a divorce to rid him at last of Caroline's presence so that he might remarry if he should wish. He hoped that his friends in the new Whig ministry would support him, and Samuel Romilly questioned the Douglases on his behalf. The papers were laid before the King in May 1806. The Privy Council decided upon what came to be somewhat ironically called a 'Delicate Investigation' and a committee of four Cabinet ministers, headed by the Prime Minister Lord Grenville, was appointed to carry it out. They were convinced that the Princess had written the anonymous letters to Sir John Douglas, but they were unable to find positive evidence of her adultery, and it was agreed that the child William Austin was not hers.[24]

[20] George to Howick, 22 and 24 Sept.; Howick to George, 24 Sept. 1806: ibid., 454–5, 458–9.

[21] Fraser, 146–8, 152.

[22] Ibid., 137.

[23] Ibid., 152.

[24] Romilly, *Memoirs*, ii, 123–6, 142–5; Statements by witnesses, 'Delicate Investigation', 1806: RA, Queen Caroline papers 8/2.

Their report, dated 14 July, reflected Romilly's opinion that Lady Douglas was probably motivated by pique at her treatment by the Princess, and that there was no evidence for the birth of a child nor of the 'criminal intercourse which preceded it' other than the uncorroborated testimony of Lady Douglas herself. The commissioners concluded that there was 'no foundation whatever' for the Princess's alleged adultery. However, they continued that her general conduct had been indiscreet and 'must . . . necessarily give occasion to very unfavourable interpretations', and recommended that the King should himself decide if any further action was desirable. The King demanded more positive advice, upon which the Cabinet suggested that he should warn her as to her future conduct, but that it was not necessary to bar her from the court.[25]

The result was to leave Caroline as free as before to cultivate the King's favour, and the Prince was furious. He quoted Lord Thurlow's opinion, that the commissioners had shown 'too great a degree of lenity' towards her and that if they had failed to discover enough evidence to have her prosecuted for high treason there was sufficient ground for a recommendation for an Act of Parliament to dissolve the marriage.[26] He characterized their proceedings as guided by 'weakness, irresolution & pusillanimity'. He appealed to the King to be allowed to respond to the Cabinet's recommendations before he decided whether to readmit her to the court, and declared his intention to place the evidence against her before his lawyers with a view to divorce proceedings. The King therefore postponed Caroline's visit, at which she threatened to publish the proceedings of the Commission to vindicate herself.[27]

A change of government in the spring of 1807 reversed positions. The new Cabinet, composed of those who had supported Caroline, agreed without further reservations that the allegations about her pregnancy were completely disproved, and added that all the remaining accusations against her were either satisfactorily contradicted, or rested upon unsatisfactory evidence. There was accordingly no reason for the King to forbear from receiving her into his presence, and indeed she should be received as soon as possible. They further recommended that she should be allowed an apartment in one of the royal palaces.[28]

The Prince swallowed the pill with as much grace as he could muster,

[25] Report of commissioners, *CGPW*, v, 401–5; Cabinet minutes, 29 July and 23 Dec.; ibid., 406–7 and 25 Jan. 1807: ibid., vi, 125–8.

[26] Under the medieval statute which prescribed the penalties of high treason for anyone convicted of adultery with the consort, and also for the consort herself.

[27] George to McMahon, 5 Aug. 1806; same to Queen, 2 Feb. 1807; King to Caroline, 10 Feb.: ibid., v, 408–9, vi, 131–3, 137n.

[28] Cabinet minute, 21 April 1807: ibid., vi, 162–3.

assuring the King that he would drop all proceedings against his wife and submit to his decision regarding the reception of the Princess, though insisting that the King should recognize that the commissioners had declared him innocent of initiating their proceedings or of taking any steps to accuse his wife. He pointed out that the present Cabinet, consisting of men who had supported Caroline's defence, had omitted to make this point in their minute of 21 April and had also dismissed as unsound the evidence on which their predecessors had recommended that the King should warn her as to her future conduct. The Princess would therefore appear to the public as utterly blameless and the Prince's continued refusal to receive her at Carlton House or allow her to visit her daughter Charlotte at Warwick House would seem to be unreasonable and vindictive. If necessary, he would (regretfully) himself publish the whole of the evidence against her, unless the King agreed to his demand for a separation: only in that case would he consent to her subsequent reception at court. On 18 May he wrote again to assure his father of his 'most unequivocal desire . . . to avoid anything which can call the attention of the World, tho' publication . . . would be infinitely desirable in other respects for me to destroy the effects which artifice has for the moment produced'. He repeated his firm determination that Caroline should neither live under his roof nor visit Charlotte at Carlton or Warwick House, and that Charlotte should have no contact with William Austin, since 'the child of a Pauper delivered in St Bartholomew's Hospital . . . is very unfit society for my daughter'.[29]

The King received Caroline on 4 June, though making it clear to her that he supported the Prince's stipulated restrictions on her access to Charlotte. Moira advised the Prince to make the best of it and not quarrel with his father, and family relationships accordingly improved for a time: George's attempt to rid himself of a wife he had never wanted was stalled for the moment, but the desire to do so never left him and it was to be renewed after he became regent, and brought to a climax when he became King.[30] Fox's death in effect ended George's association with the party he had adopted, in defiance of his father, over twenty-five years before. Despite his initial hopes, the ministry of 1806–7 had never really shown him that degree of deference he wanted, and his own circumstances and opinions had changed. He was now striving for a reconciliation with his father, which implied also a change in his political orientation. His annoyance at the failure of the 'Delicate Investigation' to condemn his wife or provide grounds for divorce had helped to undermine his relations with his former Whig

[29] George to King, 5 May 1807 and draft by Moira [n.d.]: ibid., 168–83.
[30] Moira to McMahon, 4 June 1807: ibid., 185–6.

friends, and their supposed neglect of his advice and patronage recommendations since Fox's death completed his disillusionment. Not only, he wrote to Moira, had he been made 'the mark of the most false, contemptible & at the same time the most malignant slanders' but from the time of Fox's death he had 'experienc'd the most marked neglect (to use no stronger term) from the new-constructed Administration'; he had been 'neither consulted nor consider'd in any one important instance' and had been 'a victim to the most envenom'd attacks of malice & falsehood' during the 'Delicate Investigation'.[31]

Nowhere was this neglect of his opinions more evident than in the Catholic question, into which the Cabinet stumbled in a desperate attempt to pacify Irish agitation without raising the spectre of full emancipation and so arousing again the King's wrath, as Pitt had done in 1801. Their proposal of a limited extension of toleration for Catholics holding army commissions above the rank of general and serving outside the United Kingdom was rightly seen in both countries as a feeble gesture of no real significance, but it was enough to rouse the cry of 'No Popery!' which could always inflame Protestant English bigotry, and Perceval and the Pittites were quick to use it as a political weapon.

The Prince's attitude was no longer clear. Without Fox to keep him steady and loyal, he tended to waver in his political allegiances as his natural inconstancy took over. Lady Holland remarked that he behaved 'shabbily' at the time of the ministry's resignation, and failed to give it support.[32] It was, in truth, only his personal attachment to Fox which had made him a Whig supporter: he had never shared their principles, and despite professions of friendship for Grey, Fox's successor, there was an antipathy between them that grew into active dislike.

On the other side, the long estrangement from his father which had restricted his visits to his mother and sisters had become painful to him. His relationships with them were more affectionate than ever, on both sides. The Queen always gave him her full support in his difficulties with Caroline and on his birthday Augusta wrote that 'You are well acquainted with my heart and that you have lived there from the moment instinct could act in my heart, and with rooted affection ever since reason could form my judgement'. Sophia assured him that of all the congratulations he would receive 'none will be more heartfelt & sincere than those which flow from my pen'.[33]

The desire to live more at ease with his family therefore reinforced

[31] George to Moira, 30 March 1807: ibid., 156–7.

[32] Ibid., 144.

[33] Queen to George, 6 May; Augusta to George, 10 Aug.; Sophia to George, 11 Aug. 1807: ibid., 168, 203.

the Prince's wish to '*cease to be a party man*' as he had expressed it[34] – a decision ominous for the future hopes of his former friends. For the next three years he stood aside from party conflict and gave support to his father's ministers. In private life he became increasingly infatuated with Lady Hertford. It was noticed that he was spending more and more time visiting the Hertfords, not only in London but in the country. In September 1807 he left Brighton to stay at Cheltenham, which was nearer to the Hertfords at Ragley. His excuse was that he had been unwell again and Brighton was too cold in his weakened condition. After visiting them he wrote to Lady Hertford as 'my best and ever dearest friend' and 'my dear nurse' to assure her that he would come to her as often as he could. Lady Bessborough wrote that he thought of nothing else but Lady Hertford. In town, he visited her every day: his confidant Benjamin Bloomfield told Lord Hertford that when she was not in town the Prince was very depressed, never went out, and was immovable from 'that sad room' where he sat all the time. Neither he nor McMahon, Bloomfield wrote, had ever seen him in such 'a state of lowness & depression. . . . It is not in the power of my pen to describe the sufferings of this house'. The Prince 'appears plung'd into a state of apathy & indifference towards himself which alarm more than can be describ'd' and 'scarcely speaks a word'. On the news that the Hertfords were coming, he exclaimed 'Thank God . . . now I shall be among friends who really do love me. . . . Now I shall be able to unburthen myself'.[35]

Whether the Prince had a sexual relationship with Lady Hertford is doubtful. In the first place, though she was intelligent and handsome, she was not a passionate woman. On the contrary, she was regarded as cold and frigid, and though there is no reason to suppose, as some writers have done, that a grandmother in her mid-forties was incapable of sexual passion, or that the Prince had ceased to feel any, it does seem that their relationship was more domestic – particularly as Lord Hertford was usually also present and he and the Prince remained close friends. What George now wanted was a sympathetic relationship with a woman who would listen to him, offer him understanding, guide his views, and provide a comforting environment in which he could forget the cares of his personal life. His need for a close and affectionate

[34] George to Moira, 30 March 1807: ibid., 156–7.

[35] George to Lady Hertford, 4 and 25 Oct. 1807; Bloomfield to same, 2, 10 and 15 Dec.: ibid., 215–17, 220–1 and n., 231–4. Charlotte wrote in Jan. 1812 that her father 'is *quite governed* by his mother & the Manchester Square folks, to whom he goes *regularly every day & dines there every day*. He seldom leaves his house till 4 or between 4 & 5 & then never comes home again till late *at night*': Aspinall (ed.), *Letters of Princess Charlotte*, 23.

atmosphere was not yet met in his own family circle, despite his love for his mother and sisters and theirs for him, and in spite of his efforts to seek a genuine reconciliation with his father, who was now becoming blind as well as showing occasional symptoms of his mental troubles. Lady Hertford was a refuge from all these anxieties, while Maria became more irritable and impatient with him. The Hertfords also shared George's passion for the arts and for collecting: it was at this time that what later became the Wallace Collection was being assembled by the Hertfords at their house in Manchester Square and their son Lord Yarmouth was advising the Prince on his purchases of pictures. There was more to their relationship with the Prince than what one biographer has described as 'the outcome of a disagreeable and capricious taste for elderly women'.[36] Nor could the Prince forget for a moment that the Hertfords had come to his rescue by helping him to ensure that his beloved Minny Seymour should continue to live with Maria.

Nevertheless, the Prince's eye had not ceased to rove. In December 1809, on hearing that Granville Leveson-Gower had deserted his mistress of many years, Lady Bessborough, to marry Harriet Cavendish, he attempted to make passionate love to her, declaring his willingness to leave both Maria and Lady Hertford for her and to make her protégé Canning Prime Minister. Lady Bessborough was sensible enough to laugh at him and reject his advances, which he accepted with good grace before launching into a three-hour political discussion.[37] It was habit rather than need or emotion that still led him occasionally into sexual escapades.

Maria was the one who suffered most from his inconstancy. In July 1807 one observer noticed that at a ball at the Hertfords' Maria seemed 'much deserted' by the Prince and when he went to Cheltenham in August to be near Ragley the world began to draw its conclusions. Lord Carlisle noted that Maria's situation was 'becoming more perilous'.[38] Others saw that George's visits to her were primarily intended for him to see and enjoy the company of Minny, while he ignored Maria even in public. Lady Bessborough thought that Maria now bored him.[39] She was too proud to bear this neglect and she resented the fact that she was still expected to act as his hostess at the Pavilion while Lady Hertford dined at his table and openly displayed her intimacy with him, thereby deliberately humiliating her. Maria resented the rudeness of Bloomfield, who made no secret of his preference for Lady Hertford and who was

[36] Fulford, *George the Fourth*, 99.
[37] Lady Bessborough to G. Leveson Gower [n.d.]: Granville (ed.), *Leveson Gower* ii, 349–50; Villiers, 229.
[38] Anita Leslie, *Mrs Fitzherbert*, 144.
[39] Lady Bessborough to G. Leveson Gower, 27 Oct. [1807]: Granville (ed.), *Leveson Gower* ii, 297–8.

writing frequently to her to say how low and depressed the Prince was without her company and to encourage her to visit him. Maria could bear it no longer. In December 1809 she wrote of 'the very great incivilities I have received these two years' at the Pavilion and pointed out that since 'Your Royal Highness four and twenty years ago placed me in a situation so nearly connected with your own' she owed it to herself 'not to be insulted under your roof with impunity'. She threatened to leave him. He replied with merely polite regrets and 'every possible kindness and good wishes towards you'.[40]

It was effectively the end of their relationship. Though she continued occasionally to appear at the Pavilion for another eighteen months, the old feelings were never there. When the Prince was about to become regent at the end of January 1811, he called her to Carlton House to ask her advice as to whether he should continue his father's ministers in office or send for Grey. She urged him to call in his old Whig friends, only to be rebuffed. He wished her to approve of Lady Hertford's advice to retain the Tories and refuse to emancipate the Catholics. At the end of the interview she left, cool and self-possessed, with a last injunction to him to treat his daughter Charlotte with more kindness: 'That is your opinion, Madam', he replied. She curtsied and departed.[41] She took up residence with Minny at Battersea and left him for ever.

The final break came in June 1811 when he gave a magnificent dinner at Carlton House, attended by the exiled King Louis XVIII of France and his family, to celebrate the inauguration of the regency. Maria received her usual invitation, but the Prince let it be known that there would be a change in the seating arrangements. Instead of sitting at the head of the Prince's table as his wife, which he had always insisted upon in the past either at his own table or as a guest elsewhere, she was to be seated with others according to rank: in other words at the foot of the table as a commoner. Maria rejected the invitation with spirit and dignity: as 'the person who is not unjustly suspected by the world of possessing in silence unassumed & unsustained a Rank given her by yourself above that of any other person present', she said that she could 'never submit to appear in your house in any place or situation but in that where you yourself first placed me many years ago'.[42] They never spoke again, and their infrequent contacts, usually the consequence of their common affection for Minny who continued to live with Maria, were cool and unfriendly. It was a sad end to an affair which had given both of them intense pleasure and fulfilment for over twenty years but also created strains and stresses which in the end were too strong for

[40] Maria Fitzherbert to George, 18 Dec. 1809 and reply, 19th: *CGPW*, vi, 510n; Anita Leslie, *Mrs Fitzherbert*, 147.

[41] Anita Leslie, *Mrs Fitzherbert*, 154.

[42] Ibid., 156–7.

their relationship to contain. Yet the underlying devotion was still there: on his deathbed nearly twenty years later he was found with her portrait round his neck, and he asked that it should be buried with him, while she mourned his passing with genuine sorrow. She wrote him a farewell letter a few days before his death: to her great distress, he never sent an answer, though he put the letter under his pillow.

Chapter 11

BROTHERS AND SISTERS

The Prince's association with the Hertfords, together with the decision of his old Whig friends in 1807 to commit themselves to the Roman Catholic cause and his resentment at their alleged neglect of him, contributed, as has been shown, to his decision to 'cease to be a party man'. He hoped above all to be fully reconciled with his family and this implied the abandonment of his old political associates and his pro-Catholic position. When Lord Holland remonstrated with him on the grounds that this would destroy his popularity and influence in Ireland, and put an end to the longed-for prospect of his being able to reconcile the two countries, he replied that to encourage the Catholics 'might drive his father to insanity'. He assured Holland and Lord Fingall, leader of the Irish Catholics, that he still sympathized with their cause and that he would observe strict neutrality in any political discussion of it, and in the autumn at a fête in his honour at Stowe, home of the head of the Grenville family, the Marquess of Buckingham, he expressed friendly views towards Grenville and the opposition, reserving only the need to keep the Catholic issue from the King. On the other hand, he was now seeing much more of his brother Ernest, whose anti-Catholic views might best be described as rabid and who never hesitated to press them on him.[1]

In the circumstances the opposition in Parliament was somewhat at a loss and matters were not helped by the disclosure in January 1809 by a radical MP named Wardle of the activities of the Duke of York's mistress Mary Ann Clarke in using her influence to obtain army commissions and promotions for money. The more radical Whigs, led by Whitbread once more, joined in the outcry against her and the Duke, which forced him to resign as Commander-in-Chief, though Grey and the moderate Whigs refrained from exploiting the scandal for fear that the monarchy itself might be discredited.[2] At first George assured his brother of his support, but he withdrew into neutrality when public opinion rose in condemnation, for fear of being associated with

[1] *CGPW*, vi, 246; Holland, *Memoirs*, ii, 247–51; T. Grenville to Lord Grenville, 19 Oct. 1808: Hist. MSS Comm., *Fortescue MSS*, ix, 229.

[2] Smith, *Grey*, 182–3; Harvey, 240–4.

political corruption. The King was annoyed and once again the fragile unity of the royal family wavered, while more public disclosures of all their debts threatened to associate them with personal extravagance at a time of national financial stringency.[3]

The Prince's affairs were again to the fore. Robert Gray complained in April 1809 that apart from a small reduction in expenditure on the Prince's stables, 'the general rate of expenditure is nearly as before' and 'each quarter produces fresh bills for jewellery, prints and various articles . . . wholly unconnected with the ordinary supplies'. George was quite unable to resist buying whatever luxuries took his fancy, and new debts had accumulated to the amount of old debts paid off. The attempt to set aside a further sum to help pay his wife's debts and so avoid more unfavourable publicity only added to his own financial problems and increased his resentment against the government for what he castigated as their 'mean, paltry, dirty, pettifogging' attitude. He complained of 'the prodigious excess of her Royal Highness's expenditure' and asserted that the government's plan transformed 'all the *grace & merit*' that he deserved for his 'very generous' action into 'a sort of *forced consent* extracted from me *by art & quibble*', as if she rather than he was the injured person and, he said, 'I am crying *peccavi for the past*' to make up for '*past omissions & delinquencies on my part*'.[4] To try to silence his critics George agreed to pay the Princess's debts of £41,000 and to increase her allowance, on condition that he should not be responsible for any further liabilities she might incur, a step which he asserted was designed to avoid burdening the public in these difficult times and also to do justice to his wife's creditors. They at any rate applauded his generosity and even the King agreed that it was a fair and reasonable settlement.[5]

It did not however entirely heal the troubles of the royal family. Princess Amelia's health was now giving rise to serious concern. The youngest of the daughters, now aged twenty-six, and the last of George III and Charlotte's children, she was her father's favourite and, next to Mary, her eldest brother's too. He was her godfather and there was always a tender relationship between them. George encouraged her to call herself his 'child' and was always sensitive to her troubles. These

[3] George to Frederick, 25, 27 Jan. 1809 and reply, 27th: *CGPW*, vi, 359–60.
[4] R. Gray to W. Adam, 1 April 1809; George to same, 16 and 29 May: ibid., 374–5, 383–5, 391–2.
[5] King to Eldon, 17 June 1809: ibid., 405. Aspinall, who could rarely see merit in any of George's actions, could not forbear from remarking that 'it would have been well for the Prince's reputation had he had these wholly admirable sentiments in mind during the years when he was piling up debts on a vast scale with which the taxpayer was ultimately burdened' (ibid., 391–2n.).

began in 1798 when tuberculosis developed in her knee, causing excruciating pain, and in 1801 she had the first of a series of worsening attacks of erysipelas. The two complaints were to cause her early death nine years later.[6]

Her troubles were also emotional. During or shortly after a visit to Weymouth in 1801 she fell in love with Colonel (later General) Sir Charles Fitzroy, second son of Lord Southampton and nephew of the Duke of Grafton, who was one of the King's aides-de-camp and who had been left behind as her attendant when the rest of the family returned to Windsor. Fitzroy was the same age as her eldest brother, and was thus twenty-one years her senior. Though not an ardent suitor, he returned her affection and their attachment soon became clear to those about the court. She was cautioned by the Queen to be careful of her behaviour, and it was not mentioned to the King for fear of driving him mad, as any threat of the marriage of one of his children to a commoner might well do. Her brothers and sisters soon became aware of the situation. Indeed she told the Duke of York that she considered herself married to Fitzroy, and though her biographer thought that this referred to a spiritual rather than a physical union, Mrs George Villiers was said to have been present at the actual marriage. Rumours nevertheless abounded, some even alleging that she had become pregnant. The truth seems to be that Amelia was determined to marry Fitzroy, but only after her father's death, and that the rumours of a child are unlikely.[7]

However, it was Amelia who died. Her tubercular condition spread to her lungs and her attacks of erysipelas worsened. By 1808 the signs of a fatal outcome were becoming plain to all except the King, who was never fully informed of her condition for fear of the effect of the news upon his weakened mind.

The Prince was her constant confidant. In September 1809 she wrote to him that 'I always loved you better than any of my brothers, I knew, and *now* [I know] very much more'. He visited her when she was sent to Weymouth in the hope that the sea air would help to cure her, and she gave him power of attorney over her affairs and opened her heart to him over Fitzroy. As she lay in her last prolonged illness in the early summer of 1810 she wrote: 'most tenderly do I love you, & how much I wish the *rest* of the family had hearts and feelings like yours' – a reference chiefly to the Queen and the Duke of Cumberland, neither of whom showed much concern about her true condition. She entrusted George with her will and named him her executor – a

[6] Stuart, *Daughters of George III*, 337–8.

[7] Ibid., 350; G. Villiers to Sir H. Halford, 10 Feb. 1813: RA, Regency, box 7, 20413–14.

delicate trust as she wished to leave everything except a few personal mementoes to Fitzroy. She died on 2 November.[8]

George and his fellow executor Adolphus did not carry out the strict terms of their late sister's will. Fitzroy was not given her jewels as she had asked; instead they were handed to her sister Mary, who had nursed her, and Fitzroy saw none of the 'pecuniary compensation' which the King was told by her doctor, Sir Henry Halford, he had been promised. This apparent breach of faith is attributed by Amelia's biographer to the Prince's belief that her infatuation for Fitzroy had been a contributory cause of her death and that he had not been as ardent as she in their relationship, but had received rather than given her love.[9] Yet his letter to George after Amelia's death hardly bears this out: it spoke of 'the memory and transcendental purity of affection of the adored and departed Angel'. Mrs George Villiers wrote that he was 'dreadfully and deeply afflicted'.[10] Nevertheless, he was unkindly treated. Instead of receiving Amelia's jewels and other intimate souvenirs he had to make do with a shabby collection of several wagon-loads of odds and ends of little real or sentimental value, and when he remonstrated the Prince turned his back on him. Two years later Miss Knight recorded that George burst into tears in regret that he had not complied with Amelia's wishes, but this rather maudlin attack did nothing to redress the slight.[11] Possibly Fitzroy had not been worthy of her affection, and George's actions over her will at least contributed to a reconciliation with his father and to averting more distress in the last few weeks before the final lapse into insanity.

Long before Amelia's death George had become aware of the increasing discontent felt by all his sisters with their secluded lives in the dull atmosphere of their parents' court. 'We go on vegetating as we have done for the last twenty years of our lives', Elizabeth told him in September 1808. Their daily routine was never exciting. Augusta had written earlier that 'we walk for two hours of a morning and our Instructions last from 11 till 2, then I have an hour's English reading from 3 to 4 and sometimes go out with Mama. . . . We always go to town with Papa and Mama and then go to the drawing room and to the play, sometimes we play at cards in the evening, sometimes work, and draw. You may judge from this account if I have not great reason to be happy.'[12] The Queen's solicitude for her husband's health was carried

[8] Amelia to George [*c.* 1 June 1810]: RA Add. Geo. 14/193; Stuart, *Daughters of George III*, 367, 370–1; Halford to George [2 Nov.]: ibid., 378.
[9] Ibid., 383.
[10] Mrs G. Villiers to George, 5 Nov. 1810; Fitzroy to George, 5 Nov.: Stuart, *Daughters of George III*, 383 and RA Add. Geo. 14/239–40.
[11] Stuart, *Daughters of George III*, 384–6.
[12] Augusta to William [n.d.]: RA Geo. 4/22.

to excess and cast a shadow over the whole family. She would not allow her daughters to go out in society or visit the theatre lest they should seem uncaring about their father. As for allowing them to marry or even fall in love, that was unthinkable: the King would never willingly allow any of his children to marry a commoner or even a subject, and to broach the idea with him was impossible. He had to put up with his sons' illicit if hardly secret liaisons; only Frederick was legally married by 1807, though his extramarital affair was to be notorious enough, but William's long-running relationship with the actress Dorothy Jordan, which by 1807 had produced ten illegitimate but acknowledged children, was well known, and Edward, Duke of Kent and Ernest, Duke of Cumberland also lived with ladies who were in all but name morganatic wives.[13] Augustus had defied his father and the Royal Marriages Act and actually married Lady Augusta Murray in 1794 and had two children by her, but the marriage was forcibly annulled and the children bastardized at his father's insistence and with the help of the Prince of Wales.[14] Fate took its revenge on the author of the Royal Marriages Act: no children were ever born to Frederick, to Charlotte, the Princess Royal, who married the Prince (later King) of Württemberg, to Elizabeth, who later married the Landgrave of Hesse-Homburg, or to Mary, who finally married her cousin the Duke of Gloucester: the remaining daughters never married. The Prince's daughter Charlotte and her baby died in childbed in 1817. Edward, who was forced into marriage with Princess Victoire of Saxe-Coburg in 1818, produced the eventual heiress to the throne, Princess Victoria, in 1819. Ernest had a son in 1819 who became King of Hanover after his father. Adolphus, Duke of Cambridge, who was also married off in 1818, had a son and two daughters. The fifteen children of George III and Charlotte gave them only six legitimate grandchildren.

The lives of the unmarried princesses – that is, all but one of them in 1807, five out of the six – were miserable. Not only were they kept strictly under the Queen's authority, but they felt deprived of real love and affection from their mother. They felt greater attachment to their father, but their love was mainly concentrated on their brothers, and largely on their eldest one. George returned their affection, and except for his eldest sister who went off to Württemberg in 1797 and rarely saw him afterwards, he tried to compensate them as much as his own complicated private life allowed. Their letters were always fond and it was to him they turned when life at Windsor became insupportable without outside help. In 1808 Elizabeth appealed for his support in her

13 Tomalin.

14 Privy Council minutes, 27–28 Jan. 1794: RA 48019–29; Registry of Arches Court of Canterbury, 14 July 1794: ibid., 48045–9.

desire to marry Louis Philippe, Duke of Orleans, who much later became King of France, but the Queen was adamant that none of her family should marry a Roman Catholic. George interceded but she refused to change her mind. Elizabeth submitted, but wrote heart-brokenly to her brother that she was 'very desirous to open my heart to you under the seal of secrecy' and that none of her family had shown more protection than '*your own dear self*'. 'I have taught myself so thoroughly to look cheerful with a heavy heart', she wrote: 'No words can ever express half what I feel towards you for your unbounded goodness to me . . . I am on my knees with *gratitude*. . . . Volumes wd. not suffice to express half what I feel towards you . . .'.[15] Sophia, who was in Elizabeth's confidence, assured him: 'you have proved yourself what *none of us* can *ever doubt* so kind a brother'. She continued to confide in him from what the sisters called 'the Nunnery'; in December 1811 she thanked him for his 'noble and generous intentions', describing the sisters as '*poor old wretches* . . . a *dead weight* upon You, *old Lumber* to the *country*, like *Old Clothes*, I wonder you do not vote for putting us in a *sack* and drowning us in *The Thames*'. Her niece's later addiction to underlining her words for emphasis when she became Queen was clearly a family trait. The Prince's considerate conduct towards his father during the first months of the King's illness also pleased his sisters, who were almost as devoted to their father as to their eldest brother.[16]

The lives of the princesses clearly went from bad to worse as their mother became more cantankerous and irritable. She refused to contemplate the marriage of Augusta to Sir Brent Spencer with whom she had been in love for several years, again despite George's support for his sister and, like Elizabeth, Augusta was forced to submit to her mother's authority. The situation was unbearable and the sisters determined on a coup. In April 1812 they wrote four letters – one, drafted by Augusta, was signed by all four, the other three separately by Elizabeth, Mary and Sophia. The letters were presented to the Queen at breakfast by Madame Beckendorff, her keeper of the robes.

The Queen's reaction was instantaneous and predictable. She wrote a reply that same morning declaring that she never 'felt as shattered in my life as I did by reading your letter'. She admonished her daughters, 'as this may perhaps be the last time that any one of you may be inclined to take a mother's advice . . . to consider that your situation is very different to that of your Brothers', who had public duties to perform. In their case, 'in your Sex, and under the present Melancholy Situation of your father the going to Public Amusements except where Duty calls

[15] Elizabeth to George, 25 Sept. and 2 Oct. 1808: *CGPW*, vi, 316–18, 323–4.

[16] Sophia to George, 12 Dec. 1811: Stuart, *Daughters of George III*, 286–7; Mary to George [1811]: RA Add. Geo. 12/2/104, 115; Elizabeth to George, 10 Feb. 1811: *CGPW*, vii, 222–3.

you would be the *highest mark of indecency possible*'. They were never to be in the same house alone with even their unmarried brothers unless a lady was present. The tone of injured reproach was completed by a final plea that 'the stroke is given, and nothing can mend it' and that none of their brothers or friends should ever mention the matter to her again.

The princesses were not prepared to surrender without making every effort to gain their wishes and they sent another joint letter to the Prince Regent declaring their inability to continue their present life and their refusal to tolerate the treatment they received whenever they proposed to spend a few days away from 'the Queen's Roof'. They would accept no invitations even from him 'unless it shall be in your Power to secure us from the continuation of a treatment . . . which is destructive alike to our health, happiness, and comfort'.[17]

George did all he could to make his sisters' lives more bearable but the shadow of the King's illness lay over them all and even George could not ignore the fear that his father's recovery might be prevented if he found that his daughters had not behaved with the utmost propriety and restraint. George, too, was genuinely fond of his mother and he valued her affection in return. She showed no scruple in playing on his feelings for the King. When in November 1812 Elizabeth and Mary went up from Windsor to take Princess Charlotte to the opening of Parliament the Queen was furious and, according to Augusta, 'a dreadfull scene' resulted on their return. The Prince again intervened, appealing to his mother not to subject them all to such 'scenes so distressing and so painful to all of us' and reminding her that she had agreed to the princesses chaperoning his daughter when she appeared in public: he asked for her kindness and support in *his* difficulties. She replied that his own appearance in the House of Lords, though required by duty, 'was more melancholy than the King's death' and in the case of the princesses, excepting Charlotte, it was a matter of 'female delicacy' that they ought not to go: their appearance 'appears to me a full declaration to the world that the King can never recover'. She felt even more deeply the defiance expressed by both Elizabeth and Mary (Sophia, having the excuse of her illness, escaped the crisis) when, on telling her that they intended to go, against her wishes, they asserted that 'living with me in my distress is disagreeable' and Elizabeth had a fit of hysterics. The Queen now wished the matter to be ended, and assured him that she would 'keep peace', though 'to forget it is out of my power . . . for it is so hard a blow . . . '.

George replied with a soothing but unrepentant letter, defending his

[17] Stuart, *Daughters of George III*, 99–105; princesses to George, 2 & [12] Dec. 1812; Elizabeth to George [?1 Dec. 1812]: RA Add Geo. 10/1/57, 59, 11/1/210.

sisters, 'whose general conduct has been so truly proper and affectionate' and who had met his wishes to do 'my duty to my family and to the public'. He also defended his ministers, whom the Queen had censured for presuming to advise him on what she saw as a purely family matter, saying that in such circumstances it was impossible to separate family and public interests. The Queen was mollified to the extent that she was able to discuss the question more calmly with him at dinner at Carlton House a few days later. In the interval, news of a French defeat before Moscow lightened the clouds of anxiety over the war and lifted everyone's spirits. Augusta wrote pathetically that they loved the Queen, though 'our lives have not been *too happy*, but we have never complained'. Mary added that their father had suffered much with the Queen's temper for fifty years, but he had brought up his daughters to help hide it from the world. His eldest son, however, was the only one who seemed able to soothe her temper and, Elizabeth wrote, all was '*couleur de rose*' after the dinner at Carlton House.[18]

George did his best through the following years to lighten the family atmosphere, inviting the Queen and the 'sisterhood' to parties at Carlton House and the Pavilion, suggesting new round games which they might play in the evenings. In 1818 Mary wrote that the Queen had told her that his conduct 'has been most *amiable towards* myself and Sisters . . . . You have the satisfaction of feeling you have done your *Duty* by all *parties*'. After her mother's death she assured him that 'much as I *loved* you *before* which God knows is far beyond what I can find words to express – This long protracted illness has made me if possible value you more and more every hour'.[19]

George's kindness towards his sisters made him the repository of their secrets and inner feelings. In March 1812 Augusta wrote him a long letter baring 'the Secret of my Heart' – her long-standing love for one of the King's equerries, Sir Brent Spencer, and her dearest wish to be allowed to marry him, even if privately and in secret. She wished George to talk the Queen round to it but he almost certainly decided that it would be counterproductive to attempt it. Whether in fact he sanctioned a secret marriage cannot be shown with certainty, but her biographer believes the evidence is that he did and that Augusta did find private happiness.[20]

Sophia too owed her eldest brother thanks for his support in her private difficulties. She fell in love with another of her father's equerries, General Thomas Garth, who also was several years her senior, and

[18] George to Queen, 11 Sept. and 1, 3, 6 and 11 Dec. 1812, and replies 2 and 3 Dec.: *Taylor Papers*, 78–83: Stuart, *Daughters of George III*, 105–6.

[19] Stuart, *Daughters of George III*, 120–1; Mary to George, 3 Feb. [1818] and 23 Nov. [1818]: RA Add. Geo. 12/317, 320.

[20] Augusta to George, March 1812: Stuart, *Daughters of George III*, 109–12.

it is generally accepted that in 1800 she bore him a child, also probably after a secret marriage. Greville later told the comical story that when her pregnancy could no longer be hidden, the King was told that she was suffering from dropsy, and after her figure returned to normal when she was delivered, he was told that she had been instantly cured by eating roast beef, which he solemnly declared was 'a very extraordinary thing'.[21]

Sophia wrote several affectionate letters to her eldest brother who sent her many little gifts. She thanked him in 1802 for a trinket in the form of a pansy, writing that 'I am in ecstacies with my lovely *Pensée*, yet, dear love, I will not disown that the contents of the dear letter is [*sic*] what I prize most, as it contains the assurance of your affection'. In 1803 he sent her a heart-shaped jewel on her birthday, on which she wrote 'If I may hope that I have a little corner in the *original* heart of which this dear one is a representative, it will make me happy, for I do love you, *de coeur et d'âme*'. Sophia was described by the sisters' biographer as 'the most unhappy of them all', yet her association with Garth seems to have been accepted even by her parents. Sophia herself was more independent of them than the other princesses, and inclined to be impetuous and self-willed. The Queen in her turn showed her little overt affection, despite her frail health which kept her out of the family crisis of 1812, but George treated her with loving kindness until his own death in 1830.[22]

His sisters were not the only members of the Royal family to give George concern in the years leading to the regency. His own wife and daughter were still causes of tension, Caroline taking every opportunity to discredit him in the eyes of the public and embarrass him socially and financially, while Charlotte's upbringing and education caused constant difficulty with the King. George's brothers too were a source of family and public embarrassment. Frederick's probably innocent but undeniable implication in the activities of his mistress in dealing in army patronage led to his enforced resignation as Commander-in-Chief in 1809, and stirred up a renewal of radical agitation against corruption in public life which became a running sore throughout the regency period.

A further sensation was the affair of the Duke of Cumberland. In May 1810 the Duke's valet, Joseph Sellis, was found in his own bedroom in the early hours of the morning with his throat cut. The Duke had cried out that he was being attacked, and had indeed suffered a blow from a sword (his own regimental sabre) on his head. He claimed that he had been woken by the attack, had fought off his assailant, and called for his

[21] Ibid., 273–4; C.C.F. Greville, *Diary*, ed. Wilson, i, 94 (14 March 1829).
[22] Stuart, *Daughters of George III*, 276–7, 281.

other valet, Neale, who administered some hasty first aid and with the other servants went to Sellis's bedroom and found him dead. An inquest brought in a verdict of suicide, and concluded that Sellis had first attacked his master before cutting his own throat with a razor.[23]

That was not the end of the matter. Rumours began to circulate accusing Cumberland of having murdered Sellis, who it was alleged had been blackmailing him or had found him in bed with Mrs Sellis, and of faking the attack on himself. The foreman of the inquest jury was no other than Francis Place, the erstwhile radical 'tailor of Charing Cross', who supported the verdict of suicide and was therefore suspected by his former radical associates of becoming a government spy and organizing a cover-up. The matter does not end there, for there is in the Royal Archives a document dated 1827 written by one Charles Jones, the Duke's former ADC, alleging that Cumberland had confessed to him in 1815 that he had killed Sellis to prevent his 'propagating a report' against him. The depositions presented to the inquest however support the view that the verdict was a true one and that Cumberland's confession, if it was ever made at all, may have been the result of a mind under stress when the Queen refused to receive his bride, whom he married in 1815, on the grounds that she had broken off a former engagement to his brother Adolphus after she had become pregnant by the Prince of Solms-Braunfels. On this occasion George supported his brother, though to no avail with the Queen. It nevertheless brought them closer together, possibly leading to a further stiffening of the Prince's developing anti-Catholic attitude. In 1818 Ernest wrote that 'you ALONE among eleven *brothers & sisters* have proved to me that you are really a *brother & friend*'.[24]

George's relations with his other brothers had now become less cordial. Augustus, the most liberal in political views, was estranged when George took his father's side in insisting on the annulment of his marriage, and later by the Prince's refusal as Regent to employ his old Whig friends in government. This coolness suffered a further drop in temperature in 1811 when Princess Charlotte was alleged to have appealed to Augustus in her rebellion against her father's attempt to force her to marry the Prince of Orange, though Augustus denied that he had been consulted by Charlotte or had in any way encouraged her. He declared that he suffered 'deep pain' at the Regent's attitude towards him, which nothing seemed able to alter. On the Queen's death in 1818 Augustus wrote that he acknowledged his duty to accept his brother's proscription of him. He devoted the rest of his life

[23] Halford to King [31 May 1810]: *CGPW*, vii, 34–5.
[24] RA Geo. Add. 8; Queen to George, 10 April 1818: *LG4*, ii, 260; Patterson, *Burdett*, i, 290.

to a number of worthy charities and to his immense collection of books.[25]

Edward, Duke of Kent, who had been a devoted friend of Maria Fitzherbert and on that and other accounts perhaps the closest of the brothers to George, fell out of favour on his marriage in 1818 despite his obedient abandonment of his long-standing partner Mme St Laurent. He insisted that his wife should be delivered of her child – who would be heir presumptive since Charlotte had died in 1817 – in England rather than on the continent and George attempted to prevent it by refusing to pay their expenses. The government also declined to come to his aid, Liverpool remarking that there was no necessity for children born in the royal line to be delivered in England rather than on the continent. This parsimonious atititude, as it seemed to the Duke, was circumvented by a loan of £5,000 from two whig lords, Fitzwilliam and Dundas, with additional help from Lord Darnley and Alderman Matthew Wood, later the leading supporter of George's estranged Queen. Not surprisingly in these circumstances, the former affection between Edward and his eldest brother was replaced by hostility and in later years the child – who became Queen Victoria in due course – was told by her uncle Leopold that George 'hated your father most sincerely' and wanted to get her and her mother out of the country.[26] Leopold, however, had taken a violent antipathy to George because, as widower of Princess Charlotte, he considered, most unjustly, that his late wife had been badly treated and even driven to her death by her father's neglect.

Only Frederick, William and Ernest were to remain on affectionate terms with their eldest brother after 1819. No one, William had written in 1813, is 'more sincerely attached to you publicly & privately than myself: 4 & 40 years have you invariably been to me one and the same and I should be the most ungrateful being if I did not feel yr goodness and kindness to me'. In 1830 he recalled 'the uninterrupted friendship that has subsisted . . . for *nine & fifty* years'.[27] During George's final illness he asked for daily bulletins from the doctors and after George's death he revealed his genuine affection for Maria Fitzherbert when she showed him George's 'will' of 1796 naming her as his only true wife. Despite his reputation as a drunken martinet in the navy and after he became King William IV as a buffoon without dignity, in the end he showed more heart and affection than the remaining brothers.

[25] George to Queen, 29 Jan. 1817: RA Add. 9/191; E. Livingston to King, Naples, 1 May 1798: ibid., 480; Augustus to George, 19 Nov. 1818: ibid., 48300–1.

[26] Kent to Lt.-Gen. F.A. Wetherall, Dec. 1818 to March 1819: ibid., 45605–25, *passim*; H. Twiss, *Life of Eldon*, ii, 319; Leopold to Victoria, 16 Dec. 1842 and 22 Jan. 1841: RA Queen Victoria papers, Y69/26, 30.

[27] William to George [?31 Dec. 1813]: RA 45012 and to Knighton, 21 April 1830: Add. Geo. 4/745.

Chapter 12

PRINCE REGENT

The King's final relapse into his own world of delusions occurred in the last weeks of 1810 and the ministers shortly laid out their proposals for a regency under the Prince of Wales, with limited powers for one year in the first instance, on the model of Pitt's scheme of 1788, in case his father recovered within that time. The Prince protested formally at this limitation, but accepted it without undue fuss. Early in 1812 he assumed the full powers of the royal prerogative, and so began the period known in British political, social and artistic life as the Regency.

The regency period is conventionally seen as a time of social and artistic elegance, fashion, refinement and the display of wealth. It took its character very much from the Prince Regent himself, the 'first gentleman of Europe', patron of all the arts, supporter of new ideas and innovations in painting, sculpture, architecture, decoration, literature and music. In these spheres the previous rigid codes of taste gave way to a freer, more informal and imaginative mode of expression. As the reign of George III had begun in an era of classical formality and established conventions, that of his eldest son marked the beginning of a romantic desire to stretch the frontiers of experience and explore the deeper realms of emotion. No monarch has ever better symbolized his age than George IV. As Roger Fulford remarked, 'He did more than any other man before him, or after, to develop the art of living in England'. Another biographer described the regency in this respect as 'one of the greatest and most glorious epochs in our history'.[1]

Though the regency is most often associated with elegant refinement in the arts and social manners, it was also a period of discovery and development in the sciences, technology and manufacturing industry. Paralleling the aesthetic achievements of Lawrence, Turner, Constable, Crome and Cotman in painting, the mysticism of Coleridge, Blake and Fuseli, the philosophical speculations of Bentham and James Mill, the literary efforts of Jane Austen and Walter Scott – the Prince's two favourite authors – were the scientific and technological advances of Faraday, Stephenson, Robert Owen, Telford and McAdam, Humphry Davy and many others. Man's command over his physical environment

[1] Fulford, *George the Fourth*, 156–7; D.M. Stuart, *Portrait of the Prince Regent*, 21.

in the discovery of electricity, gas lighting, steam power, and even the beginnings of mechanical flight, advanced in step with theoretical knowledge and speculative philosophy. As their titles imply, it was under royal or princely patronage and encouragement that bodies such as the Royal Institution, the Royal Society of Arts and the Royal Literary Fund in their various fields promoted the spread of intellectual and practical speculation, knowledge and experiment. Freedom of enquiry and the encouragement of originality were both spheres in which the Prince Regent's interests were engaged. He was no merely formal patron, but took an active interest in the artistic, cultural and scientific progress of the age and contributed greatly to its character as what has been called 'The Age of Improvement'.[2]

Nowhere was the aesthetic spirit of the new age more vividly expressed than at the lavish fête given at Carlton House on 19 June 1811. Ostensibly to entertain the French royal family in exile and to promote British manufacture, the real purpose was to celebrate the inauguration of the regency, though this could not be avowed publicly out of consideration for the Queen's feelings and her husband's mental condition. Charles Abbot, Speaker of the House of Commons and later to be first Baron Colchester, described the scene.[3]

Around 2,000 guests from the highest ranks in society, the men in court dress or uniforms and the ladies in the height of fashion, were summoned from 9 p.m. and admitted by tickets. At about ten o'clock the French royal family arrived and were greeted by the Prince in his splendid new Field Marshal's uniform in scarlet and gold, designed by himself to accompany his newly self-conferred rank. It was rumoured that with all the heavy gold embroidery it weighed 200lb. After receiving the King of France in a room specially set aside and decorated with furniture and blue silk hangings displaying the fleur-de-lys in gold, the Prince and his guests mingled with the crowds, the rest of the English Royal Family also moving informally among them. In the great gothic conservatory a transformation had been arranged; a large silver basin filled with water fed a stream which meandered between banks of flowers and vegetation and was stocked with golden fish and silver gudgeons, reaching the whole length of the principal supper table over 200 feet long at which sat the chief 200 guests, presided over by the Regent. Behind his table the stream widened and fell in a series of cascades into 'a circular lake surrounded with architectural decorations, and small vases, burning perfumes, which stood under the arches of the colonnade round the lake'. A 'magnificent sideboard of gilt plate three stories high' stood at the end of the Prince's table. It was all

[2] A. Briggs, *The Age of Improvement, passim.*

[3] Colchester, *Diary*, ii, 336–8.

'oriental and fanciful' as Abbot described it, though Tierney less fancifully referred to the rivulet and its fishes as 'that Sadler's Wells business'. The remaining guests were seated at tables in other rooms or in marquees in the garden which Miss Berry described as 'immense, and admirably contrived'.[4] These were festooned with flowers and lit by hundreds of lights, and after their supper the guests crowded behind the brass railings to inspect the distinguished company and gaze at the stream and the fishes, calling out the sights to each other like tourists: their 'eager and ridiculous curiosity' Abbot found 'very entertaining'.

The supper was lavish and elegant. There were hot soups, roasts, cold food in abundance, peaches, grapes, pineapples and other fruits 'in or out of season' piled up everywhere, with iced champagne for everybody. A band concealed in the garden played throughout the meal. 'Nothing was ever half so magnificent', declared the Irish poet Tom Moore who was 'enchanted half out of his mind' by the spectacle which put him in mind of the theatre, an 'assemblage of beauty, splendour, and profuse magnificence . . . women out-blazing each other in the richness of their dress'.[5] After supper the guests swarmed in a tide round the remaining rooms, 'an intolerable cram and jam' as Abbot remarked, though the whole 'supply, waiting, and arrangements were admirable'. George had an undoubted gift for organization. The crowds began to disperse and drift away after four in the morning.

The rest of London's citizenry were not forgotten. For the succeeding three days people were admitted by ticket to view the palace and gardens and the decorations and, as usually happens, the last day of all was inconceivably crowded – 30,000 were said to have 'stormed' in, the ladies so battered by the crush that they lost their shoes, their gowns and their possessions, ending 'almost completely undressed, & their hair hanging about their shoulders'. The *Morning Chronicle* advertised a large tub filled with lost and discarded shoes on the next day. The critics of course fastened on the expense – Shelley remarked that it must have cost £120,000 of the people's money, though in fact it was nowhere near so much. On the following Wednesday there was a grand ball at Devonshire House, attended by the Prince and 'brilliant', wrote Miss Berry, 'from all the women having on their Carlton House gowns, and many their feathers'.[6] The Prince enjoyed it all immensely, but inevitably it was added to the popular list of his extravagances and follies, and it set the tone for the enduring image of the regency as created by him.

[4] Miss Berry, *Journal*, ii, 481.

[5] Priestley, 40; T. Moore to his mother, 21 June 1811: Lord John Russell (ed.), *Memoirs of Thomas Moore*, i, 255.

[6] Shelley to Elizabeth Hitchener, 20 June 1811: R. Ingpen (ed.), *Letters of . . . Shelley*, 99–100.

In February 1813 Lady Elizabeth Feilding described another glittering entertainment in

> that Mahomet's Paradise, Carlton House. I do not know whether *we* all looked like *Houris,* but I for one was certainly in the seventy-seventh heaven. . . . The sight and sound were both animating, the kettledrums and cymbals, the glitter of spangles and finery, of dress and furniture that burst upon you were quite *eblouissant.*
>
> Then you turned to the right through a suite of rooms, some hung with scarlet and gold, others with blue and gold, and some decorated with portraits of all our great commanders. . . .

In the ballroom sat the Queen, flanked by the Princesse de Condé and Madame de Lieven, who was dressed for the occasion like Mary Queen of Scots, sitting demurely but outspoken in her disapproval of the 'abruptness and want of grace of the English ladies . . . these things are *mieux arrangés* at St. Petersburg'.

Later in the year, an afternoon fête was held in honour of Wellington's victory at Vittoria, the élite of London once more in full dress, the ladies 'displaying their diamonds and pearls', the men in knee-breeches and buckles. It was also the first appearance in public of Princess Charlotte and there was dancing on the lawn in the fine summer weather, with music by various military bands around the gardens.[7]

In truth the Regent influenced his age more in the cultural and artistic spheres than in politics or government. In the more serious public aspects of his role he was a dilettante: it was in the arts that he was a professional. At his lavish parties, 'in the midst of festoons, glittering lustres, painted Cupids and garlands of roses' he appeared 'brighter than sunshine . . . graciousness personified'. The leading men and women of the age testified to the splendour of his living and the refinement of his taste. Joseph Haydn was charmed by him. He delighted in the company of actors, musicians, artists and literary men, and was knowledgeable enough to impress them all with his conversation. He attended and spoke effectively at Royal Academy dinners, had his portrait painted by the leading artists of the age, and became a discriminating collector – the first and only monarch since Charles I to show an active and expert interest in the royal collection. He was a talented performer with friends at evening parties in chamber music, and was equally at home singing glees and rounds at gatherings which often ended in bouts of intoxication. He was fascinated from his youth by the stage and frequently attended the opera and the theatre: his

[7] Lady Elizabeth Feilding to her sister, 10 Feb. 1813: H.G. Mundy (ed.), *Journal of Mary Frampton,* 156–80; Grego (ed.), *Reminiscences . . . of Captain Gronow,* i, 40–1.

fascination also extended to actors and especially to actresses, from the time of 'Perdita' Robinson onwards. The contrast with the sober and secluded domestic life of his parents could not have been more extreme.[8]

The regency period is also celebrated as the heyday of George's other residence, the Brighton Pavilion. In 1814 the painter Benjamin Haydon described the town as 'gay, gambling, dissipated, the elegant residence of an accomplished Prince, with its beautiful women and light hussars, its tandems and terriers'. It had become best known as the seaside retreat of George and Maria Fitzherbert, away from the public attention of the capital, after their marriage and during the long period of political idleness which followed. During the regency Brighton came into its own as the playground of London society under princely patronage, centred on the Pavilion and its surroundings on the Steine and the seafront. George could not resist the opportunity to lavish his talents as a decorator and leader of fashion on the house, which had been remodelled by Holland, soon after George acquired it, into a rather modest Georgian country residence. He had added two bow windows at the sides of the front in 1801, and three years later he had begun a circular stables building – now the Dome – remarkable for its cupola 80 feet in diameter and 65 feet in height, with stalls for forty-four horses and accommodation for grooms above them. At about the same time he had been presented with some Chinese wallpapers, then very avant-garde, and began to redecorate some rooms in the eastern style. The Dome was designed in a predominantly Indian character and Humphry Repton, who was called in to advise on future projects, suggested in 1808 that the rest of the Pavilion might be brought into conformity with it, but George's chronic shortage of funds compelled him to lay the scheme aside. Nevertheless, he gradually introduced the desired mood into the interior decoration as opportunity offered.

The eastern, predominantly Indian but frequently misnamed Chinese, furnishings were not to everyone's taste. Miss Berry wrote critically in 1811 that 'All is Chinese, quite overloaded with china of all sorts and of all possible forms. . . . All is gaudy, without looking gay; and all is crowded with ornaments, without being magnificent'. She was somewhat prejudiced perhaps, having been deafened by the Prince's military band playing in the dining room which was really too small for 'so many loud instruments, . . . not a remedy for my headache'.[9] In 1812 Wyatt was engaged, and drew up plans in his favourite Gothic manner, but his death in an accident in 1813 put paid to that scheme. However, help was at hand. John Nash had already worked on Carlton

[8] J.W. Oliver, *Life of Beckford*, 108; H.C. Robbins Landon, *Haydn*, 122–4.
[9] Miss Berry, *Journal*, ii, 490.

House and was engaged in planning the grandest of all the Regent's projects, namely the construction of a great processional way from Regent's Park to Carlton House, together with the building of the famous terraces. Nash's work deeply impressed the Regent: it was bold, adventurous, and skilful in its use of cast iron, which enabled apparently delicate and airy façades to be applied to a deceptively strong framework. In 1815 Nash's designs, inspired largely by Sezincote in Gloucestershire, which was built by a returned Nabob, were approved and work began on transforming a classical villa into what Hazlitt described as 'a collection of stone pumpkins and pepper-boxes . . . anything more fantastical . . . was never seen'. Sidney Smith remarked that the domes made it seem as if St Paul's had gone down to the seaside and pupped, and farmer Cobbett compared it to a square box with a large turnip in the middle and four smaller ones at the corners, scattered with bulbs of crown imperial, narcissus, hyacinth, tulip and crocus.[10] The interior was no less exotic. From the new kitchen, its iron columns blossoming into large copper palm leaves, to the banqueting and music rooms with their domed decorations and the carved dragon swooping across the ceiling, the effect was startling; some thought bizarre. It suited the Prince, who revelled in the extravagant over-decoration which filled the house. It crowned and symbolized his artistic endeavours – defying the conventions of good taste, showing a degree of vulgarity, and yet achieving an overall effect of lightness and luxury. By no means everyone liked it: but George, one suspects, enjoyed shocking his subjects out of their complacency.

Politically, the Prince's acceptance of the regency came at a moment of crisis for Britain both in internal politics and in the French war. The succession of Spencer Perceval to the premiership on the retirement of the aged Duke of Portland in 1809 had offered a new opportunity to pursue that perpetual chimera, a broad-based coalition formed by the admission of the leading Whigs to office, but both Grey and Grenville, representing the two wings of the opposition, had rejected Perceval's invitation to talks about reconstruction of the administration, on the grounds of irreconcilable differences of policy and in particular the division over the Catholic question. Grey did not even condescend to come to London from Northumberland, though Grenville briefly came to town from Buckinghamshire.[11] The Whigs spoke of differences over policies and principles as if they alone professed them; but in truth they preferred to wait in the hope that Perceval would, like Addington in 1803, prove to be a weak and unsuccessful war minister and that the

[10] Quoted in Roberts, *Royal Pavilion*; Priestley, 255; Summerson, *Life and Work of John Nash*, 108.

[11] Smith, *Grey*, 172; P. Jupp, *Grenville*, 426.

whole government would fall into their hands. Their hopes were encouraged in 1809 by the duel between Castlereagh and Canning over the allegation that the latter had plotted Castlereagh's dismissal after the failure of the Walcheren expedition of British troops to the Netherlands, an episode which led to Castlereagh's departure from the government and hastened Portland's resignation. However, the expected collapse of the old Pittite regime failed to materialize.

Meanwhile, the war dragged on. The continued failure to find a weak spot in Napoleon's command of continental Europe prolonged the stalemate in military operations, while economic blockade and counter-blockade were draining the economy and leading to industrial unrest in the manufacturing districts. The crack in Napoleon's 'fortress Europe' represented by the Spanish and Portuguese risings against French occupation from 1808 seemed to have closed again when an early British success in Spain was followed by the negotiation of the Convention of Cintra, which allowed the French to retire with their forces intact. Sir John Moore's retreat and death at Corunna soon afterwards temporarily extinguished hopes of a British beachhead in the Peninsula. The opposition at home took a defeatist attitude, while the government's failures encouraged the spread of pessimism for the future. No one as yet was confident that the return of a British expedition under Arthur Wellesley, who was untried in European warfare and denigrated as a 'sepoy general' for his Indian exploits, was to foreshadow a series of successes and eventual victory. At home too the revival of radical politics after the Duke of York scandal seemed to be gathering momentum, dangerously focused on political corruption and royal extravagance. When the radical leader Sir Francis Burdett was imprisoned for supporting the newspaper editor John Gale Jones in attacking governmental corruption, London was almost set aflame with popular riots and demonstrations that aroused fears of civil war.[12] It was an ominous moment for the King to fall ill again and for a regency to be established under a Prince whose political attitude was uncertain after the events of the past four years.

However, all these circumstances at least made it essential that the regency should be inaugurated urgently, and though the proposed arrangements aroused considerable controversy in Parliament they were approved rapidly enough. Perceval proposed a limited regency in the sense that for at least one year the regent should be prevented from making any permanent changes, particularly from granting peerages, pensions and offices in reversion or making changes in the Royal Household. This was modelled on Pitt's scheme of 1788–9 and the Prince and his brothers consequently remonstrated strongly, but

[12] Patterson, i, 240–75; Harvey, 269–70.

Grenville, who had been in Pitt's Cabinet in 1788, was placed in an embarrassing position and felt bound by consistency not to object now. The Prince was even less warm towards him from thence forward. However, the Commons accepted the scheme by narrow but sufficient majorities and George made the best of it.[13] The proposal to put the care of the King and the government of his Household in the Queen's hands was, as in 1789, also objected to as being derogatory to the Prince as regent and divisive of the powers of government. The opposition managed to defeat the first version of this arrangement but in the end after bitter debates in both Houses the essence of the scheme was accepted, largely through Grenville's changing from opposition to support at the last moment.[14]

The Prince at first behaved with complete political propriety and neutrality. McMahon told the Duke of Northumberland in November 1810 that he gave no audiences to any politicians and that he abstained even from writing to any of his former political friends. However, he was angry at the implications of Perceval's proposed restrictions and when a Parliamentary deputation brought the resolutions embodying them to Carlton House he assembled all his brothers and they agreed on a protest on the lines of his answer to Pitt's similar proposals in 1788.[15] He then asked Grey and Grenville to draw up a reply, a step which appeared to presage an intention to change the administration.

Grey was sceptical, believing that the Prince was no longer a Whig, and that he had fallen under the influence of the Tory Hertfords and in particular was no longer a supporter of the Catholics, to whom the Whigs were pledged.[16] Nevertheless, when William Adam, Grey's confidential friend, called to see the Prince on 5 January he reported that the Prince had expressed his 'fixed opinion' that only an administration under Grey and Grenville 'could be really useful to the country', and when he saw Grenville on the 6th the atmosphere was friendly. Grey, who had been in Northumberland to attend the birth of one of his children, returned to London and reported 'a cordial and satisfactory' interview with the Prince, coming away with the impression that he might be offered the premiership when the regency came into operation. However, when he and Grenville prepared the intended reply to the regency resolutions Grenville was still embarrassed by his past conduct and their wording was objected to by George. Sheridan, whom he called in for consultations, substituted a draft of his own

[13] Spencer Perceval to George, 18 and 19 Dec. 1810 and reply [19th]; protest of the royal dukes, 19 Dec.; Perceval to Frederick, 20th: *CGPW*, vii, 108–15 and 116–17n.; *Parl. Debates*, xviii, 241–329.

[14] Jupp, 431–3.

[15] McMahon to Northumberland, 8 Nov. 1810: *CGPW*, vii, 76–7.

[16] Smith, *Grey*, 192–4; Romilly, *Memoirs*, iii, 12.

which gave full assent to the restrictions but reserved any opinion as to their necessity. Grey and Grenville indignantly rejected the draft, more through pique at the Prince's consulting an 'inferior counsel' to theirs than at the contents of the letter. Grey had always suspected and resented what he saw as Sheridan's long-standing attempt to supplant him and to curry the Prince's favour and this was the last straw. Sheridan's 'lying and baseness have been beyond all description', he wrote, and if this was the way the Prince was going to act he would offer him no further political advice. George tried to smooth the ruffled feathers, but could not forbear from pointing out that Grey and Grenville were not yet his constitutional advisers and should not so consider themselves.[17]

The Prince now asked the Whig leaders to draw up a list of a possible new Whig administration. It proved to be a difficult task, and they soon fell to arguing about the congenial matter of the distribution of offices and the relative weight of their respective followings. McMahon told the Duke of Northumberland that the Prince 'cannot be much in love with either' of the Whig leaders but thought nothing could be done without them.[18] Eventually they managed to agree, and were on the point of submitting their proposal to the Prince when the royal doctors declared that they saw signs of the King's likely recovery. George drew back. He discussed the matter with the Queen and, possibly under pressure, but more likely being himself anxious not to do anything to retard that recovery, he decided not to make any immediate changes in the government. Grey accepted the decision with as good a grace as he could muster, attributing the Prince's change of mind to the combined influence of 'that greatest of villains the D. of Cumberland' and Sir Henry Halford, the chief of the King's physicians. However, he and Grenville, to their credit, accepted that the Prince's decision was taken with honourable intentions and advised him not to change the administration while there was a fair chance of the King's recovery. When George informed Perceval of his decision he attributed it to his sense of 'filial duty'.[19]

The Regency Bill was now passed and on 6 February 1811 the Prince was sworn in as Regent at a Privy Council held at Carlton House. He

[17] Adam's memorandum, *CPGW*, vii, 139–46; draft reply, ibid., 154–6; Grey and Grenville to George, 11 and 21 Jan. 1811; Adam's memorandum [n.d.]: ibid., 158–64, 184–6; Sichel, ii, 338–48.

[18] McMahon to Northumberland, 28 Jan., 2 and 23 Feb. 1811: *CGPW*, vii, 188–9, 198, 246–7; reports of doctors: RA 41438–9; George's questions to doctors: *CGPW*, vii, 194–6; Queen to George, 5 Feb.; Northumberland to McMahon, 5 Feb.; Eldon to George, 10 Feb.; Elizabeth to George, 10 Feb.: ibid., 203–5, 221–3: RA 21/4/134.

[19] Smith, *Grey*, 195; George to Perceval, 4 Feb. 1811: *CGPW*, vii, 200–1, 208–9.

made his underlying feelings plain to his ministers by keeping them waiting for an hour and a half in a room where a bust of Fox was prominently placed – perhaps a deliberate reminder of the occasion in 1783 when his father, on receiving the members of the Fox–North Coalition ministry, was observed to 'put back his ears like the horse at Astley's [circus] when the little tailor he was determined to throw got on his back'.[20] In this case, the parallel did not hold. The Prince Regent did not overthrow his ministers in favour of their opponents and in the end he confirmed them in office, where they and their successors remained till the end of his reign in 1830.

There were attempts at a reconstruction of the ministry in February 1812, when the year-long restrictions on the regent expired and he entered upon the exercise of the full royal prerogative, and in the following May after Perceval's assassination. On neither occasion did the Whigs benefit. The Catholic question was becoming a more and more divisive issue. George's attitude against emancipation was hardening, while the Whigs' pessimism and apparent hostility towards the war in the Peninsula, which began to turn in Britain's favour after Wellington's victory at Salamanca, alienated him, and as he became accustomed to his present ministers his inertia and dislike of political exertion inclined him to leave things as they were. He confided to the Duke of York, who acted as intermediary in an attempt to bring the Whig leaders into the government, that although it was his sense of duty to his father that prompted him to retain his present ministers, he was 'well satisfied with them and no longer wished for a complete change'. He complained that 'he had *opened the door* for his old political friends, meaning and hoping that they would rally round him', but they had 'most cruelly stood on punctilios' and refused to listen to him, while 'the understrappers and . . . second-rates of the opposition' had abused and sniped at him without being checked.[21] He was certainly not prepared to allow the Whigs to force their way in. The Prince's personal dislike of Grey reached new heights, from which it was never to descend. In 1828, commissioning Wellington to form a new administration, he told him 'he could have any Whig he liked, except Lord Grey', whose admission to office was barred until after George's death.

The Whigs naturally blamed the Prince for deserting his old friends and the policies he had formerly supported. When on 24 May 1813 the Catholic Relief Bill was lost in committee in the Commons after having passed its second reading by 242 votes to 203, Grey attributed the defeat to the 'undisguised and indecent canvass made by Carlton

[20] Fox, *Memorial & Corresp.*, ii, 28.
[21] Smith, *Grey*, 196–204; *LG4*, i, 1.

House' against it, alleging that the Prince had said publicly at his table a day or two before that 'nobody would vote for the question who did not wish to endanger his title to the Crown'.[22] Yet his actions were defensible. Apart from the fact that public opinion in England was strongly anti-Catholic, as the general election only six years before had proved, as regent he bore the responsibility for the government of the country and for its security in Europe, and he was bound to take a broader and more responsible view of its interests than was necessary when in opposition. Filial duty also influenced him: as he came round to his father's views on the Catholic and other questions, he stressed more and more his duty to follow his father's principles and continue his policies, and his affection for his mother confirmed his attitude. In February 1812 he assured the Cabinet, somewhat grudgingly, that 'his sense of duty to his Royal father' determined his decision to keep them in office. Above all, he had ceased to trust the Whigs since Fox's death. At his last levee of the session it was apparent that there was little good feeling between him and the Whig leaders; Grey was 'Iceland' itself, reported McMahon.[23] The divisions among the opposition during the regency over the questions of radical agitation and war strategy and policy, and even in attitudes towards Napoleon himself, drew them further apart. By 1820, though he had no special affection for his Tory ministers and chafed at the dictatorial attitude of Liverpool as Prime Minister over policies and patronage, he had come to regard Grey and the Whigs in much the same way as his father had regarded Fox and his friends – as dangerous, inexperienced, and probably incompetent candidates for office. As the Member of Parliament J.W. Ward wrote in July 1812, 'If they [the Whigs] serve the Crown it must be *always* against the inclination of him that wears it . . . [but] the Tories . . . are the natural allies of the monarch'.[24] George as Prince Regent behaved responsibly in supporting ministers who prosecuted the war with energy and gave strong support to law and order against riot and revolution. Though he was in error in coming to believe in later life, as he apparently did, that he had been present on the battlefield of Waterloo,[25] he made his own contribution to victory over Napoleon and the maintenance of the British Empire at its greatest extent yet.

George's support of the war never wavered. From the outset in 1809 he had approved Wellington's campaigns in the Peninsula, at a time when the Whigs and the public in general were despondent and unenthusiastic for what seemed yet another rash adventure. The Whig atti-

[22] Thorne, *House of Commons*, i, 207.
[23] McMahon to Northumberland, 13 March 1812: RA 21/4/184.
[24] S.H. Romilly, *Letters to 'Ivy'*, 165.
[25] Hibbert, *George IV, Regent and King*, 78.

tude of appeasement towards Napoleon was indeed one of the major reasons for George's growing support for their opponents, and for the rest of the period to Waterloo his unwavering conviction of the need for a strong military policy did much to ensure British victory.

The signs of George's new attitude were quickly perceived. In his first message to his ministers after he assumed the full powers of regent, George assured them that he viewed 'with satisfaction' the situation of the country. Important acquisitions to the empire had been made, 'the national faith has been preserved inviolate towards our Allies' and Britain's arms though inferior in numbers were 'animated by a glorious spirit of resistance to a foreign yoke'. For himself, 'The Prince Regt has no predilections to indulge, no resentment to gratify, no objects to attain but such as are common to the whole nation'.[26] The approval thus expressed, by implication, of the way in which the ministers had conducted the government was a significant pointer to his inclinations to trust them to continue, and his assurances as to his own future role and conduct suggested that as Prince Regent and King he would be a different proposition from the Prince of Wales of the past.

Unlikely as it might have appeared in view of his previous partisanship and his tendency to take his political attitude from his friends, for the future he gave first place to what he considered the interests of his country. Without surrendering his personal views on men and policies, he was to prove more successful than his father in subordinating them to his constitutional responsibilities. His old Whig friends were slow to recognize this, and indeed never really did so: they accused him of betraying his old friendships from personal pique or from weakness of character and dislike of trouble, whereas it was they who, by refusing to co-operate with Perceval and the other ministers on the grounds of their differences, especially on the Catholic question, had made it impossible for any coalition to be arranged. They now believed themselves to be the victims of tory intrigue and of George's personal prejudices learned from his mistresses or his family, and particularly of subservience to the Queen. They could never give him credit for a more objective view of how the national interest should be served. Despite their own pessimistic view of the nation's prospects against Napoleon they expected him to entrust them with the conduct of a war which they never hoped to win. His refusal to countenance Catholic emancipation in order to pacify Ireland, despite his past pledges to that country, they saw as the expression of a prejudice implanted in his mind by the machinations of Lady Hertford under the pretence of a new-found affection for his father. It was not surprising that as Regent and King George IV never called a Whig administration into office, for the Whigs

[26] George to Cabinet [15 Feb. 1812]: *LG4*, i, 5–6.

never convinced him that they were capable of constructing an effective one.

The lingering hopes still cherished by Grey, Grenville and their colleagues that the new reign would bring them into power were therefore never realistic. George's inclinations to make any changes in the ministry were limited to his wish to bring particular friends like Moira or Wellesley into office and if possible to construct an all-party government, but even these hopes were given up with little regret when they proved impossible to realize and the bitter accusations of duplicity made against him by Grey and other Whigs were deeply resented and never forgiven. Moira, heavily tipped at the outset of the regency as the next prime minister, was alienated by George's volte-face on the Catholic question and, having declined his offer of the Garter, he was sent off to India, where as Marquess of Hastings he proved a successful and popular Governor-General. Wellesley, who had become Foreign Secretary in 1809, was too unpopular with his colleagues, too dictatorial in Cabinet and too lethargic in office, and he failed to arrange a coalition with the leading Whigs that might have sustained him.[27]

When after Perceval's assassination in 1812 the House of Commons narrowly passed a resolution calling for the formation of 'a strong and efficient Administration',[28] the Prince was obliged to attempt to broaden the basis of the Cabinet. He again approached Wellesley and Canning, rather than Grey and Grenville, but to no avail. Lord Melville declared that if Wellesley and Canning were admitted the majority of the Cabinet would resign. The Prince commissioned Wellesley to explore the possibility of a coalition only for him to be given the same view and when George summoned all the Cabinet ministers to give him their individual opinions the result was identical. He nevertheless authorized Wellesley to offer the Whigs four or five places in a reconstituted Cabinet, but Grey and Grenville indignantly rejected the offer as too small a share of power. On 3 June Wellesley announced to the Lords the end of his negotiations.[29] The Prince then commissioned Moira to make a similar attempt, but now the Whigs refused to treat unless they were given the power to appoint the Prince's Household as a sign of good faith, a condition which he indignantly refused.

On the 8th George cut the knot by deciding to abandon all plans for

[27] For the full account of the negotiations of Feb.–June 1812 see ibid., i, 2–116, Hist. MSS Comm., *Fortescue MSS*, x, 197–288, Holland, *Further Memoirs*, 117–50, Twiss, ii, 209–20 and *Wellesley Papers*, ii, 71–116.

[28] *Parl. Debates*, xxiii, 249–81.

[29] *LG4*, i, 78n. letters to George from Queen, Sheridan, Wellesley, Liverpool, Melville, Mulgrave and Sidmouth, 21–28 May; from Arbuthnot, Northumberland and Moira to McMahon, 18–26 May; Cabinet minute 22 May 1812: ibid., i, 80–93 and RA, Regency, 5/19672–720.

change and he reverted to Liverpool's former ministry, no doubt relieved to have avoided a prima donna Prime Minister. Moira defended him in the Lords, saying that he had never insisted on the appointment of any individual except Wellesley, had excluded no one and had 'soared infinitely above personal animosities', and in private the anti-Whig Duke of Northumberland told McMahon, somewhat fulsomely, that the Prince had shown nobleness of mind and true patriotism in being willing to sacrifice personal feelings to the public good. Some, including the modern editor of the Prince's correspondence, believed that he had intended this result all along, and had taken care to make the conditions of appointment unacceptable to the Whigs. Whether or not that is true, he had conducted the negotiations with some skill and put the Whigs at a disadvantage, while leaving affairs in the dull but safe hands of Liverpool.[30] He also had the foresight to accept Castlereagh at the Foreign Office where he became one of the most eminent of nineteenth-century foreign secretaries and was largely responsible for the pacification and long-term settlement of Europe.[31] After his death in 1822 George even managed to set aside his detestation of Canning – largely derived from his supposed sexual relations with George's wife in the period after their marriage – and to appoint him to succeed Castlereagh. Eventually Canning became a favourite Prime Minister, at the cost of the resignations of Wellington, Eldon and other 'ultra' Tories who would have protected him from submission to Catholic emancipation. For these and other reasons, George IV may be regarded as a highly constitutional monarch who did much – and not primarily from laziness, weakness of character or neglect of royal duty – to help the transition from personal monarchy as exercised by the earlier Georges to a more broadly based system of government founded on Parliamentary consent. When he died in 1830 the country was preparing for the next major step, the Great Reform Act, which, despite the fact that George would have disapproved of and resisted it, had become a necessity for which the way had been largely cleared.

[30] Smith, *Grey*, 203–4; letters from Moira, McMahon, Arbuthnot and Northumberland, 4–12 June 1812; memorandum by Canning, 9 June: *LG4*, i, 106–14; Romilly, *Memoirs*, iii, 39–43.

[31] C. Webster, *Foreign Policy of Castlereagh*; W. Hinde, *Castlereagh*; memorandum by Sir Charles Stewart [?12 June 1812]: *LG4*, i, 130n.

Chapter 13

A GLORIOUS VICTORY

The year 1812 not only saw the beginning of the regency in Britain. It also marked the turn of the tide in Europe, leading in three years to the final collapse of Napoleon's empire and the reassertion of Britain's supremacy at sea and of her Imperial and commercial world power. Britain played a subordinate role in the vital military defeat of Napoleon, which her ministers recognized could be achieved only in central Europe, where the massive armies of the allies, Russia, Austria and Prussia in particular, were alone a match for French military resources. Britain's role on land was limited to Wellington's campaigns in the Iberian Peninsula, which, despite being the centre of British attention, was never more than a subsidiary theatre. Britain had not the manpower to field the large armies by which alone France could be subdued, and her naval supremacy after Trafalgar could have only a minimal impact on the war as a whole. A major reason for the fall of the Grenville–Grey ministry in 1807, and for George's disillusionment with his former friends, had been the inability of the ministers to evolve an effective and coherent war strategy, wasting Britain's efforts by dispersing her inadequate forces in pointless diversionary expeditions to various parts of the globe. More important was the financial contribution made by Britain to the overthrow of Napoleon. Millions of pounds were poured into subsidies, in specie or in war material, to persuade the continental powers to take the field and to support their armies. Not for the last time, commentators in other countries criticized Britain for using her financial resources to pay other people to fight for her interests, but in practice it was not until the very end of the war that Britain's war aims were given much regard by her allies, who fought as much for their own interests as did Britain. Nevertheless if the Peninsular campaigns were something of a side-show they did tie down substantial enemy forces and by enabling British trade to avoid the continental blockade they played a part in weakening French resources. Nor was the British army a negligible force. The Duke of York's military reforms had made it an efficient and well-trained body whose fighting qualities made it superior to many other armies; its part in the final battle at Waterloo was alone sufficient to ensure it an honoured place

1. George IV, by Sir Thomas Lawrence, 1822.

2. George III, by Allan Ramsay, 1761.

3. Queen Charlotte, by an artist in the studio of Allan Ramsay, *c.* 1762.

4. Queen Charlotte with her two eldest sons, by Allan Ramsay, 1764. Lady Sarah Lennox remarked that George (*left*) was 'the proudest little imp you ever saw'.

5. Princesses Charlotte, Augusta and Elizabeth, by Thomas Gainsborough, 1784.

6. George, Prince of Wales, after Sir Joshua Reynolds.

7. Perdita Robinson, by George Romney, 1780–81.

8. George, Prince of Wales, by John Hoppner, 1792.

9. Mrs Fitzherbert, by Sir Joshua Reynolds, *c.* 1788.

10. Mrs Fitzherbert, by the miniaturist Richard Cosway.

11. 'Vices overlooked in the Royal Proclamation', by James Gillray, 1792, which depicts the royal family with their alleged vices at a time when the King issued a proclamation against vice. Clockwise from top left: the King and Queen (avarice), Prince of Wales (drunkenness), Clarence and Mrs Jordan (debauchery) and Duke of York (gambling).

12. 'Dido Forsaken', by James Gillray. Mrs Fitzherbert, as Dido, Queen of Carthage, is on her funeral pyre as her lover (the Prince), accompanied by North, Fox and Burke, sails away from her towards Windsor, blown by Pitt and Dundas as the wind.

13. The Pavilion and the Steyne, Brighton, 1801, as remodelled by Henry Holland.

14. The Pavilion in 1805. The Prince, on horseback, is accompanied by Bloomfield (in uniform) and on his right by Maria Fitzherbert and 'Minny'. Others depicted include the Duke of Grafton (*right*), Sir John Lade, Lord Craven and Bob Mellish, the prizefighter (*centre*), General Dalrymple, Lord Sefton and Martha Gunn (bathing attendant) (*left*).

15. The 'gothic conservatory', Carlton House, 1819.

16. Lady Hertford, by John Downman.

17. Princess Charlotte, by George Dawe, 1817.

18. The Pavilion, as converted by John Nash.

19. The Pavilion Music Room, with the Prince's band.

20. Lady Conyngham, by Sir Thomas Lawrence.

21. (a) 'The Kettle calling the Pot ugly names' (*above*), by J. Marshall and (b) 'Which is the Dirtiest?' (*below*), by William Heath: two caricatures of 1820 on the dispute between George and Caroline.

22. George IV in Highland dress, by Sir David Wilkie.

23. Sir William Knighton, after Sir Thomas Lawrence.

24. The Coronation procession of George IV, 1821, by Sir George Naylor.

25. George IV driving a curricle, from a print of *c.* 1830.

in the roll of victory, and Wellington's generalship, with few exceptions, fully justified the honours heaped upon him.[1]

The Prince played his part, as has already been argued, with decisiveness and patriotic enthusiasm, when both the more radical and whig sectors of opinion were inclined to half-heartedness and despondency. The whig attitude towards Napoleon was never wholly hostile. He was seen as the child of the French Revolution rather than as a military despot, and his 'liberal Empire' was regarded as a vast improvement on the ramshackle despotism of the Bourbons which the allies sought to reimpose. Fox had declared himself an enemy of 'the cause of Kings' and had visited Napoleon in Paris during the peace of 1802–3, and Holland House, Fox's shrine, continued to advocate allowing Napoleon to rule. As late as 1815 many British whigs and liberals were willing to settle for a negotiated peace that would leave Napoleon ruler of a territorially reduced but not impotent constitutional state. Grey himself, who had abandoned Fox's search for a negotiated peace in 1806, expressed an ambivalent attitude towards the defeated Napoleon on the grounds that the triumph of the autocratic military powers of continental Europe would enable them to suppress liberal movements across the Channel and even threaten Britain's own constitutional regime.[2]

These views however were largely restricted to certain liberal intellectual circles in England. There is no sign that public opinion in general was favourable to Napoleon, for government-inspired propaganda since the very beginning of the war in 1793 had identified the French Revolution, and later Napoleon as its embodiment, as a threat to everything the patriotic Englishman prized in his country and its traditions. George III, hardly a popular figure before the American war, had become after 1792 the personification of the British spirit against the French Revolution.[3] One of the reasons why the Prince had become unpopular since the 1790s was that in quarrelling with his father he was seen as unpatriotic as well as selfish. The final decision to exclude Napoleon from France and restore the Bourbons was therefore popular among the Prince's subjects, and it also accorded with his own strong views, which, in the case of Louis XVIII, he held to even more firmly than did his ministers.

George followed the events of the last years of the war with close attention and mounting satisfaction. He never wavered in his support of Wellington in the Peninsula and expressed delight at the news of every victory there, or by the allies in central Europe after the failure of

1 R.J.B. Muir, *Britain and the Defeat of Napoleon.*

2 L.G. Mitchell, *Charles James Fox*, 165–9; Smith, *Grey*, 86–7, 166, 176–8; Muir, 328–9.

3 Linda Colley, 'The Apotheosis of George III': Colley, *Britons*, 208–16.

Napoleon's Moscow campaign. He supported the efforts of the ministers to bring about another coalition of the powers against France, and Sir John Macpherson, though a notorious flatterer, gave him the major credit in 1813 for personally winning the co-operation of Tsar Alexander.[4] When the news arrived in September 1813 of the liberation of Mecklenburg, his mother's family home, he wrote to her in ecstasy of his 'boundless gratitude to Almighty Providence'. He asked her and all the royal household to drink a bumper to Bernadotte, the Prince Royal of Sweden, and not to forget 'poor me, who have I think, some little merit at having been the first to set them all at work'. He wrote again two months later on the 'glorious intelligence' of Napoleon's defeat at Leipzig to send her a snuff box decorated with his effigy as '*one* who I hope you will *now* think is *no disgrace to you*, to his family, or to his country'. The liberation of Hanover was another cause for celebration, and this was swiftly followed by news of Wellington's victory on the Nivelle, at which he was 'quite worn out with the joy of the business of this thrice happy day'. Finally, on the news of the allied entry into Paris in April 1814 his brother Adolphus sent his congratulations on a victory to which the Regent had contributed so much, and the Hereditary Prince of Orange acclaimed him as one 'to whose firmness we owe all this and whom the whole of Europe is obliged to acknowledge as his [*sic*] deliverer'.[5]

No doubt all this was egregious flattery, to which George was never unreceptive, but it contained a truth, for had he not shown consistent support and encouragement to ministers who were committed to victory over Napoleon the outcome might have been different. Cumberland asserted that had the Regent not been firm, a compromise peace might have been arranged at Châtillon before Napoleon's final defeat: 'You are the mainspring of the whole', he wrote. As it was, George had the satisfaction of accompanying Louis XVIII to London, where he invested him with the Garter, himself buckling it round his immense leg, which he later likened to 'fastening a sash round a young man's waist', and then seeing him off on his way back to reclaim the throne of his ancestors to the echo of yet another tribute: 'It is to the counsels of your Royal Highness, to this glorious country, and to the steadfastness of its inhabitants', declared the newly restored monarch, 'that I attribute, next after the will of Providence, the re-establishment of my house on the throne of my ancestors.' The capital was indeed delirious with joy. London was illuminated for three nights with 'every device that . . . taste and invention . . . could supply', including a repre-

4 Macpherson to McMahon, 19 March 1813: RA, Regency 7.

5 George to Queen, 22 Sept., 3 and 24 Nov. 1813, 9 April 1814: *LG4*, i, 319, 340, 346, 420 and from Prince of Orange, 20 April 1814: ibid., 430.

sentation of Wellington destroying with a puff Napoleon's house of cards. The celebrations culminated in June 1814 in the visit of the Tsar Alexander, followed by the King of Prussia and representatives of other allied sovereigns and their ministers and generals, to mark the general victory.[6]

The visit of the allied sovereigns, intended as a public endorsement of Britain's role in the defeat of Napoleon, soon turned sour for the Regent. The Tsar to begin with was distinctly uncooperative. He had previously expressed the hope that it would be a private visit and not an occasion for large-scale public rejoicing, whereas George had hoped to use it as a boost to his own popularity which was flagging, largely because of the public's sympathy for Princesses Caroline and Charlotte. Alexander refused the offer of apartments at St James's Palace, preferring to join his sister the Grand Duchess Catherine, who was already in residence at Pulteney's Hotel off Piccadilly, and he even changed his route into London to avoid the crowds which awaited him at London Bridge – a snub to the Regent as well as to the people of the capital. This was followed by other graceless acts, including his refusal to attend a banquet arranged for him at Carlton House on the evening of his arrival; expressing a wish to go to visit Princess Caroline, he invited the leaders of the Whig opposition to a long conversation on politics. He capped his offences by waltzing with Lady Jersey, the Prince's discarded mistress, at a ball in his honour. The Grand Duchess had already given great offence by interfering in the proposed marriage of Charlotte to the Prince of Orange, encouraging her to break off the engagement, it was thought in the hope of securing a marriage alliance with one of the Russian Grand Dukes, and by lecturing the Regent on his marital obligations.[7]

The Tsar's tactless behaviour towards the Prince was the more galling because all the allied visitors were popular with the crowds, whose cheers for George were pointedly less than enthusiastic. Marshal Blücher was an especial favourite – 'a nice old man', as Creevey remarked, who endeared himself to the crowd by toasting them, often apparently in an inebriated condition, from the open window of his hotel. King Frederick William of Prussia was also popular, despite his much more stiff and sober manner, and though the Austrian Emperor did not come, his representative, Prince Metternich, put himself out to be ingratiating and was well received. A born diplomat, he used the occasion to court ministers and George himself by flattering him as the architect of victory and arbiter of Europe.

[6] Ernest to George, 2 May 1814: ibid., i, 440; Priestley, 115; *Annual Register* (Chronicle) 1814, 29, 32–43; Webster, 251–2; Muir, 327.
[7] Muir, 330.

The visit was a hectic round of ceremonies, appearances, parties and banquets which taxed the stamina of all concerned. One of Creevey's friends reported that the Tsar 'grumbles at the long dinners of the Regent's' and Creevey himself noted that 'they are all sick to death of the way they are followed about'. They went to Ascot races on 10 June and attended a grand military review in Hyde Park on the 20th. On the 14th the Prince took them to Oxford for the conferment of honorary degrees, followed by 'a sumptuous dinner to 200 persons' in the Radcliffe Camera, at which the cheering public burst in and Blücher got so drunk on quantities of strong beer washed down with cognac that he could not find his lodgings afterwards and was found wandering about the streets. Four nights later the Corporation of the City of London gave a banquet in Guildhall, where they feasted on turtle and a baron of beef and drank sixteen toasts, with predictable consequences for Blücher's sobriety. London was wild with excitement: it was said that there was a milk shortage because the cows in the Green Park, who supplied the West End of the capital, were frightened out of the park by the loud cheers. It was all very frustrating for the Prince, for despite his graciousness and his imposing costumes the applause was never for him, and as Creevey spitefully and gleefully reported he was 'exactly in the state one would wish; he lives only by protection of his visitors. If he is caught alone, nothing can equal the execrations of the people [and] . . . he is worn out with fuss, fatigue and *rage*'. Even worse, he was upstaged by Caroline, who arrived at the theatre exactly at the moment to turn the cheers of the audience for the royal party into acclamations for her: '*She* . . . carries everything before her', wrote Creevey.[8] Fortunately, and to the disgust of Brougham and the Whig opposition, she was persuaded to retire to the continent by the offer of an extra £15,000 a year and she departed in early August.

The visit of the allied royalties and ministers ended on 23 June with a grand naval review at Portsmouth, where they were joined by Wellington who had just arrived from Paris and posted down from London. He was acclaimed by the crowd as the hero of the hour. The Prince escorted his guests on board HMS *Impregnable*, where they were treated to a ration of the ship's grog. It was an appropriately symbolic occasion, when the Great Duke, as he had now become, joined the Regent, who had given him unstinted and uninterrupted support to defeat the French, on board one of the great ships which had protected his country from the possibility of defeat. From this time onwards the two became firm friends. On 7 July they attended a national service of

[8] Stuart, *Prince Regent*, 82–4; Creevey to Mrs Creevey, 14 June 1814: *Creevey Papers*, i, 195–6; Richardson, 137–40; Muir, 330–1; Priestley, 121–3; Knighton, *Memoirs*, i, 151–8; Anon., *Account of the Visit . . . to the University of Oxford* [1815].

thanksgiving at St Paul's, sitting together in the Prince's carriage drawn by eight cream-coloured Hanoverian horses and attended by footmen in sumptuous livery. The Duke sat on the Prince's right throughout the service, and George paid him a further tribute by organizing a fête at Carlton House two weeks later.[9]

The fête was even more splendid than the one which had inaugurated the regency in 1811. The centrepiece was a Corinthian temple containing a bust of the Duke on a column of antique marble in front of a mirror, surmounted by a star over the letter 'W' in cut glass, and surrounded by draperies of pink and white muslin. The temple was approached through a brick polygonal structure of twenty-four sides and 120 feet in diameter, specially designed by Nash and draped with white muslin with an umbrella-shaped painted roof. Two bands, concealed within a mass of artificial flowers, played continuously 'God Save the King' and 'The Prince Regent's March'. Beyond the polygon room on the west and the Corinthian temple were two supper tents decorated with silk in regimental colours. On the east of the polygon room was a covered walk decorated with military trophies and allegorical transparencies representing patriotic scenes and leading to further supper rooms. The Queen and members of the royal family arrived at 10.30 and promenaded round the rooms. After supper Princess Mary and the Duke of Devonshire opened the ball, which went on till 6 a.m. It was a tribute unsurpassed in taste and luxury, all attributable to the Regent's talent for design and theatrical effect.

These were private ceremonies, though attended by hundreds of notable guests. The Prince however did not leave out his common subjects. For them an immense fête was prepared in the three royal parks on 1 August to celebrate peace and the centenary of the accession of the House of Brunswick. Nash was again placed in charge of the works, designed on the oriental theme now much in the Regent's mind and shortly to be adapted to the reconstruction of the Pavilion at Brighton. A Chinese bridge topped with a blue and yellow pagoda was built across the lake in St James's Park, and a medieval Gothic fortress in canvas 100 feet square mysteriously appeared in Green Park, eventually to be revealed as a setting for an immense firework display. Hyde Park was the free, popular end, with booths and tents housing hordes of pedlars, strolling players, puppet shows, acrobats and musical performers, complete with a menagerie and mock naval battles on the Serpentine representing Nelson's victory at Trafalgar, with the additional refinement of a fireship which accomplished, to great applause and general satisfaction, the destruction of the entire French fleet.

At the end of the firework display, which lasted two hours and

[9] Stuart, *Prince Regent*, 92–3; *The Times*, 27 June 1814; accounts of the festivities daily in *The Times*, 10 June–8 July 1814.

temporarily obliterated the scene in Green Park in a cloud of smoke, there magically appeared on the previous site of the fortress (now revealed to have been made of canvas) a highly illuminated 'Temple of Concord', decorated with scenes representing the origins of war in 'Strife expelled by Jupiter from Heaven', the deliverance of Europe from tyranny, the restoration of the Bourbons, the return of Peace, and the triumph of England under the regency, showing the Prince Regent 'crowned by victory . . . with Discord crouching in chains at his feet', attended by Britannia and Mars and surrounded by 'Art, Commerce, Industry, & the Domestic Virtues'. This patriotic construction was the work of Sir William Congreve, inventor of the 'Congreve rocket' which had played an interesting though not wholly successful part in wartime operations in Europe.[10] All did not go entirely smoothly: Nash's Chinese bridge and pagoda in St James's Park which had amazed and delighted the spectators with its own interior firework display, 'the canopies . . . throwing up their bright wheels and stars, the pillars enriched with radiance, every rising tower of the Pagoda pouring forth its fiery showers and rockets springing from its lofty top in majestic flights', accidentally caught fire and toppled into the water, killing two spectators. The balloon ascent from Green Park by the well-known Mr Sadler, formerly of the Liverpool Gas Company, had to take place without the company of 'a gallant lady, called Mrs Johnstone' who was to have released from it a dove as an emblem of peace; there were fears that her weight might be too much for the balloon's lifting power. Mr Sadler however took off in great style but had to make an emergency landing on Mucking Marshes near the Essex coast to avoid being swept out into the North Sea.[11]

The whole series of celebrations was a great success. Even whigs and the critical press had to admit that it was immensely popular, and it proved a spectacular triumph for the Prince himself and his artistic flair. The departure of Princess Caroline for the continent a fortnight after the grand fête crowned George's satisfaction. George was free to cast off public and private cares for a time and retire to Brighton, where, he informed his mother on 22 August, there was 'a complete stagnation & dearth of every thing, no, not even one little scrap of scandal' and he spent his time with 'a few male companions, my brother William at the head of them', walking and riding in the mornings and 'in the evening about half a dozen ladies, Mme. de Lieven &c. &c. &c. come at nine o'clock, when we have a delightful concert, Mme. de Lieven sometimes charming us for half an hour with her uncommon

[10] The 'Congreve rocket' was a rocket projectile invented in 1808 and was used at the battle of Leipzig in 1813, but it proved to be inaccurate and hazardous to the user.

[11] Fulford, *George the Fourth,* 140–2; Stuart, *Prince Regent,* 96–8; Priestley, 128–30.

beautiful talent on the Piano Forte, & at half past eleven, or twelve at the latest, all is over, & we trip away to bed'.[12]

The visit of the allied ministers had been too festive for diplomatic activity of any serious nature, and the statesmen of Europe now transferred their attention to Paris, where Wellington and Castlereagh joined them to discuss the outlines of a European settlement, and then to Vienna where the Congress to negotiate the final treaties assembled in the autumn. The leisurely pace of the discussions was suddenly interrupted in March 1815 by news which reached London on the 10th of Napoleon's escape from Elba and return to France. The flight of Louis XVIII from Paris followed on the 20th. The Powers were agreed on the necessity of resisting Napoleon's re-establishment, but sections of British opinion were hostile to the principle of forcing any government on a nation without popular consent. The Prince and the government unhesitatingly backed the second restoration of Louis XVIII but some of the Whigs, including Grey, had reservations on principle.[13] The months of April, May and early June were tense and anxious for many, not only because of uncertainty as to the defeat of Napoleon but even more because of fears that if the Bourbons were successfully restored by allied force of arms Louis XVIII might not be able to maintain himself on the throne. The four days of operations from 15 to 18 June, culminating at the field of Waterloo, settled the question of victory, and it was a decisive enough outcome for the Bourbon king to be restored, thanks largely to Wellington's firmness in the ensuing weeks.

The news of Wellington and Blücher's victory reached London on 20 June, reportedly to Nathan Rothschild who used his secret information to make a profit on the Stock Exchange. It was not until the evening of the 21st that one of Wellington's ADCs brought official news from the Duke. The Cabinet were dining at Lord Harrowby's house in Grosvenor Square when Henry Percy, the ADC, burst in in a suitably dramatic tableau shouting 'Victory!' He then went on to St James's Square where the Prince Regent and the Duke of York were attending a ball given by the society hostess Mrs Boehm. According to her daughter's account the first quadrille was forming when the shouts of the crowd came through the open windows on that hot, sultry night, and Percy dashed in from his carriage carrying a captured French standard in each hand, pushed aside everyone in his path, and rushed up to the Regent. Dropping theatrically on one knee, he laid the flags at his feet with the words 'Victory, Sir! Victory!' The Prince, overcome with emotion, promoted him on the spot but was soon reduced to tears by news of the

[12] George to Queen, 22 Aug. 1814: *LG4*, i, 477.

[13] Smith, *Grey*, 177–8; Grenville's contrary view led to the break-up of the alliance between the two groups in the Whig party.

dead and wounded, who included several of his friends. As with Trafalgar, Britain's greatest victory of modern times was bought at a price which muted the thanksgivings and rejoicings.[14]

The final act, or perhaps postlude, to the tragedy occurred when Napoleon decided to surrender to the British as the likeliest of his opponents to be chivalrous to a defeated enemy, and presented himself to Captain Maitland of HMS *Bellerophon* bearing an appeal to the Prince Regent 'as the most powerful, the most constant, and the most generous of my enemies'. Despite the ridicule of some of George's domestic opponents at what they considered gross flattery, it was not an unworthy sentiment, but the Regent and his ministers had no wish to be burdened with the responsibility of keeping the ex-Emperor and it was quickly decided to send him to the remote Atlantic island of St Helena where he ended his days in moderate comfort but in despair and frustration.[15] Meanwhile Castlereagh, with the Regent's full support, managed to persuade the allies to accept a peace settlement which, despite the inevitable imperfections of any such document, provided Europe with a hundred years of almost unbroken peace. George could look with justifiable satisfaction on a major achievement by his country.

[14] Muir, 364–5; R. Colby, *The Waterloo Despatch*; M. Glover, *A Very Slippery Fellow*, 150.

[15] J. Holland Rose, *Life of Napoleon*, ii, 520.

Chapter 14

REBELLIOUS DAUGHTER

One of the major causes of George's unpopularity as Regent was his supposed cruel treatment of his daughter Charlotte. She was growing up to be a lively, energetic and self-willed teenager with many of her father's own qualities. No doubt perceiving this, George was as severe with her as his father had been with him, attempting to shield her from the contamination of the outside world and placing her under the care of governesses and attendants whom she regarded as gaolers and who supervised her leisure as well as her education. She was given all the necessary accomplishments of a young lady, and like her father showed considerable talent as a musical performer and a knowledgeable interest in literature and the arts, but unlike him she lacked refined manners and was too cloistered to be used to the ways of polite society. As the child of a broken marriage – her parents ceased to live together even before she was born – she suffered those psychological handicaps which derive from the lack of a secure and affectionate home, and they were made worse by the fact that her parents' disputes were public property, and that she was to some extent a political victim of their quarrels. Charlotte showed the strain by bouts of violent temper tantrums which made her temporarily unmanageable. As the only child of this most disastrous of marriages she had to carry a heavy burden.[1]

George was determined from the outset that Charlotte's mother should have no say in her upbringing and education. He was convinced that Caroline was immoral and an unsuitable guardian for a young girl who was apparently destined to be Queen of England, and he always tried to restrict his wife's access to their daughter. Yet he had no better claim to be able to provide the secure background she needed, and for long periods during her childhood she was in effect brought up by governesses, her father's role being largely confined to drawing up restrictive rules to prevent her mother from having any part in her life.

George's attitude to his only (legitimate) daughter was an ambivalent one. On the one hand, he was always fond of small children and liked to play and romp with them and give them little presents. On the other

[1] Charlotte to Mercer Elphinstone, 22 Jan., 26 and 28 Oct. 1812, [1 Dec. 1813], and [2 Feb. 1815]: Aspinall (ed.), *Letters of Princess Charlotte* (henceforward *Letters . . . Charlotte*), 26, 33, 35, 88, 108; A. Plowden, *Caroline and Charlotte*, 76.

hand, he could not forget that Charlotte was Caroline's daughter. Like her mother, Charlotte showed early signs of being a tomboy, with boisterous manners – her handshake as a girl and young woman was a hearty one more suited to the society of young sportsmen than to that of genteel young ladies. She was unguarded in her language, a reckless horsewoman, and showed a liking for exuberant companions. George feared that she might turn out as her mother had done, and he thought, like his father and despite his own experience, that a strict regime would prevent his offspring from succumbing to the temptations of the world. His attitude seemed to Charlotte to alternate between neglect and repression, with only occasional displays of affection. She thought his 'sugary' letters 'after all, were but *des phrases*, without any meaning' and declared 'I *cannot* write what the heart *does not* dictate – *tho' he may*'. Sometimes he hardly spoke to her, even at family dinners, and at others he appeared 'very kind and attentive' but he rarely seemed to be able to relax in her company. His attitude contrasted remarkably with his relationship with young Minny Seymour, with whom he exchanged playful letters and affectionate banter, so that to some observers Minny seemed more like his own daughter than Charlotte did.[2]

Charlotte's uncertainty about her father's attitude and the Prince's evident reluctance to give his time to her were perceived by the King, who had developed a fondness for her as he had done for her mother. This too led to complications. The King's desire in 1804 to bring Charlotte more closely under his care by moving her to Windsor showed his genuine concern for his granddaughter, and to some extent the Prince saw the advantages of the plan. It would relieve him of the more onerous duties of fatherhood and possibly improve his own relations with the King, but on the other hand he became convinced that there was an underhand plot to allow Caroline closer access to Charlotte.[3] It was not until the King withdrew his former intimacy with Caroline over the 'Delicate Investigation' that the Prince became more favourable to Charlotte's spending time at Windsor, and after the King's relapse into insanity in 1810 he took the opportunity to limit Caroline's access to her daughter still more. In June 1812 he laid it down that Charlotte should live for part of the year at Windsor, under the Queen's eye, and might visit her mother, now installed in apartments at Kensington Palace, only once a fortnight. Caroline was not to visit her daughter under the Queen's or the Prince's roof and she was to have no say in her education or her household companions.

[2] *Letters . . . Charlotte*, xv–xvi, to Mercer on 7 March 1813: ibid., 61; Plowden, 93, 97–8.

[3] Moira to Eldon, 17 July 1804: RA, Princess Charlotte, 49275–6.

George's excuse was that he feared Caroline would corrupt her daughter's morals and as Charlotte grew up he became even stricter as to the conditions of her life and upbringing.[4]

The strain on Charlotte was considerable. She had no illusions about her mother but she was naturally fond of her and the restrictions her father placed on her tended inevitably to turn her away from him. When he moved her into a new residence of her own, Warwick House, a dilapidated mansion next door to Carlton House, she was given no more freedom than before, and during her visits to Windsor she had to endure the society of the Queen, who had always hated Charlotte's mother and supported her father, and the princesses, whose life was intolerably dull. She described Lower Lodge at Windsor, where she was housed after 1812, as 'this infernal dwelling' where she believed there were 'spies . . . everywhere' and in the Castle, 'the royal menagerie', she was surrounded by 'the whole pack of devils', as she unkindly described her aunts. She not unnaturally found life 'dreadfully dul', with her grandmother and four maiden aunts determinedly working with their needles for five hours every evening 'without a word being uttered'.[5] Her life at Warwick House too became ever more boring and depressing, and her relationship with her father took another turn for the worse when it became apparent that, as Regent, he had deserted his former Whig allies and turned against them. Charlotte had inherited, or had been taught, her father's whiggish inclinations and she was distressed by his volte-face which she attributed to his ever-closer relations with the Queen. This became even more apparent when the Queen presided at a family dinner at Carlton House to celebrate Charlotte's sixteenth birthday. The evening was pleasant and sociable enough to start with, the Regent declaring that 'he was never so happy as when in the bosom of his family', which struck his daughter as an even more unnerving sign of political apostasy. The tenor of the evening then degenerated. The Prince got drunk and abused Grey and Grenville so much that Charlotte had to be taken out of the room in tears by Sheridan.

The danger was that if Charlotte's political views became known, her popularity might be used by the opposition as a means of discrediting her father and his ministers.[6] When he took her with him to the state opening of Parliament in the autumn of 1812 she could not help noticing that he was greeted with 'dead and most humiliating silence' by the crowds in the streets, while she was cheered as she passed. It was

[4] Eldon to Princess of Wales, 17 June 1812: *LG4*, i, 116–17.
[5] Charlotte to Mercer, 5 Oct. [1811] and 26 Oct. [1812]: *Letters . . . Charlotte*, xiii, 7, 33.
[6] Same to same, 8 Jan. [1812]: ibid., 22–3; Plowden, 101; Sichel, ii, 349.

noticed too that she occasionally turned her back on him. Some of the leading Whigs were certainly hopeful that the old 'reversionary interest' – the prospect of future favours from the heir to the throne – might be revived. Samuel Whitbread, the Whig brewer and Grey's brother-in-law, who leaned towards the radical wing of the party, and Henry Brougham, an ambitious and unscrupulous lawyer who saw Charlotte and her mother as potential tools to restore the Whigs to popular favour, were foremost among her new champions. When Charlotte was shown over the Commons chamber in January 1812 she wrote to her friend and confidante Mercer Elphinstone, 'I could not *resist* sitting down in one of the Opposition benches'.[7]

The Prince was disturbed at his daughter's growing popularity. It was hard to bear when he was increasingly unpopular. He responded with even more authoritarian rules for her conduct which eventually led her to blaze out in open defiance: in December 1812 she attempted to assert her independence by demanding that at the age of seventeen she should no longer have a governess but that her attendants should be ladies of her bedchamber. She also objected to the Prince's choice of the elderly Duchess of Leeds to succeed Lady De Clifford as governess on the grounds that she would be too subservient to the Queen and 'the Castle'. George humiliated her by giving her a thorough telling-off in front of Lord Eldon, the Lord Chancellor, who declared that if she were *his* daughter he would have her locked up. Charlotte told one of her aunts in tears that she had been compared to a 'collier's daughter' – Eldon having come from a family of Newcastle coal merchants. She was also upset by her father's announcement in 1813 that her mother's conduct was again being investigated and that she might never be allowed to visit her again.[8] Charlotte obeyed, but was hurt when her father neglected her: her companion Miss Knight said he scarcely saw her once in two months. In May however he gave her permission to visit her mother on her birthday, though he stipulated that it should be a morning visit only and she should not stay to dinner, since he could not know who else might be present. He continued to keep a watchful eye on his daughter for fear of her mother introducing her to bad company, and lost no opportunity to remind her that she was subject to his sole authority. The Queen backed him up, telling Charlotte in May that 'she ought to look upon [her father] as the only source of her happiness & that it was her duty to obey [him] in everything . . . & that any of the Royal family taking a part against the Crown was lowering it most essentially'.[9]

[7] Romilly, *Memoirs*, iii, 73; Charlotte to Mercer, 7 and 8 Dec. [1812] and 6 Jan. [1812]: *Letters . . . Charlotte*, 40, 22.
[8] Queen to George, 28 Dec [1812]; Princess Mary to same, 10 Jan. [1813] (two letters); Sir H. Halford to same [?14 Jan.] 1813: *LG4*, i, 192–3, 202–4, 207–9, 222.
[9] Queen to George, 17 May 1812: ibid., i, 73.

As she reached adolescence Charlotte naturally began to take an interest in young men, and when she was sixteen she was attracted to a Captain Hesse, who was reputed to be a natural son of the Duke of York. She wrote him several indiscreet letters and sent him small presents, which Mercer Elphinstone later attempted to get back from him.[10] It was ominous to the Prince that Caroline seemed to encourage an affair between them and he was infuriated to learn that she had left the young couple alone in a locked room during a visit to her. Charlotte also showed signs of infatuation with the older Duke of Gloucester, her father's cousin, an amiable nonentity of nearly forty who was variously known as 'The Cheese', 'The Slice', or 'Silly Billy', though this was probably no more than a symptom of a determination to rule her own life. More ominous was a burgeoning friendship with the young bachelor Duke of Devonshire, Georgiana's son, who was regarded by the young ladies as the prime catch of the season. In May 1813 the Prince even censured Charlotte's attendants for allowing her to drive twice along Chiswick Road on a day when the Duke was giving a party at Chiswick House, and he was concerned to see his attentions to her at entertainments in Carlton House. The Duke's Whig connections again aroused fears that Charlotte might be drawn into opposition politics and this led to further restrictions on her social activities.[11] In July 1813 she was refused permission to go to the seaside for a few weeks for the benefit of her health, which she said had suffered from her confinement at Windsor the previous year, despite her assurances that she had no plans to meet anyone there or make any new acquaintances. Her father blandly replied that although he had not the slightest mistrust of her intentions it was 'my duty as your affectionate Father to foresee & to ward off any evils which might arise', and in any case Sir Henry Halford had assured him that 'your health does not in the least require it'. Charlotte submitted and assured him that she would think no more of it, though to make sure her father gave her a lecture on the subject which Halford thought would do good. He also advised the Queen that Charlotte had a 'natural & intuitive spirit of restlessness & premeditated systematick kind of dissatisfaction' and that she should be closely watched.[12]

George's response to the signs of Charlotte's awakening sexuality was to try to marry her off as soon as decently possible to a suitable husband. In the summer of 1813 the Hereditary Prince William of Orange came

[10] *Letters . . . Charlotte*, xv, n.4.

[11] *LG4*, i, 321–2n: Capt. Hesse to Mercer [?1814]; Charlotte to [Hesse], [1814]; George to Charlotte, 26 Dec.; Mary to Charlotte, 26 Dec. and to George, 31 Dec.; Mary's memorandum [1 Jan. 1815]: ibid., i, 436–7, 514–23; Charlotte to Mercer, 16 Aug. [1813]: *Letters . . . Charlotte*, 65; J. Lees Milne, *The Bachelor Duke*, 25–6.

[12] Charlotte to George, 20 and 22 July 1813; George to Charlotte [?21 July]: RA 49810–13.

under consideration. Politically he had much to commend him, for the two royal families had intermarried since early Stuart times, and the Dutch were traditionally seen as sound Protestant allies against threats from Catholic France. One of the strongest inducements to Britain's declaration of war on France in 1793 had been the fear of continued French ambitions in the Netherlands and the need to keep British influence paramount at the mouth of the Scheldt, the main passageway for the vital British trade to continental Europe. Unfortunately, these considerations gave Charlotte all the more reason to reject the idea. She knew that her parents' marriage had similarly originated in schemes for political alliance and she was determined not to be a pawn in a diplomatic game. She was also personally revolted by the drunken behaviour of the Hereditary Prince's father, in company with her own father and uncle William, at a dinner to celebrate the Prince Regent's birthday.[13]

Nevertheless, the Prince, aided by the sedulous and obliging royal physician and go-between Henry Halford, embarked on a campaign in the following months to pressure her into the 'Orange match', as it became known. The opposition in England affected to believe that his eagerness was explained by a desire to remove Charlotte from the political scene. When she appealed directly to Lord Grey for advice, although he was careful to avoid pushing her into extremes, and acknowledged that she was as yet too young to defy her father's authority and too inexperienced to rush into a hasty marriage with possible political implications, he advised her that George could not force her, with propriety, into a marriage for which she had no desire. She should delay any decision until she was older and more experienced.[14]

Charlotte was delighted with Grey's statesmanlike advice, but the Prince had not given up his intention to bring her round. He simply changed his tactics and, instead of acting the heavy father and threatening her, he became all kindness and affection, even telling her that she could go to see her mother whenever she liked. When the Hereditary Prince landed in England on 10 December and was invited to dinner at Carlton House, he proved to be pleasant, lively and modest, though not handsome, and made a favourable impression. After dinner Charlotte told her father that she approved of him, whereupon the Prince embraced her with tears of congratulation and declared himself 'the happiest person in the world'. Prince William came in and George joined their hands together in

[13] Charlotte to Mercer [14 Aug. 1813]: *Letters . . . Charlotte*, 63.

[14] Same to same [15 Oct. 1813] and Grey to Charlotte, 19 Oct.: ibid., 75, 80–2; Smith, *Grey*, 224.

betrothal before leaving them to talk together for the rest of the evening.[15]

Two days later he called again at Warwick House with the intended bridegroom, and left the happy pair together while he talked to Charlotte's companion Miss Knight, only to be interrupted by the sound of loud sobbing by his daughter. Her fiancé had told her that after their marriage she would have to spend part of every year in Holland, or the Dutch people would object. Charlotte had apparently assumed that she would never be expected to leave her own country; she now rather unreasonably blamed her father for deceiving her, though (or rather because) the subject had never been mentioned between them. 'My soul is wrung out to the bottom', she declared to Mercer.[16] She did not immediately withdraw from the engagement, but as the time of her wedding drew nearer she became more and more uneasy, and her mood was deepened when no celebrations were ordered for her eighteenth birthday on 7 January on the feeble excuse that the expense would be inappropriate in wartime: her father had even gone out of town and did not invite her to dinner. Charlotte thought that his kindness and affection had been only a pretence to achieve his objective of getting her married off and out of the way. For his part the Prince was annoyed at her extravagance in jewellery and her general inability to keep within her income. Small as her debts of £15,000 were in comparison with his own in his youth, it was a different matter when he found himself responsible for them.[17]

Brooding over her situation at Warwick House with no society but her two companions and with nothing to occupy her and few contacts with her fiancé, Charlotte became more unhappy. She was not consulted about the terms of the marriage treaty and it appeared that she would be expected to live in Holland for six months of the year rather than a few weeks. Advised by Henry Brougham and Lord Grey, she decided to protest to her father, who replied testily that the terms of the marriage contract were none of her business, and that it was not unreasonable that she should be required to follow her husband abroad. If she did not withdraw her demands the engagement would have to be broken off and he would not consent to a marriage with anyone else.[18]

[15] Charlotte to Mercer [24 Oct.], [1 Dec.] and [13 Dec. 1813]: *Letters . . . Charlotte*, 85, 87–8, 91–3; Plowden, 134–5.

[16] Charlotte to Mercer [14 Dec.], [16 Dec.] and [18 Dec. 1813]: *Letters . . . Charlotte*, 93–5.

[17] Plowden, 138.

[18] Grey to Charlotte, 7 Feb. and 10 April 1814; Charlotte to George, 15 April, to Mercer [16 April]; Adolphus to Charlotte [?17] April 1814: *Letters . . . Charlotte*, 109–12, 114–17.

Charlotte was capable of being as obstinate as her father and during several weeks a series of interviews and letters failed to reconcile their views, while the visit of the Tsar and his entourage and the other allied sovereigns in the summer of 1814 to celebrate the allied victory added to George's frustrations and annoyance. In the end he gave way so far as to agree that Charlotte would not be required to leave England without her own consent, but she was now turning against the whole idea of the Orange match, influenced by her mother and by her own Whig advisers. She was falling out of love, in so far as she had ever been in it, while her fiancé was neglecting her and getting drunk at parties to which she was not invited. During the summer festivities she became infatuated with the dissolute Prussian Prince Frederick Augustus and contrived several secret and indiscreet assignations with him. Using the excuse that her mother was being appallingly badly treated and that she could not desert her, she announced to the Prince of Orange that she could not possibly go to Holland with him and that their engagement was at an end. Her father remonstrated in vain: he wrote that the tales about Prince William's drunken conduct were put about by 'mischievous, false & wicked persons' and reminded her, with some feeling, that 'our station compells us no doubt to enter into matrimonial connexions guided by a superior sense of the duty which we owe to our country'. Unlike him, however, she had 'no reason to apprehend' in her proposed union 'the grievous calamity, which I alas! my dearest child have experienced from marriage with a person, whose character we have had occasion so recently . . . to gather'. It was, he asserted, 'the wicked act & deprav'd contrivancies of your mother' to ruin her for the benefit of her supposed child William Austin; 'a husband with a name and character in Europe' was her best protection. 'We cannot marry like the rest of the world', he reminded her. Charlotte replied that her feelings against the Prince of Orange were stronger than ever, so turning her father's tactics against himself.[19] Charlotte's obstinate refusal to change her mind determined him to force her to come to heel. He dismissed her attendants, ordered Warwick House to be closed up, and announced that she was to be shut away at Cranbourne Lodge in Windsor Forest where she would see no one but the Queen once a week.

Charlotte's patience snapped. Snatching a bonnet from her astonished maid, she ran down the back stairs and out into Pall Mall, found a hackney carriage, and drove off to take refuge in her mother's house in Connaught Place. Fortunately, Caroline was out, but Charlotte sum-

[19] George to Charlotte [*c.* 20–25 Feb. 1815] and reply, 27 Feb.; George to Charlotte [after 27 Feb.]: *LG4*, ii, 31–9.

moned Henry Brougham to come to advise her. Shortly after his arrival her mother returned and they all sat down to dinner.[20]

Charlotte's freedom did not last long. Brougham sensibly realized that the consequences of her impulsive act might be disastrous. The Londoners had been cheering Caroline and booing the Regent throughout the 'victory summer' and Charlotte's flight might lead to riots and bloodshed. After an all-night series of conferences and messages, including visits from the Lord Chancellor and Lord Chief Justice (who were kept waiting in their carriages in the street), the Bishop of Salisbury and other functionaries on behalf of the government, and the Whig Duke of Sussex as reinforcement for Brougham, Brougham finally persuaded the Princess to return escorted by the Duke of York to Carlton House. On meeting her father, there was a tearful reconciliation, Charlotte begging pardon for her rashness, George promising 'not [to] make [her] life miserable.' 'Your mind may be perfectly tranquil', he assured her. He would press her no further. Nevertheless, she was now closely watched and confined, with her new ladies acting virtually as gaolers and censoring her correspondence. She was removed to Cranbourne Lodge, which she found surprisingly agreeable as a residence despite its relative isolation. The Whigs, at first inclined to raise her situation in Parliament, were advised by Grey that it would be counterproductive and even dangerous to public tranquillity to do so, and his advice to her was to submit as patiently as possible until the affair blew over.[21]

Charlotte slowly became reconciled to her lot and to her father, who visited her at the end of July to tell her that her mother had decided to go abroad, feeling that her presence in England was no longer of any use. The Prince was naturally pleased at the news, though for Charlotte it was tantamount to a betrayal by the mother on whom she had hoped to rely for support. It left her with no resource but to make up the relationships with her father's family, and in fact the Queen and princesses soon became friendly and supportive. In the autumn she was sent off to Weymouth to forget the Prince of Prussia, who was certainly unworthy of her but for whom she still harboured an imagined romantic feeling. She returned for Christmas at Windsor, where she and the Regent made up their differences in a long talk after Christmas dinner.[22]

[20] Charlotte to George, 18 April, to Prince of Orange, 16 June, to Princess Mary [17 June], to Princess of Wales [17 June], to George [18 June 1814]: *Letters . . . Charlotte*, 117–19; Plowden, 154–6.

[21] Plowden, 156–60; Charlotte to Mercer [20 July 1814]: *Letters . . . Charlotte*, 131; Erskine to Charlotte, 27 July 1814: *LG4*, i, 474–7.

[22] Charlotte to Mercer [21 July] and [26 Aug. 1814]: *Letters . . . Charlotte*, 133–4, 145; Plowden, 163–73.

She was now beginning to turn her affections towards Prince Leopold of Saxe-Coburg, whom she had met the previous summer and who was a favourite with her aunts and seemed agreeable to her father. George had not given up hope of persuading her to renew her engagement to the Prince of Orange, but she remained firm and she was released from her fears on that score when her former suitor announced his engagement to a Russian Grand Duchess in the summer of 1815.[23] Charlotte made up her mind to marry Leopold, the Regent finally consented, the Queen enthusiastically approved, and both Houses of Parliament and the people gave their blessing. They were married with due ceremony on 2 May 1816, the twenty-year-old bride's father doing her proud in his Field Marshal's uniform, wearing all his orders and decorations, the crowd in the streets cheering and the guns of the Tower booming in salute. Two days afterwards he visited them at Oatlands, the Duke of York's house in Surrey, where they were spending their honeymoon, and to Charlotte's relief he spent over two hours in describing to Leopold various military uniforms of 'every regiment under the sun, wch', she added, 'is a *great mark* of the *most perfect good humor*'. The young couple set up house at Claremont in Surrey, an agreeable and comfortable residence.[24]

George had reason to be in good spirits. His unruly wife had left England and was busy scandalizing Europe by her reckless and discreditable conduct, and his daughter was safely married off and no longer likely to be a trouble to him. Although the anxieties and frustrations of the past months were by no means over and the state of the country remained worrying, his domestic life was beginning to be more comfortable.

There was one consequence of the marriage that the Prince and the country looked forward to: the birth of an eventual heir to the throne. Charlotte suffered a miscarriage a few weeks after the ceremony, and another in December, but in April 1817 it was disclosed that she was pregnant again. This time the pregnancy lasted its full term, though the old Queen, whose experience in such matters was formidable, declared misgivings when she saw how large her granddaughter was becoming. In fact the baby's arrival was considerably delayed and when labour began on 4 November it continued for two days. The Prince Regent had tired of waiting for the birth at Claremont and had returned to Carlton House, where he received a letter in the evening of 5 November from Lord Bathurst, one of the ministers in attendance, telling him that Charlotte had been safely delivered of a boy who, however, was still-

[23] Charlotte to Mercer [22 Dec. 1814], [5 Jan.], [8 Jan.] and [?11 Jan. 1815]: *Letters . . . Charlotte*, 273–8; Plowden, 174–6.

[24] Charlotte to Mercer [23 Jan.], [19 March, 1815], [4 May 1816]: *Letters . . . Charlotte*, 186, 194, 242; Plowden, 194.

born. She was 'doing extremely well'. Unfortunately it was not so: a few hours later she suffered a fatal haemorrhage.[25]

The news was a profound shock to the whole nation, the more so as the expectation of rejoicing at the birth of a new prince or princess had so suddenly given way to grief. The Duke of Wellington soberly remarked that it was 'one of the most serious misfortunes the country has ever met with' and on the opposition side of the political divide the sorrow was multiplied by the loss of the Whigs' prospects of support from a future sovereign. Samuel Romilly noted in his diary that though it could not be certain that she would have called a Whig administration to office, there was now 'no prospect of such an event taking place in a long series of years', since the heir presumptive was now George's Tory brother Frederick. In the provinces, James Losh, a Newcastle attorney and friend of Lord Grey, wrote that 'a heavier calamity could scarcely have fallen upon my beloved country'. Brougham recollected in his much later *Memoirs* that 'it is difficult for persons not living at the time to believe, how universal and how genuine' the national sorrow was: 'It really was as if every household throughout Great Britain had lost a favourite child.' And the normally cynical Dorothea Lieven described how 'in the streets people of every class [were] in tears, the churches full at all hours, the shops shut for a fortnight': the general despair was 'impossible to describe'.[26]

For the Prince Regent, the shock was devastating. Whatever his conduct towards his daughter had been and however he had mistrusted her political connections, her death was a personal blow such as he had never before experienced. Princess Mary visited him on 9 November and found him prostrated with grief in 'deep affliction'. He could not even rise from his bed of suffering to attend the funeral. The Queen wrote in sympathy that 'as I always share in yr prosperity most sincerely so do I most deeply feel your present loss & misery' and attempted to reassure him that he could take some consolation from the fact that he had allowed Charlotte to marry the man she loved and had provided her with a home 'in which she spent to the very last [in] almost complete felicity'.[27]

There is no doubt that George's distress was genuine, despite Lord Melbourne's assurances to Queen Victoria in 1839 that he had 'rejoiced' at Charlotte's death and had disliked both her and Leopold.[28]

[25] Ibid., 201, 203, 206–8.

[26] Ibid., 209; Romilly, *Memoirs*, iii, 318; E. Hughes (ed.), *Diary of James Losh*, i, 73: H. Brougham, *Life and Times*, ii, 332.

[27] Queen to George, 7 Nov. 1817: *LG4*, ii, 212.

[28] Queen Victoria's Journal, 21 Jan. 1839: RA. Leopold hated his father-in-law and never ceased to assert that George had hated Charlotte – which was patently untrue.

The sorrow may well have been mingled with self-reproach that he had not been kinder to her, but her death brought out the fundamentally affectionate nature of George's heart. The event was also one of deep importance for the future succession. She was the only legitimate descendant of any of George III's children and it became a matter of urgency that all those of his sons who had never married and were living with mistresses should look around for wives and produce a new generation of the family. Some suspected that the Regent himself would now renew and hasten his efforts to divorce Caroline and remarry for the same purpose, and it was not long after Charlotte's death that spies and agents were sent out to gather evidence of Caroline's immorality on the continent. It is in fact doubtful whether George had any serious intention of remarrying; he was eager enough to divorce Caroline in order to ensure that the throne could not descend to William Austin or at any rate that no claim on his behalf could be put forward, but he had no prospect of marriage for himself. He was keener to see his brothers regularize their marital positions and on 16 December, as soon as he could bring himself to write to his mother, he urged her to encourage William to marry and also informed her that Adolphus had already been accepted by Princess Augusta of Hesse. The story that George assembled all his unmarried brothers and told them it was their duty to marry, to be asked by William 'But who would marry us?' may be apocryphal, since several of them were already contemplating doing so, but it contains the germ of truth.[29] Charlotte's death certainly gave rise to a flurry of activity among her 'wicked uncles', at the expense of more than one royal ex-mistress, and it must have stimulated renewed attempts to discredit her mother in a way which would have upset Charlotte if she had lived. Caroline, now living in a villa on the shores of Lake Como, was not informed of her daughter's death and learned of it from a newspaper. Next to the bereft widower who had lost his opportunity to become a Prince Albert to Charlotte's Victoria, she was the chief sufferer by the event.

[29] Notes of a conversation with the Duke of Kent, Brussels, 11 Dec. 1817: *Creevey Papers*, i, 268–71.

Chapter 15

SEDITIOUS SUBJECTS AND TURBULENT WIFE

Despite the glorious success of British arms in Europe and despite the Regent's unwavering support of his ministers in bringing it about, George remained deeply unpopular with the mass of his subjects, at any rate in London where political opinions were more openly expressed. This was partly due to his reputation as a libertine and spendthrift with his people's money at a time of general financial strain, and to indignation at his allegedly cruel treatment of his wife and daughter, but it mainly derived from the economic and social circumstances of the time. From the beginning of the regency the country suffered under high taxation, not least to meet the enormous cost of foreign subsidies to carry on the war, the interruption of overseas trade because of economic warfare, and subsequent widespread unemployment in the manufacturing districts. Bad weather and harvest failures raised the price of bread and added to the distress. All these were exploited by radical propaganda, which depicted the government and the royal family as corrupt and self-seeking parasites indifferent to the sufferings of the poor. Cobbett referred to the royal family wallowing in luxury 'at the expense of a nation of industrious people'.[1] The removal of George III from active kingship laid open a contrast between his parsimonious housekeeping and care for public economy and the extravagant self-indulgence of his sons. Not for the last time, the popular press delighted in contrasting the sober and respectable life of the reigning monarch, who had become the symbol of British virtue and liberty against French wickedness and tyranny, with the sexual profligacy and financial irresponsibility of the younger members of the royal family.

Since the last twenty years of the eighteenth century a new class of business entrepreneurs and professional men had grown up, devoted to those so-called 'Victorian values' of self-help, enterprise, sober living and private morality, and often inspired by strict evangelical religion.

[1] Quoted in *The Gridiron, or, Cook's Weekly Register*, 23 March 1822. Government expenditure 1812–15 totalled £550 million, 3.5 times the equivalent in 1793–6: J.E. Cookson, *Liverpool's Administration*, 19.

They frowned on the remnants of eighteenth-century dissipation which they identified with the old aristocracy. They demanded a fair field for the development of talent and a social and political status and influence through which they could attain greater importance in society. They supported the growing demand for fairer political representation and for the new economic doctrines associated with Adam Smith which stressed individualism and freedom from old restraints on enterprise. Although these doctrines found a readier echo and acceptance in the party of Pitt, Perceval and Liverpool than in the old centres of aristocratic whiggery, they implied reform of political and economic structures at a faster pace and to a more extensive degree than the old governing élite of either party considered acceptable. The spectre of the French Revolution still haunted the British political establishment and though the new 'middle class' flirted with radical reform they agreed with the old aristocracy that it should not be carried beyond safe limits for the security of private property. Not for another twenty years was there to be sufficiently wide support for reform of the old constitution; in the meantime, and especially during the years of the regency, the 'lower orders' reacted to the hardships of the post-war years of depression by posing a threat to law and social discipline.

The period from 1812 to 1821 was one of popular disturbance, occasional rioting, a seditious and unrestrained popular press, and repeated literary attacks on the Prince Regent as the embodiment of national corruption and repressive tyranny, led by poets and intellectuals such as Byron and Shelley and journalists like Leigh Hunt and William Cobbett. The rancorous disparagement of disappointed Whigs reinforced the resentment of the poorer classes at such evils as the privations of agricultural labourers, the hardships of life in new industries and the harsh treatment of the unemployed, the insane and petty criminals driven by despair and deprivation. In associating him with the social evils of the day, they did the Prince Regent an injustice, but as the figurehead of the nation he had to bear responsibility for the sufferings of his people. The Prince was hissed and jeered in the streets of his own capital and abused even in the debates in Parliament. In 1816 Brougham declared in the House of Commons that he was devoted to vicious pleasures and indifferent to the sufferings of his people. The bluntness of the attack stunned the House. Romilly was one of the few to defend him and even that in not uncritical terms: 'With all the Prince's faults, and they are great enough, it is absurd to speak of him as if he was one of the most sensual and unfeeling tyrants that ever disgraced a throne'.[2] Leigh Hunt summed it all up in a famous passage in his radical journal the *Examiner*: George was

[2] *Parl. Debates*, xxxiii, 476–513; Romilly, *Memoirs*, iii, 236–7; Castlereagh to George, [20 March] 1816: *LG4*, ii, 161.

> a violator of his word, a libertine over head and ears in debt and disgrace, a despiser of domestic ties, the companion of gamblers and demi-reps, a man who has just closed half a century without one single claim to the gratitude of his country or the respect of posterity.[3]

The verdict has passed into the popular history of the time, and as one recent commentator has remarked, 'it became something of a classic text for the Whig legend of George IV and its last statement was repeated time and again for well over a century'[4] – aided by the success of Thackeray's grossly exaggerated caricature of George IV in his influential but biased lecture in *The Four Georges* in 1855. Hunt and his brother John, who edited the *Examiner*, were brought to trial, charged with intention 'to traduce and vilify His Royal Highness'. Despite Brougham's vigorous defence they were sentenced to two years' imprisonment, which made them martyrs to the cause of the liberty of the people and the press. Many other figures in the literary world joined the ranks of the Prince's detractors.

Critics among the poets and essayists of respectable society were hurtful to a man who had devoted considerable energy to the patronage of literature, but they did not threaten the fabric of the polite world. Discontent boiling up among the unpropertied working classes was a far more dangerous matter. Luddite riots in 1812, Corn Law riots in 1815–16, nocturnal meetings and drilling of men on the moors above the Yorkshire woollen towns in 1816 and 1817, threats of violence against employers and Anglican clergymen – the 'black dragoons' as they were christened – all aroused the fears of men of property and kept the troops on the alert night and day.[5]

The Luddite movement which emerged in the manufacturing districts of the north and north midlands in 1812 owed little to any political stimulus. It was a protest against unemployment and poverty which was ascribed to the increasing use of machinery and resulting trade practices by employers in such industries as the knitting of stockings and manufacture of woollen cloth. It was probably a spontaneous movement amongst craftsmen who saw their old skills being displaced by the employment of women and children to work machines. However, it did suggest an awakening political consciousness among the working classes and the authorities were always ready to imagine the presence of secret agents and agitators who were supposedly using the opportunity to politicize the common people. Repression was consequently severe. Machine-breaking was made punishable by death and

[3] 22 March 1812.
[4] C. New, *Life of Henry Brougham*, 91.
[5] J. Stevenson, *Popular Disturbances*, 155–62; F.O. Darvall, *Popular Disturbances*, *passim.*

many hundreds of working men were sentenced, though in the great majority of cases the death penalty was reduced to transportation or confinement in the hulks – prison ships moored in the Thames.

Nevertheless, the atmosphere of panic among the upper ranks of society was easily aroused and, once aroused, difficult to calm. Local magistrates, some of them employers whose property was threatened, or clergy who were often associated with the putting down of dissent in any form, felt themselves to be particular targets. Samuel Bamford, the Lancashire weaver and radical leader, recorded in his memoirs instances of manufacturers keeping cannon and muskets in their factories day and night for fear of attack by mobs.[6] Though the improvement of trade after the repeal in 1812 of the 'Orders in Council' which had strangled trade with the continent helped to calm agitation in the manufacturing districts, and the last years of the war brought better news of victories in Europe and hopes of peace and prosperity to follow, social and economic conditions were slow to improve. High levels of taxation to finance the huge subsidies to European allies that formed a major element in the British war effort affected the upper and middle classes and despite frantic efforts by the government to economize and reduce expenditure after Waterloo the House of Commons, representing those classes, insisted on abolishing the property tax, a form of income tax and a mainstay of government finance. This placed a proportionately heavier burden on the lower classes. At the same time the hated Corn Law of 1815, which tried to protect English agricultural interests from competition by cheap foreign imports, was seen as a blatant kind of class discrimination, protecting landowners and farmers while raising the price of bread to the poor.

The immediate post-war years were a time of economic depression and social unrest with which the central and local authorities were ill-equipped to deal except by force.[7] The government thus became more and more unpopular. Demands for reform of the representative system, to make parliament more responsive to the people at large, were suspect as being the first steps along the road to democracy and the redistribution of property. Agitation by public meetings, or suspected plots to overthrow the government, were countered by the suspension of the Habeas Corpus Act and the billeting of troops in the 'disturbed districts'.

The Prince Regent, presiding to all appearances over this repressive regime, had to bear a large share of the resulting unpopularity. He had been greeted by absolute silence from the crowds which came to witness

[6] Bamford, *Passages in the Life of a Radical*, vol. 1, *Early Days*, 301–2.

[7] N. Gash, *Aristocracy and People*, 76–89; Cookson, 102–16; Romilly, *Memoirs*, iii, 75.

the opening of Parliament in both November 1812 and 1813 and this turned into outright hostility after Caroline's departure in 1814. Yet he was not insensitive to the plight of the poor and the unemployed. Moira, the Regent's spokesman in the Lords, declared in a debate on the Framebreaking Bill in 1812 which proposed the death penalty for the offence, that while Parliament should take measures to stamp out the offences, it should also 'endeavour to prevent those distresses which gave rise to them, and to try to ameliorate the situation of the starving manufacturers' (i.e. artisans). Most people shared this more humanitarian attitude but felt themselves, and the state, to be helpless in face of the trade cycle and the after-effects of the war. 'These evils', the Regent declared in his speech opening the session in 1817, 'are of a nature not to admit of an immediate remedy'. Poor relief expenditure, the responsibility of local and not national authorities, rose to its maximum but it was never more than a palliative. The year turned out to be one of the worst, in terms of popular distress, in the whole of the first thirty years of the nineteenth century, though distress and disaffection were sporadic in nature and varied in intensity from place to place. Government however was always liable to panic, and anxiety was kept on the boil by exaggerated reports from spies and informers set to watch for signs of danger – and paid by results. The situation culminated in an apparent assassination attempt in January 1817, when the Regent's carriage window was pierced by either a bullet or a stone when he was on his way to open the session of Parliament. The Cabinet was shaken by the outrage: Peel considered it a sign that 'the general spirit of the country is worse, I apprehend, than we understand it to be'. The attack seemed a prelude to a general insurrection. Both Houses rushed to pass loyal addresses expressing their horror at the attempt, and though in his reply George assured them that he felt 'no other sentiment on the occasion but deep regret at the violation of the laws and the breach of good order', Lord Fitzwilliam caustically expressed the hostility of the Whig opposition when he remarked that 'minds differently constituted might perhaps under similar circumstances have lamented that they could not show themselves to their subjects without being hiss'd, hooted and pelted'.[8]

The government decided to take no chances and the attack provided a pretext for stronger measures of repression. Secret committees of the two houses claimed to have found evidence of extensive disaffection in London and the manufacturing towns and declared the existence of a 'traitorous conspiracy' for the overthrow of government and 'a general

[8] Peel to Lord Whitworth, 29 Jan. 1817: C.S. Parker, *Peel*, i, 237; *Parl. Debates*, xxi, 1167; Darvall, 334–7; *Commons Journals* lxxii, 4; Smith, *Whig Principles*, 335, quoting Fitzwilliam to Milton [29 Jan. 1817]: Fitzwilliam papers, Northamptonshire Record Office, X515.

plunder and division of property' among the 'lower orders'. On the basis of these somewhat unreliable assertions Parliament suspended Habeas Corpus, passed an Act to forbid 'seditious' meetings of more than fifty persons without the authority of a magistrate, and two years later, after the 'Peterloo massacre' of 16 August, 1819, when the crowd at a peaceful demonstration in Manchester was ridden down by yeomanry cavalry and eleven people were killed, passed the 'Six Acts' against various forms of radical activity. The Prince's action in sending a message of congratulation to the Manchester magistrates after Peterloo without waiting for full information, much less an enquiry into the episode, seemed further to emphasize his lack of sympathy for his own subjects and their plight.[9]

George's action was certainly hasty, but on the other hand ministers believed that the mood of the country was dangerous and that any apparent lack of support for the forces of law and order would demoralize those on whom the maintenance of the country's institutions depended. Though much of the appearance of disaffection and potential uprisings was later shown to have been manufactured or exaggerated by government spies and informers, the mood at the time was near to panic and Sidmouth, the Home Secretary, was taking no chances.

Thus George came to be associated in the popular culture of the time with the repressive acts of the central and local authorities and the refusal of ministers and Parliament to make concessions to popular demands or modify the discriminatory system of taxation which bore most heavily on the poorer sections of society. The identification was not altogether unjust. George was kind to his personal servants as individuals, but he gave little thought to general social problems. He was not an 'enlightened despot' who could set his own policies or rule without reference to the interests of the upper classes who dominated society and government, even had it been the practice of the age for governments to concern themselves with social welfare beyond the necessary maintenance of order and subordination. Nor was he, unlike his father, an active, businesslike monarch who took the trouble to inform himself on political details. He lacked interest in routine business and could barely be persuaded to attend to his papers and boxes. He was content to leave to others the smooth working of the machine. Ministers were theoretically his personal servants, but in practice they were increasingly responsible from day to day to Parliament rather than to the monarch, who was fast becoming a constitutional figurehead. The monarch's views and opinions might be taken into account, but if

[9] *Parl. Debates*, 18 Feb. 1817, xxxv, 411–19 (Lords) and 19 Feb. 438–47 (Commons); second reports ibid., 12 June, xxxvi, 949–56 and 20 June, 1088–98; Read, *Peterloo*, 181–5.

they were at variance with those of ministers and Parliament it was expected that he and not they would give way. It was becoming the accepted principle that the Crown should not resist the will of Parliament, at least in matters of real significance.

Whether a king could enforce his will in the minor matter of appointments or grand views of policy depended on personalities and the nature of his relationship with the Prime Minister and his colleages. Thus, to associate the repressive policies of Liverpool's government and Sidmouth in particular with George personally is unfair: he followed rather than led his ministers' actions. Radical propaganda did focus on the ministers, particularly on Liverpool, Sidmouth, Castlereagh – who as leader of the House of Commons was seen as sharing in the responsibility for repressive legislation – and Canning, and might even appeal to George as Regent to exercise his prerogative to rescue the country from them. 'You have been beloved and respected by people and can be again', the *Black Dwarf* wrote in 1817. In fact, after the Leigh Hunt trial in 1812 editors were cautious about attacking the Regent personally and adopted an oblique way of associating him with ministers' actions. The same article referred to him as adored by the people once, when Fox was alive, but now led astray by his 'own passions, and the pernicious flattery of sycophants'.[10]

In one respect, however, George was saddled with the whole responsibility for what was seen as his tyrannical conduct, and was pilloried unmercifully in the press. This was the treatment of his wife in the months following his accession to the throne in January 1820. In February the radical newspaper the *Republican* came out in support of

> this injured woman – this victim, first to unbridled lust, and now to despotism. . . . This innocent, injured, and unfortunate Princess, had her future happiness sacrificed at the altar of profligacy. . . . Her husband has decoyed her into a marriage to answer his own private views, without the slightest affection towards her, he just condescends to consummate the marriage, and then drives her from his house, studies to insult her, by every means that can be devised, and utterly forsakes her by a public avowal that he will never meet her in public. What tie can a woman feel towards such a husband as this . . . when she perceives that the man who has seduced her into this situation, is daily revelling in adulterous harlotry?[11]

Whatever the rights and wrongs of the case, the public was to take her up as an injured woman suffering under the persecution of a profligate

[10] *The Black Dwarf*, 21 Dec. 1817.
[11] *The Republican*, 25 Feb. 1820.

tyrant who was as guilty as she was of adultery. Cobbett wrote that the parting with Caroline was the real cause of the unpopularity which George had to endure for the rest of his life; and the attempt in 1820 to divorce her reduced his reputation to its lowest ebb. Even Sarah Lyttelton wrote that the King 'is so unpopular, his private character so despised, and everything he does so injudicious as well as unprincipled that one can hardly wish him well out of it, except for the fear of a revolution'.[12]

Princess Caroline's departure from England in 1814 had dashed at least temporarily the hopes of the Regent's political opponents that she might provide them with further opportunities to embarrass him. By removing herself voluntarily from the scene at a time when George's popularity, despite the victories in Europe, was still low, and about to fall even lower because of the hardships of the post-war recession, she deprived herself of the opportunity to exploit his misfortunes to her own advantage. Looked at more objectively, her decision was understandable. Without the King to protect her, and in face of the hostility of the Queen and most of the royal family, she was vulnerable to plots and machinations which might provide pretexts for the Prince to divorce her, while the approaching prospect of Charlotte's being married off to a foreign suitor freed George's hands from any restraint which his daughter's presence might impose on him. In any case, eighteen years of fighting against the frustrations of her life were enough. Abroad, she might have the chance of avoiding constant publicity and of being able to enjoy herself without the need to observe the restraints of English society. She knew she was unlikely ever to become queen and if she could manage to live comfortably on her increased income she might pass her time agreeably enough.

Accompanied by a retinue of mainly English friends and supporters, Caroline embarked on 8 August 1814 on what became a hectic and picaresque tour of the pleasure spots of Europe in the company of notorious adventurers and obscure Italian hangers-on who soon replaced the more respectable of her English companions.[13] Her behaviour, freed from whatever had remained of the barriers imposed by prudence and convention, reflected her determination to enjoy her new freedom to, and beyond, the limit of acceptable conduct. Reports, which hardly underrated the spectacular side of her activities, attracted attention in England, not least that of the Prince, while his agents, or spies, who trailed after her reported back the full details. The Prince was overjoyed, not only that she was now out of the way, but also

[12] E.B. Wilbraham to Colchester, 20 June 1820: Colchester, *Diary*, iii, 141–3; Sarah Lyttelton to F. Spencer, 7 and 24 June 1820: Wyndham, *Lyttelton*, 224.

[13] Caroline's narrative of her travels, Queen Caroline papers, RA 13/7; Fraser, 263–87.

that she was providing evidence which might be useful in the divorce proceedings on which he was still determined. Baron Ompteda, a former Hanoverian court chamberlain, who was recommended by Count Münster, the Hanoverian minister in England, undertook to 'give proof to the Prince Regent of Great Britain and Hanover of his zeal and devotion' by providing 'an exact account of her conduct' and 'sufficient proofs to legitimate' any reports of particularly scandalous behaviour. Evidence was to be forthcoming soon enough. Meanwhile, foreign courts were encouraged to refuse to receive her or recognize her royal status, the papal court being particularly helpful and co-operative.[14]

Reports from Ompteda and others, particularly describing Caroline's supposed intimacy with her Italian major-domo and favourite Pergami (or Bergami) and their frequent occupancy of adjoining or communicating bedrooms, encouraged George to hope that the necessary evidence for divorce would soon be available. If nothing else, the possibility that Caroline might have a child, in addition to the existing doubts about the status of William Austin, who was accompanying her and being widely regarded as her son, aroused fresh concern about Charlotte's succession to the throne. The Prince's Hanoverian ministers were particularly concerned because of the Salic law which would forbid Charlotte's succession to the German kingdom in any case. They urged the necessity of a divorce but, as Count Münster pointed out, a divorce in Hanover under local law might not suffice in England. There was also a doubt whether her adultery with a foreigner abroad would subject her to the penalties of high treason in England.

The Prince sought a legal opinion from the ecclesiastical lawyers at Doctors' Commons, and was advised that proceedings in the ecclesiastical courts might be lengthy, taking perhaps three years or longer, and that if it were to be proved that he had committed adultery himself there would be a bar to divorce proceedings against his wife under the principle of 'recrimination'. The law officers agreed that the facts produced were not sufficiently well-founded to ensure the success of divorce proceedings in England, and the Cabinet pointed out that the evidence, coming from foreigners in a 'low station of life', might be difficult to prove, considering the xenophobic attitude of the English in general, particularly towards Italians, who were regarded as especially frivolous, untrustworthy and venal. Lengthy proceedings in an ecclesiastical court were also ruled out as being likely to stir up public agitation against the Prince, proceedings for a parliamentary Bill of divorce were likely to fail because of the nature of the witnesses and proceedings for a verdict of high treason would be even more unreliable. The Cabinet

[14] Fraser, 261, 309, 343–5, 359; Queen Caroline papers, RA 8/6.

concluded that they were 'decidedly adverse' to any proceedings either in the ecclesiastical courts or in Parliament without further and more reliable evidence.[15]

So matters rested until after Charlotte's death, when her father determined to renew his efforts. 'Much difficulty in point of delicacy', he wrote to Lord Eldon, had been 'set aside in my mind by the late melancholy event which has taken place in my family': in other words he was no longer deterred from disgracing his dead daughter's mother. He was determined

> to extricate myself from the cruellest as well as the most unjust predicament that ever even the lowest individual, much more a Prince, was ever placed in, by unshackling myself from a woman who has for the last three and twenty years not alone been the bane and curse of my existence, but who now stands prominent in the eyes of the whole world characterized by a flagrancy of abandonment unparalleled in the history of women, and stamped with disgrace and dishonour.

He could not bear the thought that 'such a monster' should continue to bear his name and he had determined to rid himself of her by any means. He laid the latest reports of Caroline's conduct before his ministers, confident that they would endorse his wishes, only to receive the same answer: moreover such proceedings would be seen as the vindictive pursuit of a woman no longer protected by the status of her daughter as a future Queen of England. In the delicate state of the country, with sedition and discontent rife, it would be foolhardy to take the risk.[16]

George turned to other tactics. New efforts would be made to gather conclusive evidence in Italy. Three commissioners were appointed under the authority of the Vice-Chancellor, Sir John Leach, to investigate the matter on the spot. The chosen members of the commission were William Cooke, KC, formerly an authority on the bankruptcy laws, but now almost retired from the bar, John Allan Powell, a younger solicitor hoping for preferment, and Major James Browne, a military attaché at the British embassy in Vienna who was selected for his knowledge of Italian language and customs. They were instructed that there must be no possible doubt about their evidence: witnesses must not be given money except for bona fide expenses and no other inducements must be offered for them to testify. The mission was enthusias-

[15] Münster to George, 2 June 1816; Legal opinion 1 Aug. 1816; minute of Cabinet, 11 Aug.; legal opinion, Hanover [n.d.]: RA 8/2; Cabinet minute, 24 July 1819: C.D. Yonge, *Liverpool*, iii, 19–22.

[16] George to Eldon, 1 Jan. 1818: RA 21/179/159; Twiss, ii, 304–5; Fraser, 302–4.

tically supported by the Prince, but only reluctantly and partially by the Prime Minister and Cabinet, who feared the impact of more scandal on public opinion. The 'Milan Commission', as it became known from its base of operations, was thus of doubtful constitutional legality.[17]

The commission began work in the autumn of 1818 but it soon degenerated into farce. The witnesses, called to Browne's lodgings in Milan to give their testimony, made it clear that scandalous stories about Caroline were freely available at the right price, and they gossiped unrestrainedly in the inns with the eager Englishmen. Clearly no reliable or untainted evidence was going to emerge. Nevertheless, Caroline herself was frightened that she would be irretrievably damaged by these disclosures, many if not all of which were in fact quite true, and offered a compromise. She told James Brougham, Henry's brother, who visited her in Pesaro where she was now living, that she would agree to a divorce provided she received an adequate sum to enable her to live comfortably in Italy with Pergami. She no longer wished to return to England.

James Brougham was sceptical as to her motives but passed on the offer to his brother, who consulted Lord Lauderdale, the Prince's friend. They concluded that no divorce was possible without proof or her confession of adultery, and this Caroline ruled out. She hoped that Henry Brougham would secure her an agreement on her terms: the Prince's intransigence forbade that, but Caroline still hoped that he might be forced to agree at least to a formal separation in return for an income and her agreement to give up her hopes of becoming Queen – which had no longer any value for her since Charlotte's death. Brougham formalized these notions into a proposal that Caroline would remain abroad, renounce the right to be crowned or take the title of Queen, and receive £50,000 a year. He put the proposals to Lord Hutchinson, a friend of the Prince, but George again refused to agree to such terms. Only a divorce would satisfy him, based on the report of the Milan Commission which was now almost ready and which condemned Caroline's conduct. The furthest he would go was to consider a divorce by consent and arrangement, but the Cabinet stepped forcefully on that idea and insisted that divorce could be obtained only on proof of adultery before a recognized court. Since any attempt of that kind was likely to lead to public controversy and a threat of riot and disturbance, the Cabinet repeated their veto on anything further than a separation by agreement, without public proceedings, which the Regent again refused to consider.[18]

[17] Memoranda by Powell and by Leach, 4 Feb. 1821: RA 13/7; Leach to Cooke, Browne and Powell, 8 Aug. 1818: *LG4*, ii, 252.

[18] Memoranda by Leach and Powell on the Milan Commission; James Brougham

The affair was leading to a breakdown of relations between the Prince and his government, while Caroline, increasingly frustrated by the delay and uncertainty, and probably already in touch with the Prince's English radical enemies, was making ostentatious preparations to return to England to demand her rights. Her journey came to nothing for the present, possibly, as her biographer suggests, because the Peterloo affair diverted the attention of her radical advisers and provided an alternative and more productive channel for their attacks on the Regent and his government.[19] The question of a royal divorce or separation hung fire until, after Christmas, the old mad King at Windsor caught a cold which turned to pneumonia and carried him at last peacefully to the grave on 29 January 1820. The 'Queen's affair' was about to begin.

to Henry Brougham [1819]: ibid., ii, 410–17, 272–85; Fraser, 311–12; Brougham to Hutchinson, 14 July 1819; cabinet minute 17 June 1819; George to Liverpool, 22 June: Yonge, iii, 15–19.

[19] Fraser, 332–8.

Chapter 16

CROWNED WITHOUT A QUEEN

George IV became King on the 29th and was proclaimed on 31 January 1820, the intervening day being set aside for commemoration of the execution of Charles I, which some might have thought an ominous coincidence. The new monarch was in fact seriously ill with a chest infection which turned to pleurisy and seemed to place him, as Henry Bankes, MP wrote to his friend Lord Colchester, in 'imminent danger of following, instead of succeeding, his father on the second and third days of his reign', so that, as another friend wrote, 'the longest reign in our annals would be followed by the shortest known in history'. The King was 'much reduced by illness, very pale, very weak and tottering'. Charles Arbuthnot, Secretary to the Treasury, told his wife that at the accession council he was 'extremely ill' and 'so much agitated he could hardly get through' the proceedings.[1] Nevertheless, he wasted no time. He sent for all available copies of the Anglican Prayer Book and ordered that the Queen's name be omitted from the prayer for the King and Royal family. This deliberate insult angered Caroline and it more than anything determined her to come to England to claim the throne and the right to be crowned with him. She wrote indignantly to the Prime Minister to demand why her name was omitted 'to prevent all her subjects to pay her such respect which is due to the Queen, . . . as if she was no longer for this world'.[2] (One can always tell from the grammar and spelling whether she had written her letters herself.)

Henry Brougham, now deep in his involved intrigue to use the occasion for his own advancement, intervened to try to prevent her from coming, partly to gain credit with the ministry for keeping her away, partly to forestall those 'less discreet parties in England' who were uging her on and trying to recruit her to their own radical cause to the detriment of Brougham's Whig colleagues. As Caroline approached the Channel, Brougham travelled to St Omer to intercept her before she embarked, taking with him his brother and Lord Hutchinson, whom he (mis)represented as the King's accredited envoy. Despite their pleas

[1] H. Bankes to Colchester, 15 Feb. and H. Legge to same, 16 Feb. 1820: Colchester *Diary*, iii, 115–16; *Arbuthnot*, i, 1.
[2] Queen to Liverpool, 16 March 1820: Yonge, iii, 46–7.

and two urgent letters, with a hurried draft by Hutchinson of a proposed deal offering an annuity of £50,000 in return for her giving up the title of Queen and agreeing not to visit England, Caroline ignored the terms and set out for Dover. The die was cast, and Brougham's attempt to ward off the crisis had failed. He was forced to throw in his lot with hers, in the hope of emerging as her leading counsellor and legal representative and keeping her under Whig control.[3]

She arrived on 5 June, to the acclamations of crowds of people and a royal salute of guns. On the evening of the 6th she reached the capital, passing through streets lined with cheering crowds all the way from Deptford, through Greenwich and Blackheath to South Audley Street in Mayfair where she lodged at the house of Alderman Matthew Wood, ex-Lord Mayor, leader of the city radicals, and now appearing in public as her chief adviser. Her enthusiastic reception was ominous. It showed that, whatever happened, she had extensive support among the middle and lower classes, who were eager for another opportunity to demonstrate their sympathy for 'an injured and unprotected female' pitted against the forces of corruption and tyranny in the person of her husband. As one of Colchester's friends noted, 'The first subject, perhaps the only one about which the English world talks and thinks, is the Queen.' Whether she was worth their loyalty was hardly a consideration: she had become a symbol of the wrongs of the common people in general and of women in particular, and to George's radical enemies a powerful tool in their political campaigns.[4] The proceedings of the next six months were a purely political affair, in which the moral rights or wrongs of the individuals involved were subordinate to the interests of the parties, loyalist and conservative or militant and radical, who contended for the public's support. To George it was always a deeply personal question, an opportunity at long last to rid himself of the intolerable burden of his marriage, buttressed by what he considered, not without justification, incontrovertible proof of his wife's scandalous conduct and open infidelity. The desire of his ministers to avoid public disorder and scandal seemed to him cowardice at best and even disloyalty to their monarch. He insisted on proceedings for divorce and to disqualify Caroline from taking her place beside him on the throne,

[3] Brougham, *Life and Times* ii, 355–65, 370–2; Caroline's narrative, RA 13/7; Fraser, 358–61; Hutchinson to Bloomfield, 6 June: *LG4*, ii, 339–42.

[4] Wilbraham to Colchester, 20 June 1820: Colchester, *Diary*, iii, 141–3; Croker to Peel, 1 Sept.: J.W. Croker, *Corresp. and Diaries*, i, 177–8. For observers' accounts of Caroline's reception in England, see Smith, *A Queen on Trial*, 30–7. Addresses to the Queen ibid., 50–2 and *The Times*, 12, 17 Aug., 20 Sept.; Mme Lieven to Metternich, P. Quennell (ed.), *Lieven–Metternich Letters*, 3 Oct.; Lady C. Lindsay to Miss Berry, 13 Aug.: Miss Berry, *Journal*, iii, 247–9; J. Hatsell to Colchester, 9 Sept.: Colchester, *Diary*, iii, 161–2.

which would in his eyes, and again not unjustly, have disgraced the monarchy itself. Preliminary attempts at a negotiated compromise were rejected by both parties, and the evidence against the Queen was presented to Parliament in what became a symbol of her persecution, a 'Green Bag'. On 17 August the House of Lords assembled to hear the evidence and to determine the fate of the government's Bill of Pains and Penalties, introduced at George's insistence, which would dethrone her as queen and end her marriage.

The story of what quickly came to be known as 'the Queen's Trial' has been told elsewhere.[5] George himself played little part in it, except to appear as the butt of satires and caricatures, often of an obscene kind, which depicted him as a monster of depravity and a wicked and cowardly schemer against his injured wife. The subject of the 'trial' obsessed everyone and was the constant talk from society dinner parties to street-corner gossip. The prudish Harriet Arbuthnot considered the salacious details of the evidence too disgusting to mention in her journal. She was led to wonder whether the postponed Coronation would ever take place. The young Robert Peel was not the only one to ask what would be the end of it and whether the monarchy could survive. Revolution seemed in the air. The Queen was showered with petitions from all over the country, several from groups of women, and many of the peers in the House of Lords, though undoubtedly convinced of her guilt, shrank from voting in favour of the Bill of Pains and Penalties for fear of the public reaction. The proceedings, widely reported in full detail in the press, took up three months from mid-August to mid-November. The evidence of Caroline's immorality seemed overwhelming, but she still appeared to the crowds as a wronged and persecuted victim. The final vote revealed a Lords majority of only nine for the Bill and Liverpool immediately announced its withdrawal rather than face the prospect of violent popular disorder if the government tried to force it through the Commons. Caroline was still Queen.[6]

The effect on George was predictable. Charles Arbuthnot declared that 'his language and manner were those of a Bedlamite' and that he held forth in private for two hours at a time against his ministers, whom he accused of dragging him 'through the mire'. According to Lady Granville, 'He shuts himself up, [and] will see nobody'. In a memorandum of 22 November he blamed 'the conduct of my

[5] The story is told in detail in Fraser, 413–44 and Smith, *Queen on Trial*, *passim.*

[6] Account of trial by Lady Charlotte Lindsay, 17 Aug.–10 Nov. 1820: Miss Berry, *Journal*, iii, 252–60; *Arbuthnot*, i, 32–3, 37; Croker to Peel, 1 Sept.: Croker, i, 177–8; George spent over £2,500 in buying up obscene caricatures between May 1820 and March 1821: RA 51382(a). On the aftermath of the trial see *Arbuthnot*, i, 51–3 (10–17 Nov.); *The Black Dwarf*, 15 Nov.; Lady Erne to Lady Caroline Stuart-Wortley, 12 Nov.: Grosvenor and Stuart, *First Lady Wharncliffe*, i, 286.

Government' for his difficulties, castigating their 'irresolution in the 1st instance in settling their plan of Proceeding, & the folly of abandoning their own measures when once they had resolv'd upon them'. He accused them of 'indifference, not to say apparent insincerity to their sovereign, at any rate of rank Cowardice', and castigated Canning in particular for virtually admitting 'what everybody before believ'd, almost an open avowal of a criminal intercourse with the *P[rince]ss*'.[7] Yet within a short time the public mood, ever fickle, began to swing. The Queen had not been acquitted, and although proceedings against her had been dropped, the accusations against her moral character still stood, confirmed by a positive if small majority of the peers and corroborated if anything by the witnesses she had called in her own defence. George was justified in sticking to his vow that she should never be crowned nor acknowledged as Queen, in the Anglican liturgy or otherwise.

In truth, the ground was shifting under her feet. Once the Bill collapsed, her alliance with the political radicals fell apart. Despite their propaganda, Caroline was never interested in, nor did she ever understand, their political programme of parliamentary reform, which was their primary and almost sole objective. Her case had served its purpose: to expose injustice, tyranny and corruption – the three pillars of her campaign. There was no further mileage in her cause when the radicals moved on to a more positive programme. As the personal element which she had provided gave way to more abstract argument, the press and people lost interest, and began to tire of the endlessly repeated cries of scandal at the disclosures of her doings. After all, most of those who had been drawn to her support had backed her because she was legitimately Queen, but she had been exposed as the lover of low-born foreign servants. Even William Cobbett, doyen of the radical cause, admitted that though she may have been an injured wife, she was undoubtedly a depraved woman. The satirists turned against her, denigrating her as 'Mrs Muggins'.[8]

By Christmas the tide was turning. At the beginning of December loyal addresses to the King, even if possibly no more spontaneous than most of those which had supported the Queen, were coming in even from Alderman Wood's strongholds in the City. A service of thanksgiving for her at St Paul's on 29 November disappointed her by the crowd's diminishing applause – Lord Donoughmore called it a 'contemptible burlesque' – and the ever-loyal Brighton greeted George on his Christmas visit, though officially private, with displays of enthusiasm

[7] *Arbuthnot*, i, 53; Lady Granville to Lady G. Morpeth, 12 Nov. 1820: Granville (ed.), *Letters of Countess Granville*, i, 191; memorandum by George, 22 Nov. 1820: RA 22584.

[8] Fraser, 450–1; Aspinall (ed.), *Diary of Henry Hobhouse*, 47–50.

and an official reception and general illumination: 'most effulgent was the aggregate and glittering effect', exulted the local (ministerial) paper. On his accession day in January 'God Save the King' was received 'with rapture and waving of hats' in the London theatres and calls for 'God Save the Queen' were hissed. At Drury Lane in February the King and the Dukes of York and Clarence were received with 'immense acclamations, the whole pit standing up, hurrahing and waving their hats'. Only one man called out from the gallery 'Where's your wife, Georgy?' and was promptly sat on. At Covent Garden on the following evening there were equally wild scenes of enthusiasm, 'the house crowded almost to suffocation, and the whole standing up & waving their hats & handkerchiefs for near a quarter of an hour. I am sure,' commented Harriet Arbuthnot, 'if the King wd shew himself more in public, he wd always be equally well received.' Caroline had destroyed what was left of her popularity with the masses by accepting with alacrity a sum of £50,000 to follow what seemed to be the advice of the satirical versifier who adapted the unfortunate reference by Thomas Denman, her defence counsel, at the end of his closing speech, to the words of Christ's injunction to the woman taken in adultery, to 'go away and sin no more':

> Most Gracious Queen, we thee implore
> To go away and sin no more;
> But, if that effort be too great,
> To go away, at any rate.[9]

On 11 February, the Commons rejected by a majority of 120 an opposition motion to restore her name to the liturgy. It was the final humiliation. George was recovering the affections of his subjects; the coronation was about to demonstrate that the loyalty of the people to the institution of monarchy was greater than the effects of temporary scandal.

While still awaiting Caroline's arrival in England in May 1820, and while still believing that in the end she would have to accept the terms which had been offered to her, George had broached with Lord Eldon the subject of his coronation, which he was determined should be a spectacle of a magnificence never yet seen on such an occasion. He was

[9] Newspaper reports in Smith, *Queen on Trial*, 165–9; Lady Erne to Lady Caroline Stuart-Wortley, 6 Dec. 1820: Grosvenor and Stuart, *First Lady Wharncliffe*, i, 289; Donoughmore to Bloomfield [29 Nov. 1820]: *LG4*, ii, 396–7; Lady Cowper to F. Lamb, 1 Feb. [1821]: T. Lever (ed.) *Letters of Lady Palmerston*, 67–8; C.C.F. Greville, *Journal* i, 43; *Arbuthnot*, i, 69–70; The St Paul's service is reported in *The Times*, 30 Nov. 1820. Richard Rush, the American ambassador, summed up the significance of the affair in *A Residence at the Court of London*, i, 346–7.

equally resolved that his wife should not be present. Eldon was disinclined to co-operate since he expected that the ceremony would have to be postponed until the Queen's business was settled, and sure enough on 8 July an indefinite delay was announced.[10] The King made the best of it, in the confident expectation of ultimate success. He spent the summer at Windsor, away from the excited crowds of London, staying with his new favourite Lady Conyngham and her daughters in the newly furbished Royal Lodge, boating on Virginia Water, and toying with his ideas for the coronation.

Elizabeth, Lady Conyngham was the wife of the first Marquess (so created in 1816) who, like Lord Hertford, was a courtier married to an attractive wife. She was Elizabeth Denison, daughter of a Yorkshire businessman who had risen from the lowly status of a clerk in a counting house and accumulated great wealth by his 'unabated industry and rigid frugality'.[11] His son, William Joseph, banker and Whig Member of Parliament, became a double millionaire. Elizabeth's marriage to an Irish peer was an advance in the social scale, for though her husband had inherited only as a baron in 1787 he came of Anglo-Norman ancestry and owned a castle in County Meath. He rose in the Irish peerage and in 1821 was advanced to the more highly regarded British peerage as Baron Minster and appointed Lord Steward of the household through his wife's influence. In English society, however, Elizabeth was regarded as a parvenue and considered vulgar and mercenary. She loved diamonds and, according to the waspish Mme de Lieven, had a 'most limited mind', though this criticism may have chiefly arisen because she did not share Mme de Lieven's obsession with politics. She was a good-looking woman, though like George running to stoutness, and her age – fifty-four in 1820 – was no disadvantage in his eyes. As in the case of Lady Hertford, George was not so much in need of sexual gratification as of calm, warm companionship and stable affection. Lady Hertford had been cold and passionless: Elizabeth Conyngham, her husband and four grown-up children formed a ready-made family circle which appealed to the King, especially as Minny was growing up and could not be a daughter-substitute for ever, and reconciliation with Maria Fitzherbert had long been out of the question.

Lady Hertford's day came to its close with the regency. At the last Christmas before George's accession the new favourite's reign was announced to gossips in London. Harriet Arbuthnot's ear was close to the ground, as ever. She noted that Lady Hertford was 'very unhappy at the total desertion of the King' but could not forbear from adding 'I am

[10] Report of committee of Privy Council: *LG4*, ii, 329; Eldon to Mrs E. Bankes, [29 May 1820]: Twiss, ii, 365–6.
[11] Richardson, 201.

astonished she should not be very glad'. Madame de Lieven however remarked of the King that 'I have never seen a man more in love'. Lady Hertford was certainly capable of getting her own back: Charles Greville recorded that when someone enquired of her whether George had ever spoken to her of his feelings for Lady Conyngham she replied that 'intimately as she had known the King, and openly as he had always talked to her upon every subject, he had never ventured to speak to her upon that of his mistresses'. She reportedly said that 'she always had and still has the greatest regard for the K but there are things *one cannot do* & she cannot consent to visit his mistress'.[12]

Lady Conyngham was soon installed as the King's favourite, though for propriety's sake they never lived under the same roof and did not appear in public together. The Conynghams lived in Marlborough Row, near to Carlton House, where Elizabeth and, usually, her daughter dined every day, and the whole family had the use of his horses and carriages bearing the royal arms. 'She comports herself entirely as mistress of the house', Greville declared, both in London and at Brighton. In fact, Lady Conyngham came nearer than any of George's mistresses to filling Maria Fitzherbert's place in his affections. He was infatuated with her. He loaded her with jewels and other tokens of affection. She used the royal sapphire, once the property of the Stuarts, to ornament her head-dress. Harriet Arbuthnot recounted Madame de Lieven's story of an evening at Brighton when George sat between her and Lady Conyngham, and told her

> that he had never known what it was to be in love before, that he was himself quite surprised at the degree to which he was in love, that he did nothing from morning till night but think what he could do to please Ly C & make her happy, that he wd do anything upon earth for her that he owed his life to her, that he shd certainly have died in his illness if it had not been for her, & that she was an angel sent from Heaven for him.

The three of them ended in floods of tears together – 'such folly!!' as Harriet snorted. In May she again censured the King for spending the whole evening at the ball given at Carlton House to celebrate his (official) birthday with Lady Conyngham and finally retiring alone with her to one of the rooms to which no one else was admitted with a page on guard at the door: 'I really think he might controul his passion & not behave so indecently in public'.

[12] Temperley, *Diary . . . of Princess Lieven*, 117–18; *Arbuthnot*, i, 10; Quennell (ed.), *Lieven–Metternich Letters*, 2 June 1820: 36; C.C.F. Greville, *Journal* i, 29; Fanny Williams Wynn to Mrs C. Williams Wynn, 24 April [1820]: Charlotte Grenville, *Williams Wynn*, 238.

In 1821 George's infatuation was at its height. 'He sits kissing her hand with a look of the most devoted submission', wrote Lady Granville, and his determination to exclude his legal wife from the coronation was reinforced by his insistence that Lady Conyngham should not only attend the ceremony but be seated as near to him as decency allowed so that he could see her throughout. Indeed, he spent much of the time ogling her with significant, and to observers like Harriet Arbuthnot, indecent looks. Her presence acted as a stimulant during the long ceremony.[13]

The public too were becoming 'Coronation mad', as Lady Williams Wynn wrote on 12 May, and the King 'is *comme toujours* absorbed in the Care – of inventing the new dress for the Peers for the Coronation'. There was some concern at the possible expense. George III's coronation had cost £70,000, which seemed unlikely to be sufficient to cover the new King's extravagant tastes. The same correspondent reported that the two royal robemakers were visiting Brighton to discuss proposals for the peers' robes which 'together with the vests are to be of the richest & purist [*sic*] Virgin white Satin', and that £18,000 had been provided for a new setting for the royal crown.[14] The crown was to be the most brilliant ever made. As was customary, the frame was adorned for the occasion with gems hired from the royal jewellers, Rundell, Bridge and Rundell, for a fee of £6,500 per annum. No fewer than 12,532 diamonds were used in the setting, twice as many jewels as ever used in a royal crown before or since, and George was so delighted with the result that he tried, unsuccessfully, to persuade Parliament to buy them for him, and kept them for two years before agreeing to their return.

George's love of theatre and magnificence needed little encouragement to run far beyond the dictates of economy even at such a time of distress: interestingly, however, the public was growing tired of austerity and was ready to respond to the opportunity to enjoy a lavish spectacle and forget the troubles and privations of the immediate past. George provided a foretaste by ordering a grand procession for the state opening of his first regnal Parliament, using for the first time a new processional route from Carlton House, down the Mall and through Cockspur Street, Charing Cross and Whitehall to give maximum opportunity for public spectacle. He was 'better received than we had expected', said Harriet Arbuthnot. He also displayed his new royal crown and was attended by the usual sovereign's escort of cavalry, while the

[13] C.C.F. Greville, *Journal* i, 46, 48; Lady Granville to Lady G. Morpeth, 11 Feb. 1821: Granville (ed.), *Letters of Countess Granville*, i, 207; *Arbuthnot*, i, 81–2, 91, 108.

[14] Lady Williams Wynn to Mrs Henry Williams Wynn, 12 May 1820: Charlotte Grenville, *Williams Wynn*, 239–40.

band of the Coldstream Guards played outside the House of Lords. So great was the wish to attend the occasion that a queue of peers' and peeresses' carriages caused a traffic jam the length of Parliament Street for two hours before the official opening time at 12 noon. It was, Lady Williams Wynn wrote, 'more display than ever was yet known'.[15] George was well aware of the value of spectacle as a means of stimulating the loyalty and excitement of his subjects and from the start his coronation was to be a major contributor to reviving the popularity of the monarchy.

The ceremony took place on 19 July amid scenes of impressive pageantry. The extra time had allowed more lavish preparations. Sir Walter Scott noted that 'the most minute attention must have been bestowed to arrange all the subordinate parts in harmony with the rest; so that, amongst so much antiquated ceremonial — imposing singular dresses, duties, and characters, upon persons accustomed to move in the ordinary routine of society, nothing occurred either awkward or ludicrous which could mar the general effect . . .'.

Parliament, equally impressed by the value of the spectacle in promoting loyalty, had granted the unprecedented sum of £240,000 to meet the cost, and George had taken the opportunity to provide what Scott was to describe as a 'degree of splendour which [foreign visitors] averred, they had never seen paralleled in Europe'. Every costume had been specially designed on an Elizabethan and Jacobean theme to pick up the allusion to England's great historic heritage. 'Cloaks, ruffs, slashed-doublets, hose, and plumed caps of carefully constrasted colours' were worn by all the attendants, from dignitaries of the Royal Household to the waiters, ushers and menial servants. A band of herbwomen, society ladies and their daughters, dressed in 'a decorative combination of ruff and high-waisted Regency dresses and scattering rose-petals as they went', headed the King's procession, which culminated in the royal personage himself. At his entry into Westminster Abbey he wore robes 'of enormous size and richness', heavily trimmed with gold and crowned with a black velvet hat adorned with a 'monstrous plume of ostrich feathers, out of the midst of which rose a black heron's plume'. From his shoulders hung a train of crimson velvet 'adorned with large golden stars and a broad golden border' so long that it took nine pages to support it, and so heavy that 'he would infallibly tumble backwards with his gouty legs, if they [the robes] were ever left for half a minute to his own shoulders'. W.H. Lyttelton described it as one of the 'most magnificent and affecting spectacles that ever were beheld' and Mrs Arbuthnot wrote of 'the nobles and sages of the land decked out in velvet and satin, gold and jewellery,

[15] Same to same [1820]: ibid., 240–1; *Arbuthnot*, i, 64.

passing in procession among countless thousands, the sun shining without a cloud, all uniting to do homage to that Constitution under which we have so flourished!' Sir Walter Scott, who was to prove himself twelve months later no mean hand at inventing lavish spectacle, declared that the scene in the Abbey was 'beyond measure magnificent . . . the sides filled even to crowding with all that Britain has of beautiful and distinguished'. The cross-galleries were filled by the boys of Westminster School in white surplices, 'the aisles crowded with waving plumage, and coronets, and caps of honour, and the sun . . . beaming in full lustre on the rich and varied assemblage'. The King was 'much affected . . . and bore . . . the fatigue of the day very well . . . nothing could exceed the grace with which he accepted and returned the various acts of homage rendered to him in the course of that long day'. Even the ageing Privy Councillors, fantastically adorned in a 'fancy dress . . . of white and blue satin, with trunk-hose and mantles, after the fashion of Queen Elizabeth's time', provided an impressive and harmonious spectacle. A modern commentator, Mark Girouard, has remarked that it had 'the character of a gigantic fancy-dress pageant on the theme of the Faerie Queen, in which George IV played the part of a male Gloriana'.[16]

One who was not present to enjoy the spectacle in the Abbey was the Queen. The final indignity heaped on her was George's adamant refusal to allow her to be crowned. She had attempted to recover her position and popularity after the 'trial' by demanding (unsuccessfully) the restitution of her name to the Prayer Book, paying visits to the theatre to stimulate applause and public sympathy, and re-entering society by giving dinners and parties. All this merely infuriated her husband, who refused to receive her at court. Caroline then declared that she would attend the coronation and even requested that the King should advise her as to her dress for the occasion. (Mrs Arbuthnot suggested in her journal that a white sheet would be appropriate.) George had ordered research as early as November 1819 into the question of whether a queen had the right independent of her husband to be crowned, and precedents were carefully studied. Supported by the outcome, he declared to Liverpool that she 'should *never* be suffered by the King, under any circumstances, to appear at that most solemn ceremony, the law having placed the entire control upon that head in the hands and at the pleasure of the King'. Her counter-demand to be

[16] Walter Scott to the editor of the *Edinburgh Weekly Journal*, 20 July 1821; Lockhart, *Scott* [1900], iv, 35–46; M. Girouard, *The Return to Camelot*, 26–8; Sir George Nayler, *Coronation of . . . George IV, passim*; George Spencer to Frederick Spencer, 14 July 1821; W.H. Lyttelton to Sarah Lyttelton, 20 July: Wyndham, *Lyttelton*, 236–7; A. Wright and P. Smith, *Parliament Past and Present*, 194; Priestley, 284–6.

crowned as a right either with, or separately from and a week after the King was rejected by the Privy Council despite threats from Matthew Wood of riots in the streets. Brougham advised her to drop the matter but she persisted in her intention and was escorted to the Abbey by Lord and Lady Hood and Lady Anne Hamilton on the morning of the ceremony. She was refused entry and the door was slammed in her face. (George had arranged for a number of well-known prize-fighters to act as stewards.) She was cheered by the crowd on her way to the Abbey but hissed and hooted when she gave up and turned away: Lady Cowper considered it 'a complete victory' for the King, and so it turned out, for it was her last public appearance before sudden illness ended in her death three weeks afterwards.[17]

The coronation ceremony therefore passed off well for George, despite the anxiety which Caroline's actions must have caused at first, and despite too the oppressive weight of his costume and the fatigue of the long ceremony. Mrs Arbuthnot noted that from the start he seemed 'excessively pale & tired but soon recovered' when he was received

> with the loudest cheers, which were repeated with increased vehemence when the crown was placed on his head &, particularly, when the D. of York did homage & kissed him. It was a magnificent sight, that fine building full of people as it could possibly hold, all magnificently dressed, peers, heroes & statesmen all joining in one unanimous hurra.

More poetically, the painter Benjamin Haydon recalled the concluding procession: 'The distant trumpets and shouts of the people, the slow march, and at last the appearance of the King crowned and under a golden canopy . . . we were all huzzaing, and the King was smiling . . .'. During the ceremony, much of which, according to Lady Cowper's taste, was 'Monkish and twaddling and foolish and spun out', though the music 'had a grand effect', the King was observed, according to the censorious Harriet Arbuthnot, 'continually nodding and winking at Ly Conyngham & sighing & making eyes at her'. She thought his figure enveloped in 'the weight of his robes & his 60 years' quite a sickening sight: but Lady Cowper noticed that a look from Lady Conyngham

[17] Queen to Liverpool, 3 March 1821; Liverpool to Queen, 19 March and reply, 19th; Queen's petition to King, 21 March; George to Liverpool, 21st; Queen to Liverpool, 29 April: Yonge, iii, 121–6; Holland, *Further Memoirs*, 293–5; RA Queen Caroline papers, 13; *Arbuthnot*, i, 92; notes on coronations, RA 223–34, 22346–7, 22392–8; Queen to Archbishop of Canterbury, 15 July 1821; Sidmouth to Queen, 20th: RA Add. Geo. 5/1–2; *The Times*, 20 July 1821; Lady Cowper to F. Lamb, 20 July: T. Lever (ed.), *Letters of Lady Palmerston*, 86–7: Croker to Peel, 24 July: Croker, i, 196–7.

'revived him like Magic or Ether' and when he put on the ruby ring 'he cast up a most significant look at her'. The occasion was agreed to be magnificent and wholly impressive and the King 'did all with much grace & dignity', though his brothers were 'a deplorable spectacle', 'waddling in their tight, plain uniforms'.[18]

There followed in the evening the state banquet, for 312 persons besides the royal family, in Westminster Hall, revived with full ceremony for the occasion. Mrs Arbuthnot noted with glowing affection how her adored friend the Duke of Wellington performed to perfection his duty as High Constable, riding a white Arabian horse up to the King's table and backing out again. Lord Anglesey said that he was 'the only man in England who can back his horse down Westminster Hall'. All traditional ceremony was observed, 'a great many services done, caps given & returned, falcons presented by the D. of Atholl'. The King's Champion appeared in 'bright armour' with helm and gauntlet. The banquet itself was lavish: 160 each of tureens of soup (turtle, rice, or vermicelli), dishes of fish (turbot, trout, and salmon), hot joints (venison, roast beef, including three barons, mutton, and veal), and dishes of vegetables. Eighty dishes each of braised ham, savoury pies, dishes of goose, of savoury cakes, of braised beef and of braised capons were accompanied by 1,190 side dishes. For dessert there were 320 dishes of 'mounted pastry', 320 of small pastry, 400 of jellies and creams, 160 of lobster and crayfish, with 160 dishes of cold roast fowl and 80 of cold lamb. A total of 7,742 lb. of beef, 7,133 lb. of veal, 2,474 lb. of mutton, 75 quarters and five saddles of lamb, 160 lambs' sweetbreads, 389 cow heels, 400 calves' feet, 250 lb. of suet, 160 geese, 720 pullets and capons, 1,610 chickens, 1,730 lb. of bacon, 550 lb. of lard, 912 lb. of butter and 8,400 eggs were provided, so lavishly that large quantities of leftovers were distributed to the poor of St Margaret's. Everyone drank to everyone else and the evening concluded at eight o'clock with a choral performance of 'God Save the King' in which everyone joined.

There followed scenes of plunder and disorder as the King left and the hunt for souvenirs began. The golden cutlery and plate were the chief prize: some of it was rescued by the Lord Chamberlain's staff, but the mob then proceeded to claim 'coronation privileges' in the form of all the drink they could lay their hands on and the stripping of the tables of the remains of their decorations, glasses, cutlery and pewter ware. The exhausted diners then collapsed into the various rooms of the Palace, 'peers and peeresses, judges and privy councillors, knights of all orders, and commoners of all degrees lay promiscuously, some on sofas, some on chairs, and a still greater number on the matted floors

[18] *Arbuthnot,* i, 107, 108; A.P.D. Penrose (ed.), *Autobiography . . . of B.R. Haydon,* 266–7; Villiers, 347.

of the rooms and passages', where 'many were overtaken with sleep'. Their carriages only slowly forced their way through the crowded streets, so that it was 3 a.m. before they all departed, and some of the ladies had to be carried out. The crowd from outside now clamoured to enter and join the plunder, but were dispersed by soldiers. It was not surprising that neither William IV nor Victoria chose to revive the banquet and that this was the last one to be held.[19]

The citizens of the capital were treated, in compensation, to a great fête in Hyde Park which it was estimated was attended by half a million people, ending with fireworks: 'Nothing was to be seen or heard but sounds of pleasure and festivity', Scott wrote. It was all, noted Croker, a mixture of splendour, good order and good luck.

The coronation restored things to normal. It effectively completed the revival in the people's loyalty to the crown and constitution after a period of doubt and anxiety. George himself sought to capitalize on the event by showing himself more to his people, and in particular by embarking on tours to Ireland and Scotland, where, despite the long past history of tensions between the kingdoms, the disaffection prevalent in London was less evident and the personal response to the monarch more welcoming.[20] George was determined that his reign would restore the prestige and traditional magnificence of his throne and the people's response heralded the creation of a new royalism which was to carry the monarchy through the next century and beyond. It was not the least of his services to his country.

[19] Wright and Smith, *Parliament Past and Present,* 198–9.

[20] Lockhart, Scott (1902), vi, 318; Croker to Peel, 24 July 1821: Croker, i, 196; Webster, 5–6.

Chapter 17

KING OF THREE DOMINIONS

Even before he became Regent, George IV had nursed a desire to visit his Irish subjects and an ambition to try to heal the religious and political differences which divided his kingdoms. As far back as his marriage to Maria Fitzherbert who, though not Irish, was a Roman Catholic, he had taken a sympathetic view of the Irish cause, and during the 1790s he had twice offered to go to try to bring that unhappy country into a closer relationship with England and to form a common cause against the (anti-religious) French Revolution. Every time, his interest was ignored by the King and Prime Minister and his offer rejected. The Act of Union which came into force on the first day of the new century was designed by Pitt merely to bring Ireland under more direct British control and owed nothing to the Prince's advocacy of conciliation. Whatever faint resemblance it bore to his views was vitiated by his father's stubborn refusal to consider the slightest concession to or conciliation of the Catholics.

After 1807, George too drifted away from his former sympathetic attitude. Most contemporaries followed the Whigs, towards whom he also now cooled, in attributing his change of mind to the malign influence of the Protestant-minded Lady Hertford who had displaced Maria Fitzherbert in his affections, though not, in the end, in his heart. This, as has already been argued, is a superficial view. George's political attitude was more influenced by his growing desire as he grew older to stand better with his father and family, his disillusionment with the Whigs after Fox's death, and his commitment to the Protestant Anglican Church as the centre and safeguard of English national independence. The increasingly radical attitude of many Irish Catholic leaders towards the connection with England, and the building up of organizations like the Catholic Committee and, later, Daniel O'Connell's radical agitation among the peasantry, also played their part.

Yet George's old sympathies were dormant rather than dead, and it was suspected that they might revive under the influence of Lady Conyngham, who was called 'a protectress of the Catholics'. Mme de Lieven found her studying tomes of theology in an attempt to prove to George that his coronation oath did not forbid him to allow Catholics into public office[1] – a more useful and praiseworthy occupation, one might think, than those usually ascribed to royal mistresses. George however was no more willing to take his opinions from his notional mistress than he had been with her predecessor. He had a sincere belief in the supremacy of the Anglican faith, which, like many, he regarded as intimately bound up with the legitimacy of the Protestant succession and therefore the lawful title of the Hanoverian dynasty to the throne. Opposition to legal equality for the King's Catholic subjects was grounded in political expediency rather than in religious bigotry. There was no necessary conflict between affection for the Irish people and political proscription of their religion.

George had always professed himself 'Irish at heart'. He was attracted to the qualities which many Englishmen found congenial in their conventional view of the Irish character – warmth, impulsiveness, generosity, a degree of fecklessness, and intense personal charm. They were in truth qualities which George himself possessed in full measure. At the time of the first regency crisis, when the Irish parliament had begged him to accept the unrestricted power of Regent of Ireland, he had announced himself as 'a most determined [sc. complete] Irishman',[2] and in a sense it was so. He had always admired talented Irishmen – Burke, Sheridan, Tom Moore – and appreciated the light-heartedness of the Irish approach to life. Like a true Irishman he loved music and singing, drinking and carousing, parties and the uninhibited enjoyment of the company of like-minded friends. As soon as he became King he determined to visit his Irish kingdom and as soon as he was free of the toils of the 'Queen's affair' and safely crowned he set off.

His journey was momentarily delayed by his wife's last hindrance – her sudden death as he was on his way to Holyhead. The news hardly dismayed him: there is the famous story that when a courtier had brought him the news of Napoleon's death in May 1821 with the words 'Sire, your greatest enemy is dead', the King exclaimed 'Is she, by God!' However, he declared that 'every regard to decorum and decency' would be observed and, whether genuinely or not, he did appear to be affected. He took the Home Secretary's advice and broke off his journey for a few days to stay at Lord Anglesey's house, Plas Newydd, as a mark of bereavement.[3] He could not, however, disguise his true feelings for long. In an extraordinary letter written from Holyhead to Sir William Knighton who had now become his intimate confidant, he wrote:

[1] Richardson, 215; Quennell (ed.), *Lieven–Metternich Letters*, 4 March 1821: 124.

[2] Richardson, 95, 228.

[3] George to Knighton [7 Aug. 1821]: RA 22533–4; George to Liverpool, 27 July 1821; Liverpool to George [7 Aug.]: *LG4*, ii, 451–2; Aspinall (ed.), *Diary of . . . Hobhouse*, 71–3.

> The blessing, which the protecting Hand of God, in his mercy, has bestowed upon me, in this recent event, is so great, & so incalculable in every point one can consider it & view it, whether as to the past (but what is of more importance, in all its consequences for the future, especially as I trust that it affords me a fair prospect, of real & true happiness for the rest of my days) that I even yet can hardly bring myself to believe that it is really so . . . it has literally turned one almost quite topsy-turvy. . . .

He assured his correspondent that 'You may however depend my best & Dst of friends, & mentors, upon my observing the utmost caution in my conduct, during the whole of my stay in Ireland'. The news must nevertheless have contributed to the happiness he was to express in his public utterances at his pleasure in visiting this island.[4]

The steam packet bearing him across St George's Channel sailed on his birthday, and his equerry recorded that 'we drank his health in sight of Irish land' during a 'most delightful passage of six hours and a half'. Croker, in attendance as Secretary to the Admiralty, another Irishman who developed an affection for his royal master, observed that he was 'uncommonly well . . . and gayer than it might be proper to tell' and 'partook most abundantly of goose pie and whiskey'. It was an appropriate prelude to a visit which was a roaring success from the start: 'a strange madness' seized the Irish and 'there was nothing thought of but processions, and feasting, and loyalty'. 'Never was Ireland so unanimous in its past history as it was in 1821, when giving a reception to their beloved monarch, George the Fourth', wrote a later nineteenth-century commentator.[5]

The royal party landed on Irish soil at Howth at 4.30 in the afternoon of 12 August and drove to Viceregal Lodge in Phoenix Park, escorted not by soldiers but by crowds of the Irish people on horseback, in carriages and other conveyances or on foot, the crowds growing by the minute as they passed. A Mr Palmer of Norwich who was present estimated that at least 6,000 horsemen rode to Dunleary to welcome him. At the Lodge the King made an impromptu speech expressing 'the gratification I feel . . . by your escorting me to my *very door*' and declaring that despite the 'particular circumstances [which] have occurred . . . this is one of the happiest days of my life. . . . My heart has always been Irish. From the day it first beat, I have loved Ireland'. He dismissed them to drink his health as he would drink theirs – 'in a bumper of Irish whiskey punch'. He then shook hands with everyone

[4] George to Knighton, 10 Aug. 1821: RA Add. Geo. 3/50.

[5] Sir A. Barnard to Lady Anne Barnard, 13 Aug. 1821: A. Powell, *Barnard Letters*, 294; Croker's diary, 11–13 Aug.: Croker, i, 201; V., Lord Cloncurry, *Personal Recollections*, 277; S.H. Burke, *Ireland 60 Years Ago*, 1.

who could reach him, a gesture which won the hearts of all, including the lowliest who were present. He then remained in seclusion as a gesture of respect to the late Queen until the 17th, when his royal entry into Dublin took place amid scenes of enthusiasm.[6]

The procession contained, Croker said, 'more carriages and horsemen than I thought Dublin could have afforded', stretching for at least an Irish mile. Harriet Arbuthnot heard that 'it beat the Coronation . . . in crowd & in the enthusiasm of the people'. The Lord Mayor offered the keys of the city at the end of Sackville Street, the King wearing the Order of St Patrick over his regimentals and standing up in his barouche, holding up his hat prominently adorned with a large bunch of shamrock and laying his hand over his heart. The crowd milled round the barouche for an hour, shaking it with their movements so that the noblemen in the carriage had to steady him with their arms. At last they moved on to the Castle where he received several loyal addresses. The weather was fine if hazy; the King declared it was 'just the day he wished for'. It was spoilt only by the arrival of news from London of the casualties at the confrontation at Hyde Park between the troops and the crowd trying to divert Caroline's funeral procession from the official route. Croker reported that George was greatly distressed – 'it affects him certainly more deeply than I should have expected' – and it confirmed his determination to get rid of Liverpool and his government, whom he blamed for bungling the affair.[7]

On the next day there was a military review in Phoenix Park, including a march-past by the children of the Soldiers' Orphan School which Croker found very touching, and on the 19th a church service 'where, what with chaunting long Te Deums and anthems, they kept him exactly three hours'. On the 20th he held an investiture and received various addresses, including one from the Catholic bishops which Croker disapproved of as in 'bad taste; it talked too much of politics' in an 'unseemly . . . tone'. A levee followed, attended by 2,000 people, 'wonderfully crowded'. The following day there was a drawing room where Croker thought upwards of 1,000 ladies, all rich and respectable, were presented. It was 'quite equal, except as to jewels and titles, to any we had seen at St James's'. George added to his popularity by specifying 'Irish manufacture to be worn' on the invitations. On the 23rd the City gave a splendid dinner with 400 guests in a specially built room representing 'the interior circular court of a Moorish palace open to the sky; the battlements were a gallery filled with ladies, music, and a company of halberdiers, in spanish dresses of light blue silk as a guard of honour to the King'. George's taste for the theatrical was no doubt

[6] Burke, 4–7.
[7] Ibid., 14–15; Croker, i, 202.

gratified: 'the whole was gay, graceful, and grand', reported Croker, though the music was 'poor and scattered'. This was not the end of the festivities, for on the 24th Dublin society was treated to 'a splendid and profuse breakfast in a royal pavilion and in about thirty other tents' containing seats at tables for 900, with a further 300 present, presumably standing. George was now tiring of the endless round of formalities and was anxious to get away for his private visit to the Conynghams' castle at Slane. His haste in cutting short the civilities to his guests at the close of this function caused some criticism.[8]

At Slane the King was able to relax for three days in a more intimate atmosphere. Besides his hosts, the company comprised the Esterhazys, Fagel the Dutch ambassador, Bloomfield, the Attorney and Solicitor-General, and Croker, who thought it 'the pleasantest dinner I almost ever was at'. The King was 'in excellent tone and spirits' after his triumphs in Dublin, despite heavy rain and 'some oppressive loyalty' displayed by great crowds in the morning at church. On the final Monday back in Dublin there was another formal dinner at Trinity College but though the King was 'much pleased' he was visibly tiring and retired half an hour too soon, again apparently displeasing some of the guests and undergraduates. As before, he was anxious to get away from the formalities and retire to the domestic scene.[9]

George's visit aroused demonstrations of affection from those Irish who came to cheer and enjoy the festivities, but it contributed little if anything to the course of Anglo-Irish relations in the longer term. On his side, it gratified his love of grand and spectacular ceremonies and made him feel loved by his people, an emotional response very typical of his character, but essentially superficial. It did not convert him to the cause of Catholic emancipation, despite the address of the Catholic bishops which pointed out that four-fifths of the population were of that religious affiliation, nor did it touch on the deep-seated economic and agrarian problems of Ireland which unrestrained population growth and land shortage were leading towards the ultimate disaster of the Great Famine twenty-five years in the future. The King did try in his speeches to promote Irish cloth manufactures and encourage the Irish gentry to live on their estates but if George felt that his visit had contributed anything more than a temporary and essentially transitory glow he would have deceived himself. There is indeed no evidence that he considered it in any other light than that of a personal triumph. Croker thought that the visit had soothed Anglo-Irish relations for the moment, but 'Human passions will break out again'.[10]

[8] Croker, i, 203–6; Burke, 24; *Arbuthnot*, i, 115.
[9] Croker, i, 206–7.
[10] Ibid., 214–15.

There was no doubt about the popularity George himself had aroused. The first of the Hanoverian monarchs to visit Ireland and the first to show publicly affection to his Irish subjects, he captivated the crowds by his manners and the gentry and nobility by his courtesy and familiarity. Whether, as the address of the citizens of Dublin on his departure declared, he had 'banished every bad passion and united six millions of a grateful people in a bond of brotherly love to one another, and of affectionate attachment to your Majesty's person and throne' was any more than flattery may be questioned, but as Scott wrote to Maria Edgeworth, 'If there was no better result to the King's journey than that single temporary union of feelings and interests it cannot have been made in vain'. It showed too that he had the ability and the genuine qualities to appeal to the people and to be a well-loved monarch. It was sad that he created so few opportunities in his lifetime to show that side of his character and that circumstances as well as his own failure always to live up to the best he was capable of robbed him of the popularity he could have had.

The King left Dunleary (named Kingstown in his honour, to revert to the Irish equivalent of its original name after the separation in 1922) on 3 September, to the accompaniment of the cheering and waving of immense numbers lining the hills and beaches. Even Daniel O'Connell joined in the tributes, presenting a laurel crown at the head of the Catholic deputation: the King shook his hand 'in a friendly manner'.[11] Reality awaited him at the end of his voyage from what had seemed almost a Utopian interlude. The aftermath of Caroline's death and funeral had now to be faced. Caroline's death had not spoiled his visit but the bungled Hyde Park incident angered him: it was, Liverpool told Croker, 'the *great sin* of which the King now accused the ministers'. Croker believed it merely reinforced George's existing belief that Liverpool was 'captious, jealous and impracticable' and objected to everything the King wanted. He still blamed his ministers for the failure to get him his divorce, and for the public obloquy he had been subjected to during the 'trial'. Now the blame for Hyde Park was laid at their door. His stay at Slane had probably confirmed his feelings, for Lady Conyngham was suspected to be whiggishly inclined and, according to Croker, was being assiduously courted by Lord Grey, though George's own dislike of the Whig leader was too strong for that to be effective. Nevertheless, George's irritation with his Prime Minister was very obvious as he set off only three weeks afterwards for a visit to another of his dominions, the Electorate (now the kingdom) of Hanover.[12]

[11] Burke, 27–8; Scott to Maria Edgeworth, Oct. 1821: *Letters of Maria Edgeworth and Anna Letitia Barbauld*, 25–6.
[12] Croker, i, 209, 198.

George's departure just before one o'clock on 24 September was clouded by these worries and by ill health. He intercepted Croker on his way, saying 'he was not well, and that he was tired of his journey before he began it'. He complained that he was not up to the exertions of a state visit, and the beginning of his travels seemed to bear out his forebodings. He left Ramsgate – he was determined not to show any favour to the citizens of Dover who had given a rapturous welcome to Caroline in June 1820 – and embarked for Calais on the 25th. The crossing was rough, and on the other side the King's yacht could not get into the harbour and he had to transfer to a French fishing boat which also stuck on the bar, half filled with water and nearly sank. The King showed considerable courage and presence of mind. The royal party, which included his friends and close advisers Knighton and Bloomfield, as well as Lord Conyngham, were welcomed by the duc d'Angoulême on behalf of Louis XVIII at Dessin's Hotel, a popular halting place at Calais for English tourists passing to and from the continent. Here another minor personal tragedy took place. Beau Brummell, once George's close friend and companion but now in disgrace and exile, was in Calais and had sent George some maraschino brandy and snuff and written his name in the hotel visitors' book. George however ignored him. That chapter in his life was closed, and they never met again.[13]

Despite George's forebodings his journey to Hanover was enjoyable and highly successful. At Brussels he was entertained to dinner by the King and Queen of the newly united Netherlands, and kept them in fits of laughter with his talent for mimicry. Travelling on, they reached the field of Waterloo where the King examined minutely the battle positions in pouring rain in the company of Wellington and visited the spot where Lord Anglesey's leg was buried. Two days later at Düsseldorf the garrison marched out by torchlight to salute him, and when they reached Osnaburg there was a general illumination and a welcome from the citizens 'almost mad with joy'. On the evening of 7 October they arrived at Hanover to a salute of 101 guns and more festivities. Hanover had been promoted to a kingdom in 1814 and George was the first of its kings to appear there in person, as well as the first British monarch to visit the territory since his great-grandfather George II. His father George III had called it 'that horrid little Electorate' and never set foot outside England. Now George had a second coronation, less lavish than in Westminster Abbey though fatiguing nevertheless, but again accompanied by the applause of the crowds. Again he made a conquest of his subjects' affections, especially by speaking German, in which he was fluent, and publicly weeping with emotion when the

[13] Ibid., 213–14; Richardson, 237–8.

University of Göttingen, where his brothers had been educated forty years ago, presented him with an address.[14] It was an historic occasion, and as events turned out the one and only time when a British monarch of both kingdoms was present in his German capital. William IV never visited it as King and after Victoria's accession George's next brother Ernest inherited Hanover, where Salic law forbade the accession of a woman.

George's Hanoverian excursion restored his health and spirits, refreshed as always by the experience, too rare in recent years, of popular adulation. He was to have an even headier dose of the same medicine in the following year, when he completed the circuit of his dominions (excepting Wales) by visiting Scotland's capital, Edinburgh. As with Ireland, the political relationship of the two kingdoms had been stormy in the recent past and was still delicate. It was only seventy-seven years since the last Jacobite rebellion and the brutal suppression of the remnants of Scottish nationalism. More recently, the Highland clearances had fed Scottish resentment against English landlords in particular. In the later years of the eighteenth century political relations had been more peaceful and harmonious, and the cultural renaissance of the Scottish Enlightenment had raised Edinburgh to the status of a major European city rivalling or surpassing London in some respects, and creating a closer affinity between the intellectual circles of both cities. Scots had also made many distinguished contributions to British life, in the wars of the later eighteenth century and the expansion of Imperial power, in economic development and inventions, in literature and pictorial art, to name but a few spheres in which they acted: and Scots had prospered financially as individuals from the exploitation of these opportunities. Scotland's political life however was closely subordinated to England, for the extreme narrowness of her representative system had confined power to a few families and interests who had proved to be largely susceptible to English control through patronage and corruption. Would Scotland, then, welcome their English-German monarch who sat on the throne rightfully that of the Stuarts?

No one need have worried. To begin with, Scottishness was in fashion among their southern neighbours, and with none more than George IV. His tastes in architecture and the decorative arts might be ruled by oriental and continental fashions, but in literature, painting and philosophical ideas Scottish practitioners were dominant. Sir Walter Scott was beginning his reign as the literary colossus of the day, and no one admired his novels and poetry more than did the King. In painting he favoured, next to Lawrence, Raeburn and Wilkie. In the lighter reaches

[14] Richardson, 239; Stoddard, *Personal Reminiscences by . . . Thomas Raikes*, 187–8; Sir William to Lady Knighton, 1 Oct. and 1 Nov. [1821]: *Memoirs*, i, 160–1, 181.

of social life Scottish dancing and traditional airs were more popular than ever, and these were favourite diversions. The 'Waverley' novels – not yet identified as products of Scott's pen – expressed the new Scots romanticism of the age and tied it to notions of medieval chivalry which called up associations with the 'gothick'. It was in truth almost the perfect moment for an English monarch who loved art, literature, music and poetry to visit Scotland and experience its culture at first hand.

It was Scott who had originally suggested the visit and who took charge of all the arrangements. His countrymen had so far shown little enthusiasm, but Scott changed their attitude by frenetic activity in three weeks. It was said that he planned and arranged everything and, as his biographer Lockhart wrote, 'the Waverley and Rob Roy animus was allowed to pervade the whole'. His more sober countrymen deprecated any show of popular enthusiasm such as had been seen in Dublin: that, wrote the *Scotsman*, 'ought to be a lesson to us'. The newspaper reckoned without Scott's talent for stimulating the imagination of his fellows. He was, wrote Sir Humphry Davy, 'in fact, master of the royal revels; and I was very much amused to see the deep interest he took in the tailors, plumassiers, and show dressmakers, who are preparing this grand display of Scotch costume'. This attention to the smallest details ensured the success of the whole enterprise.[15]

George set out from Greenwich on his yacht the *Royal George* almost exactly a year after he had sailed from Holyhead to Ireland. In Edinburgh, meanwhile, preparations had been hurried ahead. The Scottish compiler of the account of the visit, published in 1822, noted that 'various buildings offensive to taste' were quickly demolished, new prospects opened up, roads, triumphal arches and viewing platforms were built, the Castle buildings were repaired, a 'handsome portico' was erected at the entrance to Holyroodhouse House, and the hall of the Parliament House was decorated and fitted up for a banquet. Members of many trades and professions set about preparing their loyal addresses, being careful to omit or delete any awkward political references, and the bards and poets got to work to celebrate the king's arrival. Scott was nominated, as 'the bard of chivalry and romance', to greet the King and present a jewel, designed and embroidered by the ladies of Edinburgh, in the form of a silver St Andrew's cross embroidered with pearls on a blue velvet ground within a belt of gold. It had a diamond buckle and a magnificent (Scottish) pearl, surmounted by the imperial crown picked out in brilliants, rubies, emeralds and topaz.

[15] Scott's Diary, 11 May 1828: Lockhart, *Scott*, [1900] v, 198; J. Davy, *Fragmentary Remains*, 156–7; Richardson, 256.

George wore it on his hat or his breast throughout the public appearances he was to make.[16]

The crowds gathered from all parts of Scotland from the 10th onwards, his actual date of arrival having not yet been announced. Rumour took the place of up-to-date news in the age before the telegraph, and many made sure of arriving early. It was said that a large part of the population of Glasgow flocked to Edinburgh, leaving their town almost deserted, and it was estimated that 300,000 persons, one-seventh of the entire population of Scotland, were eventually present at the ceremonies. The Waterloo Hotel was reserved for the royal suite, and at Dalkeith, where the King was to stay at Dalkeith House, a dairy and a laundry were set up to serve the royal party.

The royal yacht reached Leith, after delays from contrary winds and under tow by steam vessels, on the afternoon of the 14th. Scott, in Windsor uniform, boarded the yacht to greet his sovereign and to dine with him and present the St Andrew's cross. It was raining heavily, and Peel's arrival with news of Londonderry's suicide added to the momentary gloom, but the bonfire on Arthur's Seat was successfully lit and the King condescendingly donned what was supposed to be Highland costume, made for him by the clothier and mercer George Hunter of Princes Street. The ensemble cost £1,350 18s. and comprised 61 yards of satin, 31 of velvet and 17½ of cashmere. It was topped by a Glengarry bonnet set with diamonds, pearls, rubies and emeralds in a wreath of golden thistles surrounding a sea-green emerald. The sporran of soft white goatskin was ornamented with the royal arms and a thistle in gems, and accessories – powder horns and a dirk – were similarly bedecked. It was perhaps a little vulgar. This fittingly set the mood for the visit, for though the Highland dress was still strictly limited to the clans of the northern and western parts of Scotland it quickly became the fashion to adopt it as a mark of Scottish national pride. It is hardly too much to say that George IV and Scott, together, invented the kilt as Scots ceremonial and recreational dress. It was not without opposition: one observer was later to remark that the Lowland Scots were offended at George's wearing this dress at his levee – 'Sir Walter had ridiculously made us appear a nation of Highlanders and the bagpipe and the tartan was the order of the day . . . I daresay he thought the country all Highland'. George added a taste for the Glenlivet as his favourite drink and chief ingredient of Atholl brose to which he took a strong fancy. Hitherto

[16] R. Mudie, *Historical Account of HM's Visit to Scotland* describes the visit in detail, as does Lockhart, *Scott* [1900], iv, 35–46 and Scott to Lady Abercorn, 13 Sept. 1822: Scott, *Letters*, vii, 241–3.

also limited to the Highlands, it established a wider market through royal patronage.[17]

On the 15th the royal party disembarked and travelled in procession to the sound of bagpipes and a band playing 'God Save the King', from Leith to Edinburgh Castle, passing through dense crowds, including the local magistrates and trades and 'the beauty and fashion of Leith'. All Edinburgh was 'joy and breathless expectation' as the King, in the full-dress uniform of an admiral, passed in a low open landau – the rain had stopped – drawn by eight bays. At the Castle a royal salute of guns greeted him as he entered to ascend the throne and receive the Scottish regalia and the first of the inevitable series of loyal addresses. He then left for Dalkeith with an escort of Scots Greys for a select dinner where the King was in 'good appetite and excellent spirits'. He had already charmed the spectators with his evident delight at the scenes and the compliments he paid to 'a nation of gentlemen'. The 16th was a rest day, while Edinburgh itself was splendidly illuminated, and on Saturday the 17th he appeared again in his Highland dress, which suited his portly but handsome figure, for the levee at Holyroodhouse. An Edinburgh lady, Mrs Fletcher, and her three daughters watched the procession from a window over a shop in Princes Street and thought it 'certainly a most imposing and gorgeous sight' though she added with true Scots candour that 'it was not the gilded coach or the fat gentleman in it which made it an affecting one: it was the vast multitude assembled . . . animated by one feeling of national pride and pleasure in testifying their loyalty to their Sovereign'.[18]

A full week of festivities followed. There was a court at Holyrood on Monday the 19th, where the Church of Scotland and the five universities presented their addresses, and a drawing room at the Palace on the 20th, attended by 500 ladies 'of the most distinguished rank, fashion and beauty of Scotland', who formed 'a flowing sea of silk, satin, velvet, lace, and muslin, wave-topped by great ostrich plumes in fashionable colours'.[19] The King was in Field Marshal's uniform. This was followed on Wednesday by a select dinner entertained by 'Gow's celebrated band' who 'delighted his Majesty by their masterly performance of a number of favourite Scottish airs'. So taken was the king, who was observed beating time to the music, that he personally congratulated the bashful Gow, who declared himself 'ready to die now'. George sent the band a supply of Atholl brose to drink his health and they took ample advantage. On Thursday the 22nd there was a procession to the Castle on a wet, overcast day and on the 23rd, countering the charges

[17] Eliza Dawson (Mrs Fletcher) in J.G. Fyfe (ed.), *Scottish Diaries and Memoirs*, 505–6; J. Prebble, *The King's Jaunt*, 73–4, 269.
[18] Fyfe *Scottish Diaries* . . . , 321–2.
[19] Prebble, 277.

that he paid too much attention to the Highlanders, the King reviewed the Volunteer cavalry and yeomanry of the Lowland districts in the sunshine on Portobello sands. A great ball and supper at the Assembly Rooms concluded the day, the ladies in white dresses and ostrich feathers. The King greatly enjoyed the Scots music and dances. On Saturday the 24th the great banquet in the Parliament House took place, the King again in Field Marshal's uniform enjoying turtle and grouse soups, stewed carp and venison in his first course followed by grouse, and apricot tart, washed down with Moselle and a little champagne, followed by claret and dessert. He was 'most affable and dignified' and conferred a baronetcy on the Lord Provost, to that dignitary's surprise and delight. He proposed a number of toasts including 'All the chieftains and all the clans of Scotland, and may God bless the Land of Cakes!' with three times three. The King left at 9 p.m. but the guests stayed to drink a formidable number of further toasts till midnight.

On Sunday the 25th he attended divine service and heard a good Presbyterian sermon at St Giles, preached by the Moderator of the Church of Scotland on what might have been thought the somewhat sensitive subjects of fornication, concupiscence, anger, wrath, mendacity and the obligation on all husbands to love their wives. There is no record of any comment by the King but he did admire the music. On Monday a grand ball was given by the Caledonian Hunt, where he commanded that the majority of the dances be reels and strathspeys, and on Tuesday the 27th he visited the theatre for a command performance of *Rob Roy*, which he enjoyed immensely and visibly. His last engagement was a large dinner party at the Marquis of Lothian's seat, Newbattle Abbey, at which he knighted Henry Raeburn, now President of the Scottish Academy, and commanded him to come to London to paint him in Highland dress. It was a highly popular honour, which Raeburn's biographer declared 'conferred equal credit on the giver and the receiver'.[20] Sadly, Raeburn, now sixty-six years old, did not live to carry out the engagement. On Thursday the 29th the royal entourage departed from Queensferry, arriving back at Greenwich on 1 September and driving to Carlton House.

The visit was, again, an enormous success for what would now be called 'public relations'. The King was at his best – gracious, dignified, but affable and condescending to all. He showed a deep interest in the institutions of the country and city, received many hundreds of his subjects at drawing rooms, levees and other functions, and by his presence and enthusiasm contributed to raising the national pride of his Scottish subjects. He won the hearts of all. Mrs Fletcher remarked that 'if he had been the wisest, bravest, and most patriotic of Kings that ever

[20] Ibid., 324; W.R. Andrew, *Life of Sir Henry Raeburn*, 75–9.

wore a crown, he could not have been received with more loyal devotion'.[21] It was a personal triumph for him – if the last such public accolade of his reign. If, as one commentator has complained, the enduring effect of the visit was to impose a permanent 'bogus tartan caricature' of Scotland which was taken up by Victoria and Albert and future English monarchs, Sir Walter Scott's 'Celtification' created a 'Romantic myth' and a national self-consciousness that united the whole country and provided the basis for the future rise of Scottish nationalism as a political and social movement.[22]

[21] Fyfe *Scottish Diaries* . . . , 321.
[22] Prebble, 363–4.

Chapter 18

THE KING'S SERVANTS

It has been said that eighteenth-century monarchs 'ruled as well as reigned'. From William III onwards, and like his predecessors, they supervised the making of domestic and foreign policy, could appoint ministers without reference to 'party' connections and alignments, and expected to control the distribution of patronage. No important decision could be taken without their consent. The efficiency of the system depended upon the ability and conscientiousness of the ruler, but although the first two Georges were notoriously deficient in some respects, they retained, and exercised, considerable power over policy and the composition of their ministries. Even Sir Robert Walpole, who was the leading minister for twenty-one years, depended for his security in office on the King's continuing confidence in his ability and on his own skill in cultivating and retaining that confidence. He was always vulnerable to a royal change of mind or the rise of a talented rival, and he fell from office in 1742 when he showed himself less capable as a war minister than he had been in peacetime. The great Chatham, who dominated the first administration of George III, fell from office in 1762 after disagreeing with the King's far less able but favourite politician the Earl of Bute. Chatham's son the younger William Pitt remained George III's Prime Minster for eighteen years after 1783 partly because of his great talents and political skill, but also because the King could never find an alternative whom he was prepared to employ: and even Pitt fell from office in 1801 when the King refused to accept his advice on a major question of policy, the Catholic question.

George III was the most hard-working and politically determined monarch since William III. He was successful for most of his reign in maintaining ministries of his own choosing and acceptability and excluding or limiting the tenure of personally objectionable ministers who in unusual circumstances 'stormed the closet', as the contemporary phrase was. Yet he was the last British sovereign to sustain this position for any length of time. The year 1807 was the last occasion when a ministry objectionable to the King was forced out of office by the King's personal action. It has been alleged that the real culprit was George IV, who as Regent and as King is said to have allowed his ministers to dominate him because of his own lassitude, weakness of character and lack of political skill. Furthermore, the 'influence of the crown' – the patronage resources which sustained ministers of the King's choosing – diminished rapidly during the first thirty years of the nineteenth century, partly through reforming legislation and partly because of changing attitudes, so that in 1830 William IV was compelled to employ a ministry which owed its strength to parliamentary and popular support and which forced him to accept a degree of constitutional reform, setting Britain firmly on the path of parliamentary rather than royal government.

However, there were underlying realities and compulsions which accompanied the reduction in royal power under George IV. An increasingly articulate 'public opinion' was expressed and stimulated through the expansion of the newspaper press, which catered for a public advancing in material wealth, sophistication and political awareness. The growth of the 'middle ranks' of society, of professional, mercantile and industrial fortunes, was beginning to outpace the social and economic dominance of the old landed élite and led to a demand in consequence for a greater political voice through representation in the House of Commons. The financial strains and economic dislocations of the long French wars worked against the landed sector more than against the commercial and industrial interests and weakened their resistance to political change. Governments now had to satisfy the various interests represented in the lower House of Parliament rather than the personal prejudices of the monarch. It was against these developments that George IV had to carry on his government. His reign stood midway between the 'personal rule' of George III and the monarchy of Queen Victoria as defined by Walter Bagehot in the 1860s as a consultative and not executive body.

Nevertheless, there was still scope for the exertion of the King's personal preferences. When George became Regent it was widely expected, as we have seen, that he would replace his father's ministers by his own former friends who were currently in opposition, and few doubted his ability to do so and to sustain the new men in office. It was George's own decision to continue Perceval's cabinet; whether this was because of feelings of responsibility towards his sick father or because he had begun to change his own opinions was in this respect immaterial. Again in 1812 he had a genuine choice whether to keep the existing ministers or replace them by some other arrangement. On this occasion too the personal difficulties which arose in contemplating change were closely associated with matters of policy: the Regent's wish to support the war effort and his growing reluctance about Catholic emancipation lay behind his attitude to the two major parties as they were beginning to emerge. The issues had begun to predominate: George's personal views might operate to exclude or to include particular individuals – Canning or Wellesley, for example – but he was becoming more wedded to the ministry in general because he had greater confidence in its policies than in those of its rivals.

On his accession to the throne George IV again had the choice of whether to continue the existing ministers in office or to replace some or all of them with men more agreeable personally to him. He was never wholly content with Liverpool and his Cabinet, especially since they were apt to thwart his wishes in matters of patronage and occasionally on policies, but his dislike of their opponents had deepened since 1810 and he was inclined to prefer the devil he knew. Nevertheless, the 'Queen's affair' sowed dissension between him and his Cabinet. He resented their initial refusal to countenance his wish for a divorce, and he was enraged by their reluctance over the exclusion of the Queen's name from the liturgy. Charles Greville, Clerk to the Privy Council, alleged that they were forced to the brink of resignation within three weeks of George's accession and that harsh words passed between King and Prime Minister. Only Caroline's headstrong action in refusing the Cabinet's offer of a compromise and coming to England to claim her rights induced them to agree to a parliamentary process against her. Even then the King was not placated. He was furious that the ministers proposed no increase in his Civil List allowance and he had to be soothed by the Duke of Wellington, though in the end the settlement proved a generous one and he was able to live comfortably without getting into debt again. He also resented parliamentary opposition to the Divorce Bill and blamed Liverpool for allowing it to succeed, and he accused his ministers of weakness and vacillation and what he interpreted as their inability to protect him from public criticism.[1]

Relations with Liverpool sank to their lowest level, with King and Prime Minister barely on speaking terms and the King threatening to call in the leader of the opposition, Lord Grey, and to dismiss his ministers on his own initiative. Liverpool however was not to be got rid of so easily. He was now a politician of considerable experience and well used to handling awkward relationships. He had been a member of Parliament since 1790, had begun his official career in a minor office shortly afterwards, and in 1801 became Foreign Secretary under Addington. He was thus responsible for negotiating the Peace of Amiens and for the resumption of the war the following year. When Pitt returned to the Premiership in 1804 Hawkesbury, as he was during the lifetime of his father, the first Earl of Liverpool, moved to the Home Secretaryship and leadership of the House of Lords. He was marked out

[1] *Arbuthnot*, i, 2, 25–6; C.C.F. Greville, *Journal*, i, 24–6; Bankes to Colchester, 15 Feb. [1820]: Colchester, *Diary*, iii, 116; George's memorandum, 22 Nov. 1820: *LG4*, ii, 386.

as one of the main contenders, with Castlereagh, Canning and Perceval, for the succession to Pitt, which he achieved in 1812 through election by the Cabinet after Perceval was assassinated. He held the Premiership for fifteen years, one of the longest continuous tenures of that office on record.

By 1820 Liverpool (as he became in 1808) was a long-established head of government and a figure of much consequence. He was rarely happy in his duties, which frequently oppressed him. In Cabinet he was not so much a leader of his colleagues as a chairman and former of consensus. Unlike Pitt, he did not impress his personality on his age: he was an Attlee or a Major rather than a Churchill or a Thatcher. Yet like them he was no nonentity, and certainly not the 'Arch mediocrity' of Disraeli's phrase. He had a clear conception of economic policy and administrative method. His strength lay in his doggedness, persistence, firmness against adversity, and in undemonstrative efficiency rather than showy presentation. As Henry Hobhouse, Under-Secretary at the Home Department, wrote in his *Diary*,

> It is a most curious fact that a Govt wch carried with it the confidence of the country to a greater degree than any wch has existed for many years, should have been formed of such discordant materials as to have been kept together by one individual, and that individual a man who had fewer personal friends and less quality for conciliating men's affections than perhaps any Minister that ever lived.

It was in no small measure Liverpool's quiet determination that carried his country through the trials of the last battles against Napoleon and the radical disturbances of the Peterloo years, promoted the beginnings of recovery from post-war recession and economic expansion, and held together governments containing personalities as diverse as Lord Chancellor Eldon and George Canning. In the true Pitt tradition which he always kept before his eyes, he was a pilot who weathered many storms.[2]

He and George were in many ways perfectly matched, and though the affair of the Queen at the beginning of the reign led to a near-breakdown of relations between them George could never quite bring himself to dismiss Liverpool. In November 1820 he drew up a memorandum, probably intended for his new confidant Sir William Knighton, in which he reviewed the possible advantages of a change of administration, which might deprive the Queen of the opposition's support and placate the public. He quickly reconsidered: in a second undated memorandum he reminded himself of the Whigs' favourable

[2] N. Gash, *Lord Liverpool*; Aspinall (ed.), *Diary of . . . Hobhouse*, 135–6.

feelings towards Napoleon and of their likely change of 'the system and spirit of my foreign policy – a policy, the successful application of which, has brought back everything to this country, and established a power and friendship with the Sovereigns and Govts of Europe, which England never before possessed' – a policy, he claimed, 'the happy foundation of which . . . I have laid during my Regency'. He also feared that they would insist on Catholic emancipation, against which 'my own conscientious feelings' had been strengthened by 'the pure and exalted spirit of my ever revered father'. They were also pledged to financial retrenchment and the reduction of the size of the army, neither of which commended itself to him. Finally, he conceded that although Liverpool's government 'might have consulted my feelings more' and had subjected him to 'vindictive persecutions, [and] the lowering abuse to my character' which he had had to suffer, nevertheless 'they have been a good Govt for the country'. He concluded that he must maintain 'a determination to persevere, a thorough trust in Providence, a good conscience, a high principle and sentiment of honour, and a firmness of action in decision' and that 'yielding in the smallest particular' would mean '*instant perdition to me*' and loss of personal character as well as of 'all political and moral influence, weight, and authority to the Crown, for ever'. These high-flown sentiments showed clearly enough the direction the King's thoughts were taking under Knighton's influence. The approach to Grey was never made, though the Whig leader was said to have delayed his departure for Northumberland for the purpose.[3]

Relations were still tense, however. In December 1820 Canning at last resigned. The government's refusal to adopt his advice, to give the Queen what she asked for in the confident expectation that she would cease to cause trouble and would retire to Italy for good, determined him to part company with them. The King's response, Charles Arbuthnot told his wife, was 'very cold, merely saying he was not surprised, tho' sorry to lose so able a servant'. George was angry that Canning's followers in the Lords had voted against the second reading of the Bill of Pains and Penalties, and he had never forgiven him for what he called, in his memorandum of 22 November 1820, his 'open avowal of a criminal intercourse with the Pcess'. Harriet Arbuthnot, who always disliked Canning, thought it good riddance and hoped that Peel, 'who certainly has many partizans', would replace him. Liverpool also hoped to bring in Peel in Canning's place, but Peel hung back, waiting to see how matters would turn out, and the government was temporarily patched up.[4]

[3] George's memoranda [Nov. 1820]: *LG4*, ii, 388–93; *Arbuthnot*, i, 57, 59.

[4] *Arbuthnot*, i, 55–7, 60; Hinde, *Canning*, 303, 305; Liverpool to George, 4 Jan. [1821]: *LG4*, ii, 401; Aspinall (ed.), *Diary of . . . Hobhouse*, 45.

Liverpool saw Canning's retreat as temporary. In the longer term he wanted to strengthen the Cabinet by bringing Canning back and also bringing in Peel and the Grenville group who were now disenchanted with their previous alliance with Grey and the Whigs, and anxious to enjoy the fruits of patronage again. However, personal jealousies stood in the way and, not least, the King was obstructive. His relations with the Prime Minister were still abrasive: in late February he was reported to have 'abused Lord Liverpool, called him all sorts of names' for three hours in an interview with William Wellesley-Pole, Wellington's elder brother, and though Harriet Arbuthnot tartly commented that 'the King was such a blockhead nobody minded what he said', Liverpool said 'he was weary of office & of serving such a master' and would resign as soon as he could. Wellington declared that 'no men with the feelings of gentlemen could go on being talked of by the King as they were'. He thought however that George merely 'liked to talk grandly to make people imagine that his Prime Minister was a sort of *maitre d'hotel* which he might dismiss any moment that it happended to suit him' and that it was mere meaningless bravado.[5]

Matters did not improve during the summer, and even before George's return from Ireland in September the Arbuthnots were told that 'we shall have a great storm when the King returns', with the prospect of 'a complete breach'. Castlereagh (now Marquess of Londonderry) foretold that Liverpool would be dismissed, because the King 'hates Lord L, & there is constant & incessant bickering between them', while the Prime Minister 'abhors him & takes every opportunity to thwart & vex him, & often fails most seriously in the attention & respect that is due to him'. But he thought that the King's dissatisfaction was 'entirely personal to Lord Liverpool' who, Harriet Arbuthnot wrote, 'has a disagreeable, cold manner & a most querulous, irritable temper . . . but he is a most upright, honest, excellent man, conscientiously devoted to the service & to the real good of his country'. His fault, she considered, lay only in his refusal 'to bend obsequiously to an impudent, avaricious mistress'. Whatever the reason, the breach remained and after his return from Ireland George actually refused to see Liverpool to discuss ministerial arrangements. The King apparently believed that his ministers wished to reduce him to powerlessness, while on the other side the ministers resented what they saw as the atmosphere of intrigue and personal ambition around the sovereign. The unpleasant atmosphere was no doubt partly responsible for the King's mood as he set out for the next stage of his tour of his dominions, the visit to Hanover.[6]

[5] Aspinall (ed.), *Diary of . . . Hobhouse*, 58; *Arbuthnot*, i, 75, 79.
[6] *Arbuthnot*, i, 116–17, 121; Croker, i, 212.

While abroad, George was brought round, partly by his confidential advisers Bloomfield and Knighton, but principally by Londonderry, the minister in attendance. All were partisans of Liverpool and despite the King's indiscretion in complaining to Metternich of all his ministers except Londonderry himself, they succeeded in reconciling him to his existing government. Although George let off steam in a letter from Herrenhausen expressing a determination to maintain what he regarded as his right to name the ministers as 'personal servants' of the Crown, Londonderry reported that the King was now '*apparently* in better humour' and Liverpool 'very well received'.[7] Further sugar was added to the pill by the addition of Peel to the Cabinet in place of Sidmouth at the Home Office, for Peel had attracted George's favour. Though George never acquired his Home Secretary's efficient habits of business, they had a common interest in the arts and Peel's resistance at this stage of his career to the Catholic claims for emancipation commended him. They also shared a common humanity in dealing with the sometimes savage penalties of the criminal law. While in Hanover, George had acted to abolish the legal use of torture in his German dominions, and during Peel's tenure of the Home Office they agreed on the need to bring the criminal law into closer conformity with public opinion. They met on regular occasions at the so-called 'Hanging Cabinets' to consider the extension of the prerogative of mercy to criminals condemned to death. George's tender instincts often led him to try to commute these sentences by royal prerogative whenever there was any pretext to do so, particularly in the case of younger offenders. He did not always carry Peel with him, for the Home Secretary had the responsibility to administer the law as it was, and the King's prerogative was now firmly subject to ministerial advice and responsibility in this as in many other fields of governmental activity.

So for the time being the government was more at ease with itself and with the King, who, reported Londonderry, 'says he has *never* felt *so happy*'. He was placated by Liverpool's agreement to Conyngham's appointment as an English baron and Lord Steward of the Household. 'Such a changed man as the King you never saw', wrote Londonderry: 'Complete harmony has been restored between the King and his Government, and he has received Liverpool with cordiality'. The King was ready to set off for Scotland in a benevolent frame of mind, but on the day before his departure worrying signs appeared. Londonderry had been under severe strain both through overwork, and, apparently, as a result of being hounded by a blackmailer with allegations of homosexual behaviour. His attitude at his farewell audience so

[7] Quennell (ed.), *Lieven–Metternich Letters*, 30 Nov.: 143; George to Londonderry, 12 Oct. 1821; Londonderry to his brother, 21 Nov. 1821: *LG4*, ii, 466, 471–2n.

disturbed George that he urged him to see his doctor at once, and on the way north he also wrote to Liverpool to warn him of Londonderry's mental state. He told him that he must not be left alone for a moment lest he take his own life. It was to no avail. Liverpool dismissed the King's note as unnecessary panic: but early in the morning of 12 August Londonderry cut his own throat as his doctor, hurriedly summoned by Lady Londonderry, rushed into his dressing room.[8]

The post of Foreign Secretary was far too important to be left vacant, but it opened up a difficult problem. Canning was the obvious and almost universal choice, but George's ill-feeling towards him still persisted. He had consented six months before to Canning's appointment as Governor-General of India, which would have taken him away from the domestic political scene. The Foreign Office, with the leadership of the House of Commons, would have placed him at the heart of the government, in the most important office next to the premiership, and close to the King himself. Liverpool had no doubt that Canning must be appointed, but he recognized that his own relations with George were still too fragile for him to be the best person to cajole the King. Peel was in great favour, but it was Peel himself whom many – including the King – considered the best candidate. Fortunately Peel was more attracted by his present office – Peel 'cannot talk French' was the reason assigned by Wellington – and he agreed to be Liverpool's agent in persuading the King, while George appealed to the Duke for advice on how to get round the problem of his 'private honour': Wellington assured him that 'the honour of your Majesty consists in acts of mercy & grace'. Within a week of George's return from Scotland he gave his consent to Canning's appointment, though he later confessed that it was a 'measure . . . which was of all others the most disagreeable to me'.

Liverpool thanked both Wellington and Peel for their 'handsome and disinterested conduct' in the matter and George acknowledged in particular the Duke's friendly assistance. He was sensible enough to recognize that Canning's abilities so far outshone his other immediate rivals that it would be to the King's own advantage and credit to appoint him. He satisfied his feelings by writing in his letter of appointment to Canning that 'the brightest ornament of his crown is the power of extending grace and favour to a subject who may have incurred his displeasure'. It was written, as Liverpool admitted, 'with as much delicacy as, considering the King's strong personal feelings, could reasonably be expected', but Canning resented it and even contemplated refusing the office. It hardly laid the foundation of a cordial relationship, but George could never bring himself entirely to forgive those who had supported Caroline. As Charles Greville waspishly noted, 'it is

[8] Hinde, *Castlereagh*, 279.

one of the phenomena of the present times that the King should have Ministers whom he abuses and hates, and who entertain corresponding sentiments of aversion to him', though they were compelled to appear in public as harmonious.[9]

Relations between the King and Prime Minister were further strained by Lady Conyngham's activities and by suspicions of her influence. Caroline's death in August 1821 freed George IV from his recurrent worries about what more she might do to discredit him or about the possibility of her becoming a focus for the discontented who might try to do so. In other respects it made little difference to his way of life. Though he was free to remarry, he does not seem to have harboured any thoughts in that direction, being content to continue his association with Lady Conyngham and her family. Whether he would have proposed marriage if she had been free to do so is doubtful: their relationship was as intimate as either seemed to wish and George was well used to a relationship outside wedlock, having never had any other to speak of, except for the ambiguous example of Maria Fitzherbert. Nor was there any 'reason of state' for marriage as she was presumably past child-bearing. The succession was bound to pass via one of George's brothers to any surviving child of the next in line. George settled into a comfortable existence with his mistress who (unlike Lady Hertford) was almost certainly so in reality as well as in name.

She certainly took full advantage of her position. Harriet Arbuthnot thought she 'has no sense of shame about her connection with the King; she continually boasts of her influence over him & of her knowledge of public affairs'. She was thankful that it was to 'our own power as a party & not to the King's good will' that the ministers owed their places. On the personal level, at any rate, Lady Conyngham undoubtedly governed George's predilections: she was annoyed that she was not invited by ministers' wives to their houses and that ministers blocked her wishes for patronage for her family and favourites. She wanted a court appointment and an English peerage for her husband, and had settled on a canonry at Windsor as a suitable berth for a young protégé, the Revd Charles Sumner, who was tutor to her sons. Liverpool refused to agree, in the latter case on the very proper grounds of Sumner's youth (he was twenty-eight years of age) and inexperience for such an important preferment. George tried to insist but Liverpool was having no nonsense. Eventually he went down himself to Brighton and absolutely refused to give way. He returned to London victorious but on an empty stomach: the King had shown his resentment by refusing

[9] George to Wellington, 5 and 7 Sept. 1822 and reply 7th; Eldon to same, 8 Sept.; Liverpool to same, 8 Sept.; George to same, 13 Sept.: *DCM*, i, 273–6, 278–9; Liverpool to Peel, 8 Sept.: Parker, *Peel*, i, 335–6; C.C.F. Greville, *Journal*, i, 44; Aspinall (ed.), *Diary of . . . Hobhouse*, 62–5.

him any refreshment – not even a glass of water, according to Mme de Lieven.[10]

Lady Conyngham was furious, and spent two hours telling all her grievances to Wellington. She 'cried nearly the whole time', and made it apparent that her objective was 'to turn the Ministers out whenever she could'. The Duke read her a lecture on constitutional propriety, pointing out that 'it was known to the most ignorant that the King of this country could only act thro' the medium of his responsible advisers'. He added, for the King's benefit, for he knew she would repeat the conversation to him, that the real cause of the difficulties between the King and his ministers was George's refusal to communicate directly with them and that he never saw them, but used Bloomfield, his private secretary, 'or some such subordinate agent' as intermediary. His ministers had 'the greatest possible desire to accommodate and please him' but it could not be done under such conditions. A month later the Duke had a two-hour conversation with the King in which he told him bluntly that 'if he did not like his ministers he had much better turn them out at once': the King dropped the subject and 'sat grinding his teeth' in silence and finally 'went off to some gossipping story about Lady Jersey & Mad^me de Lieven'.

The Sumner affair nevertheless added significantly to the tension between the King and his ministers. Wellington warned Liverpool in October that he had never been forgiven for his opposition to Sumner's appointment and that it had 'influenced every action of [the King's] life in relation to his government from that moment'. Sumner's elevation was only postponed: he was taken into the royal household as a chaplain and, Mme de Lieven alleged, 'exercises spiritual and temporal control over all the King's movements'. He even introduced prayers before dinner. He seemed 'very anxious to become a bishop'. He finally achieved his ambition (and promotion to Winchester in 1827) but forfeited George's favour by voting for Catholic emancipation in 1829.[11]

Thus, relations between George IV and his leading ministers at the start of his reign were often volatile, if not actually antagonistic. The King did not always get his own way, and in matters of minor patronage he often had to concede mastery to his titular servants. In greater matters, however, he attempted, not unsuccessfully, to preserve the constitutional prerogatives and the political authority of the Crown, despite the counter-pressures of changing times. He tried to insist upon

[10] Aspinall (ed.), *Diary of . . . Hobhouse*, 52–3; *Arbuthnot*, i, 86–8; Quennell (ed.), *Lieven–Metternich Letters*, 17 and 20 April, 1821: 131, 133.

[11] *Arbuthnot*, i, 97–9, 103, 105; C.C.F. Greville, *Journal*, i, 45; Wellington to Liverpool, 26 Oct. 1821: *DCM*, i, 195; Quennell (ed.), *Lieven–Metternich Letters*, 8 Jan. 1822: 147–8.

his right to make important appointments in Church and State, and especially to determine who should be his Prime Minister. On several occasions, he carried his determination in that respect. His reappointment of Perceval in 1810 and his refusal to admit a Whig alternative despite the expectations of his former friends testified to his stoutness under pressure. He was able, without difficulty, to exclude from office men whose policies or persons he disliked. Grey had no hope of resuming his political career as long as George was alive, nor did the Whigs have any prospect of forming their own administration or even holding the predominant power in one. The later history of the reign was to confirm this revival, for such it was, in the central importance of the monarchy in the political system.

Chapter 19

'THE INVISIBLE'

Behind the public façade of the King's government by his responsible ministers lurked the possibility of more sinister 'secret influence' such as had been suspected in George III's first years as King, when that monarch was alleged (without foundation) to be trying to revive the independent power of the crown through the agency of unknown advisers 'behind the curtain'. By the end of George III's reign the King had given up, if he had ever really cultivated, this kind of influence, though there is no doubt that he used underhand means to get rid of the 'Talents' ministry in 1807. His son was tempted by the heady prospects of secret intrigue to get his own way, but he was sensible enough in reality to recognize that this was little more than a game, a safety valve for frustrated feelings in the face of the realities of politics.

Nevertheless, echoes persisted in the controversy which soon developed over the constitutional implications of the office of private secretary to the monarch. The post was unknown until George III's failing eyesight during the last few years of his active life made it necessary for him to have someone to read his correspondence and write letters and memoranda for him. Sir Herbert Taylor, a retired army officer and formerly secretary to the Duke of York as Commander-in-Chief, performed these routine duties from 1805 until the King became incapable of ruling, but he seems never to have used his position improperly to influence or advise the King independently of the ministers. As Regent, George IV had found it useful to have his own confidential factotum and, despite constitutional objections in Parliament, Sir John McMahon continued to serve him in this capacity, with the office of Keeper of the Privy Purse to the Duchy of Cornwall. A contemporary described him as 'an Irishman of low birth and obsequious manners; a little man, his face red, covered with pimples . . . always ready to execute any commission'. It was alleged that he had furthered the Prince's intrigues with numerous women previous to this period and engineered the ruin of innocent virgins for his master's pleasure.[1] He was privy to George's most private and sensitive papers, as well as acting as intermediary in his political correspondence.

[1] T. Raikes, *Journal*, iii, 55; Huish, ii, 68–81.

In 1817 McMahon became ill – partly through over-indulgence in alcohol – and on the Regent's initiative he was attended by Sir William Knighton, who had been appointed one of the Regent's physicians in 1812 on the introduction of Lord Wellesley. Knighton, seeing his opportunity to ingratiate himself, persuaded McMahon to resign, and established his own strong position by quickly securing McMahon's papers. They were alleged to contain secret and damaging correspondence relating to George's affairs, including letters from Mrs Fitzherbert. He passed them to George, who quickly destroyed them. He then took full advantage of his knowledge of their contents. George told Charles Arbuthnot in 1823 that to his astonishment Knighton introduced himself to him shortly after McMahon's death as '"the depository of all Your Royal Highness's most secret affairs, & perfectly acquainted with every part of your concerns"' and, George wrote, he 'came to make his own terms'. The King offered him £25,000, which was refused as not enough, and he was obliged to double it and also to give him the office in the Duchy of Cornwall held by his new Private Secretary, Sir Benjamin Bloomfield, to whom he had to pay £12,000 to persuade him to relinquish it.[2]

Whether in gratitude for Knighton's prompt action with McMahon's papers or, as this story implied, from threats or fears of blackmail on Knighton's part, George accepted him as 'his confidential friend in all those secret concerns which a life of pleasure and sensuality had exposed him to', as Knighton expressed it. His reward was to be the succession to Bloomfield as the King's closest confidant as soon as the latter could be removed from his post of Private Secretary.

Bloomfield had served as George's chief equerry since 1806, when he charmed the Prince by his musical talent (he must have been the only man to become a king's right-hand man through a performance on the cello). In 1816 he was made Auditor of the Duchy of Cornwall and in the following year was given McMahon's office of Keeper of the Privy Purse, and shortly afterwards the title of Private Secretary. A handsome Irish ex-soldier with plenty of charm, he served George loyally for twenty-five years, but his irascible temper and over-familiar manner began to be irksome. Among his services, it will be remembered, was that of driving Maria Fitzherbert to leave George because of his insulting behaviour to her. As Mrs Arbuthnot remarked, he 'has always done all his dirty work, such as buying up caricatures & the newspapers to keep his own & Ly Conyngham's name out of them'.[3]

[2] Knighton, Diary, 5 Nov. 1830: *Memoirs*, ii, 184–6; Knighton's account of his relationship with the King: *LG4*, iii, 477–83; *Arbuthnot*, i, 270; *Aspinall* (ed.), *Diary of . . . Hobhouse*, 76.

[3] *Arbuthnot*, i, 147.

Knighton sought Bloomfield's disgrace by cultivating Lady Conyngham, whom he perceived as the likely successor to Lady Hertford. After George's accession Knighton promoted the King's relationship to the new mistress: Henry Hobhouse, the Under-Secretary of State at the Home Office, wrote that among his duties was that of conveying Lady Conyngham secretly to Carlton House so that her visits should not be known even to Bloomfield. It was a rather unsavoury association. Harriet Arbuthnot remarked that Knighton was 'a great rogue & a blackguard, with great softness & plausibility of manner'.[4]

Knighton's intrigues ensured that as the Conyngham influence grew, Bloomfield's declined. Charles Greville noted in 1821 that Elizabeth's son Lord Francis breakfasted with the King almost every day and received all his orders, so bypassing Bloomfield's influence.[5] Knighton proposed a method of getting rid of him altogether, by the simple expedient of abolishing his office of Private Secretary. It was argued that the post was inappropriate in the case of a king whose constitutional advisers were expected to be ministers responsible to Parliament and not personal servants. Objections had been raised to Bloomfield's position on these grounds during the regency and they were more forceful now. Bloomfield however knew too much for George to take the risk of his retaliation. He was therefore to be treated generously, with the gift of an Irish peerage and a diplomatic or colonial appointment abroad. In January 1822 the King disingenuously told Liverpool that, as the government was now satisfactorily settled, 'perhaps it might be desirable to get rid of the office of Private Secretary' which 'has always been looked upon, I know, with a jealous eye, both by the Govt. and the country'. Presumably with tongue in cheek, he assured the Prime Minister that 'my feelings are naturally tender and delicate', so Bloomfield must be generously provided for, to avoid 'all the natural and innumerable inconveniences of misrepresentation &c. &c. &c. which must otherwise devolve upon me'. Liverpool agreed that the governorship of Ceylon would be quite suitable as compensation.[6]

The King disclosed his fate to Bloomfield shortly afterwards, in a letter drafted for him by Liverpool. It put the stress on the constitutional principle that all communication with the King on public affairs should be through his responsible ministers, and that the duties of a private secretary should be limited, as in Sir Herbert Taylor's time, to purely clerical functions. As Bloomfield could not be expected to

[4] Ibid., i, 186: Aspinall (ed.), *Diary of . . . Hobhouse,* 20, 85–6.

[5] C.C.F. Greville, *Journal,* i, 49–50.

[6] George to Knighton, 30 Dec. 1821; to Liverpool [Jan. 1822]; Liverpool to George, 5, 7, 8 March; George to Liverpool [*c.* 8 March]: *LG4,* ii, 484–5, 490, 503–5.

accept so diminished and menial an office, and in return for his 'long, meritorious and faithful services', he would receive the governorship of Ceylon. It was not an ungenerous compensation but, as Aspinall wrote, it hardly excused 'the cool, calculated manner of his disgrace . . . for having offended Lady Conyngham and aroused the concealed jealousy of Sir William Knighton', and it might also be seen as an attempt to forestall any threat to make embarrassing disclosures about George's past life.[7]

Bloomfield well knew where his disgrace had been planned: he told Charles Arbuthnot in January 1822 that Lady Conyngham was at the bottom of it and 'attributed all his [the King's] alteration in feeling towards him to his infatuation about Lady Conyngham, which quite amounted to madness'. When the blow finally fell in March, it was generally considered, as Harriet Arbuthnot wrote, 'the most scandalous transaction that ever was heard of', while Bloomfield declared that 'tho' he hoped always to retain feelings of duty & allegiance to the Sovereign, that every other feeling towards the King was completely extinguished in his breast'. The King told Knighton that it was absolutely essential that Bloomfield be '*got rid of*' and sent out of the country 'at all costs' but he refused to be bought off cheaply, declined the governorship of Ceylon, and tried to insist on a British peerage. He eventually accepted an Irish one, with the Order of the Bath and a diplomatic post in Sweden.[8]

After long negotiations and correspondence involving Liverpool, Wellington and Knighton, the King's design was accomplished, and Bloomfield expressed 'his humble submission to your Majesty's Royal will and pleasure, his deep sense of the favours your Majesty has been graciously pleased to confer upon him, and the pain which he must feel at those expressions in your Majesty's letter which convey your Majesty's dissatisfaction with any part of his conduct'. Liverpool agreed with George in refusing Bloomfield a British peerage as compensation and Wellington urged him to take the governorship of Ceylon instead, but Bloomfield stood out for a diplomatic appointment in Europe. Despite his assurances to Liverpool that he appreciated the wisdom of abolishing 'the inordinate power of the late office of p.s.' the King was suspected of wishing to revive the post for Knighton. The Prime Minister warily reminded him, 'to prevent any possible misapprehension in future', that it was George himself and not the ministers who first proposed the abolition of the private secretaryship. He was well aware of the King's future intentions, and it quickly became apparent

[7] Bloomfield to George, 10 March 1822: *LG4*, ii, 506; Aspinall, 'George IV and Sir William Knighton', *EHR*, 63.
[8] *Arbuthnot*, i, 138, 152–3.

that the King was equally determined not to be trapped into a commitment to complete abolition. He asserted that his intention from the first had been only to get rid of Bloomfield, but that it was Liverpool himself who had proposed the abolition of the post because of 'the power and influence which it had attained' since the time of Taylor's appointment to his father. He had assented to the suggestion despite the 'great personal inconvenience' which it entailed: he was ready either to agree to 'try' the abolition or to consider a successor, as his ministers would advise. Liverpool repeated the desirability of abolition, accepted the responsibility for advising the step and expressed the belief that it would create 'no serious personal inconvenience'. George had to submit.[9]

Nevertheless, Knighton quickly assumed the role of private secretary in all but name. He wrote to the King on 7 April, two weeks after Liverpool's letter, to say that 'There is no personal attention, there is no sacrifice, there is no pain or penalty that I am not ready to undergo to shew my sincere devotion, my affection and the real purity of all my motives in what relates to your Majesty's happiness'. Shortly afterwards he was given the office of Keeper of the Privy Purse, from which Bloomfield had also been dismissed, and quickly assumed what George called 'the entire management of my private affairs'. The relationship between the two men had deeper roots than that of master and servant. Knighton certainly appealed to George as 'a very agreeable companion, a competent [medical] practitioner, and an excellent man of business' but his extraordinary hold over the King's mind must have gone even deeper. As a physician, Knighton was well known for his notoriously smooth and effective 'bedside manner'. Sir Denis Le Marchant wrote that 'he was remarkable for the ascendancy he exercised over the minds of his patients. . . . The same faculty followed him to Court.' George had become a considerable hypochondriac, suffering from some real and some imaginary illnesses, constantly demanding to be bled to relieve his symptoms, taking quantities of laudanum, and at the back of his mind afraid that he might have inherited his father's dreadful insanity. His relationship with Knighton was more than that of patient and physician; it anticipated that of a twentieth-century dependent patient to a dominant psychotherapist. He relied on Knighton's advice, counsel and support in every aspect of his life, personal and public. His will seemed to be at Knighton's disposal. He had always craved a guide and supporter since his youth when he lost the companionship of his brother Frederick and his friend Lake in 1781, and the many

[9] George to Knighton [1822]: RA 51266–7; Wellington to George, 13, 14, 16 and 18 March 1822; George to Wellington, 14th and to Londonderry, 14th; to Liverpool, 21, reply 22 March: *LG4*, ii, 508–15; Aspinall (ed.), *Diary of . . . Hobhouse*, 94.

misfortunes he had suffered in the interval had confirmed his belief in his own inadequacy. He was soon writing to Knighton that 'It is utterly impossible for me to tell you how *all abroad, how uncomfortable & how miserable I always feel when I have not you immediately at my elbow*', and assuring him that his 'pure and genuine feelings of affection would never cease to live in his heart as long as that heart continued to beat'. He hated it when Knighton was not at his side, or quickly available when needed. 'I cannot stir one step without your advice', he wrote in July 1822. On his journey to Hanover in 1821 Knighton not only travelled with the royal entourage but was told to sleep in the King's dressing room 'so that he has access to me at all hours'. Even Lady Conyngham became jealous of Knighton's influence and he was nicknamed 'The Invisible' as a testimony to his powerful but shadowy position 'behind the throne'. Knighton's astute knowledge of George's character served him well. He wrote in February 1822:

> I trust that the Almighty will give you peace, and that your afflicted mind will cease to be tortured by the overwhelming inquietudes which have of late made such painful inroads on your health. . . . Do not let your mind, Sir, be tied down by the fetters of apprehension: anticipate, I beseech you, no ill, for I will not believe that any is to happen to us. . . . If you knew, Sir, what I really and sincerely felt, your Majesty would scarcely believe the *extent of my anxiety* and *misery respecting you.*

More than a letter of friendship and gratitude, this bears witness to the exceptionally intimate emotional dependence which lasted till George's death.[10]

For the rest of his reign, George IV's affairs were transacted in the shadow of Knighton's presence and activities. Liverpool had warned the King in 1822 that Knighton should 'have no other character, than that of domestick physician', but on his appointment as Keeper of the Privy Purse in the same year he gave up his medical practice and henceforth appeared at the King's side in all the business of the reign. His influence was unbounded and he knew so much of George's private affairs that, as Le Marchant declared, he 'was [both] loved and feared by his master in an almost incredible degree'. Whether openly or more commonly in secret, he played a part in everything that happened, and ministers had to learn to take him into account. Canning

[10] Aspinall, *EHR*, 60, 64; D. Le Marchant, *Althorp*, 217n; George to Knighton, 10 Aug. 1821: RA Add. Geo. 3/50; George to Liverpool, 23 March 1822; Liverpool to George, 24 & 25 March, Knighton to George, 7 April, George to Knighton, 17 July; Knighton to George, 12 Feb. 1822: *LG4*, ii. 516–19, 521–2, 527–8, 501–4 & n.

courted his favour, and undoubtedly owed his promotion to Prime Minister in 1827 in a considerable degree to Knighton's support and influence.[11]

Unconstitutional or not, Knighton was essential to the King's peace of mind. When the Duke of Clarence's infant daughter died in 1821, George in distress called to him to 'come to me with as little delay as possible' and to advise him on 'other subjects *most dear and important to all my happiness and very existence.* You will be *a great consolation to me*'. More sinister was the fact that Knighton was politically ambitious. It was noticed that during the Scottish visit he was reproved by Peel for making suggestions to the King which lay outside his proper sphere, and that he was allowed to stay in the room during private audiences. The Duke of Wellington tried to warn him after Bloomfield's dismissal not to meddle in politics, but to no avail. He was suspected by Mme de Lieven of putting absolutist notions into George's head. In December 1823 George asked Canning to provide a spare key to the Foreign Office boxes so that Knighton could have access to confidential papers and dispatches, and no doubt the King discussed highly confidential business with him. Mme de Lieven wrote in 1824 that he was the real Prime Minister; Aspinall even suggests that he was rather the real Sovereign. He intrigued to get rid of Liverpool and hoped to further the appointment of his old patron Lord Wellesley as his successor, though Wellesley lacked the political weight to be a serious prospect. In 1823 he persuaded the King virtually to command Liverpool to make him (Knighton) a Privy Councillor: 'I wish to have no conversation on the subject', George wrote: '. . . there are occasions in which I must use my own judgement'. Liverpool consulted Wellington, who was inclined to concede it in order to have Knighton bound to secrecy by the Privy Councillor's oath – he was suspected of leaking information to the press – and both McMahon and Bloomfield had been Privy Councillors. Liverpool, however, supported by Peel and Canning, refused to budge. Harriet Arbuthnot reported that the Prime Minister 'does not consider the accoucheur of all the ladies in London exactly fit to be in the Privy Council'. Knighton was incensed, and his attitude of co-operation and assistance towards the Prime Minister rapidly changed. Charles Arbuthnot warned him that Knighton was almost mad with rage and disappointment and would 'seek occasions and make occasions of doing you all the evil that he can', unless he was given 'his bauble'.[12] Knighton even approached Arbuthnot in search of allies against

[11] Liverpool to George, 5 and 7 March: *LG4*, ii, 503–5; Le Marchant.

[12] Knighton, *Memoirs*, i, 198–9; *Arbuthnot*, i, 186–7, 236–7, 245–6; Quennell (ed.), *Lieven–Metternich Letters*, 188, 324; George to Liverpool, 16 July 1823 and to Canning, Dec. 1823: *LG4*, iii, 9, 50–1; Aspinall, *EHR*, 65–8; Wellington to George, 16 July 1823: *DCM*, ii, 102–3, 105–6.

Liverpool and Peel and in favour of Canning, an unlikely alliance in view of the Arbuthnots' wholly contrary views.

The relationship with George was curiously inconsistent, oscillating between closeness and dislike. Knighton complained about the King's attitude, saying that he never saw him except on business and that he seemed rather pleased at his failure to attain the Privy Council. In October he repeated his criticism of George, 'abused the King, called him a great beast who liked nothing so much as indecent conversation' with 'no regard for anybody but himself, & did not care a pin whether he (Knighton) was in the Privy Council or not'. The King in turn abused Knighton in conversation with Arbuthnot and, wrote Mrs Arbuthnot, 'shewed evidently that he feared & hated him as a madman hates his keeper'. The King told Arbuthnot his version of Knighton's first approach to him after McMahon's death and said that he 'was certainly very clever & managed his private affairs excessively well', but had absurd social ambitions which he thought would be furthered by his being a Privy Councillor, but that that would not be the case: 'He does not know how to behave himself in good company & he will never be the least raised by honours & titles', the King was reported as saying. The Arbuthnots concluded that the two hated each other but could not extricate themselves from their mutual dependence, so that Knighton still had great influence. 'It is really too bad', confided Harriet Arbuthnot with typical disdain to her journal, 'to reflect that all this intriguing & ill humour is going on because Ld Liverpool refused to admit into the Privy Council a fellow who, 15 years ago, carried phials & pill boxes about the town of Plymouth'. She thought him ridiculously vain, for 'all his importance is confined to petty court squabbles, to settling whether I shall go to Lord Hertford's box at the Opera, or whether Madme de Lieven shall be invited to Windsor'. Nevertheless, Knighton kept the King's ear and he was clearly a key figure in any possible change in George's political preferences. As Knighton had said to Wellington, who told him of the decision not to admit him to the Privy Council, 'he hoped you [Liverpool] did not consider him as a *Nobody*'. Liverpool would have been foolish to do so.[13]

Apart from his political intrigues, Knighton served the King in his intimate personal interests. He was entrusted with a number of secret and delicate missions to the continent, whose purpose is still somewhat mysterious, for his confidential papers were afterwards destroyed by his widow, and the volume of *Memoirs* of her husband which she published mentions nothing of his secret activities and little of his relationship with the King, which lay at the root of his influence. In 1826 Knighton

[13] *Arbuthnot*, i, 269–70, 255–6, 317; Wellington to Liverpool, 28 July 1823: *DCM*, ii, 106.

visited Lord Granville, the British Ambassador in Paris, on business 'upon which the King is most deeply anxious' and attempted to get the Paris police to put certain (unnamed) individuals under surveillance. In the following autumn he met the Ambassador to the Hague at Aix-la-Chapelle, on his way to Berlin on another secret mission, and the Ambassador subsequently went to meet a secret agent with directions to interview the famous ex-courtesan Harriette Wilson, now known as Mrs Rochfort, and to discover all her movements and put a stop to 'those annoyances which she had long and particularly of late been in the practice of directing against a quarter . . . in which it was not possible that they should be endured', on pain of 'inconveniences to which she had probably never looked'. Presumably she was attempting to extend her notorious blackmailing activities by threatening to expose to the public the old relationship between Lord Ponsonby and Lady Conyngham, who had once been his mistress. Harriet Arbuthnot speculated in January 1826 that Harriette Wilson was about to publish the story, which would be acutely embarrassing both to the lady and to the King. According to rumour, Canning supplied money from the foreign secret service fund to bribe Harriette Wilson to keep quiet: this, Ponsonby's appointment abroad, and Knighton's appointment as receiver of the revenues of the Duchy of Lancaster, which enabled the King to tap substantial sums for his building works at Windsor, all contributed to the warmer relationship between the King and Canning which Knighton was anxious to promote. Liverpool's health was becoming steadily more precarious and Knighton hoped to further Canning's candidature as his successor. 'Mr Canning is now the entire master not only of Lord L[iverpool] but of the King', Harriet Arbuthnot wrote in May 1826. His influence was seen in the number of his supporters who were given peerages in the current batch of new creations, after, as the snobbish Mrs Arbuthnot alleged, searching 'the highways & hedges' for possible candidates. 'Mr Canning has completely succeeded in gaining the King's favour, & still more that of the *accoucheur*', she wrote. An unmistakable sign of his ascendancy was the adulation of Mme de Lieven, whose nose never missed the signs of where power lay.[14]

Other missions concerned a different ghost from the past. In 1790 George and his two eldest brothers, York and Clarence, had relieved their financial crises by raising a 'Dutch loan' of some £300,000 through an agent named J.J. de Beaume. Bonds had been issued but they were never honoured, and a number of French *émigrés* who had taken them up were got rid of and expelled under the Aliens Act, and on returning to France were sent to the guillotine, while three agents

[14] Note on Knighton's missions to the continent, *LG4*, iii, app., 501–5; *Arbuthnot*, ii, 4, 24, 27, 28, 31, 47.

involved in the loan committed suicide. In 1828 the affair surfaced when an allegedly fraudulent copy of one of the bonds was produced. The Duke of Wellington pointed out that others might follow and that it would save a great deal of embarrassment if the securities were bought up as cheaply as possible. George authorized Knighton to offer £5 apiece for them to hush the affair up. Also in 1828 a report from a secret agent mentioned a French smuggler called Merle who was employed in the 1790s in defrauding and betraying French would-be *émigrés* from Dieppe, and converting their jewellery and French currency into English money. His son Gibbons Merle, who now edited a radical evening newspaper in London, discovered Knighton's secret journeys, which he said concerned 'some money transactions and other business of the King's when he was Prince of Wales'. He described Knighton as frequently passing through Dover to and from Paris, travelling incognito as a member of his courier's staff. A secret service agent reported that the doctor received a succession of large boxes from France which were never opened at the Customs House. The agent doubted if Knighton was smuggling, 'although the boxes look like it'. It was all very mysterious. Was Knighton buying and smuggling art treasures for the King, or was he engaged in even more underhand transactions linked to his employer's murky past? The evidence is lacking, but whatever was going on, Knighton must have increased his hold on the King both through gratitude for his endeavours and also through George's knowledge of his secret information.[15]

Knighton was valuable in other material ways. He was an efficient 'man of business' and as Keeper of the Privy Purse he set himself to unravel George's tangled finances. The King's income, settled by the Civil List in 1816 and in 1821, was now securely established and his expenses under control, but the threat of royal extravagance was by no means negligible and his building ventures at Brighton, where the Pavilion was his personal property, and the continual drain of Carlton House, also his own responsibility, might at any time reduce him again to financial chaos. Knighton reduced even these costs to order, sometimes, as he wrote in 1822, opposing 'some of your Majesty's schemes' but being assured by his master of 'those pure & genuine feelings of affection which will never cease to live in my heart'. By the end of his reign George was clear of debt and had a small surplus of income. As the first man ever successfully to manage his sovereign's expenditure Knighton must deserve great credit, but his constant presence at his master's side never ceased to arouse speculation and resentment.[16]

[15] *Supra*, p. 217; Wellington to George, 2 April 1828; warrant to Knighton 23 May 1828; memos by a secret agent, n.d.: *LG4*, iii, 400–1, 406–11.

[16] George to Knighton, 11 July 1822: Knighton, *Memoirs*, i, 187–8; Aspinall, *EHR*, 81–2.

Chapter 20

CONSTITUTIONAL MONARCH

Professor Aspinall once remarked that the reign of George IV, in particular the year 1827, marked 'an important stage in the long process whereby the quasi-"personal" Monarchy of George III was transformed into the constitutional Monarchy of Queen Victoria'.[1] The whole period from the institution of the regency until George IV's death occupies a critical phase in that process. It was a period in which, while most of the Crown's traditional powers and prerogatives were maintained, their exercise in certain respects became increasingly dependent on circumstances and personalities. Yet the transition was by no means complete, or even inevitable, by 1830, and the monarch still retained much influence. In one of the crucial attributes of 'personal monarchy' – the sovereign's ability freely to choose his own ministers – George as regent and king was able to exercise considerable authority: he was less successful in attempting to dictate their policies and control their actions.

Nowhere was this more evident than in the case of Canning.[2] George's initial resistance to his appointment as Foreign Secretary stemmed, as we have seen, from his anger at Canning's earlier involvement and continued sympathy with Caroline and it was strengthened by the fear that Canning would follow a 'liberal' course in Europe, possibly leading to isolation from Britain's current allies and even European war. George, who had enthusiastically supported the restoration of the Bourbons in France, naturally sympathized with the legitimist cause in Europe, considering that the wars of 1793–1815 had been successfully fought to defeat revolutionary Jacobinism and republicanism. He was also sensitive to Britain's own predicament in Ireland, where the growing campaign for Catholic relief and equality of civil rights was apparently turning, under O'Connell's leadership, into a radical political movement. Canning, however, remained a tory at home, or at any rate enlisted under the banner of Pitt and Liverpool. He was a liberal abroad in that he had no wish to associate Britain with repressive

[1] A. Aspinall, *Formation of Canning's Ministry*, xxv.
[2] For Canning, see Hinde, *Canning*, and H.W.V. Temperley, *Foreign Policy of Canning*.

autocracies but he was no promoter of revolutions, nor could he accept that it was in Britain's interests for absolutist Powers to interfere in the internal politics of other countries, any more than it was their business to concern themselves with the British constitution. He was prepared to withdraw from the 'Congress system' rather than associate Britain with such intervention. At the Congress of Verona of 1822, the first of the European 'summit meetings' after Canning's appointment, Wellington as the British representative alone refused to support allied intervention against the constitutionalist party in Spain. The French, supported by the other powers, insisted on doing so, leaving Britain no other course but to stay neutral. Canning nevertheless spoke in favour of the Spanish liberals and won an overwhelming vote of support in Parliament. From that time, Canning had the backing of patriotic and liberal British public opinion and his political position at home was greatly strengthened.

However, George did not yet see eye to eye with his new Foreign Secretary. He had been forced to accept the appointment by the united persuasion of his ministers, but he had not developed a cordial relationship with him. For the first three or four years of Canning's foreign secretaryship tensions remained and George continued to be suspicious of his liberal attitude. During 1822 and 1823 the King repeatedly told Madame de Lieven that he disliked Canning, thought he had no tact or judgement, was unpopular with his colleagues in the Cabinet, was difficult to work with, and didn't know the first thing about his job: 'I pursue my own policy', she alleged the King said. He gathered around him at Royal Lodge, known as the Cottage, in Windsor Park, a group of personal friends who became known as 'the coterie'. Meeting usually at weekends, their social occasions were lively. Lady Granville reported 'gay doings' at the Cottage in August 1820, with Lord Francis Conyngham making 'a great fool of himself, showing off the presents' he had received from the King, and George himself 'in outrageous spirits'. Their ulterior purpose seemed more sinister. The guests were mainly foreign – Esterhazy the Austrian ambassador, the Russian ambassador Count Lieven and his wife, Count Münster the Hanoverian minister, and the French ambassador Prince Polignac – together with, on occasion, Wellington, the Duke of York, and other English Tories.

Their discussions centred on European affairs, which George, on the pretext of his capacity as independent King of Hanover, could discuss in the absence of his British ministers. Fears that this might enhance the King's personal role or even lead to a 'double system' of foreign policy akin to that once pursued by Louis XV of France were, however, unfounded. Canning alleged that the purpose of the meetings was more personal – 'a plot to change the politics of the government by changing *me*' – but it was more an opportunity for George to let off steam. When he proposed to invite Metternich to stay, Canning was able to warn the

Austrian Chancellor off and the King submitted. It seems most likely that George's purpose was simply to make Canning aware that he had a mind of his own and was not a mere puppet-king, and possibly to annoy Canning by making provocative gestures against alignment with liberal ideas. Canning saw through the game and said to the French chargé d'affaires that it was only an attempt 'to avenge himself for his impotence'.[3]

The issue of legitimacy versus revolution arose in its most acute form over the government's proposal in 1824 to recognize the independence of Spain's former South American territories which had thrown off their colonial status. Recognition held out the inviting prospect of benefits to British commerce, but George again saw the shadow of the 1790s coupled with the threat of another Irish rebellion. As he pointed out to Wellington, it seemed inconsistent to be putting O'Connell on trial while 'making a treaty with Bolivar', the liberator across the Atlantic. He protested strongly to the Cabinet and to Liverpool at what he regarded as the abandonment of Castlereagh's policy of co-operation with the continental monarchies to maintain European peace and the Vienna settlement, pointing out that he had abandoned his former Whig friends in 1810 because of their 'liberal and anti-Monarchical sentiments' only to find their opinions being now acted upon by his own ministers. He saw parallels with the revolt of Britain's American colonies fifty years ago. That rebellion, he maintained, had brought about the French Revolution and all its evil consequences: 'The Revolutionary spirit of those days . . . is by no means extinguished', and 'the Jacobins of the world', he wrote, were 'now calling themselves the Liberals'. He threatened to dismiss his ministers unless they changed their policy.[4]

It was an empty threat. Faced by a unanimous Cabinet he backed down. The most he could do when the independence of the major republics was recognized in December 1824 was to refuse to read the King's speech announcing the fact at the opening of the next parliamentary session, pleading a disabling attack of gout and an accident to his false teeth which impaired his speech. Liverpool, who was less of a liberal than Canning, nevertheless sourly commented that the King ought to be made to realize that 'the opinions which he sometimes avows on the subject of legitimacy would carry him to the full length of

[3] Quennell (ed.), *Lieven–Metternich Letters*, 7 and 13 Jan., 5 March 1823, 4 Oct. 1824: 218–19, 223–4, 241–2, 330; Lady Granville to Lady G. Morpeth, 18 Aug. 1820: Granville (ed.), *Letters of Countess Granville* i, 157; Temperley, *Canning*, 240, 243, 248–9, 256.

[4] Wellington to Peel, 26 Dec. 1824; George to Liverpool and encl., 27 Jan. 1825: *DCM*, ii, 377–8, 401–4; RA 23422–4, 23154–5; George to Cabinet [1824]: *LG4*, iii, 97.

the principle of the Emperor of Russia and Prince Metternich'. The affair demonstrated that the Cabinet, if backed by Parliament and public opinion, in this instance the powerful commercial interest, could impose its policy against the King's personal wishes. It was a lesson George did not forget.[5]

A similar issue had arisen a few months earlier, in May 1824, when Canning accepted the usual invitation to a government minister to attend the annual Lord Mayor's banquet at the Mansion House. The new Lord Mayor was none other than Robert Waithman, who had been a leading supporter of Queen Caroline and, as George considered, had publicly insulted him and the monarchy. This circumstance aroused recollections of Canning's own attitude at the time and the King feared a resurgence of city radicalism under the patronage of one of his own ministers. Liverpool defended Canning, pointing out that since Pitt's time the Prime Minister had normally attended such functions, regarding it as a political occasion and not an endorsement of any individual's views or conduct. If he had not been out of town he would have gone himself: Canning attended as his representative. He forwarded a letter received from Canning in which he protested that he had only followed precedent in attending the City banquet, which was a compliment 'to the Magistrate, not the individual', and that his presence had in fact done useful service in preventing any hostile or embarrassing event or demonstration taking place. He added indignantly that 'I have as good a right as any publick man of the present day not to be suspected of courting popularity by a compromise with Jacobinism', having 'passed near thirty years in fighting the battle with it'. He concluded, in his usual vein, by tossing a compliment to the King, with an assurance that 'there is no feeling nearer my heart than that of affectionate gratitude to His Majesty for the kindness and confidence with which His Majesty has invariably treated me since he was graciously pleased to recall me to his service'. It was a typical Canning touch of the kind which helped to reconcile George to him as a faithful servant.[6]

These feelings gradually ripened into friendship. The Cannings took a house on the Marine Parade at Brighton (now the Royal Crescent Hotel) and as near neighbours to the Pavilion were able to cultivate the royal acquaintance. Canning's private secretary soon afterwards wrote that 'nothing could surpass the good faith and kindness which the King manifested in the whole of his conduct towards him'. George was always gracious and considerate towards those who were loyal to him; it was

[5] E.A. Smith, *House of Lords*, 21; Liverpool to Wellington, 8 Dec. 1824: *DCM*, ii, 366 and Yonge, iii, 305.

[6] George's memorandum, 1 May 1824; Liverpool to George [n.d.]: Yonge, iii, 280–3; George to Wellington, 1 May 1824: *DCM*, ii, 251; RA 23152–3; Liverpool to George, 5 May; Canning to Liverpool, 5 May 1824: *LG4*, iii, 72–5.

one of the best sides of his character. The relationship was cemented by Canning's tact; he appointed Lady Conyngham's son as his Under-Secretary of State, and when the notorious Harriette Wilson of the scandalous memoirs seemed to be threatening to disclose the old relationship between her and Lord Ponsonby, formerly her lover, Canning posted him off to Buenos Aires on a diplomatic mission. Madame de Lieven noted that the King 'nearly swooned with gratitude'. 'I must . . . do Mr Canning the justice to say', he told Londonderry in April 1827, 'that, since he has served me, I have found him considerate and behaving well towards me in every respect.'[7]

George's acceptance of Canning's foreign policy was not the surrender of a weak man to a stronger personality. As the (generally hostile) historian of Canning's foreign policy, Harold Temperley, admitted, the King 'had qualities far above mediocrity . . . was well informed on foreign policy, quick at seizing a point, and still quicker at turning it to his advantage'. He kept in touch with foreign diplomats for his own ends, and discussed policy with them to learn their secrets. He was particularly assiduous in courting Mme de Lieven, to whose charms he was by no means impervious, though much of what seemed his foolish weakness in her hands was probably rather his skill in playing the game to acquire her encyclopaedic knowledge and information for his own purpose. She told stories of his demonstrations of affection towards her and in 1826 alleged that he said he had been secretly in love with her for the past thirteen years, the disclosure 'accompanied . . . by would-be amorous glances'. There was more calculation in this than perhaps she realized. She was a notorious gossip and intriguer and a channel to the ear of her former lover Metternich. In fact both she and the King were trying to make use of each other. It was thus not lacking in significance that by 1826 she wrote that she was getting to know and like Canning, who had fallen into the habit of visiting her for two hours every Sunday and confiding to her his political ambitions.[8] Liverpool's long premiership was unlikely to last much longer, and since the death of his wife he had been increasingly irritable and difficult with his colleagues. In February 1827 he collapsed with an apoplectic stroke.

Canning had clearly set his sights on the succession for which Liverpool had always intended him, but the King, though assuring him in his first interview after Liverpool's incapacity that he was the fittest man to be Premier, warned him that his pro-Catholic inclinations would create difficulties with his colleagues and in the country. He wished to appoint him, but he must agree not to agitate the Catholic question and to have

[7] A.G. Stapleton, *Canning and his Times*, 444–5; Quennell (ed.), *Lieven–Metternich Letters*, 8 Nov. 1825: 355.

[8] Quennell (ed.), *Lieven–Metternich Letters*, 28 March, 14 May 1826: 366–8, 363–4; Temperley, *Canning*, 241.

a 'Protestant' (anti-emancipation) majority in the Cabinet. Canning realized that the Tory group in the Cabinet would not accept him as Premier, and looked towards a junction with at least the moderate Whigs who shared his views on the Catholic question, and he warned the King that a 'Protestant' administration would trigger disorder in Ireland. He could not guarantee to restrain agitation of the Catholic issue.[9]

The King now acted with skill. At first he held back, ostensibly waiting to see if Liverpool would recover, but in reality giving the Tory faction time to discover that they lacked the political strength or support to form a Protestant Cabinet. He first proposed that the remaining members of the Cabinet should elect their chief, as had been done in 1812 when Liverpool was chosen, but Peel objected that this would be unconstitutional, as depriving the King of his rightful prerogative. It soon became clear that Peel, even if he had wanted the post, would not have sufficient support and that Canning would refuse to serve under him. In turn, Peel had scruples about serving under Canning because of their differences over the Catholic question. The King, still pursuing his tactic of what Aspinall called 'masterly inactivity', refused to be drawn into an appointment until the moment was ripe. When the Tory Duke of Rutland pressed him to appoint Wellington he turned the conversation to horse-racing. Towards the end of March the ultra-tory Duke of Newcastle weighed in with the assurance that he spoke for 'a great number of Peers' who wished 'to see an administration formed on anti-Roman Catholic principles and that . . . it would be certain of support and success'. The King answered cautiously that he was pledged not to hurry the appointment of Liverpool's successor and that 'he would act fairly by all'. He would not appoint 'a Roman Catholic premier' but he would not 'plot against my ministers'. He continued to be evasive as Newcastle urged 'the effect which it will have upon the nation' if he did not appoint 'a Protestant Ministry'. 'H.M. seemed to think I was pushing him', Newcastle commented, and 'gradually led me off the conversation' to talk of the rebuilding at Windsor.[10]

Eventually on 4 April, almost on the eve of the end of the parliamentary session, George ended his apparent hesitation and commanded Canning to draw up a plan of arrangement – a rather ambiguous phrase which might or, as in the precedent of 1812 with Wellesley and Moira, might not mean designation as Prime Minister but simply a commission

[9] Lansdowne's memorandum [19 April 1827]: Aspinall, *Formation of Canning's Ministry*, 118–23.

[10] Rutland to Mrs Arbuthnot, 4 April 1827: ibid., 52; Aspinall (ed.), *Diary of . . . Hobhouse*, xxxvii–viii, 52, 127–8; Newcastle, memorandum of 24 March 1827, Newcastle papers, Nottingham University Library (I am grateful to Professor P.J. Jupp for this reference).

to negotiate. Wellington now sought clarification, and was informed rather brusquely by Canning that of course it did mean that he was intended to be Premier. The Duke and his friends promptly sent in their resignations.[11]

The King was furious at, as he put it to Lord Londonderry, the 'desertion by those who forced Mr Canning on him originally', Peel and Wellington in particular, since it put him in peril of a wholly pro-Catholic administration. Even Wellington, so often the recipient of his assurances that 'the glory of my reign is . . . identified with you' and of 'the affection I have for you', was coolly received when he insisted on resigning also as Commander-in-chief. The resignations of the six 'Protestant' Cabinet ministers meant, as Mme de Lieven wrote, that 'Party spirit now reigns supreme', though the King was 'perfectly fair, calm, and resolved'. When Canning went to him, he was in bed, but called out: 'Well, if you are not frightened, I am not. . . . After this usage, if you were to present to me a list of names entirely Catholic, I should accept it, and say . . . that you had done everything in your power to avoid driving me to this extremity'. The King's tactics were paying off; all that remained was to stipulate that Canning's Cabinet should be formed on the same basis as Liverpool's, namely that the Catholic question should remain 'open' – that is, while individual ministers were free to follow their own judgement, the government as such must be neutral and not put forward any official measure on the subject.[12]

George had made up his mind that a 'mixed' ministry would serve his purposes best, since it would provide a safeguard on the Catholic issue, and he made his resentment against the Protestant 'seceders' quite plain. He sent for Lord Bexley, the last to resign, after church on Good Friday and harangued him for three hours, 'complaining of the desertion of his Protestant counsellors' while at the same time professing 'so strong a Protestant feeling' that Bexley wondered if after all he 'ought not to leave him till I could form a clearer judgement of the formation and measures of the Govt'. Bexley feared that any disrespectful conduct by the Protestants would drive the King altogether to the views of his 'Catholic' ministers – which in fact George had not the slightest intention of allowing to happen, as his reaction to Wellington's proposal for emancipation in 1828–9 was to prove. He was, however, determined to show his extreme displeasure towards the 'seceders' and he now sent

[11] Wellington to Canning, 10 April 1827 and reply, 11th; memorandum 'on quitting the Cabinet', 13th: *DCM*, iii, 628–9, 636–7; Aspinall (ed.), *Diary of . . . Hobhouse*, 129–31.

[12] Minute of Londonderry's audience with the king, 13 April 1827; Wellington to George, 12 April; minute of Cabinet, 23 April: *DCM*, iii, 632–5, 630–1, 657–8; Mme Lieven to Alexander, 19 April 1827: D. Lieven, *Letters in London*, 95–7; Sandon's memorandum, 12 April: Aspinall, *Formation of Canning's Ministry*, 67.

for the Archbishop of Canterbury and the Bishop of London and held forth for six hours on the subject, though assuring them 'that he was as sincere and determined in his opposition to it [emancipation] as his father had been, and that he should always remain so'. The Archbishop passed the message on to all the bishops.[13]

The affair showed, as Canning's friend Lord Binning remarked, that 'the King has immense power' when he chose to exert himself. He succeeded in securing the appointment of his own choice as Prime Minister, but also in tying his hands with respect to his major policy – at any rate in the eyes of all but Lord Grey, who had always distrusted Canning and considered him insincere on the Catholic question and more interested in power. Grey's refusal to join the main body of the moderate Whig opposition in supporting the new administration may have originated in personal dislike and pique, but it preserved the continued integrity of the Whig party after Canning's death.

Canning defined the constitutional position on 23 April: the Catholic question was 'to remain, as in Lord Liverpool's government, an open question, upon which each member of the Cabinet is at perfect liberty to exercise his own judgement', but the government would not be committed: in other respects, there were to be no 'open' questions and (in accordance with the King's wishes) there was to be no parliamentary reform and the Test and Corporation Acts which limited the civil rights of Protestant Dissenters were to remain on the statute book. Even with these provisos, as Lady Cowper reported, the Tories at White's Club abused the King and said he ought to be in a strait waistcoat. The Duke of Cumberland agreed. Writing from Berlin on 6 July 1827 he declared that 'I never felt anything more deeply or ever suffered greater anxiety of mind than I do . . . when I see my brother in the hands of such a man as Mr Canning, who is the most ambitious, wrongheaded and insolent man I have ever met with' and a government of 'those very men who for the last 20 years have been trying to dethrone his late father & overturn the Monarchy'.[14]

The King's stipulation about the Catholic question reflected not merely his own strong views, but also the practical situation in Parliament. In the House of Commons at any rate, opinion was very equally divided on the issue, though not in the Lords. In the Upper House, however, as events were in due course to show, votes were much more frequently determined by the Lords' susceptibility to royal or governmental influence. Once the government, in 1829, produced its own bill

[13] Bexley to Sidmouth, 16 April 1827; G.G. Vernon to Lansdowne, 18 April: Aspinall, Formation of *Canning's Ministry*, 90–1, 112–13.

[14] Binning to Bagot, 6 March 1827; Canning's memorandum, 23 April; Lady Cowper to F. Lamb, 24 April; Cumberland to Wellington, 6 July: ibid., 33, 158, 176–7, 250–3.

to emancipate Roman Catholics, presumably demonstrating the King's approval of their doing so, the previously hostile majority against emancipation in the Lords was miraculously transformed into a substantial one in its favour.

The King's attitude towards the Catholic question was still crucial and George knew that it was not necessary for him to command his ministers to oppose it. As long as the Lords remained hostile, whether through covert or assumed knowledge of the King's attitude or because of the Lords' own opinions, the question could be blocked simply by not allowing the government to support it. The maintenance of the 'open question' principle was therefore both essential and all that was necessary. Things would be different two years later, but circumstances were different then.

George was happy with the administration which Canning headed, consisting of a mixture of his own followers or 'Canningites' and moderate Whigs, but excluding six of the 'Tory' members of Liverpool's Cabinet – Eldon, Wellington, Peel, Bathurst, Westmorland and Bexley. This marked an important stage in party development: the Tory party which had looked to the legacy of Pitt was now bitterly divided, and so, on a less profound issue, was the Whig party of Fox, Grey and Holland. This loosening of political bonds naturally suited the King for it might give him more freedom of action and more influence over a less united Cabinet. The price he had to pay was the breaking of the bond, established early in his father's reign, between the monarchy and a united Tory party which was now divided not only on account of the Catholic question but also because of Canning's 'liberal' foreign policy. The consequence in one respect was the weakening of the monarch's political base; there was no major party which regarded support of the Crown as its natural posture. On the other hand, George was well aware that, as Aspinall wrote, 'in choosing Canning as Prime Minister he was fighting over again his father's battle against the pretensions of the great aristocratic cliques who had sought to monopolise office and to deprive the Crown of its ancient right to nominate its servants'.[15] The construction of Canning's administration was a victory for George's conception of monarchy as the unifying bond between separate parties, and had Canning lived it might have endured; but his death, from this point of view, was a disaster. Canning might well have brought George round to accept Catholic emancipation as willingly as he had eventually brought him round to his view of foreign policy, and a new and more permanent set of political alignments, more favourable to the constitutional headship of the monarch, might have ensued. Would parliamentary reform in 1832 and the Victorian monarchy have followed? Who

[15] Ibid., xxvi–xxvii, xlix.

can tell? At any rate George IV is not to be written off as a weak, indolent and cowardly King, but as one who, but for the untimely death of Canning only four months after he became premier, might be celebrated as a truly effective constitutional monarch.

Canning's death threw the situation back into the melting pot, but George was again equal to the task. Many observers thought that Wellington must be Prime Minister, and that he might complete Canning's work by bringing Lord Grey into office, but George was not prepared to accept this. As Sir Henry Hardinge wrote, the King was anxious not to fly to 'those men whom he so lately stigmatised as deserters and conspirators', against whom, Hobhouse wrote, he had taken 'violent umbrage', while his dislike of Grey, 'so far back as when they crossed in each other's way with the Duchess of Devonshire', remained in full force. George hoped to perpetuate Canning's system under Lord Goderich, formerly Chancellor of the Exchequer as Frederick John Robinson and a colleague of Canning and Huskisson in the 'liberal Tory' ministry of 1822–7. Goderich was generally liked: as Lord Bathurst remarked, he was 'as amiable and as honourable a man as the King could have selected', but he was weak and indecisive and 'too good-humoured to control his colleagues'. Lord Lauderdale said he was 'not . . . fit to manage a poultry yard'. He was nevertheless acceptable to the 'seceders' as being free from the suspicions of intrigue which clustered round Canning's reputation, and Wellington was ready to agree to return to the Horse Guards as Commander-in-Chief as the King had been trying to persuade him to do since his resignation.[16]

Goderich however proved to be another 'might-have-been'. The task of controlling his colleagues did indeed prove too much for his nerves, and in a famous scene he is said to have wept in audience with the King and had to borrow the royal handkerchief. According to Mrs Arbuthnot, the King 'got into a violent passion' and 'called Ld. Goderich a blubbering fool'. The Whigs refused to serve when J.C. Herries, a strong Tory, was appointed Chancellor of the Exchequer at the King's insistence, possibly in the hope that he would look kindly on the royal expenditure at Windsor and Buckingham Palace. The Cabinet was at sixes and sevens with, as Mrs Arbuthnot also wrote, Goderich 'laughed at & despised by every body' and the King having 'the greatest contempt for the Ministers. . . . Tho' he rules them, he must despise them'. He later described his Prime Minister as 'a weak and foolish person'. Goderich could not even make up his mind to resign: he did so in December but then said he had not meant to, was taken back, and

[16] Sir Henry Hardinge to Wellington, 9 and 11 Aug. 1827; Bathurst to same, 12 Aug.; Lauderdale to Bathurst, 24 Dec.: *DCM*, iv, 74, 80–1, 174; Aspinall (ed.), *Diary of . . . Hobhouse*, 141.

finally resigned again and for good in January. The King, wrote Mrs Arbuthnot, 'is getting tired of these perpetual worries & of their weakness; he complains that he is 66 years old & ought to be allowed a little repose. He shd have thought of that before he formed such a govt'. They had discredited themselves by their jobbery in patronage and by their mishandling of the 'Navarino incident' when the country was brought to the verge of war with Turkey, who was a British ally. Everyone was relieved to see the government resign. The King accepted the inevitable and sent for Wellington, hoping that the Duke would see acceptance of the premiership as a service to his King and country and not a party appointment.[17]

The King laid down his conditions: he had no objections to anyone except Lord Grey, apart from whom the Duke had *carte blanche*; the Catholic question was not to be a Cabinet question: and 'Protestants' were to fill the offices of Lord Chancellor, Lord Lieutenant and Irish Lord Chancellor. Wellington noted in a memorandum in January that 'Every member of the government is at liberty to take such part as he pleases respecting the Roman Catholic question, whether in Parliament or elsewhere, but he acts upon this question in his individual capacity.' Apart from this issue, the Cabinet was to act 'as a body' and each member was obliged to support its policies. This was the same convention as under Canning's ministry and indeed until 1828 three former followers of Canning served in the Duke's Cabinet. Thus, when the Commons approved Lord John Russell's motion for the repeal of the Test and Corporation Acts, which limited the holding of offices in central and local government to Anglicans (though it was rarely enforced), Wellington insisted that the Cabinet's decision to accept the repeal was binding on all its members. This did not refer to Roman Catholics, and here the King's stipulation held good: the rule that the Cabinet was not even free to consider the Catholic question as a body without the King's prior express permission had been in force since 1807 when George III laid it down with the 'Talents' ministry and it was confirmed in 1810. George told Eldon in 1829 that when Wellington's administration was formed 'no reason was given him to suppose that any measures for the relief of the R. Catholics were intended or thought of by Ministers'.[18]

George IV was not a bigoted anti-Catholic on principle: he had been prepared forty years before to see a measure of emancipation as an essential part of the strengthening of ties with Ireland and the healing

[17] *Arbuthnot*, ii, 141–2, 149–51, 154; Eldon's note of his interview with the king, 28 March 1829: RA George IV, 3/503.

[18] Wellington to Peel, 9 Jan. 1828; Wellington's memorandum on the Catholic question, Jan. 1828; Wellington to Montrose, 30 April 1828; same to Anglesey, 28 Sept.: *DCM*, iv, 183–4, 194, 411–12, v, 92–3.

of divisions between the two kingdoms. His resistance to the measure had grown up on largely political grounds. Protestantism, as Professor Linda Colley has recently pointed out, was regarded as the symbol of British identity in this time of the greatest war Britain had ever had to fight to preserve her independent national existence.[19] Nor was there any doubt that anti-Catholic feeling remained strong in both the highest and the lower ranks of society. The gradual growth of support for emancipation among the middling, intellectual and commercial classes was beginning to change the balance of opinion in the House of Commons. Since 1807 there had regularly been a small majority in favour of considering emancipation in every House elected except one, in 1818, and then it was negatived by only two votes. In 1820 the Commons passed two bills for emancipation, and in 1828 voted in favour by 272 to 266, though in every case the Lords prevented further progress.

Wellington was aware that the tide had set in, and in an undated memorandum in the Royal Archives surveying the whole question he concluded that resistance to all change was no longer a viable option in the state of the House of Commons.[20] In the meantime, the King's Speech for the opening of the session in February 1828 contained a paragraph on the need to review the laws relating to Roman Catholics. Wellington's attitude was, as always with him, pragmatic and more concerned with the maintenance of public tranquillity than with abstract principles. 'I look to realities, not to names', he wrote. 'If emancipation, limited by necessary safeguards for the position of the Anglican Church Establishment and the Protestant state, would give strength to the government in Church and State', it should be accepted. He devoted himself to working out proposals which would achieve that end and put a stop to the Catholic agitation. Above all, he was aware that since the County Clare by-election in 1828, when O'Connell had been returned, although a Roman Catholic, the Catholic Association was bound to succeed in carrying a large number of constituencies at the next general election in Ireland, and that it would do so by the return not merely of supporters of emancipation but above all of O'Connellite radicals who would threaten the government's majority in the Commons and dangerously increase the radical vote. Emancipation must be conceded, not because of the moral justice of the Catholic cause, but because it was the only way to preserve order in Ireland and avert the radical threat to the existing form of government in the United Kingdom.[21]

[19] Colley, *Britons*, 329–34.

[20] Wellington's memorandum on the Catholic question [n.d.]: RA 24648–9, and dated 29 Jan. 1829: *DCM*, v, 475–6.

[21] *DCM*, v, 475–6.

It was another matter to convince the King. Wellington could march his political troops through the 'Aye' lobbies in both Houses, but the King's resistance was uncompromising. Lyndhurst, the Lord Chancellor, admitted to Lord Ellenborough that 'the King was the real difficulty'. Peel also wrote that it would be impossible to sustain the 'open' rule much longer and sooner or later there must be a 'satisfactory adjustment'. Wellington concurred, and forwarded Peel's memorandum to the King. George gave way so far as to accept the necessity to allow the Cabinet to consider the question, but reserved his own position in regard to any proposal they might make, professing 'the greatest possible pain & uneasiness: a pistol was pointed at his breast and he had nothing to fall back upon'.[22] He had sought Eldon's advice on the coronation oath in 1825 and he told Londonderry in April 1827 that he had warned his late brother Lord Castlereagh in 1820 that once he took the coronation oath, with its promise to maintain the Protestant established Church, he would be 'for ever a Protestant King, a Protestant upholder, a Protestant adherent, and no power on earth will shake me on that subject'. His father could have said no more, and he had sacrificed his favourite minister Pitt in 1801 rather than give way. Should there be any doubt, George's brother Ernest was determined to keep him in line. He told Knighton in May 1828 that 'my services are always at my brother's command, and there is no *personal* sacrifice that I am not ready to make at any time to be of the smallest use to him', which he interpreted principally as stiffening his resistance to concessions. Wellington was well aware of the danger, and as the critical moment drew near, he wrote in February 1829 to beg him not to come to England until the matter was settled – which was enough to bring the Duke hotfoot to London by the 14th.[23]

George was now in the middle of a tug of war between Wellington and Cumberland, pulled this way and that in real agony and distress of mind. Lord Ellenborough chronicled events in his diary. On 19 February Cumberland made 'a violent declaration of his opinions' in the House of Lords the day before the Cabinet began consideration of a relief bill. On the 25th Wellington travelled to Windsor and had a 'very disagreeable' conversation with the King: 'the Duke of Cumberland has had great effect upon him', Ellenborough wrote. George however caved in when Wellington went again on the following day and in an interview lasting six hours 'had *entire success*' to the extent that the King agreed not only to the Cabinet's proposal but to asking

[22] Peel to Wellington, 12 Jan. 1829: ibid., v, 435–40; Edward, Lord Ellenborough, *Diary*, i, 142.

[23] Eldon's minute on the coronation oath [?1825]: *LG4*, iii, 117–23: Cumberland to Knighton, 17 May 1828: RA 51068–9; Wellington to Cumberland, 2 Feb. 1829: RA Add. 15/126 and *DCM*, v, 482–3.

Cumberland to go abroad. George was 'in a very agitated state, and even spoke of abdicating'. Wellington said that he was obliged to speak in 'very peremptory language' and that 'he never witnessed a more painful scene. He was so evidently insane.' Ernest however was not done yet, and for another week the battle raged to and fro, ending with another three-hour interview between Wellington and the King, from his bed. The Duke made it plain that the government would resign if he did not accept their advice; and of course the opposition was equally committed to the Catholics, so that, as Lady Conyngham and Knighton assured the King on 4 March, 'he could not make another Government; that he was left alone'. After further hesitation he at last wrote to the Duke that 'As I find the country would be left without an administration, I have decided to yield my opinion to *that* which is considered by the Cabinet to be for the immediate interests of the country. Under these circumstances you have my consent to proceed as you propose with the measure. God knows', he concluded, 'what pain it costs me to write these words', and at 7.15 the following morning he wrote again 'from my bed' to declare his 'feelings of distress . . . such as I scarcely know how to support myself under them'. On 13 April as he signed the Catholic Relief Act he wrote that he 'never *before* fixed his name, with pain or regret, to any act of the Legislature'. Cumberland, to whom Lady Conyngham attributed all the blame for George's vacillation, was, Ellenborough said, 'a beaten man': George seemed relieved that it was all over. However, it was the final ignominy: the principle he had adopted during the regency, with all the zeal and conviction of the convert, and with the affirmation of his father's memory, was in ruins, and to George it seemed the ultimate defeat of his conception of kingship.[24]

To others, it might seem the final vindication of the principle of constitutional monarchy: that the Sovereign must subordinate and if need be sacrifice his personal opinions to the necessities of the time and the majority in Parliament. George III would have refused to do so, and if driven to extremities might well have abdicated, as he had more than once threatened to do. He had twice forced governments to resign when they attempted to press on him a policy he would not accept and he had shown no scruples about consulting advisers outside the circle of the ministry. It was his conception of monarchy, which he had handed down to his eldest son, that was defeated in 1829. George IV's ultimate acceptance of his constitutional position, however unwilling, was a landmark. He might bluster and threaten to dismiss his ministers

[24] Ellenborough, *Diary*, i, 361, 376–7, 384, 399–400, ii, 16, 41, 43; Wellington to George, 27 Feb. and 5 March; George to Eldon, 13 April 1829: *DCM*, v, 511–12, 518, 580.

and call in the opposition, but in the end he was sensible enough to accept the limits beyond which he could not safely go. In both 1820 and 1829, his sense of reality prevailed. The change came about not because the resources of the Crown in influence and patronage which had lain behind George III's kingship had diminished drastically since 1782; royal influence, both tangible, in offices and preferments, and intangible, in sentiment and the force of tradition, was still strong, especially in the House of Lords but also in the Commons.[25] Ministers from Liverpool to Wellington were apt to treat the monarch as a cipher in politics and made it clear that they expected his influence and patronage to be placed at their disposal and not exerted against the policy of the government. They anticipated the future rather than reflected their present. Ministries and cabinets were not yet the creatures of a democratic electorate working through party machines, and there remained a vital role for the monarchy in politics: George IV would never sacrifice the dignity of the Crown, but when matters came to a crisis between King and ministers, he was malleable enough to accept what was necessary to keep the ship on an even course.

So, at George's death in 1830, the royal power to appoint and sustain a Prime Minister of the Crown's choice was still intact, with the long-established proviso that the choice must not be unacceptable to Parliament. George's willingness to bow to what was politically inevitable saved the country from a confrontation between monarchy and what might be called democracy. In the next reign, his brother was to be taught the same lessons. The appointment of Grey, with a largely Whig Cabinet, the acceptance of their policy of parliamentary reform, and the royal support of the measures needed to overcome the resistance of the House of Lords showed that the power of the Crown was still a force in politics, provided that it was exercised in conjunction with ministers backed by a parliamentary majority. The reign of George IV was the first one to make this clearly apparent, and in this respect at least it marks a vital transitional stage in constitutional history. It was George IV, rather than his niece Victoria, who took the decisive role in creating the constitutional monarchy of the age of Gladstone and Asquith.

[25] Sir Richard Vyvyan, a leading Tory, told Cumberland in July 1829 that 'the influence of the Treasury must always be paramount in a general election' and that as long as the King determined the composition of the ministry he held a strong card in any crisis: quoted in A. Aspinall and E.A. Smith (eds), *English Historical Documents*, xi, 1783–1832, 123.

Chapter 21

THE ROYAL BUILDER

If George IV's political services to his country are matter for debate, there can be no question that his role in the adornment and enhancement of his capital in the age of Britain's military and naval triumphs was an outstanding contribution to the country's glory. The diarist Henry Crabb Robinson wrote that the master-plan for the development of the Regent's Park/Westminster area when completed would be 'more felt by remote posterity than the victories of Trafalgar and Waterloo, glorious as these are',[1] and though later generations were to alter the outward appearance of much of the work, not, on the whole, to advantage, the present character of the political heart of London still bears the stamp of George's creative imagination. Architecture and building had been a lifelong obsession, limited only (and not always) by shortage of funds and by the parsimony of the Treasury and public towards what seemed mere self-gratification and reckless extravagance. As Prince of Wales, George had embellished Carlton House and carried out the first rebuilding of the Pavilion at Brighton but had succeeded mainly in arousing resentment at the enormous cost rather than admiration for his artistic achievement. Neither was a public building, so the country seemed to be held to ransom for a Prince's private pleasures. Nevertheless, both were important in the long run as fields for experiment and the development of style, providing opportunities for George and his first major architect, Henry Holland, to modify the rigours of Palladianism by the application of baroque, rococo, and even 'gothick' and oriental decoration to produce the unmistakable 'regency' effect which is associated with the royal impresario. This offended purists by dispensing with the 'rule of taste' which had dominated the arts in eighteenth-century England but it was in keeping with the character of the period in its introduction of a freer, less hidebound and more elaborate 'picturesque' style into everyday life. George's personal contribution to this change makes the term 'regency' wholly appropriate as a description of the artistic personality of his age.

The great age of regency building began in 1813. From the 1790s

[1] Henry Crabb Robinson, *Diary*, i, 310.

until that year the exigencies of wartime, financial constraints, and shortages of Baltic timber and other materials almost put an end to public building works in England apart from naval and military necessities. It was also the period when James Wyatt was Surveyor-General and Comptroller of the Office of Works, the government department responsible for building, under whose chaotic headship and neglect of public duty for private commissions the Office fell into confusion. He was George III's favourite architect and was responsible for the refurbishment and extensive additions in the 'gothick' style at Windsor Castle but he was an 'incurable absentee', 'certainly one of the worst public servants I recollect in any office', as Liverpool, the Prime Minister, declared, through carelessness rather than dishonesty. He was nicknamed 'the Destroyer' for his disastrous work at Durham, Hereford, Lichfield and Salisbury cathedrals. His unfortunate death in a road accident in September 1813 opened the way for the appointment of a successor who would be more amenable to the Regent's designs. Despite the desperate efforts of all three of Wyatt's sons to get their father's post – the youngest, Philip, rushed to Ragley where George was staying and burst into his bedroom at 3 a.m. to announce his father's death and reportedly moved him to tears – George had no hesitation in appointing his own favourite architect, John Nash, who had already been given responsibility for recent works at Carlton House and Windsor and who now acquired personal oversight of all the royal palaces pending a Treasury decision as to Wyatt's offices.[2]

Nash was born in 1752, the son of a millwright in Lambeth, was apprenticed to the architect Sir Robert Taylor, and after some vicissitudes went into partnership with Humphry Repton as a designer of country houses, mainly in Wales and the west country. In 1806 he was appointed Surveyor to the Office of Woods and Forests, the department charged with the responsibility of administering the revenues from the Crown lands, which were mainly appropriated to the maintenance of Crown estates. Soon afterwards he married for the second time and emerged as a man of some wealth and property, though his wife, young and attractive, was of obscure origin. The suggestion that she was the Prince of Wales's mistress and that the relationship was responsible for Nash's rise in the social scale seems unlikely.[3] Whatever the truth, Nash became one of the Carlton House set and an intimate of the Prince, just at the time when the Marylebone Park estate to the north of London reverted to the Crown and became ripe for development. A plan for such development had already been drawn up and it was referred to Nash and his colleague in the Woods and Forests for elaboration. The

[2] J.M. Crook and M.H. Port (eds), *History of the King's Works*, vi, 49–52.
[3] Summerson, *Life and Work of John Nash*, 151; *Georgian London*, 166.

scheme, largely Nash's in conception, was approved by the Treasury in 1812 and awaited only a suitable opportunity to be carried into effect.

Nash had grandiose ideas which appealed naturally to the Regent, who became his enthusiastic patron. Both were inspired by the grand rebuilding of parts of the French capital under Napoleon and wished to make London not merely a rival but, naturally in the age of Anglo-French contests for supremacy, a greatly superior city worthy of the capital of the world's greatest empire. Nash's plan embraced the whole area from what became Regent's Park in the north down to Carlton House and St James's, taking in the area between Bloomsbury and Soho and creating 'a daring and highly picturesque conception of a garden city for an aristocracy, supported by charming panoramas . . . of alluring groves and elegant architecture'.[4] It was to be completed after George IV's death by the creation of Trafalgar Square, and supplemented by the remodelling of Buckingham Palace, the construction of the National Gallery and the British Museum, and the furbishment of the royal parks to make an aristocratic playground and a vital lung for the population of a crowded city. The coming of peace in 1815 and the revival in the property market, the increase in the attraction of the capital for commerce and finance and as a social centre in the 'season' all stimulated demand for building, and the Regent added his contribution by example as well as precept. As the historian of *Georgian London* has written, 'it was George IV's superb breadth of view, his intolerance of projects of less than regal scale, that fortified the initiative of others and lent propriety to extravagance'. For once, public opinion approved, and Parliament provided money on what by comparison with the past was a munificent (if never quite sufficient) scale for the public works involved.[5]

The development of the park – soon to be the Regent's Park – proceeded slowly. Nash envisaged 'one entire park compleat in unity of character' consisting of villas 'considered as Town residences not Country Houses' as being more likely to appeal to 'the higher classes' whose presence would give the area the required tone. His initial plan for quite intensive building was however modified at the insistence of Spencer Perceval, the Prime Minister, who considered it preferable to retain the park-like character of the estate; even so, plots were taken up slowly, until the cutting of the new street – Regent Street – eased communication with the West End and government offices and made the new estate more attractive to the middle and upper classes. The cutting of the Regent's Canal which was finally opened in 1820 after

[4] Summerson, *Georgian London*, 164.
[5] Ibid., 191.

many vicissitudes by a grand procession of barges, also served to make the whole project more viable. The consequence was the beginning in 1821 of the construction of the Terraces, containing series of gentlemen's houses, which gave the Park its distinctive character and elegance.[6]

As in the case of the park, much of Nash's work was done as a speculation and not directly for the Crown. Most of the building on the new Regent Street which provided the main artery through the area was necessarily financed by and erected for private individuals and companies and Nash's original plans had to be made flexible to accommodate their requirements, but it was Nash who cajoled, persuaded, negotiated and intrigued to achieve success in carrying out the scheme. As is the way with builders and developers, all the costs escalated, and his original estimate of £385,000 for Regent Street was a fraction of the ultimate cost, estimated at over £1,533,000 in 1826. Nash himself became notorious for the purely notional character of his estimates and the work at Buckingham Palace which he began in 1825 so far exceeded the estimated costs that he was frequently in trouble with the House of Commons and was ultimately dismissed after George's death. Even so, his scheme was carried on by others so that in the end it could be claimed that he initiated and largely achieved the only major coherent town-planning scheme ever put into effect in London.[7]

It was in this context that George's rebuilding of the public face of the West End of London took place. He worked through the Office of Woods and Forests and the Office of Works, the latter being officially responsible for all building on Crown land but in practice being obliged to look to the Woods and Forests for finance. George too took more than a general interest. As Liverpool warned Colonel Stephenson, the Surveyor-General and head of the Office of Works, in 1823 when the latter incurred the royal displeasure by reprimanding workmen for removing a pulpit from the King's private chapel in Windsor Great Park to Windsor Castle, not knowing that the King himself had ordered the removal, the King 'happens to have a Personal Taste and Pleasure in making His own Arrangements and giving His own Orders'. The Colonel was fortunate not to be dismissed and was saved only by the intervention of the Prime Minister himself.[8] George was notoriously apt to change his mind frequently over details and even larger matters and to expect his changes to be implemented, so not all overrunning of estimates was the fault of his architect. It was no wonder that he got on better with Nash, who was imaginative, 'good-natured but

6 Summerson, *Life and Work of John Nash,* 115.
7 Summerson, *Georgian London,* 162.
8 Crook and Port (eds), vi, 106–7.

unmethodical', than with Stephenson who was a stickler for forms and discipline, a rather rigid bureaucrat.

As a corollary and indispensable consequence of Nash's 'metropolitan improvements', changes were made in the arrangement of streets and buildings at the southern end of the new street which affected the royal and ceremonial uses of the area. The widening of the east end of Pall Mall and of Cockspur Street and the formation of an open space – later to be Trafalgar Square – facilitated the connection of Regent Street to Whitehall and helped to provide a grander setting for public occasions. These developments also encouraged George IV and his architect to embark on their design to provide the monarchy with a suitably dignified milieu.

The responsibility for the building and maintenance of the royal palaces was divided among the three 'Attached' or Official Architects to the Office of Works. Nash was responsible for St James's Palace, Carlton House, The King's Mews (the site of the present National Gallery), Kensington Palace and Gardens, St James's Park, Green Park, Hyde Park and Windsor Great Park. Sir John Soane was the architect for Buckingham House – though the responsibility was transferred to Nash when rebuilding began – Whitehall, including the Houses of Parliament, Hampton Court and Bushey Park. Smirke was appointed architect to Windsor Castle, Greenwich Park, Somerset House, the Tower, the Mint, the Rolls House and Chapel, the British Museum, and the prisons. The Pavilion at Brighton was regarded as a private commission and financed from George's privy purse but the remaining sites were catered for by parliamentary grants. Under this heading 'the Cottage' at Windsor, the Castle, and Buckingham Palace were the subject of major building works, St James's Palace was extensively repaired and considerable repairs were carried out at Westminster Hall, the Banqueting House, and numerous government offices. New buildings were provided for the Board of Trade and the Privy Council Office. The reign of George IV proved to be one of the busiest in English history for the building and repair of public architecture.[9]

The main problem facing George when he came to the throne was to find a suitable place to live as King. Carlton House was too cramped and inconvenient, lacking space and facilities for a royal palace, and being situated on a public road, it lacked privacy. Buckingham House, which had been Queen Charlotte's residence, needed considerable enlargement and refurbishment, particularly of its state rooms. At Windsor Castle the private apartments needed major improvement, while Wyatt's alterations no longer commended themselves. George at first intended to make use of Windsor as his main home, but found that

[9] Ibid., 109–11.

more alterations were needed. He did not go into residence until 1823, and then for only two months. For the first three years of his reign he continued to make The Cottage his living quarters while plans for his other residences were considered, Windsor Castle by Nash, Soane, Smirke and Jeffry Wyatt, James Wyatt's nephew, and Buckingham House by Nash at George's express command, much to the resentment of Soane, who considered it his responsibility. Money too was the problem. The country had not yet fully recovered from the financial strain of the French wars and at a time when both the government and private landowners were being forced to retrench, a scheme to lavish taxpayers' money on more royal fancies was unlikely to commend itself to the suspicious backbench members of the Commons. Liverpool declared in 1819 that the most that could be hoped for was £150,000 spread over three years for Buckingham House, and that to be taken from the Office of Works budget supplemented by the proceeds of the sale of Crown properties, including the site of St James's Palace which would presumably become surplus to requirements. George considered this 'altogether inadequate', as indeed it would have proved to be, and asked the Prime Minister to bring before the Commons a proposal to raise half a million. Nothing was done for two more years.[10]

An alternative solution would have been to start afresh and build an entirely new palace befitting the splendour of a new reign, and indeed Nash had already considered possible plans for such a project in Green Park, but George turned it down: he was too old to build a palace, he said, and in any case he had taken a fancy to Buckingham House with its memories of his mother and father and his early youthful years. 'There are early associations which endear me to the spot', he told Charles Long, Lord Farnborough, who had become his adviser on building matters.[11] Another plan by Colonel Trench of the Woods and Forests for a vast palace in Hyde Park was ruled out by the likely cost. Meanwhile, work was 'absolutely necessary' if Buckingham House was to be habitable but no major project was undertaken until 1825. In that year, with the economic outlook now more promising, Nash submitted plans for extensive rebuilding, including the demolition and rebuilding of the former wings, the reconstruction of the hall and great staircase, the addition of a throne room and a circuit of state rooms, a drawing room, music room and picture gallery, galleries on two floors and a new range of rooms on the west side, capped by a triumphal arch and a Corinthian portico at the entrance front. With the addition of work in the gardens and domestic offices the cost was estimated at £252,000, allowing for the use of materials from Carlton House, which was to be

[10] Ibid.
[11] Summerson *Life and Work of John Nash*, 161–2.

demolished. The cost did not include sculpture, which was naturally to be lavishly added and applied, with panels in relief and statues at the garden front. The plans were approved by the government and work was put in hand immediately even before the Bill to allocate money from the land revenues was approved by Parliament. The final scheme heralded a change of mind by the King: no longer a private residence, in spite of George's earlier declaration, it was to be a palace.[12]

George's enthusiasm for his new regal residence was perhaps premature. The final shell was complete, ready for the internal work, by February 1828 but the expected cost had risen to £432,926, despite assurances to the Chancellor of the Exchequer in 1826 that Nash would observe 'those necessary forms and regulations connected with expenditure, which are so essential not only to the Government but to your Majesty'.[13] Work slowed down because of shortage of funds while costs continued to escalate, some at least due to the King's insistence on continual alterations. Nor was the work considered satisfactory. The elevation was awkwardly designed and the wings of the new building had to be pulled down and rebuilt. The Duke of Wellington, now Prime Minister, characteristically declared that 'it was no business of his; they could pull down as much as they liked' but 'if you expect me to put my hand to any additional expense, I'll be damned if I will'.[14] Nash was fiercely attacked in Parliament and the whole project, instead of contributing to the public approval of George's beautification of London, earned him further criticism for extravagance and reckless misuse of public funds. Not long after George's death Nash was dismissed with the estimated cost by then topping half a million and another £100,000 in prospect. Nash was accused of 'inexcusable irregularity and great negligence' and one critic deplored placing the Sovereign's residence 'at Pimlico, in the neighbourhood of shabby houses, breweries, factories, and steam engines; with all the filth, and smoke, and dirt which belonged to that part of the town'. The work was handed over to Edward Blore, whose later front was never admired and was eventually remodelled and replaced in 1913 by the present almost equally unattractive design. William IV, a man of simple tastes, never moved in, preferring his old residence at Clarence House, and he suggested to Wellington turning it into a barracks. The suggestion was turned down, and George's niece Victoria became the first sovereign to make it her main home.[15]

George's continued failure to make his grandiose building projects popular with his subjects was underlined by the demolition of Carlton

[12] Crook and Port (eds), vi, 169.
[13] F.J. Robinson to George, 18 Jan. 1826: *LG4*, iii, 137.
[14] Creevey to Miss Ord, 20 March 1828: *Creevey Papers*, ii, 156.
[15] Crook and Port (eds), vi, 272–87.

House in 1827. There was some justification for this in that it had never been in entirely sound condition since George first occupied it. Nash pointed out that the whole ground floor on the garden side was 'very weak' and that on levee and court days the floor had to be supported with temporary beams. George's bedroom had sunk and the famous gothic conservatory needed extensive repair. In any case it was too small for state occasions and demolition, with the re-use of materials and disposal of the site for housing development, was the sensible course. Several chimneypieces were used at Windsor, the Ionic columns of the screen and the magnificently carved 'trophy doors' went to Buckingham Palace, and eight of the Corinthian columns of the portico were incorporated by Wilkins in the side porticos of his National Gallery, completed in 1838. Despite these economies, there was some public resentment that after the huge sums spent on the house during George's lifetime it should finally have been disposed of.[16] The decision to demolish it also removed what had from the first been intended as the southern culmination of Nash's Regent Street and the focus of the new Waterloo Place. The site was placed in the hands of the commissioners of Woods and Forests under whose direction Carlton House Terraces, designed by Nash and described by his biographer as 'monumentally regal', and Carlton Gardens were built, followed by the Athenaeum and United Services (now Institute of Directors) Clubs, the former designed by Decimus Burton. The whole scheme was completed by Nash's remodelling and replanting of St James's Park.

George was well satisfied with his new palace but his wish to reward his architect by conferring a baronetcy on him was thwarted by Wellington, who used the excuse that Nash's financial failings were still under investigation by Parliament. In his letter to Knighton, the Duke set forth what was the real reason: 'There are at least one hundred pressing applications from gentlemen, many with hereditary claims from officers of the army and navy and others in the Civil Depts, all of whom would be offended by this preference of Mr Nash': besides, Nash's nephew, to whom he wished the baronetcy to descend by special remainder, was a mere attorney – and, though the thought was unspoken, Nash was a mere architect.[17] Wellington was happy to abandon him to parliamentary censure – 'making a hash of Nash', as he put it – and George was unable to protect him.

Of the other royal palace, St James's, little need be said. For some time it had been used only for state and ceremonial occasions such as levees, drawing rooms, state balls and royal marriages and christenings. Within its grounds were several grace and favour residences and offices

[16] Ibid., 320–1, 369.
[17] Wellington to Knighton, 16 June 1829: *LG4*, iii, 460.

of Court functionaries and other ceremonial dignitaries. Some of the royal princes had been provided with apartments in the Palace, including Cumberland, Cambridge and, further in the past, Clarence and Mrs Jordan and their offspring. Nash repeatedly proposed its demolition and in 1826 when he decided to make Buckingham Palace the official headquarters of the monarchy George joined in, but Liverpool objected, partly because it was not yet certain that Buckingham Palace would be finished, or suitable. George did reside there temporarily in 1826–8 for lack of anywhere else in London to lay his head and St James's continued to be used for ceremonial occasions until the 1850s.[18]

Windsor Castle had been one of the favourite residences of George III and his family and since the 1780s the old King had carried out several improvements and alterations to make it more comfortable. James Wyatt completed extensive work on the state apartments as late as 1813. In early February 1805 there was a housewarming party 'of great magnificence' worthy of his eldest son's talent for entertaining. The King revived the Garter installation ceremony and from this time onwards Windsor became the focal point for royal public occasions. The Castle grounds and terrace were open to the public and were thronged by the townspeople and visitors, a facility which George IV quickly brought to an end (except on Sundays) in order to preserve his privacy when he began to reside there. He rejected what he declared was the 'impertinence' of the Dean and Chapter of Windsor in claiming the right of access to the terrace at all times – 'a more offensive and troublesome set of individuals to the King personally it is impossible to imagine', he wrote to Liverpool.[19] He found Windsor still in need of major refurbishment and enlargement of the state and private apartments. After a short experimental period of residence in 1823 he decided to embark on what became one of his major and most spectacular projects, creating the castle which still dominates the Windsor skyline at the present day.

In the meantime, George used 'The Cottage' in Windsor Park, formerly a dairy farm attached to Cumberland Lodge, later known as Royal Lodge, as his private residence and from here he supervised the building at the Castle. During the regency it was transformed by Nash into an elaborate '*cottage orné*', predictably at enormous expense, 'stuccoed and thatched outside, totally replanned within and enormously enlarged' and again altered and enlarged by Wyatville in 1823. It suffered from dry rot and was continually in the hands of builders, but it was here that

[18] Crook and Port (eds), vi, 361–71.

[19] George to Liverpool, 19 Oct. 1823: *LG4*, iii, 30n. (from Add. MS 38190, fo. 79–80).

George's social life and his intrigues with foreign ambassadors and friends against Canning were carried on.[20]

Work on the Castle was decided on in 1824. A master-plan was drawn up by Sir Charles Long, an experienced politician and public servant, and Nash, Soane, Smirke and Jeffry Wyatt were also invited to submit designs. It was decided that the exterior should conform to the period of Edward III, and be modelled on the Welsh castles, Bodiam and Haddon, rather than on the fanciful 'modern' Gothic of James Wyatt, and that Raby, Warwick and others should provide examples of interior décor and arrangement. Jeffry Wyatt was awarded the commission and Parliament voted £150,000 for the work, Wyatt obligingly adjusting his (very approximate and speculative) estimate accordingly. When work began, he requested the royal permission to change his name to Wyatville, in order, as he claimed, to prevent confusion with his uncle and, no doubt, considering that it sounded suitably medieval. 'Ville or mutton, call yourself what you like', the King good-humouredly replied.[21]

A 'Committee of Taste' was appointed, to make sure that matters were kept under proper control. It was headed by the Prime Minister, with the Chancellor of the Exchequer and Charles Arbuthnot, formerly Secretary to the Treasury and now First Commissioner of Woods and Forests, the department responsible for the finances of Crown Lands, as representatives of the Treasury. The Duke of Wellington, Lord Aberdeen, Long, and a number of other parliamentarians knowledgeable in matters of connoisseurship were added. If, however, Parliament thought that these precautions would prevent further expense they were soon disillusioned. Wyatville discovered that the state of the structure was far worse than had been expected. The wall and floor timbers were rotten, the walls cracked and weakened by generations of alteration by successive occupants, and the roof timbers also in need of replacement. Neither he nor his employer was a man to neglect the opportunity for further expenditure and within two years the £150,000 was doubled and further sums were called for, despite the re-use of doors and other fittings from Carlton House, where demolition began in 1827. By 1830 the cost had risen to £800,000 and another £100,000 was needed. Parliament rebelled at what seemed another example of George's profligacy and refused to pay until a select committee had examined the position. The committee recommended that the money be granted for what they saw as an 'object of national concern' but deplored the disregard of economy. Wyatville continued to work on the Castle, which was completed after George's death.[22]

20 Summerson, *Life and Work of John Nash*, 95; Crook and Port (eds), vi, 399–401.
21 O. Morshead, *Windsor Castle*, 47.
22 Crook and Port (eds), vi, 373–93.

Wyatville's alterations brought the Castle into generally its present state. His supreme achievement was the construction of the magnificent sequence of state apartments in the north-eastern corner of the Upper Ward of the Castle, where Charles II and his architect Hugh May had changed Edward III's creation of a great chivalric theatre of knightly display into a baroque fantasy, richly ornamented in the dominant European style of the seventeenth century. Wyatville, under the influence of the medieval romanticism nurtured by Sir Walter Scott, destroyed May's Royal Chapel and St George's Hall, recently described as 'perhaps the greatest baroque interiors ever created in this country', a step condemned by many since and leading the present Prince of Wales to castigate him as 'the greatest vandal ever to have worked at Windsor', but the result was to restore a more harmonious medieval appearance to what was intended to be a symbol in architecture of England's historic past, and to create something of unsurpassed dignity and richness. The Waterloo Gallery, to house the Lawrence portraits of the soldiers and statesmen responsible for the defeat of Napoleon and the resettlement of Europe, the Grand Reception Room, the new St George's Hall and Garter Throne Room, the Crimson, Green and White Drawing Rooms and the State Dining Room made an impressive whole, reflecting his royal patron's taste for magnificence and display to celebrate the prestige and historic achievement of the British monarchy over the centuries. Much of this was burnt down in the great fire of 1992, but fortunately restored in essence, with significant modern modifications, by 1997.[23] Externally the building of Edward III's Tower (then the Devil's Tower), the Brunswick Tower and a new St George's Gate completed the 'medieval' fabric. The raising of the exterior of the Round Tower by 33 feet brought the whole into better proportion, though it was criticized by some. Finally, Wyatville formed the sunken garden below the East Terrace.

The new Castle met with a 'favourable opinion', though some naturally disagreed. Visitors in 1827 included Charles Greville who thought it a 'fine house' but not worthy to stand beside Versailles or St Cloud as a royal palace, considering the expense, and Thomas Creevey who agreed that it was no more than 'a very good Gentleman's or Nobleman's house'. J.W. Croker thought the style of interior decoration too Frenchified – which reflected George IV's own taste. Benjamin Haydon later complained that the decoration in the public rooms was disappointing, but praised the effect of 'a fine, gloomy old Gothic palace'. Harriet Arbuthnot however declared herself 'quite delighted with it', the new apartments 'quite beautiful' and the new George IV gateway 'perfection'. Wyatville had justified his appointment, and George's

[23] Adam Nicolson, *Restoration: the Rebuilding of Windsor Castle.*

choice, by creating what a modern authority has described as 'a magnificent and comfortable residence which . . . retained all the external characteristics of a castle . . . a palace worthy of the British monarchy . . . of picturesque grandeur allied to internal convenience and comfort . . . the image of what the early nineteenth century thought a castle should be'.[24] Not all modern critics agree. The castle has been criticized for insensitivity, crudity of construction and 'architectural deceits' such as false machicolations and portcullis-grooves on the walls, and the raising of the height of the round tower, though from a distant viewpoint the general effect is of a fine and romantic medieval fortress, 'one of the most distinctive monuments in the world'.[25] It was largely George IV's creation and remains perhaps his most splendid memorial.

[24] C.C.F. Greville, *Journal* i, 181; Creevey to Miss Ord, 11 Aug. [1826]: *Gore, Creevey*, ed. J. Gore, 265; Croker's diary, 30 March 1828: Croker, i, 414–15; *Arbuthnot*, ii, 150, 193; Penrose (ed.), *Haydon*, 557–8; Crook and Port (eds), vi, 391–2; Morshead, *Windsor Castle*, 45–52.

[25] C. Hibbert, *Court at Windsor*, 163–6.

Chapter 22

PATRON AND COLLECTOR

From his earliest adult years George had been fascinated by the arts and indulged himself as a patron, collector and friend of artists, writers, actors, singers and musicians. They in turn were charmed by his graciousness, his manners, which never seemed merely condescending, and by his knowledge of all branches of the arts. As Mrs Papendiek, the observer of court life under George III, remarked, he 'showed an elegance indescribable in everything that he did' and he impressed hardened professionals like Joseph Haydn, John Philip Kemble ('one of my earliest friends', he later recalled) and Thomas Gainsborough as more than a mere dilettante. He delighted in their presence and he showed it. He was a talented performer on the cello and played 'quite tolerably', as Joseph Haydn remarked after accompanying him on the pianoforte. His fine singing voice was prominent at his evening parties, whether these were gatherings of musicians and society ladies or drunken revels with his male cronies after a day's sport or outdoor adventures on horseback or driving his curricle. His pursuit of pleasure was incessant, whether physical or intellectual; as one of his biographers remarked, 'He did more than any other man before him, or after, to develop the art of living in England'. The Duke of Wellington who knew him only in his later years told the House of Lords after his death that 'He was admitted by all to be the most accomplished man of his age'. Only in the time of Charles I has the English throne been graced by a monarch so deeply versed in and appreciative of the arts in every branch, and who made so full a contribution to their prominence in national life.[1]

The theatre was the Prince's first love. He always enjoyed dressing up and in later years as Prince Regent and King he delighted in designing elaborate uniforms for his regiment and for himself. His designs for his coronation in 1821 were spectacular, making it the most splendid such occasion in British history. The make-believe of the theatre appealed to one whose own life was lived as on a stage, where everything seemed possible and where no such tedious considerations as expense were

[1] Richardson, xi, 22–4, 53–4; Delves Broughton (ed.), *Papendiek*, i, 229; Robbins Landon, *Haydn*, 122–4; Fulford, *George the Fourth*, 156–7.

allowed to interfere with the realization of the latest fancies. He could not perform on the theatrical stage himself, for actors and actressses were little esteemed socially and the life of the profession was generally regarded as immoral and unbecoming, but he made friends of the most distinguished of them and helped to overcome the social prejudice they suffered. Sarah Siddons became a regular guest at the Pavilion whenever she played at Brighton and the Prince was there, and the rising star Elizabeth Farren owed much to his overt patronage, so that she even rivalled Siddons herself. Kemble was a lifelong friend, and George's friendship with Sheridan which was so important in Whig politics owed a great deal to their common passion for the theatre. George kept a box at Covent Garden and attended that and other theatres regularly to see all the latest productions. In 1804 he went to see the young William Betty, at thirteen years old the new sensation on the stage and nicknamed 'The Young Roscius', at his first performance at Covent Garden. Afterwards he received him at Carlton House with Sheridan and described him as 'graceful and unaffected' in manners. 'Without the Sanction of your Royal Highness,' wrote a pamphleteer in 1795, 'the Theatres, and every Place of general Amusement would lose their force of Entertainment, and Pleasure would cease to be'.[2] The vital part played by the theatre in later eighteenth- and early nineteenth-century London society was to a great extent the consequence of George's interest and patronage.

The theatre was also one of the foremost settings for the display of royalty and for demonstrations of popular feeling towards it. George's visits to the theatre provided occasions for the populace of London to exhibit their sentiments uninhibited by any polite restraint. People were accustomed to parade their feelings not only towards the play and performance but also towards the notables in the boxes who were as much on display as the actors and actresses. The boos and hisses which greeted George during the regency when his unpopularity was at its height provided a barometer of public feeling just as much as the cheers and applause at his visits after the coronation in 1821 showed for the first time that popular feeling had turned around and that loyalty was now the order of the day. Calls for repeated performances of 'God Save the King' were a sure sign of royal popularity, and the absence of cries for the estranged Queen was the first proof that Caroline's appeal to the crowd had suddenly evaporated. The theatre was more than a venue for popular entertainment: it had a place in the political culture of the time no less significant than organized parades and ceremonies.

Less publicly obvious but no less important in George's cultural life

[2] Quoted in Richardson, 53.

was his love of literature. His education had not prepared him to any great degree for literary appreciation: his father had kept a sharp eye on his reading and proscribed all but a very few classical authors for his son's lessons. The Prince's patronage of literary affairs first showed itself in 1796, when he presented two gold medals for English composition together with two silver medals for elocution to Winchester College. His acute critical sense was displayed in the same year when he exposed the forgery of a mass of supposedly Shakespearian manuscripts by acute questioning of their pretended discoverer. George's best-known gesture of literary patronage is perhaps his support of the Literary Fund, established in 1790 by the Revd David Williams for the benefit of distressed and unfortunate writers lacking means of support. He set up a fund from the Duchy of Cornwall revenues to provide 200 guineas a year for the rent and taxes of a house and in 1818 he helped to establish the fund on a permanent basis and allowed the use of his crest on its arms. On his accession to the throne he became patron of the fund and altogether during his lifetime gave sums amounting to over £5,000 to this charitable body.[3]

The Prince also established his own library, which was put in the charge of the Revd James Stanier Clarke, a former naval chaplain who in 1799 became his domestic chaplain and in 1812 was dignified with the title of Royal Historiographer. With John M^c^Arthur he wrote a *Life of Admiral Lord Nelson, K.B.* which he dedicated to George and when the Regent managed, after considerable searching and negotiation, to obtain the Stuart papers from Rome, whence they were smuggled through the Italian customs and reached London via Tunis and Malta in an adventure worthy of that troubled dynasty's past, Clarke was charged with the task of editing them and publishing from them a *Life of James the Second*, in which herculean task he was fortunately assisted by Walter Scott. George's persistence was almost wholly responsible for the return of the Stuart papers to Britain; they are now housed in the Royal Archives.

George's scholarly interests extended to Roman antiquities. The discovery of the buried city of Herculaneum in the early years of the eighteenth century had begun a long series of excavations on the site and in 1752 an ancient library of papyrus rolls was uncovered. The kings of the Two Sicilies however were neither wealthy nor interested enough to pay for the unrolling and copying of the scrolls and it was George who came to the rescue in 1800, offering to pay for the venture at his own expense. He sent out another clergyman, the Revd John Hayter, Fellow of King's College, Cambridge, who began work at the Royal Museum of Portici, near Naples, but who made little progress of

[3] Ibid., 95–6.

any value, partly due to faulty techniques but mainly because of his idleness and notorious dissipation – habits no doubt deeply ingrained from his university days. He returned to England after nine years, bringing 94 facsimiles of papyri and numerous engravings from the 200 papyri that were opened and nearly a hundred copied. 'To you yourself alone', he declared to the Prince, was due the credit for the preservation of these remains of antiquity. George presented the papers he had rescued to Oxford University, and received in return the deserved tribute of a degree of Doctor of Civil Law.[4]

George was also a patron of some of the best-known novelists and poets of his time. As Walter Scott wrote to Byron in 1812, 'It is a fortunate thing for the Prince himself that he has a literary turn, since nothing can so effectually relieve the ennui of state, and the anxieties of power'. George certainly possessed a low boredom threshold as far as cares of state were concerned, but he had a genuine literary taste and he enjoyed meeting and conversing with men, and women, of letters, with whom he could hold his own without strain and on whom he worked his customary charm. Byron, who was by inclination no royalist, was captivated on his first meeting with the Prince Regent in 1812, when George sought him out at a ball and held a long discussion with him on the subject of Walter Scott, whom Byron had attacked mercilessly in *English Bards and Scotch Reviewers* (1809). As a direct result of the conversation the breach between the two literary lions was healed when Byron told Scott of the episode and of George's 'great delight' in his work. They had spent more than half an hour discussing poetry and poets, about which John Murray, Byron's publisher, wrote, the Prince 'displayed an intimacy and critical taste which at once surprised and delighted Lord Byron'. Speaking of Scott, both agreed they preferred *The Lay of the Last Minstrel* to his other works, George revealing a close intimacy with the poem by quoting passages learned by heart. He also quoted Homer 'and even some of the obscurer Greek poets', leaving Byron impressed with the belief that he had read 'more poetry than any prince in Europe'. His 'tone and taste', wrote Byron, 'gave me a very high idea of his abilities and accomplishments, which I had hitherto considered as confined to *manners*, certainly superior to those of any living *gentleman*'.[5] However, Byron's acquaintance with George went no further and it was terminated when Byron wrote two verses entitled 'To A Lady Weeping' attacking his conduct towards Princess Charlotte, justifying her rebellion against her father and referring to 'a sire's disgrace'. Byron remained an admired poet in George's eyes but as his

4 Hayter, *Report upon the Herculaneum MSS.*

5 Smiles, *Publisher and his Friends*, 89; J. Murray to Scott, 27 June 1812, and Byron to same, 6 July: Byron, *Works*, ed. Prothero, 132n., 134–5; Lockhart, *Scott* [1837–8] ii, 402–3.

anti-monarchism developed and his sympathy for Charlotte and her mother grew more blatant it became impossible for them to meet again and by the end of the regency he was attacking his former admirer as a cruel despot and libertine. George's conflict with his wife and treatment of his daughter turned many of the poets of the day against him, Shelley most famously (and unjustly) categorizing him as 'Swellfoot the tyrant'. It was one of the injustices which he had to bear, for like royalty in all ages he was unable to reply to defamation, however undeserved.

Others too forfeited the royal regard by turning against his private conduct. Tom Moore, the young Irish poet, like Byron was captivated on meeting George in 1800 and by the Prince's remark that in accepting Moore's dedication of his translation of Anacreon he was honoured by having his name connected with such a fine work, and hoped to extend his acquaintance to share their common love of music. George's Irish sympathies and particularly his love of the company of boisterous and companionable Irishmen drew him to Moore who became a favourite, like Sheridan, and the recipient of George's generosity. Again, however, the relationship turned sour. Moore had tied his hopes of advancement to George's friend Moira, but the latter's fall from favour after the political negotiations of 1812 and his departure to India blasted those expectations, as did the failure of the Whigs to attain power. True to his volatile Irish temperament, Moore rushed to the other extreme and blasted off a book of squibs and satires which mercilessly ridiculed George and his relationship with Lady Hertford, depicting him as a ridiculous old roué interested only in the cut of his coat and falling foolishly in love at his advanced age. He made fun of the Regent's unpopularity with his people, only to recant when George's Irish visit in 1821 aroused the affection of his subjects across St George's Channel.

Moore now became the King's devoted slave once more and appealed to Croker to put in a word for him, assuring Croker that he would 'praise him with all my heart for his wise and liberal conduct in Ireland'. George however was not prepared to return to their old intimacy and Moore again cooled. In 1825 he published his *Life of Sheridan*, in which he declared that George had allowed his old friend to die in want and had sent him only a derisory sum for his relief. George was deeply hurt, and defended himself in a long diatribe to Croker, detailing his numerous acts of generosity and favour to Sheridan over many years. He supplied notes to Croker and Knighton, and to Lockhart who wrote a review of Moore's book for the *Quarterly* justifying George's conduct. Moore refused to retract and the affair soured recollections of another of George's friendships with notable Irishmen. The venerable actor O'Keefe was to experience the other side of George's character. When eighty years old, blind and destitute, his plight came to the King's notice and he took steps to relieve him, in memory of his presence at 'parties of my juvenile recreation and hilarity'. George had a kind heart and never forgot a friendship or a good deed, though he rarely forgot a bad turn or an insult, as Beau Brummell discovered.[6]

If George's experiences with the poets was a mixed one, with the chief novelists of his time his relations were cordial and appreciative on both sides. His admiration of Jane Austen's work led him in 1815 to offer her permission to dedicate her next novel to him, and *Emma*, which was already in the press, accordingly appeared with his name. He assured her, through Stanier Clarke, that he kept a set of her novels in each of his residences.[7] Scott, however, was the prime favourite. His romantic recreation of a mythical Scottish past appealed to George's love of pageantry and imaginative adventure and fed his desire to link his two British kingdoms in a union of hearts as well as of politics. An early partisan of Princess Caroline, Scott had disapproved of George's 'public defiance of morality' until Byron told him of the Regent's admiration of his work and Stanier Clarke told him also of the Prince's desire to meet him. This was accomplished at one of George's 'snug little dinners' with 'just a few friends of his [Scott's] own, and the more Scottish the better', as his host remarked.

The occasion was a great success, the two principals took to each other and swapped anecdotes – to the delight of Croker, who was present. He declared that the Prince and Scott were the two most brilliant story-tellers he had known. George presented his guest with a gold snuff box as a tribute to his 'genius and merit'; henceforward Scott was a frequent guest on his visits to London. For his part, the author described his host as 'the first *English* gentleman of his day'. His allegiance was cemented by George's decision in 1820 to make him a baronet – the first such creation of the new reign – which delighted his snobbish soul and made him his Sovereign's slave: Lawrence painted him in his rapture, at the King's command. Scott's Jacobite sympathies were no obstacle to the friendship; George was also fascinated by the Scottish past, had rescued the Stuart papers from Rome, and was delighted when Scott discovered the Stuart royal regalia locked away in Edinburgh Castle. Scott's brilliant stage-management of George's Scottish visit in 1822 crowned their relationship and created the modern legend of the northern kingdom as the land of the mountain, the glen and the kilt. The King returned Scott's services by restoring, at his

[6] T. Moore to his mother, 4 Aug. 1800, 18, 28 March 1801; diary 16 June 1825, 15–23 Jan. 1826; to Dr Bain, 17 April 1826: Russell, *Moore*, i, 107–8, 111–13, 271, iv, 261, 292–3, v, 40–1, 54, vii, 263–4; Croker, i, 288–9.

[7] J. Stanier-Clarke to Jane Austen, 16 Nov. 1815; Jane to Stanier-Clarke, 11 Dec. and to Murray, 11 Dec. [1815]: J.E. Austen-Leigh, *Memoir of Jane Austen*, 146–55 and R.W. Chapman, *Jane Austen's Letters*, 429–30, 446.

request, the attainted Jacobite peerages from the '45 and, more personally, by bestowing his friendship and frequently calling Scott to visit him at Windsor during the later years of the reign. Sir Walter exploited his advantage to the full; in 1827, after his disclosure of the authorship of the 'Waverley novels' he was awarded a gold medal of the Royal Society of Literature and a few months later secured, by George's personal favour, a clerkship in the Foreign Office for his son. When in April 1830, two months before George's fatal illness, Scott suffered 'an awkward fit . . . somewhat like a paralytic affection' and resigned his office in the Court of Session at Edinburgh, he was given the headship of a commission to edit the Stuart papers and offered the rank of Privy Councillor, which he declined because of ill health. He survived his royal patron by two years.[8]

Music, literature and the theatre were George's interests throughout his life; he was also a notable collector of fine furniture, porcelain, bronzes and *objets d'art* in general as evidenced in the contents of Carlton House, the Pavilion at Brighton, Windsor Castle and later, Buckingham Palace. But he is renowned above all else for his patronage and appreciation of the visual arts. No monarch since Charles I had so devoted himself to the Royal Collection of painting and sculpture, and no one since George IV has shown a similar expertise and care for its expansion and development. He had a particular fondness for seventeenth-century Dutch painting and he added works by Rembrandt, Teniers, Rubens and Van Dyck to the collection, including Van Dyck's triple portrait of Charles I, for which he paid £1,000. He was a connoisseur of the work of that great painter of the Stuart family and besides inheriting the two great full-length portraits of James I and Charles I he bought two of his finest religious pictures – *The Mystic Marriage of St Catherine* and *Christ healing the Paralytic*, which were hung at Carlton House and later adorned the new Picture Gallery at Buckingham Palace. Of the work of other Dutch masters, his collection of cabinet pictures was especially notable. He acquired seven paintings by Aelbert Cuyp and others by Pieter de Hooch, seven genre paintings by Jan Steen, and in 1814 he purchased the Baring collection of no fewer than eighty-six pictures.

He was less enthusiastic about the conventional classical landscapes of the schools of Claude and Poussin, but he did acquire some notable examples. Nevertheless, his taste, as Prince of Wales and Prince Regent,

[8] Scott to Lady Abercorn, 14 Sept. 1809 and 23 March 1813; to C. Carpenter, 3 Sept. 1813; to J.S. Clarke [4 Sept. 1813]: Scott, *Letters*, ii, 240, iii, 241–2, 341–2; 344–5; to Byron, 16 July 1812; J.S. Clarke to Scott, 19 Jan. 1815: Lockhart, *Scott* [1837–8], ii, 402–3, iii, 340–1; Lockhart's account and Scott's diary, 4 March and 20 Oct. 1826, 27 June 1830: ibid., iii, 344–5, iv, 366, vi, 254, 360–1, vii, 212–15; Richardson, 185–9.

was for the art of his own day and it was in his patronage of living artists, which was constant and discriminating, that he made a distinctive contribution to connoisseurship. In his younger days when the great Sir Joshua was alive, specializing as he did in portraits of the Whig aristocracy with whom the young Prince politically identified himself, he admired Reynolds greatly and chose him to paint him in one of the most romantic poses of his youth, standing full-length with his favourite charger, as well as in a head and shoulders which was 'much approved of' at the Royal Academy exhibition. Reynolds was 'mighty pleased' with the young Prince. Reynolds also painted 'Perdita' Robinson for him and many portraits of George's friends and family, including the Duke of York, Lord Southampton, and the Earl of Moira, and the Prince also purchased several others including a half-length of Garrick for Carlton House.

Gainsborough too received early patronage. He painted the Prince, young and slim, fashionably and calmly posed leaning against his horse beneath a tree. The picture was for exhibition at the Academy with a companion portrait of his friend Colonel Anthony St Leger. The same painter depicted the Cumberlands, who may have introduced him to their nephew, and he received several commissions, including one of the Prince in military uniform as a hussar and a delightful one of his three eldest sisters for the saloon at Carlton House. He also commissioned Beechey to paint the well-known series of the young princesses. When George married Mrs Fitzherbert, Gainsborough was called on to depict them together *en bateau* sailing with Lord Radnor and Richard Brinsley Sheridan. George also bought *The Blue Boy* and *Peasants Returning from the Market*, an example of a genre of which he was always fond. After the painter's death he tried to persuade the public to buy his neglected landscapes, and himself bought two for Mrs Fitzherbert. She was painted several times for him. She sat to Cosway for a miniature which made the painter's reputation and which George liked so much that he gave him 'more than common patronage', amounting to twenty portraits of the Prince and several of Mrs Fitzherbert, including pictures of their eyes to be set in a ring. They also became personal friends, and Cosway for a time became his chief adviser on paintings, though the painter's disreputable lifestyle, eccentric appearance and familiar manners eventually became too tiresome. John Russell, a minor artist but a clever portraitist in pastel, also provided charming pictures of the Prince and of Maria, the latter of which William IV returned to her after his brother's death, and others of people from their Brighton days, including 'Smoaker' Miles and Martha Gunn, their bathing attendants.

Another favourite portraitist, George Romney, also began with a picture of Mrs Fitzherbert in 1789 and was commissioned by the Prince to produce another one and then two of Emma Hamilton who was to become one of his most frequent sitters. Hoppner too benefited from the Prince's notice and the consequent custom of the fashionable world. He painted five portraits of the Prince, one of Frederick and a full-length of his brother William, but the social and political partisanship of the time meant that he fell out of favour with the King despite rumours that his parentage might have been royal – his mother had been an attendant at the Palace. Hoppner became the Prince's principal painter of his friends and associates and famous men of the day, 'the ministers of his serious business, and the companions of his looser hours': he painted Haydn, Nelson, St Vincent, Moira, Sheridan, Jack Payne, Fox, the Duchess of Devonshire, Lady Melbourne and George Hanger among others for his patron. George also acquired portraits of Pitt, Rockingham, Thurlow and Spencer Perceval. When Lawrence succeeded to the position of his chief painter, he added portraits of Eldon, Scott and many others. 'No other Prince or King in the history of the royal collection has ever assembled such a distinguished contemporary portrait gallery', one of the modern Surveyors of the Queen's Pictures has remarked; 'but no other Prince of Wales has been at the heart of such a galaxy of talent, charm and high spirits'.[9]

Lawrence was linked at first with Princess Caroline. He was a frequent visitor at Blackheath and was the target of some of the gossip about the Princess's amours. That alone was enough to deny him George's favour, but later Lawrence's merits as an artist overcame any prejudice that might have lingered. In 1811 Croker recommended him to the Regent as 'the only man to paint him' and three years later the artist portrayed him for the Sheldonian Theatre at Oxford, to hang between the Russian Emperor and the King of Prussia to commemorate their visit. In 1814 George adopted Lady Anne Barnard's idea of commemorating the victorious end of the French wars with a gallery of portraits of the sovereigns, soldiers and statesmen of Europe who had contributed to the defeat of Napoleon, and it was Lawrence whom he chose to execute it. No one could have been more suitable: Lawrence's gift for the romantic portrait and his sensitivity to the epic moment (together with his unremitting industry) produced the collection of canvases which still line the Waterloo Gallery at Windsor. Lawrence was told to name his own terms, and on the Duke of Wellington's suggestion asked £1,000 as expenses for two months' absence at Aix-la-Chapelle where the congress was meeting, with his usual terms of 500 guineas for a whole-length and less in proportion for smaller pictures. George immediately accepted, Joseph Farington praising his 'known kind

[9] Richardson, 17, 23, 36–7; Sir Joshua Reynolds to Duke of Rutland, 30 May 1785: Hilles (ed.), *Letters of . . . Reynolds*, 124–5; W.B. Boulton, *Gainsborough*, 244; J. Farington, *Diary*, ii, 234; C. Lloyd, *The Queen's Pictures*, 182–3; O. Millar, *Pictures in the Collection of HM the Queen: Tudor, Stuart and Early Georgian*, and *Later Georgian*.

nature . . . and the liberality of his disposition' in addition to 'His particular regard for you'. That commission occupied Lawrence until his death. Lawrence was summoned to Rome on the same terms to paint the Pope and Cardinal Gonsalvi. The resulting portrait of Pope Pius VII is regarded as his great masterpiece. While there he was employed to value, in confidence, the collection of Cardinal Fesch which was up for sale. He was now established as George's main adviser on matters artistic and as the leading portrait painter of his time. He was knighted by the Regent in 1815 with the assurance that 'he was proud in conferring a mark of his favour on one who had raised the character of British art in the estimation of all Europe'. As one biographer has remarked, 'No court painter could have been more generously encouraged, more eagerly watched, than Lawrence was by the Regent'. The Prince's admiration was apparent to all: 'He talked in wild rapture of all the delight he expected from your treasures on your return', the British ambassador to Austria told the painter during his stay in Vienna to paint the Emperor's portrait.

Lawrence arrived in England with eight full-length portraits for the King, as he now was, in March 1820 and was immediately elected President of the Royal Academy, Benjamin West having just died. On arriving at Brighton he received George's congratulations and a gold medal of the King in profile crowned with a laurel wreath, to be worn on a gold chain by all future Presidents. George's biographer again declared that 'it is doubtful whether any English artist has enjoyed such patronage, such personal interest as Lawrence was consistently shown by George IV'. It was more than enough to ensure that the painter was no longer a partisan of the soon to be disgraced Queen: arriving for a dinner engagement to find her present, he immediately turned round and left. At the coronation the next year, Lawrence, as President of the Royal Academy, walked in the royal procession by his own entreaty, alongside Sir Humphry Davy, who represented the sciences.

George also greatly admired the work of David Wilkie, which appealed to him partly because it was so much in the style of his favourite Dutch artists, and in 1828–9 he purchased a sequence of four pictures of scenes – three of them imaginary – of events during the Spanish insurrection against Napoleon which had provided British armies with a foothold against the conquering emperor. Nearer to home, Wilkie painted his King entering Holyroodhouse in 1822 and one of George in his Highland costume.[10]

All George's many interests were reflected in the pictures he commissioned. He acquired sporting pictures from Sawrey Gilpin, George Garrard – who painted seven large pictures of his horses for the hunting

[10] Richardson, 136, 191–2, 200, 206; Lloyd, 184–5; Farington, vii, 242.

lodge at Kempshott – Henry Chalon, who painted his racehorses at Newmarket and his hounds and huntsmen on Ascot Heath, James Ward and, inevitably, Stubbs, who painted him riding in Hyde Park as well as pictures of the notorious Lady Lade and several of his favourite horses being exercised by his grooms. George's collection of wild animals in Windsor Great Park also provided subjects.

George thus, as Oliver Millar has written, 'enriched the [royal] collection with some of its finest English pictures'. He also did much to encourage the art of painting in Britain in general. He was particularly proud of his association with the Royal Academy, which enjoyed his enthusiastic patronage before and throughout the regency and during his reign. Lawrence declared in his address to the students of the Academy in 1823 that he was 'at all times the munificent patron of this establishment' and praised his role in the encouragement of the fine arts and their appreciation by the public. He regularly attended the annual exhibitions and the Academy dinners and often spoke to the assembled distinguished company. In 1811, on the first such occasion of the regency, Wilberforce described his speech as the best king's speech he had ever heard, and Farington recorded its main theme: 'When He saw so much which manifested the great improvement in art He felt proud as an Englishman that He might with confidence expect that as this country had risen superior to all others in Arms, in military and naval prowess, so would it in Arts.' He concluded that none could 'exceed him in his love of the arts, or in wishes for their prosperity'. No Academy dinner, observed Farington, had ever shown 'so much cordial warmth for the prosperity of art' nor for their patron. The Prince crowned the occasion by offering the Academicians a great bronze chandelier, specially designed by Vulliamy, to light the room at the annual dinners and to make the pictures more conveniently viewable than in the past, when only candles on the tables had provided illumination. The following year he stayed two hours at the exhibition, accompanied by his brothers York and Cumberland, when, Farington noticed, he gave most of his attention to the portraits, paying little to 'fancy pictures'. He was attended by a guard of soldiers and the rooms were carpeted with green baize. In 1813 he went to the Reynolds exhibition which followed Sir Joshua's death and dined as President, seated in a gilt chair. The dinner of two courses lasted only an hour, during which a band of music played 'soft airs': the Regent rose at 9.30 and returned to the exhibition rooms.[11]

George remained a regular visitor to the Academy exhibitions, though in 1814 he stayed away from fear of hostile demonstrations by

[11] Farington, vii, 1, 93: Lloyd, 185–6: *Address to Students of the Royal Academy*, 10 Dec. 1823.

the mob. He sought out Lawrence on these occasions, signifying his favour to him as the leading artist of the day. He is said to have regarded Lawrence's portrait of him in his robes as Regent as the best ever painted of him. He also praised the portrait of Mrs Wolff as 'exhibiting fine female beauty and taste'. His conversation, Lawrence noted, was always 'easy and entertaining': the painter William Owen, RA said that when he was with him his manner was so easy and familiar, putting his hand on Owen's shoulder, that he had to be on his guard 'not to forget his situation'. In truth the Prince was never happier than when in the company of artists. Farington noted that he always expected to be shown proper attention and respect but afterwards dispensed with formality and behaved 'easily and pleasantly', unlike the rest of the family. He had an 'easy grace' in conversation, tapping his snuff box and touching his nose slightly with a pinch of snuff to put those he conversed with at their ease in his presence. Lord Thomond spoke to Farington of George's manner in society as 'the most finished that can be imagined. His look, His address, the tone of His voice, are captivating in the highest degree. He has read a good deal, & is ready at quotation; Has a respectable share of classical learning, and holds conversations most agreeably.'[12]

His favours were not limited to visiting the exhibitions. He had approved the establishment of the Academy's school and in 1816 he allowed the loan of one of the Raphael cartoons and a Rembrandt from the Royal Collection for the instruction of the students. He also presented to the school the twenty-six casts from marbles in the papal museum which had been given to him and ten casts of antique statues, the Lycomedes, acquired from Berlin. Only in his later years when he became a martyr to gout and quailed at the climb up the Academy steps to the exhibition rooms did his visits come to an end. In the last year of his life, on Lawrence's death, George contemplated proposing a nobleman to succeed as President of the Academy rather than a practising artist, but he was dissuaded by Peel from affronting the Academicians' susceptibilities and gave in with good humour, saying, 'Well, perhaps we had better not meddle with the Royal Academy.' It was a fortunate end to a long and beneficial relationship.[13]

George IV's artistic patronage was not limited to painting from the past or to academic art. As early as 1804 Farington recorded that the Prince had spoken to Benjamin West about 'advancing [contemporary] art in this country' and declared that 'there shd have been a Gallery erected many years ago for modern works' as well as for Old Masters. Governments in wartime were hardly likely to respond to such a need

[12] Farington, vii, 263, viii, 21, 92, iv, 2–3.
[13] Richardson, 159–60; Peel to Farnborough, 20 Jan. 1830: Parker, ii, 142–3.

and private benefactors were also impoverished by wartime taxation and economic hardship. Private collectors, amongst whom the financier John Julius Angerstein was pre-eminent, were continuing to build up distinguished collections and with the returning prosperity after 1821 the idea of a national gallery sited in the heart of the new metropolis gained currency. Samuel Woodburn, a leading collector and dealer, wrote in 1823 to Lawrence of his concern that foreign agents were 'purchasing fine things which ought to adorn the present Capital of the Globe' and urging him to speak to the King to persuade him to 'forward the Arts' by establishing such an institution. Neither Lawrence nor the King needed persuading, though they were more aware of the financial and bureaucratic obstacles in the path. Angerstein's death later in that year brought his collection on to the market and the Government was persuaded to buy it for £57,000 'for the use of the public'. At the same time Sir George Beaumont, another connoisseur and patron of art, gave sixteen of his pictures to the nation which, added to the Angerstein purchase, formed the nucleus of a national collection. It was housed at first in Angerstein's former house in Pall Mall. Wilkins's building for the gallery on the site of the old Royal Mews was begun in 1832 and completed six years later. The gallery was not, of course, solely devoted to contemporary art but its establishment greatly furthered the role of London as an artistic centre, a cause always dear to George's heart.[14]

George IV's services to the arts in his kingdoms were notable and distinguished, and are a major element in his importance as prince and monarch. John Young, Keeper of the British Institution, described him as 'one of the best monarchs this country ever knew, whose consummate taste and munificence has done more for the arts during his short reign, than could have been expected in a century'. Peel told Lord Farnborough, George's chief artistic adviser, that 'he stood high in the estimation of British artists and was universally admitted to be the greatest patron the arts had ever had in this country'. Fulsome flattery may be the lot of monarchs, but it is incontestable that no later sovereign has emulated his achievements in this area and none has possessed the flair and taste to stand in comparison with him. Even his father, who was interested in painting and was a notable book collector, did not match his achievements, and his brothers, George dismissively told Benjamin West, 'had no feeling' for art. Alone in his generation of the royal family George IV upheld the arts as a vital national asset. The present Royal Collection and the public collections in this country bear the mark of his connoisseurship and of his paramount influence on their development and character.

[14] Stuart, *Prince Regent*, 187; Farington, ii, 234; Summerson, *Georgian London*, 200–3; Richardson, 268–9, 279–80.

Chapter 23

THE KING IN SECLUSION

At 4 p.m. on 9 December 1828 George IV moved into his new apartments in Windsor Castle. At 5 p.m. Sir William Knighton presented Wyatville, his architect, who handed him the keys in a crimson bag and received a knighthood. The King and the royal party processed through the Grand Corridor, furnished, as Greville later said, 'with the luxury of a drawing-room', full of busts, bronzes, pictures and 'curious antiquities', viewing the lavishly gilded woodwork, the tapestries and brocade on the walls, and the furniture. It was all in George's favourite Louis XV style, in curious contrast with the architecture but magnificent and comfortable. It might have been the setting for splendid entertainments, musical parties and grand dinners even finer than Carlton House had housed during the regency. At last the monarchy had a worthy setting for its position at the head of a rich and ostentatious society.

Unfortunately, however, the King made out little of the magnificence around him for he was now nearly blind, with cataracts in both eyes. His bad health often confined him to his bedroom, or he walked through the rooms in a shabby dressing gown, none too clean, his face plastered with make-up, keeping to his own company or that of Lady Conyngham and Knighton, in alliance for their own advantage. For some time past George had lived a retired life at the Cottage or the Pavilion with his few intimates, spending his days in bed in the mornings, getting up to lunch and a drive in his carriage during the afternoon, dressing for dinner with a small company and ending the evening with cards or music until bedtime before midnight. Lady Conyngham, Mme de Lieven said, was bored and stayed with him because of 'his diamonds, pearls, handsome furniture and good dinners' while he kept up the relationship simply because he disliked change and 'needs a habit'. In the evenings he gazed at her 'with an expression in which somnolence battled against love' while she and her daughter toyed with their jewels for lack of any other occupation. The King admitted to Mme de Lieven that his mistress bored him. Lady Granville found the Pavilion 'dull. There is nothing to speculate upon, nothing to laugh at . . . we eat too much, and there is no variety of society'. The band played during the evenings and the King joined in the singing and music-making and played patience after supper, but of the wild parties of his youth nothing remained. It was all very decorous.[1]

A few weeks after the King moved into his new residence, just before Christmas, Mme de Lieven visited the Castle and was greatly impressed by the building and by her host's amiability; but, she wrote, 'I am rather troubled . . . by the apparent state of weakness in which his last attack has left him'. There had been concern about the King's health since September, when his arm had been so swollen that he was unable to dress, and he seemed to have all the symptoms of dropsy, although conflicting reports of his condition continually circulated: 'The newspapers give him a mortal disease once a week', wrote Joseph Jekyll. Lady Conyngham confessed to Mme de Lieven that she was uneasy about him, although she remarked that 'he is not happy unless he is ill' – which was characteristic of her frequent impatience with her notional lover despite his bouts of wild generosity towards her and her family. Greville noted that he 'continues to heap all kinds of presents upon her, and she lives at his expense' but that 'at Windsor the King sees very little of her except of an evening; he . . . some times goes to her room for an hour or so in the afternoon, and that is all he sees of her'. She more than once threatened to leave him but her mercenary nature drew her back. George was well aware that her affection had long since palled, and yet he was afraid of losing her company and being lonely and bored, for he had few real friends. He tended to keep people at a distance and since Maria Fitzherbert no one had shared his life or given him real devotion. Greville, who had a very low opinion of the King, wrote that he liked 'to be treated with great deference . . . and that people should be easy with him, and gay, and listen well' but he was 'tired to death of all the people about him' and constantly irritable. His lifestyle, Greville wrote, was 'most extraordinary': he

> never gets up till six in the afternoon. They come to him and open the window curtains at six or seven o'clock in the morning; he breakfasts in bed, does whatever business he can be brought to transact in bed too, he reads every newspaper quite through, dozes three or four hours, gets up in time for dinner, and goes to bed between ten and eleven. He sleeps very ill, and rings his bell forty times in the night; if he wants to know the hour, though a watch hangs close to him, he will have his *valet de chambre* down rather than turn his head to look at it. The same thing if he wants a glass of water;

[1] C.C.F. Greville, *Journal*, i, 279; Quennell (ed.), *Lieven–Metternich Letters*, 13 Jan., 14 Aug. 1823, 4 Oct. 1824, 14 May 1826: 223–4, 280–1, 330, 367–8; Lady Granville to Lady G. Morpeth, 26 Dec. 1823: Granville (ed.), *Letters of Countess Granville*, i, 238–9.

he won't stretch out his hand to get it. . . . He is in good health, but irritable.[2]

Others, too, found him irritating and predictable only in his unpredictability. He had become wilful and selfish, kept his visitors and ministers waiting while he chatted to his valet or other servants, and refused to carry out routine tasks, which he regarded with impatience. Greville alleged that he took 'pleasure in thwarting his Ministers on every possible occasion' and Peel told Lord Ellenborough that George had signed no commissions for two years. It was partly because he disliked signing parchment but also because gout in his hand or arm made it difficult to write or hold a pen and he was hampered by cataracts. Wellington noted in September that one eye was almost completely blind and the other partially so and he could not be prevailed upon to sign in this condition, although his father had done so. Eventually it was decided to have a stamp made with his signature on it so that it could be applied to documents, but even then there were piles of papers awaiting attention: some hundreds were found unsigned after his death. Greville summed up with his customary animosity:

> The fact is that he is a spoiled, selfish, odious beast, and has no idea of doing anything but what is agreeable to himself, or of there being any duties attached to the office he holds . . . he only wishes to be powerful in order to exercise the most puerile caprices, gratify ridiculous resentments, indulge vulgar prejudices, and amass or squander money; not one great object connected with national glory or prosperity ever enters his brain.

It was a spiteful and in many ways an unjustified portrait but George did little to invite a better one.[3]

The last two years of George's life were dominated by his ill health, and by his increasing reclusiveness. The struggle over Catholic emancipation in the early months of 1829 left him exhausted. He insisted on holding his usual children's ball in May, at which the young Queen of Portugal and Princess Victoria danced, but on his birthday in August 1829 he made his appearance only late in the day, Jekyll declared because 'the lacing he requires would not be endurable if he underwent it early'. He spent most of his time in bed, though he still managed to drive out in his phaeton almost every day. (His 'almost oriental

[2] Mme Lieven to Alexander, 5 Jan. 1829: Lieven, *Letters,* 169–70; to Lady Cowper, 27 Nov. [1828]: Lord Sudley (ed.), *Lieven–Palmerston Corresp.*, 6; Algernon Bourke (ed.), *Corresp. . . . Jekyll,* 186; C.C.F. Greville, *Journal,* i, 189, 207.

[3] Ibid. 214, 246; Ellenborough, *Diary,* i, 1, 19, 101–2, ii, 250, 259, 261; Wellington to Lyndhurst, 3 Sept.: *DCM,* vi, 126.

seclusion' was preserved by posting soldiers to exclude the public from Windsor Great Park when he went out.) Wilkie, who painted him in the last months of his life, told Lockhart that it was 'the most difficult and melancholy business for the man was wasting away frightfully day after day' and though he looked well enough across a room when 'dressed up in robes and hung about with orders and ribbons', at close quarters it was 'parfaitly frightful'. It took three hours to dress him, 'to lace up all the bulgings and excrescencies'. He looked 'like a great sausage stuffed into the covering'. In April he had written to Knighton that 'as to myself, I am sorry to say [that I am] but little improved in my corporeal suffering, and very much worried & distress'd *indeed*, in *body* & *mind*, with *all* that is passing in the busy & clamorous scene . . .'. Six months earlier he had suffered much pain and anxiety from attacks in the bladder and had consequently greatly increased his doses of his favourite cherry brandy or of laudanum, which he was taking in such quantities that he sometimes spent almost the whole day in a drugged condition which severely handicapped him mentally. He sometimes talked incessantly for hours, as he did in March 1829 to Wellington at the height of the Catholic crisis; at other times he was lethargic. In May 1829 he sent for the Lord Chancellor but when he arrived George was asleep after taking a large dose of laudanum and he was advised to go away again as the King would not wake for two or three hours and would then be too irritable to speak to. A year later Wellington found him in a good humour despite his having taken over 250 drops in 36 hours: the Duke suspected that he had done it in order to avoid having to attend the levee and drawing room. Maria Fitzherbert, writing from long memory, told Minny that he 'always liked to make himself out worse than he was to excite compassion, & that he always wished every one to think him dangerously ill, when little was the matter with him'. When he rallied from one of his attacks she wrote that she never thought the case was as desperate as others believed 'because I knew *the Man*'.[4]

The spring of 1830 marked the beginning of his final decline. Bulletins, vague and uninformative though they were, began to be issued at the end of April. He suffered spasmodic attacks in his chest, with such difficulty in breathing that he could no longer lie down in bed but had to sleep propped up in a chair, and his doctors prescribed frequent tapping to drain water from the swollen pericardium. The Duchess of

[4] Moore, diary, 12 Aug. 1829: Russell, Moore, vi, 69–70; Mme Lieven to Alexander, 24 Sept. 1829: Lieven, *Letters*, 198; Maria Edgeworth to Mrs Edgeworth, 5 Jan. 1831: Edgeworth, *Letters from England*, 462–3; Ellenborough Diary, i, 376–7, ii, 91, 100; George to Knighton, 3 April: RA 51346; Cumberland to same, 19 Sept. 1828: RA 51097; Wellington to Peel, 14 and 17 April 1830: *DCM*, vi, 569, 572; Anita Leslie, *Mrs Fitzherbert*, 212.

Gloucester said that he had 'become enormous, like a feather bed' and his legs 'also swollen, are as hard as stone; his face is drawn and his features pinched, and he has attacks of choking'. Yet occasional remissions seemed to offer hope of recovery and he might for a short time appear cheerful, but these fluctuations in his condition were typical of his state of health for some time past and the overall trend was downwards. In March Mme de Lieven had found him 'in good health – much in love with his big lady and much in dudgeon with his big Minister'. Harriet Arbuthnot reported that 'his mode of living is really beyond belief. One day last week, at the hour of the servants' dinner, he called the Page in & said, "Now you are going to dinner. Go down stairs & cut me off just such a piece of beef as you wd like to have yourself, cut from the part you wd like to have yourself, & bring me it up". The page . . . fetched him an enormous quantity of roast beef all of which he eat, & then slept for 5 hours'. Another night he drank 'two glasses of hot ale & toast, three glasses of claret, some strawberries!! and a glass of brandy' and another, three glasses of port and one of brandy after taking his medicine. The mixture of ale and strawberries, she thought, was 'enough to kill a horse'. Yet Wellington told her that 'his voice is quite strong, his eye clear & that, as far as appearances go, he seems perfectly well. Lady Conyngham thinks he *shams*'. He still took his customary interest in racing, and though there was no question of holding his racing dinner for the Jockey Club as he had done for the past two years or of his attending Ascot races this year, he had the results brought to him regularly and talked of horses he wanted to buy for his stables.[5]

His health fluctuated for the whole of May and June. At times he became 'very uneasy & anxious about himself' and thought he was dying, at others the physicians thought the drawing of water from his system so successful that he might recover as 'his constitution seems so good & so unimpaired', but his condition quickly worsened again and Harriet Arbuthnot despaired once more. A few days later Wellington found him in good spirits, his legs healing and the swelling subsiding, and the physicians optimistic. 'No man clung to life with greater eagerness than George IV', wrote Thomas Raikes, 'or was more unwilling to hear from those about him any hint or suspicion of his apparent decay. When confined to his room, and his case had become evidently hopeless, he still felt the vital stamina so strong in him, that he would not believe his own danger.' Wellington admired his courage and Croker wrote on 11 May that he was 'aware of his own situation, and contemplates it . . . boldly'. He received the sacrament from the Bishop of

[5] Mme Lieven to Alexander, 19 March 1830: Lieven, *Letters*, 217; *Arbuthnot*, ii, 351–64; C.C.F. Greville, *Journal*, i, 211–12, 134–5.

Chichester, a former Vicar of Brighton, with Knighton and Lady Conyngham, and it seemed to comfort him. He three times repeated 'Amen' 'with the utmost fervour and devotion' after the prayer which the Bishop read to him, which was prescribed in the churches for his recovery; it was 'in very good taste', he declared. Knighton had discreetly placed a Bible in his bedroom, and he read it constantly. He confessed to Archdeacon Glover that he repented of his early life, but he had tried to benefit his subjects in later years and had always shown mercy to others and hoped it would be shown to him.

From the beginning of June he deteriorated again, his appetite was failing and he began to await death with his usual courage. He sent for his sisters to take leave of them and dictated his last will, leaving all his plate and jewels to Lady Conyngham. Another rally in the middle of June seemed likely to confound the fear of early death – 'his Doctors don't know what to make of it', Mrs Arbuthnot wrote – but his condition remained precarious. On the 7th Knighton sat up with him and, Croker reported, several times thought he was dying, but 'in the waking intervals he was as clear, as communicative, as agreeable, nay as *facetious* in his conversation as he ever had been'. To his friend Lord Farnborough he 'appeared to balance in his own mind the probabilities of life and death as almost equal' and spoke of the latter calmly. He asked what the public thought of him and declared that 'he had always endeavoured to do his duty' and 'had never willingly done harm to any one'. Wellington 'was astonished at his strength, both of body and mind', and Ellenborough wrote that 'In constitution and in mind he is certainly a wonderful man': he behaved 'in the face of death as a man would on a field of battle'.[6]

The final attack came in the early hours of Saturday, 26 June. He had slept since just before midnight, attended by Sir Watkin Waller who sat up with him, holding his hand as the King leaned forward on a table set before his chair. At a quarter to two he woke, took his medicine and some clove tea, and slept again until a quarter to three. He woke again, asked for his attendants and was helped to the night-stool. After purging, he struggled back to his chair, asked for the windows to be opened, and feeling breathless, tried to drink some sal volatile and water but was unable to do so. He looked directly at Waller, still holding his hand, exclaimed 'My boy, this is death!', and fell back in his chair. His doctors, Halford, Sir Matthew Tierney and Brodie, and Sir William Knighton entered the room in time to witness the end at 3.15 a.m. He

[6] Raikes, *Journal*, iii, 58; Ellenborough, *Diary*, ii, 234, 244, 249, 258, 266; Knighton to Lady Knighton, 27 May [1830]: Knighton *Memoirs*, ii, 140, 143; Bishop of Chichester, 1 June 1830: RA 24821–2; Croker to Vesey Fitzgerald, 11 [misdated 3] May, 11 June: Croker ii, 57, 61, 64–5; Creevey to Miss Ord, 11 June: *Creevey Papers*, ii, 211; A.M.W. Stirling, *Letter-bag . . . Spencer-Starhope*, ii, 134.

died, Knighton told his wife, 'without any apparent pain or struggle. . . . There will be many to deplore his loss.'

One who undoubtedly did so was Maria Fitzherbert. She could not be present at the end, although she came up to Tilney Street in case he asked for her. She had not set eyes on her former lover for a long time, but on hearing of his illness she wrote him a last letter:

> After many repeated struggles with myself from the Apprehension of appearing troublesome or Intruding upon your Majesty after so many Years of Continued Silence, my Anxiety respecting your Majesty has got the better of my Scruples and I trust your Majesty will believe me most sincere when I assure you how truly I have griev'd to hear of your suffrings. . . . *No one* will feel more rejoiced to learn your Majesty restord to complete convalescence. . . .

George sent no reply, though she had dearly hoped for a last word from him: but he placed the letter under his pillow, and after his death her portrait by Cosway – one of those they had exchanged at the beginning of their marriage – was found in a locket round his neck. Lady Conyngham spent Saturday morning hurriedly packing and left at midday for her brother's house near Dorking on the way to Paris.[7]

Another who mourned him, despite their sometimes strained relationship, was William Knighton. Visiting Windsor again five years to the day after George's death, he wrote afterwards:

> The Castle look'd magnificent – but nevertheless to me dreary and melancholy; I thought I saw at every corner of the corridor, the dear King; I thought I heard his voice calling Sir William! – my feelings were much agitated; I wish'd myself away & every thought told me that no consideration could make me endure a renewal of my residence & my services in this Palace.

Sir Walter Scott added a tribute:

> He spoke of his intellectual faculty, which he considered of a high order. He said his exalted and good breeding bespoke nothing but kindness and benevolence: but he also observed that, when he was roused every inch of him was a King.

The Duke of Wellington told the House of Lords that on all occasions when dealing with his ministers the King showed 'a degree of

[7] Sir Watkin Weller's memorandum, RA 24827–8; Maria Fitzherbert to George, 23 May: ibid., 24823; Anita Leslie, *Mrs Fitzherbert*, 214; Langdale, 136.

knowledge and of talent much beyond that which could reasonably be expected of an individual holding his high station'.[8] *The Times*, reporting his death on the 28th, added that 'Personally, the King has distinguished himself by some of the finest acts of generosity and benevolence' despite his pecuniary difficulties and the 'extravagant companions, and advisers' who surrounded him: had he acquired 'real friends, studious of his happiness and honour, his private character would have equalled his public one, and the virtues of the man would have kept pace with those of the regent and the sovereign'.

Yet the general mood was hardly one of mourning at his passing. Greville, as usual, led the critics: 'Nobody thinks any more of the late King than if he had been dead fifty years, unless it be to abuse him and to rake up all his vices and misdeeds', he wrote two weeks after George's death: 'nobody ever was less regretted . . . and the breath was hardly out of his body before the press burst forth in full cry against him, and raked up all his vices, follies, and misdeeds, which were numerous and glaring enough'. Mme de Lieven agreed: George was

> completely forgotten, and if remembered, it is only to criticise his morals. It is in the middle and lower classes especially that this side of his character has left a very unfavourable impression – an impression which overshadows much that was striking and brilliant in his reign. His glory is forgotten, and his vices exaggerated; so true is it that what a nation most appreciates in its sovereign is domestic virtue.

The Times excelled itself: its obituarist attacked the late King's 'most reckless, unceasing and unbounded prodigality . . . indifference to the feelings of others . . . [and] the tawdry childishness of Carlton House and the mountebank Pavilion, or cluster of pagodas at Brighton', reminded his readers of his treatment of Princess Charlotte and of her mother – the paper had not forgotten that it had been one of Caroline's foremost supporters – and his profligate lifestyle 'little higher than that of animal indulgence'. Three weeks later, after the funeral, it printed the famous verdict: 'There never was an individual less regretted by his fellow-creatures than this deceased King. . . . An inveterate voluptuary, . . . of all known beings, the most selfish. . . .' Righteous indignation poured from its columns but of George himself there was hardly even a partial portrait.[9]

The funeral, held in the evening of Thursday, 15 July was, according

[8] Knighton's memorandum, 29 June 1835: RA 51237–8; *Hansard*, N.S., xxv, 707–9 (Wellington, 29 June 1830); Knighton's diary, 3 Oct. 1831: Knighton (ed.), *Knighton*, ii, 231–4 (Scott's tribute).

[9] C.C.F. Greville, *Journal*, ii, 1–2; Mme Lieven to Alexander, 20 July 1830: Lieven, *Letters*, 225; *The Times*, 28 June and 16 July 1830.

to Greville, 'a fine sight, the military part particularly, and the Guards were magnificent' – which would have pleased the deceased monarch. The attendance however was 'not very numerous' and the mourners not particularly grief-stricken; in fact, Greville wrote, they were 'all as merry as grigs' except for Lady Conyngham's son Mount Charles who alone was 'deeply affected'. Lord Ellenborough wrote in his diary that

> King George IV is gone to his grave with all the pomp of royalty, and splendid the pageant was; but it was considered a mere pageant even by his household, who had lived so intimately with him for years. There was no regret. A coronation could hardly be gayer; but the procession was gravely done and decently. The magnificence of the castle aided the spectacle and made royalty appear almost as imposing in death as at the moment when the Crown was assumed in the Abbey. We had supper and they all went to London.

The Times reported that there was 'not a single mark of sympathy' in the congregation. The new King, William IV, hardly set an example: he walked immediately behind the coffin but on entering St George's Chapel he rushed over to shake hands with an acquaintance and walked up the chapel 'nodding to the right and the left' to the congregation. During the ceremony he chatted 'incessantly and loudly to all about him'. After two hours he decided to leave although the anthem was still in progress and the coffin had not yet been lowered into the vault. Afterwards he slept at Frogmore and on the following day went all over the castle which he had never explored thoroughly before, savouring his new position as he had done since his accession.[10]

The order for the funeral was as impressive as George would have wished. The body lay in state in the Crimson Drawing Room, attended by various functionaries, officers and members of the Yeomen of the Guard, from the morning of the day before the funeral. The State Apartments, the Guard and Presence Chambers, and the Grand Staircase were hung with black cloth and lined by Gentlemen Pensioners and Yeomen of the Guard. The body was covered by a black velvet pall bearing the royal arms and the imperial crown and the royal crown of Hanover beneath a canopy of purple cloth. The Royal Standard, the banners of the Union, of St George, of Scotland and of Ireland, of Hanover and of Brunswick, were arranged nearby. Lords and grooms of the bedchamber, gentlemen ushers and officers of arms were stationed round the coffin. The public were admitted from 10 a.m. to 4 p.m. on the Wednesday, and from 10 a.m. to 3 p.m. on the day of the interment. Then the procession to the Chapel left at 9 p.m. to the sound of the Dead March in *Saul*, the pall borne by six dukes and four

[10] C.C.F. Greville, *Journal*, ii, 4–5; Ellenborough, *Diary*, ii, 312.

eldest sons of dukes, attended by the knights of the several orders who walked in the procession wearing collars and white rosettes, and by grenadiers of the Foot Guards, every fifth man lighting the way with a flambeau. 'The music was sublime', Harriet Arbuthnot wrote, 'the procession very fine'. Seeing the new apartments and St George's Hall in its restored beauty, it made her 'quite melancholy to think the poor King wd never enjoy it any more'. On a fine summer evening by torchlight and to the sound of minute guns George IV was laid to rest in the vault beside his father.[11]

The post-mortem examination, carried out by the late King's physicians, showed a tumour 'of the size of an orange' attached to the bladder and a large deposit of fat around the heart, which was greatly enlarged. It appeared that he had suffered for some time from arteriosclerosis: there was considerable 'ossification of the valves of the Aorta which must have existed for many years'. The final cause of death was the rupture of a blood vessel in the stomach. George's illnesses were certainly far from imaginary and it is probably a wonder that he survived as long as he did; he must, as some observers had noted, have been blessed with a strong constitution and will to live.[12]

George's first will, written in 1824, was not found for some time but when it turned up it was seen that Wellington and Knighton as executors were required to examine all his papers and destroy all they considered appropriate. They carried out these instructions thoroughly, so that a great deal of the private and personal correspondence has disappeared, to the regret and disappointment of historians and biographers ever since. Mrs Fitzherbert however did retain in her keeping the so-called 'marriage certificate' of 1785 which is now preserved in the Royal Archives, though their correspondence was burnt by Wellington and Knighton at Maria's house in 1833. No original correspondence, if there ever was any, regarding any children of that marriage, nor of any other possible illegitimate children of George IV, survives. Numerous 'pretenders' have appeared from time to time claiming descent from him, by Maria Fitzherbert or others, but none has established any solid proof.

Apart from his correspondence, George had kept almost everything he possessed. He could never bear to throw anything away and when his pages came to collect his clothes, which were their perquisite, they found

> all the coats he has ever had for fifty years, 300 whips, canes without number, every sort of uniform, the costumes of all the orders in

[11] 'Ceremonial for the interment of his most sacred Majesty': RA 24845–9; *Arbuthnot*, ii, 371.
[12] RA Geo. Add. 21/27.

Europe, splendid furs, pelisses, hunting-coats and breeches. . . . His profusion in these articles was unbounded, because he never paid for them, and . . . he recollected every article of dress, no matter how old . . .

In 1831 Wellington fell to talking with Greville after dinner and told him that

When he died they found 10,000l in his boxes and money scattered about everywhere, a great deal of gold . . . above 500 pocket-books, of different dates, and in every one money – guineas, pound notes, one, two, or three in each. There was never anything like the quantity of trinkets and trash that they found. He had never given away or parted with anything. There was a prodigious quantity of hair – women's hair – of all colours and lengths, *gages d'amour* which he had got at balls, and with the perspiration still marked on the fingers, notes and letters in abundance . . . .

At the time the Duke told Harriet Arbuthnot that the late King's effects contained

volumes of love letters, chiefly from Ly Conyngham, some *foul copies* of his own to Ly [Conyngham] descriptive of the most furious passion, trinkets of all sorts, quantities of women's gloves, dirty snuffy pocket handkerchiefs with old faded nosegays tied up in them; in short, such a collection of trash he had never seen before. He said he thought the best thing wd be to burn them all.

This was in addition to the quantity of jewels and trinkets which Lady Conyngham reputedly had carried off and the compromising letters which Knighton had rapidly destroyed after his master's death. The latter at any rate showed himself at the last to be a faithful servant. Elsewhere, life went on almost unaffected. Neither grief nor regret seemed in evidence among the crowds who thronged the streets in Windsor after the funeral, or in London in the following days. It seemed, Mme de Lieven recorded, as if George had 'never sincerely inspired anyone with attachment' and his successor pointed up the contrast by making himself approachable, cordial and benevolent, dashing about the streets and inviting familiarities from all and sundry in a way which contrasted with the dignified manner and reclusive habits of his brother. 'Wellington said to me quite truly,' Mme de Lieven wrote, ' "This is not a new reign, it is a new dynasty".'[13]

[13] C.C.F. Greville, *Journal*, ii, 23, 189–90; *Arbuthnot*, ii, 369; Mme Lieven to Alexander, 20 July: Lieven, *Letters*, 224–6.

CONCLUSION

I
FATHER AND SON

Throughout George's life, he was in his father's shadow. In his youth he chafed against rigid parental discipline, when he came of age he resented what he believed to be his father's unreasonable restrictions on his choice of friends and his way of life, and although in his later years he tried to reconcile himself to his father and to follow his policies and principles he rarely gained his approval. His father's recurring illnesses threw a shadow over George's life both by arousing the fear that he might follow his fate and by forcing him to confront the question of filial duty against personal friendships formed in the course of defying his father. George's nature was fundamentally affectionate but in his early life he became convinced that his father hated him and preferred his brother Frederick – a not unusual circumstance in the Hanoverian royal family – and this set up anxieties and resentments which, consciously or not, deeply affected his outlook. George III had set out to be a fond father, and he was capable of expressing affection towards his sons, as was shown by the letter he wrote to George and Frederick jointly in 1778, when he and the Queen were visiting Portsmouth dockyard to inspect the fleet on the eve of its departure to America. He began with a quite chatty account of their journey down from London and their subsequent doings at Portsmouth, but he could not help ending with the familiar exhortations to duty and religious obligation, clothed in the naval idiom appropriate to the occasion:

> I cannot conclude without just adding that I know very well I have a difficult time to steer the helm, but the confidence I place in Divine Providence, the attachment I have for this my native country, and the love I bear my children, are insentatives [*sic*] sufficient to make me strain every nerf [*sic*] to do my duty to the best of my abilities. My dear sons, place ever your chief care on obeying the commands of your Creator. . . . Act uprightly and shew the anxious care I have had of you has not been misspent, and you will ever find me not only an affectionate father but a sincere friend.

Typically, he appealed to their filial affection in terms of mutual obligation and reward for benefits conferred by his own performance of his duty towards them. His sons were made to feel that their father's love was always conditional on their own obedience to his will and precepts. When George replied to his father's letter in affectionate and obedient, if somewhat stilted language, the King wrote that 'Nothing could have given me more real joy' than his letter and the Queen also wrote to say that 'il est extrementent *content* & me dit "*I am proud of my two boys' letters*".' The following month when George wrote to tell his father that he had had a chance encounter with the proscribed Duke and Duchess of Cumberland in the Park and to assure him that it had been unsought, the King replied approvingly that 'The more open you are in your conduct towards me, the more cordial will always be mine in return. . . . Your conduct has been most proper'.[1]

Duty was indeed George III's watchword. It reinforced the rigidity of his inflexible temperament and explained his inability to tolerate filial defiance or understand other points of view than his own – qualities in evidence in his political as well as his parental activities. His response to obstructive behaviour, whether by politicians or by his offspring, was a stubborn appeal to self-righteousness: 'I know that I am doing my duty and can therefore never wish to retract.' Sir Lewis Namier's perceptive psychological study of that 'much misunderstood monarch' rightly places 'duty' at the forefront: allied to extreme conscientiousness it led to inflexibility and refusal ever to compromise, while equally strong religious views made him see all questions in a wholly moral context.[2] As a father, George III could not understand filial disobedience – he had been an obedient and submissive son himself – and it appeared as something evil, to be eradicated by stern punishment, just as in politics opposition to his ministers was seen as immoral as well as disloyal behaviour by 'bad men as well as ungrateful subjects', as he once put it. In both cases, the consequence was to nurture the very evil he complained of.

George's childhood, largely spent at Kew, was marked by the rapid appearance of brothers and sisters in the atmosphere of a private family home where parents and children alike lived away from the pressures of politics and the ceremonies of the court. The King tried to instil into his children the values of respectable bourgeois society, liberally dosed with religion and centred on moral values. The boys cultivated their little garden plots, ate simple meals, took gentle exercise, and played the normal children's games and in the evenings joined their parents for cards or conversation. It was a model life for a devout middle-class

[1] See Chapter 1, n.17.
[2] Namier, 125–40.

family. Unfortunately the boys, especially the two eldest, found it boring and dreary. They longed for more exciting company and for diversions among companions of their own age and they quickly tired of moral exhortations from their pious father backed up by physical punishment for transgression. Before they were into their teens they were showing signs of rebelliousness, longing to break out of their comfortable but frustrating prison. They were well aware of the temptations they might encounter in the outside world, no doubt informed and encouraged by those about them or those they met on their visits to London to accompany the King in his duties. As they grew to puberty, the presence of young attractive maids of honour or of female servants in the household provided temptation: when George's mother discovered that he had been consorting with one of her attendants behind the bushes she drew the inevitable conclusion.

The arrival of George's eighteenth birthday was the occasion for his father to renew his expressions of concern for the development of his character along the lines he expected. His joy at his son's growing maturity was mixed with 'anxiety that this period may not be ill spent'. He referred again to 'The numberless trials and constant torments I meet with in public life', which profoundly affected him, 'as I have no other wish but to fulfill my various duties' and he pointed out once more that it was on his eldest son that 'the [future] prosperity of my dominions as well as of the rest of my progeny must greatly depend'. There followed a catalogue of George's shortcomings, beginning with a fear that 'your religious duties are not viewed through that happiest of mediums, a gratitude to the Great Creator, and a resolution to the utmost of your power implicitly to obey His will as conveighed [*sic*] to us in the Scriptures'. After injunctions to apply himself more diligently to his studies, the King assured him: 'Believe me, I wish to make you happy, but the father must, with that object in view, not forget that it is his duty to guide his child to the best of his ability through the rocks that cannot but naturally arise in the outset of youth . . .'.[3] George replied rather curtly that he was 'sensible . . . of the parental attachment & kindness you profess towards me' and promised to be worthy of it: the King's next missive four months later laid down the rules his son was expected to follow in his personal and social life for the future – rules to be honoured more in the breach than the observance, as he pointed out in his next letter in May 1781, urging him to read over again the letter containing them. 'Examine yourself and see how far your conduct has been conformable to them . . . I wish to live with you as a friend, but then by your behaviour you must deserve it.' He was, he asserted, 'an affectionate father trying to save his son from

[3] See Chapter 1, n.18.

perdition'.[4] George's youth was dominated by the conflict with his father's ambitions for him and by his own unwillingness to accept the rigid rules laid down for his conduct. George was now launched on his youthful career of dissipation and he no longer even pretended to listen to, let alone observe, his father's directives. He told Frederick in October 1781 that 'the unkind behaviour of both their Majesties . . . is such that it is hardly bearable' and his explanation, to his friend Lord Malmesbury in 1785, was that 'The King hates me; he always did, from seven years old'. On reading some of the King's letters Malmesbury was inclined to agree; they were 'void of every expression of parental kindness or affection'.[5]

Matters did not improve when George acquired his own household. Those very faults which his father had identified in him seemed to grow even greater when he was no longer directly under the parental eye. His habits of extravagance and over-indulgence in worldly pleasures matured with his age, fostered by the company he kept. Either in deliberate reaction against his father's rules or simply as a consequence of his own weakness of character, he threw himself into the dissipated lifestyle of the companions who thronged around him, exploiting his partiality for amusing company and unrestrained gratification of sensual appetites for their own enjoyment and benefit. His father's anger at his extravagance, all the more marked because the nation was still suffering from the financial strains of the American war and George III was acutely aware of the royal family's responsibility to set a good example, was merely the surface expression of the King's distress that his eldest son, on whom all his hopes for the future of a benevolent monarchy were centred, should be so callously indifferent to the welfare of his country and so determined to encourage what his father saw as the immorality and corruption of the age. Carlton House itself became a symbol of the Prince's betrayal of his father's aspirations, so that demands for additional expenditure to make it a showplace for the artistic achievements of the time and a suitable setting for the magnificence of royalty were seen as a means 'to gratify the passions of an ill-advised young man'.[6] The King's blunt refusal to abet this desire for grandeur did not, however, moderate the Prince's behaviour; it merely increased his indebtedness and confirmed his father's refusal to come to his aid. Both showed that streak of stubbornness which George III handed down to his offspring.

George's relations with his father had broken down by the time he was eighteen and they did not improve during his young manhood and

[4] King George III to George, 14 May 1780 and reply, 15 Aug.; same to same, 6 May 1781: *CGPW*, i, 33–6, 60–2.

[5] Harris, Malmesbury *Diaries*, 27 April 1785: ii, 71–2.

[6] King to Portland, 16 Jan. 1783: *CGPW*, i, 117.

middle age. A succession of affairs of the heart, some trivial but others more serious, a refusal to moderate his expensive way of life and the princely magnificence to which he thought himself entitled, and outright defiance of his father's injunctions led to the breakdown of their relationship. It was sealed by George's friendship with Charles Fox, whom the King regarded as a personal enemy as well as a depraved character, especially when this led to his son's alignment with the parliamentary faction which, in George III's view, supported the American rebels who were trying to break up the Empire. That his own son and successor, on whom, as the King reminded him, the future prosperity of his people and his dominions would depend, should behave in such a way was a crushing blow to a father as conscientious as he was. In June 1783 the King wrote of 'how little reason I have to approve of any part of his conduct for the last three years', instancing 'his neglect of every religious duty . . . his want of even common civility to the Queen and me . . . besides his total disobedience of every injunction I had given'.[7] He refused to agree to what he considered the reprehensible proposals of the Foxite ministry to give the Prince an enormous income to waste on idle pleasures and corrupt politicians, and forced them to retract. The Prince's pursuit of and marriage to Maria Fitzherbert was another example of defiance of his father, since apart from the constitutional obstacle to marriage to a Roman Catholic, it was a violation of the Royal Marriages Act which George III had personally promoted thirteen years before. He himself had been compelled to put aside his attachment to Lady Sarah Lennox in his youth in order to marry a less attractive German princess – another 'duty' which subjected George III's life to his treadmill – and he was determined to prevent future alliances of that kind. It was a testimony to his sense of duty and his determination to enforce it on his descendants; its consequences were disastrous for his own children, making it impossible for all his sons to marry the women of their own choice, forcing them to cohabit with mistresses rather than sire descendants to the throne or, in the Prince of Wales's case, to contract a marriage with a wholly unsuitable woman merely because she was a German princess. In the case of the King's daughters, it forced them into prolonged spinsterhood or secret liaisons, resulting in unhappiness for all the family.

Many of the troubles which beset George III's children can thus be traced to over-conscientious attitudes by their parents, and in the case of their eldest son they were exaggerated by the King's deep and entirely genuine concern for the future and his legacy to his people. He had conceived from the start of his reign a mission to rid his country of corruption and political as well as moral depravity. He had been

[7] King to Col. Hotham, 15 June 1785: ibid., 113.

brought up to believe that his predecessors had allowed these to flourish by neglecting their duties and responsibilities, so that the whole fabric of the country had become rotten; he was also taught that only a patriotic king could eradicate the worm at the heart of the state. To see his eldest son repudiating his example and abetting those same wicked men who had since Walpole's time exploited the weakness of the monarch to foster their own power and wealth at the public's expense was a blow from which he never really recovered and which may have had some connection with the mental illnesses from which he suffered. In his turn, George IV was damaged by his conviction that his father had withdrawn his affection from him and turned his back on his needs. Emotionally he was damaged by the inability of his father, and in his earlier years of his mother, openly to show him love and understanding. He badly wanted to stand well with all his family and he lavished affection particularly on his sisters, who returned it in full measure. Mary wrote in 1818 that his care and concern for her in her protracted illness had 'made me if possible *value* you more and more every hour', 'much as I *loved* you *before* which God knows is far beyond what I can find words to express', and the affection of Sophia and Amelia had been similarly expressed at the time of the latter's fatal illness.[8] George's character needed affection and encouragement and, as he confessed on one occasion, he felt the need of guidance and advice from others, but he could not turn to his father for it and so fell victim to those who were less devoted to his interests. For King and Prince of Wales just once in the history of the Hanoverian family to form a union of affection and political agreement is perhaps asking too much of human nature. It is certain at any rate that George III and George IV could never do so. The son could argue that his father rejected him; the father believed that the son had done the same to him. Only George III's mental illnesses brought out his son's deeper feelings for him. In 1804 Lady Bessborough declared that he

> has great faults . . . but, indeed, I believe they are more *head* than heart. He listens more to the bad advice of the strange set of people he lives with than to his own feelings. This very day, as I was urging him strongly to abstain from any thing that could bear the least appearance of indelicacy towards the K., he answer'd, quite with warmth: 'As heaven's my witness, I love my Father to my heart, and never think of his sufferings without tears (and as he spoke the tears really did run down his cheeks). But is it not hard to be denied the pleasure of attending on him, of even seeing the Q. or my Sister? . . .'.

[8] Princess Mary to George, 23 Nov. [1818]: RA Add. Geo. 12/320; Princess Amelia to George [*c.* 1 June 1810]: ibid., 14/193.

I never heard the P. at any time mention the K. but with respect and affection. . . .[9]

On the first occasion of his father's mental breakdown in 1788 the Prince rushed to Windsor from Brighton, wept over his father's condition, and tried to preserve some semblance of political neutrality until, as he believed, he had been forced by Pitt and the Queen to throw himself into Fox's arms. In the outbreak of 1804 he had tried to obtain details of his father's condition from ministers who, he believed, were hiding the truth in order to hang on to office, and he protested that his only desire was to promote the King's well-being. When the final onset of madness came in 1810, having detached himself from the political opposition after Fox's death, he avoided the errors of 1789 and made it clear that he could not make any political changes that his father would disapprove of, at least until the King's recovery was out of the question. Unfortunately his father never recovered to the extent that he could appreciate his son's concern.

So the career and character of George IV were deeply influenced by his father's personality and conduct towards him. Well-meaning as George III was, his judgement of his son was harsh and too much governed by a rigid code of piety and conscientiousness which made him censorious where he might have been more successful by showing patience and understanding. The son's weaknesses of character – his lack of confidence in his own judgement, his reliance on advisers who were more concerned with their own interests than with his, his tendency to avoid trouble and responsibility and seek pleasure above duty – can all be shown to have a root in the relationship with his father. The search for affection which his father could not show led him to seek it in extramarital relationships which ultimately lacked stability and damaged his reputation. The tragedy was that he was never able to marry legally and settle down with the only woman he ever truly loved. The mistresses with whom he associated in his middle and later years were mature women in whom he sought companionship and domestic comfort rather than sexual passion, but he now lacked the qualities needed for a permanent relationship. His life was thus a lonely one at bottom. Since his teenage years when he had been denied the company of his brothers, who were all sent abroad to remove them from his influence, and even at the last, when as a sick invalid he was shut away at Windsor without friends save for a selfish mistress and a devoted but scheming servant, he found no resources outside himself to help him overcome his condition. George IV's life ended in tragedy and in squalor, in striking contrast to the princely magnificence with which he

[9] Lady Bessborough to Lady Stafford [n.d.]: Granville (ed.), *Leveson Gower*, i, 454.

had tried to surround himself. The 'Prince of Pleasure' died a forsaken and unloved recluse, unmourned by friends or subjects and unjustly despised by posterity. Yet his reign left a not unworthy legacy to his country in terms of culture, material advancement and prosperity.

II
'THE MOST ACCOMPLISHED MAN'

The phrase was the Duke of Wellington's: speaking in the House of Lords three days after George's death, he reminded their lordships that 'He was admitted by all to be the most accomplished man of his age'.[10] The Great Duke was not normally given to eulogy but though spoken in a funeral tribute the words rang true. No monarch before or since has shown the versatility, the grasp of so wide a range of the arts, including the arts of conversation and of condescension, the ability to fascinate others, the love of elegance and of gracious living, of food and drink, of pleasure in all its forms. A connoisseur of painting and sculpture, a collector of wide taste and discrimination, a lover of literature and poetry, of music and the theatre, he impressed even the professionals in those fields with his knowledge. The public at the time were more aware, through the popular press and caricature, of his faults and his vices. He drank a great deal, especially in his youth, he pursued women unceasingly even in a licentious society, he could be fickle in his friendships, and neglectful of his royal duties through indolence or sometimes the consequence of his dissipation. In everything he was and did, there was no shrinking from excess.

The best-known aspect of George IV's life and character is his devotion to pleasure and his almost frenzied search for it throughout his life. Whether that pleasure was aesthetic, in his love of the arts and building, sexual, in his pursuit of women, convivial, in his love of good company and its diversions, or corporeal, in his fleshly appetities, it filled a large part of his existence. He was constantly depicted in contemporary satires and cartoons as a libertine, a glutton, and a self-indulgent roué with no thought for others or for the welfare of his subjects. At times of popular distress he was hissed and hooted in the streets or at the theatres, and hardly dared show himself in public. When he tried to divorce his wife in 1820 he was portrayed as an unfeeling monster of depraved habits and infamous character. The first purported biography by Robert Huish, the malicious *Memoirs of George IV*, rushed out soon after his death, dwelt salaciously on his alleged scandalous behaviour in

[10] Quoted thus by H.E. Lloyd, *George IV, Memoirs of his Life and Reign*, 470. *Hansard* N.S., xxv, 707 and *The Times*, 30 June 1830 offer slightly different wording.

pursuing and deflowering a succession of innocent young girls, giving the impression that his life was 'all one huge orgy, with drunken feasts every night and with gay girls or bewildered virgins hurried along secret passages'. As J.B. Priestley remarked, it was all so much nonsense.[11] George was certainly susceptible to female charms and possessed a full measure of the Hanoverian libido which his father had sternly repressed in himself – only for it to break out during his attacks of derangement, to the distress of the Queen – but which had reappeared in his descendants. In his youth, as he himself later admitted, George lived as dissipated a life as any young man about town, behaved irresponsibly with money, and cultivated the pleasures of the table and the bottle. But it was part of the life of a 'set' of wild young bloods and not a solitary vice. He loved music and singing, enjoyed witty company, and adored being the centre of attraction, seeking the affection denied to him at home by his severe and repressive parents.

His extrovert conduct however masked a personality that was by no means domineering and insensitive. He was sometimes unwise and unfortunate in his choice of friends, and was too susceptible to flatterers and companions only anxious to embroil him in scandalous escapades and too generous towards them, as if trying to buy their affection, but he was faithful to them unless they took liberties which outraged his sense of dignity and decorum, and to those who served him well he was ever kind and considerate. When, for example, he learned in 1823 that Charles Arbuthnot, who had spent nineteen years in the service of his government and had never asked for anything beyond his official salary, was in financial difficulties because of his losses during his embassy to Constantinople in 1804–7 and might have to sell his small estate, George arranged to make a present to him of £15,000 to clear his debts, and asked Wellington to 'say everything kind and affectionate to Mr and Mrs Arbuthnot, because I know how much you love and regard them'. 'My beloved sovereign has made two beings happy', wrote Charles Arbuthnot in acknowledgement, '& . . . those two beings were even long since devoted to him'. At times he was capable of harsh and unfeeling conduct, as in his breaches with Maria Fitzherbert, when his method of ending their relationship caused great distress, but it was largely because of his inability to face a 'scene' rather than from real heartlessness. His relationship with Lady Conyngham was fraught by her rapacity and his fear of losing her and being left alone in his last years. He was more deluded than demanding and his open and generous nature was too often taken advantage of. He was at bottom a lonely man who needed someone to share his life and give him affection; the position of a prince or a king was too public and too

[11] Priestley, 26.

vulnerable. His sister Elizabeth wrote after his death that he was '*all heart*, and had he been left to his own judgment would ever have been kind and just . . . a more generous creature never existed, and had his talents been properly called out he would have been very different from what he was', but he was spoilt by flattery and being 'made much of' when young. He was not a strong character but he was not a bad one.[12]

He was also unfortunate in his times. He governed when his subjects were suffering from wartime hardships and post-war depression, and was tainted with responsibility for their distress, though it was something he could do little to alleviate. He was charitable to others, and rarely refused help to individuals, but he could not bring prosperity to the whole nation. Through his patronage of all the arts, science and scholarship he did embellish the cultural life and reputation of his country beyond all expectation and for this alone he deserves credit. 'A man of extraordinary natural distinction,' wrote the most perceptive of his biographers, 'he drew men of distinction to him'. Another wrote of his 'Extraordinary charm of manner . . . [with] also a curious feminine vanity and caprice'.[13] He could fascinate learned and unlearned alike, showing a vast and intimate range of knowledge of literature, art and poetry and yet he could talk knowledgeably of everyday matters and particularly of horses and horse-racing where his knowledge was equally encyclopaedic. 'The Druid', a pamphleteer of the turf, writing after George's death,[14] remarked that 'the one character, in which he pre-eminently shone, [was] that of an English sportsman' and a devoted lover of the 'sport of kings', as he helped to make it. 'Horses, and everything connected with them, were his idols, and no man had a finer eye for them'. He was said by his physicians to have talked in his sleep in his last illness of horses: 'it was all horses, horses, with him, by night and by day, to the very last'. On his deathbed he sent Jack Ratford, a racing crony, to Epsom for news of the Derby, which one of his horses had won in years past.

George was 'the most human and approachable of princes', as the historian of Castlereagh's foreign policy declared, quoting George Russell's view that he was 'magnificent, sumptuous, stately; majestic and yet benignant, chivalrous with women, playful with children, gracious and cordial with men'.[15] A man of many parts and unlimited interests, gifted far beyond the common capacity of monarchs, it is easy to see him as a connoisseur of the arts and sport, of society and conversation, but to ignore his political capacity: too often he has been written off as a king who presided over the loss of the royal power and influence

12 E.A. Smith, *Wellington and the Arbuthnots*, 101; Stuart, *Daughters of George III*, 193.
13 Richardson, 360; Fulford, *George the Fouth*, 22.
14 'The Druid'.
15 Webster, 5–6; Shane Leslie, *George the Fourth*, 11–17.

in government through indolence and lack of industry. There was, however, a positive side. His coronation and his visits to Scotland and Ireland unleashed a wave of royalist sentiment among the people which went some way to repairing the damage done to the image of the monarchy by his earlier financial irresponsibility, by the popular misconception of his relations with Caroline, and by the conduct of his disreputable brothers. His father had overcome his own earlier unpopularity by his symbolic role as the personification of British virtues during the French Revolution and wars, and the more public role of the princes in serving their country in wartime had given the royal family more favourable attention, despite occasional scandals in their private lives. George laid the foundations of a recovery in popular esteem for the monarchy which was of great importance for the future, although his own failure to continue the process during the rest of his reign and the early unpopularity of Victoria and especially of Albert meant that the recovery was not cumulative: when Victoria celebrated her jubilees she discovered that the republicanism of her mid-reign had been superficial and that the monarchy was, after all, close to the hearts of her subjects.

As a working monarch, George took a constant interest in political affairs and in government, but unlike his father he was wise enough to understand that the monarch no longer possessed the resources to impose his will without reference to the economic and social interests of his subjects, and that he must be prepared to bend when necessary to the force of public opinion when that was reflected in the advice of his servants or the majority in Parliament. He did not, as a man of his age, approve of 'democracy' or the rule of the majority, but he understood when to give way to necessity without losing the proper constitutional power of the Crown. His reign marked a vital stage in the transition from the personal rule of the king to the rule of the Cabinet and Parliament. In that long process George IV was neither parent nor midwife, but he helped to make the birth possible. The nineteenth-century achievement of constitutional progress without political upheaval in an age of European revolutions was the legacy of a monarch and politicians who were able to work out a fundamentally harmonious personal and political relationship.

Sir Walter Scott perceived something of the truth. Visiting George at Windsor in October, 1826, he wrote in his diary:

> He is in many respects the model of a British monarch – has little inclination to try experiments on government otherwise than through his Ministers – sincerely, I believe, desires the good of his subjects – is kind towards the distressed, and moves and speaks 'every inch a King.' I am sure such a man is fitter for us than one who would long to head armies, or be perpetually intermeddling with *la grande*

> *politique.* A sort of reserve, which creeps on him daily, and prevents his going to places of public resort, is a disadvantage, and prevents his being so generally popular as is earnestly to be desired. This, I think, was much increased by the behaviour of the rabble in the brutal insanity of the Queen's trial, when John Bull, meaning the best in the world, made such a beastly figure. . . .[16]

George IV's many virtues were overshadowed in the perception of his subjects by the biased and unfavourable attitude of the press, and have been hidden from posterity by the vengeful propaganda of the Whigs who dominated British politics for a century after his death. Those who knew him best saw a different man. Sir Herbert Taylor, private secretary to William IV, wrote in 1838 in reply to a whig attack by Brougham in the *Edinburgh Review* that

> George IV's natural temper was neither sour nor revengeful: that his abilities were far, very far, above mediocrity; that he was quick, lively, and gifted with a retentive memory and ready wit, and that he possessed a natural taste for music and the arts which was improved to a power of discrimination which few surpassed; [and] add to this, the advantage of person and grace of manner which all acknowledged . . .

Sir William Knighton wrote to his wife on the afternoon of George's death that he was 'one of the cleverest and most accomplished men in Europe – full of benevolence! There will be many to deplore his loss.' Selfish and yet generous to a fault, proud yet capable of arousing affection, a dignified monarch yet an amusing companion, George IV was, as Wellington famously remarked, a 'most extraordinary compound of talent, wit, buffoonery, obstinacy and good feeling – in short a medley of the most opposite qualities, with a great preponderance of good'.[17]

[16] Lockhart, *Scott* [1837–8], vi, 360–1.

[17] *Taylor Papers,* 501–3; Knighton to Lady Knighton, 26 June 1830: Knighton, *Memoirs,* ii, 143–5; Raikes, *Journal,* i, 92.

APPENDIX: GEORGE IV'S CHILDREN

George IV had only one legitimate descendant, Princess Charlotte, born of his disastrous marriage to Caroline of Brunswick. Her death and that of her stillborn son in 1817 meant that he had no legitimate issue and the royal line descended through his brothers. Yet it has often been supposed that he must have had illegitimate children through mistresses, lovers, and above all through his unlawful but canonically legitimate marriage to Maria Fitzherbert. There has never been any acknowledgement of such descendants and from the beginning their putative existence was hidden from public knowledge. Proof of their parentage has never been available and in some cases seems to have been destroyed, or at least concealed or falsified. Rumours nevertheless were always prevalent, though the discretion which contemporary social convention dictated was carefully maintained among those who might have had any knowledge. What follows therefore is the nearest one can approach to the truth of the matter.

In investigating the possibility of children having been born to Maria Fitzherbert by the Prince of Wales, as he was during their association, several clues are important. They are negative rather than positive in character: for example, she was a devout Roman Catholic and it is extremely unlikely that she would have allowed any children born to her to be brought up in any other faith. Suspicion has fallen upon a child, Mary Anne Smyth, who was alleged to be the daughter of Maria's brother John, one of the witnesses at her marriage to the Prince, who was maintained by his family to have been without issue. It would have been the normal practice in such a situation for the illegitimate child to be brought up as the child of a relative who could plausibly be regarded as the parent. In the now well-known case of Charles Grey's daughter by the Duchess of Devonshire, she was even brought up by his parents as though she was his sister and the secret seems to have been well kept. Further supposition is promoted by the fact that two pages of the Catholic register of baptisms at Brighton referring to the period of George and Maria's residence there were torn out and have presumably been destroyed. It was alleged by a reviewer of Wilkins's biography of Maria in 1906 that a midwife had admitted that she delivered children of Maria and the Prince who were taken away immediately after their birth and, presumably, adopted without any hint of their parentage.[1] In the case of Mary Anne, she later married the Hon. Edward Stafford-Jerningham, a member of the well-known and

[1] Father Thurston, *The Month*, Jan. 1906.

related Catholic family and brother of Lord Stafford. It is a family tradition that she was George IV's daughter by Maria Fitzherbert. Maria certainly took a close interest in her and welcomed her marriage as 'everything we could wish for or desire except for that odious commodity money' – a hindrance which she did her best to minimize by giving her £20,000. She afterwards spoke of Edward as 'my son-in-law'.[2] She also lavished affection on two nieces, Louisa and Georgina Smythe, daughters of another brother, whose mother was a Protestant and who were so brought up, which is suggestive that they were in fact legitimate children of their putative father.

Another candidate at the time for parentage by George was Minny Seymour, for whom he showed what was alleged to be a fatherly devotion. She was officially the daughter of his friends Lord Hugh and Lady Horatia Seymour but Lady Horatia had been his mistress for a short time before the child's birth in 1798. Again, no proof has ever been discovered and the supposition of her royal parentage has been based on the common knowledge of George's infatuation with Lady Horatia and in particular his notorious anxiety in and after 1801, when both the Seymours died, that Minny should remain under the guardianship of Maria Fitzherbert, who gave assurances that she would not interfere with her Protestant faith. The long-drawn-out legal battle to ensure Maria's guardianship attracted much attention and may have had a formative influence on George's desertion of the Catholic cause and of his former Whig political allies as well as of Maria herself and his attachment to the Hertfords in her place. Though Maria was undoubtedly fond of Minny it is not likely that she was her natural mother: she never showed her the degree of affection she gave to Mary Anne. Nor is it at all certain that George was Minny's father. He was always fond of little children and he seems to have selected Minny as a future companion for his legitimate daughter Charlotte rather than seeing her as a real daughter of his own, though he made no secret of his affection and played and romped with her as if she were. It was alleged during the struggle over Minny's guardianship that George had dropped hints that he was indeed her father, but no one quite believed this was anything other than a desperate attempt to win over the peers to vote as the Prince wished on the case in the House of Lords.[3]

There is one more plausible candidate as a daughter of George and Maria Fitzherbert, though again the evidence is indirect. A certain Commander Horne, RN, who appears to have left the navy and taken up the trade of builder, claimed to be the son of a natural daughter of George IV and towards the end of the King's life attempts were being made to get him a position as Inspector of Stores or Overseer of Building construction, presumably on the strength of his royal descent, but no proof has survived.[4] Other claimants to descent from George and Maria have cropped up from time to time, but none has been substantiated.

[2] Bence-Jones, *Catholic Families*, 129–30.
[3] Anita Leslie, *Mrs Fitzherbert*, 131–40.
[4] RA, P.P. Reg. Vict. 6092 and Edward VII c. 14564.

Whether or not George had children by Maria Fitzherbert, there can be little doubt that other liaisons during his life must have been productive. The most probable candidate is George Seymour Crole, born in 1799 to Elizabeth Fox who was the mistress of Lord Egremont at Petworth and who was also mistress for a time of the Prince of Wales. She was the daughter of the manager of the Brighton theatre and later of two other theatres which he built himself, one at Lewes and one in Duke Street, St James's. He died in debt in 1791 leaving his daughter in the care of Lord Egremont, who fathered four children born to her. She adopted the surname Crole and became George's temporary mistress during the period after his separation from Caroline. Their son was born on 23 August 1799 but the relationship with George ended when he was reunited with Maria the following year. He did not forget Elizabeth, but ensured that she would be looked after by Egremont and settled a pension of £500 from the Privy Purse on her for the rest of her life. Her son was discreetly looked after: his fees at the Royal Military Academy at Sandhurst were paid from the same source and in 1817 a commission in the 21st Dragoons was purchased for him. He transferred to the 11th Dragoons in the following year and accompanied his new regiment to India where he remained for ten years, becoming ADC to the governors of Bengal. After returning to the home country he was attached to the 28th Foot and served in the Ionian islands. He was granted occasional sums from the Privy Purse and in 1823 when George was drawing up his will he told Lord Eldon that he had a natural son serving in the East Indies to whom he was obliged to leave £30,000. In 1831 Knighton and Wellington, George's executors, paid him £10,000 and he received a pension of £300, being described as 'natural son of George IV'. His mother continued to receive £500 per annum. Crole left the army in 1832 and went to Chatham, where, it is said, he took up residence at the Sun hotel, intending to stay one night but remaining for thirty years. Obviously an eccentric character, he never married: was this part of the bargain, one wonders, to ensure that no embarrassing claims were made by future descendants? Curiously, his half-sister, one of Egremont's children, married George Fitzclarence, Earl of Munster, son of William IV by Mrs Jordan, who committed suicide in 1842.[5]

Others were to claim descent from George IV, including William Francis, son of a Mrs Davies, born in 1806, who also enjoyed a pension from the Privy Purse for a time, but George disowned him in 1823 and he received nothing further. George is also quite plausibly alleged to have had a child by Lady Melbourne, who was his mistress in his youth, and who had a number of children, some acknowledged and regarded as legitimate, others not, and by a variety of fathers. It would be tedious to speculate further, for no doubt careful precautions were taken to conceal whatever evidence there was during George's lifetime: these were presumably among the secrets kept by MacMahon and later by Knighton to protect their employer from further scandal. All that perhaps needs to be said is that it

[5] Lydia Collins, 'George Seymour Crole – A Son of King George IV', *Genealogists' Magazine*, xxi, Sept. 1984, 7, 228–35 and material in Royal Archives.

was by no means uncommon for members of the aristocracy (and indeed of other classes) and of the royal family to father or to bear illegitimate children in an age of sexual licence and lack of efficient means of contraception. The 'world' of society was well used to such circumstances and curiosity was discouraged: the descent of titles, estates and wealth was too important a consideration in an age when inheritance was crucial to be endangered by mere gossip and scandal, however titillating to the onlooker at the time or in later times. George, here as in other respects, was a man of his age and indulged his proclivities in the same way as his subjects and no one thought much less of him as a result. In any case, there is no ground for a challenge to the legitimacy of the royal descent after George IV under the law of England as then in force.

BIBLIOGRAPHY

MANUSCRIPT SOURCES

The Royal Archives at Windsor

Correspondence of George IV as Prince of Wales, Prince Regent, and King, and of his brothers and sisters. Much of George IV's private correspondence was destroyed after his death by his executors, Sir William Knighton and the Duke of Wellington, on the grounds that it contained many indecent passages. Almost all the remainder of George's correspondence has been edited and published by the late Arthur Aspinall. Reference to passages printed in Aspinall's volumes has been made to the published text, which has been checked with the original MSS.

Correspondence of King George III.

Queen Caroline, Princess Charlotte and Queen Victoria papers.

Papers referring to Mrs Fitzherbert.

Duke of Northumberland papers.

Other MS Collections

Aberdeen University Library: Arbuthnot papers.

The British Library: Papers of C.J. Fox; Lord Goderich; Lord Grenville; Holland House papers: Princess Lieven; Second Earl of Liverpool; Sir Robert Peel; Spencer Perceval.

Chatsworth: Devonshire muniments.

Devonshire Record Office: Sidmouth papers.

Duke University, North Carolina: Croker papers.

Durham University Library: Charles, Second Earl Grey papers; Ponsonby papers.

Leeds City Library: Harewood (Canning) papers.

Lincolnshire Record Office: Fane papers.

Northamptonshire Record Office: Althorp papers.

Northern Ireland Record Office: Anglesey papers.

Nottingham University Library: Newcastle papers: Portland papers.

The Public Record Office: Chatham papers.

Sheffield City Library and Northamptonshire Record Office: papers of Second Earl Fitzwilliam; Burke papers.

Southampton University Library: Wellington papers.

University College, London: Brougham papers.

PRINTED SOURCES

Place of publication is London unless otherwise stated

Newspapers and Periodicals

Annual Register
The Black Dwarf (1817)
Cobbett's Parliamentary History (later *Hansard, Parliamentary Debates*)
The Gridiron, or, *Cook's Weekly Register* (1822)
The Oracle
The Republican (1820)
The Times

Printed Correspondence, Journals, Biographies and Secondary Sources

ANDREW, W.R. *Life of Sir Henry Raeburn.* 1886.
ANON. *Carlton House. The Past Glories of George IV's Palace.* 1991.
—— *Account of the Visit of HRH the Prince Regent . . . to the University of Oxford . . .* Oxford [1815.]
ARMSTRONG, W. *Lawrence.* 1913.
ASPINALL, A. (ed.) *The Formation of Canning's Ministry.* Camden Society. 3 ser. 59. 1937.
—— *The Letters of King George IV, 1812–1830.* 3 vols. Cambridge 1938.
—— 'George IV and Sir William Knighton'. *EHR.* 55. 1940.
—— *The Correspondence of Charles Arbuthnot.* Camden Society. 3 ser. 65. 1941.
—— *Diary of Henry Hobhouse (1820–1827).* 1947.
—— *Letters of the Princess Charlotte 1811–17.* 1949.
—— *Three Early Nineteenth-century Diaries.* 1952.
—— *The Later Correspondence of George III, 1783–1810.* 5 vols. Cambridge 1962–70.
—— *The Correspondence of George, Prince of Wales, 1770–1812.* 8 vols. 1963–71.
—— and SMITH, E.A. (eds) *English Historical Documents,* xi, 1783–1832. 1959.
AUSTEN-LEIGH, J.E. *A Memoir of Jane Austen.* 1870.
AYLING, STANLEY *George the Third.* 1972.
BAGOT, JOSCELINE *George Canning and his Friends.* 2 vols. 1909.
BAMFORD, F. and the DUKE OF WELLINGTON (eds) *The Journal of Mrs Arbuthnot, 1820–1832.* 2 vols. 1950.
BAMFORD, S. *Passages in the Life of a Radical.* 2 vols. ed. H. Dunkley. 1893.
BARNES, D.G. *George III and William Pitt, 1783–1806.* New York 1939.
BELL, N. *Thomas Gainsborough.* 1897.
BENCE-JONES, M. *The Catholic Families.* 1992.
BERRY, M. *The Journal and Correspondence of Miss Berry, 1783–1852.* 3 vols. ed. Lady Theresa Lewis. 1865.
BESSBOROUGH, LORD (ed.) *Georgiana, Duchess of Devonshire.* 1955.
BICKLEY, F. (ed.) *Diaries of Sylvester Douglas* (Lord Glenbervie). 2 vols. 1928.
BISHOP OF BATH and WELLS (ed.) *Auckland, Lord, Journal and Correspondence.* 4 vols. 1861–2.

BLOOMFIELD, LADY (ed.) *Memoir of Benjamin Lord Bloomfield.* 2 vols. 1884.
BOLTON, G.C. *The Irish Act of Union.* Oxford 1966.
BOULTON, W.B. *Thomas Gainsborough.* 1905.
BOURKE, ALGERNON (ed.) *Correspondence of Mr Joseph Jekyll with . . . Lady Gertrude Sloane Stanley, 1818–1838.* 1894.
BRABROOK, E.W. *The Royal Society of Literature . . .* 1897.
BRETTELL, J. *George IV, The Patron of Literature.* RSL Lecture. 1831.
BRIGGS, A. *The Age of Improvement.* 1959.
BROOKE, JOHN *King George III.* 1972.
BROUGHAM, H. *The Life and Times of Henry Brougham, written by himself.* 3 vols. 1871.
BUCKINGHAM and CHANDOS, DUKE OF (ed.) *Memoirs of the Court and Cabinets of George III.* 4 vols. 1853–5.
BURKE, S. HUBERT *Ireland 60 Years Ago.* 1885.
BURNEY, FANNY *Diary and Letters of Mme D'Arblay.* 7 vols. 1842–6.
BURY, LADY CHARLOTTE *The Diary of a Lady-in-waiting.* 2 vols. ed. A.F. Stewart. 1908.
BYRON, GEORGE, LORD *Works.* ed. R.E. Prothero. 1908.
CAMPBELL, JOHN, LORD *Lives of the Lord Chancellors . . .* vol. iv. 1868.
CASTLE, E. (ed.) *The Jerningham Letters.* 2 vols. 1896.
[CAWTHORNE, J.] *A Candid Enquiry into the Case of the Prince of Wales . . .* 1786.
CHAPMAN, R.W. (ed.) *Jane Austen's Letters to her Sister Cassandra and Others.* Oxford, 2nd edn, 1952.
CHENEVIX-TRENCH, CHARLES *The Royal Malady.* 1964.
CLARKE, JAMES STANIER *The Life of James the Second.* 1816.
—— and MCARTHUR, JOHN *The Life of Admiral Lord Nelson, K.B.* 1809.
CLONCURRY, V., LORD *Personal Recollections.* Dublin 1849.
COLBY, R. *The Waterloo Despatch.* 1965.
COLCHESTER, LORD (ed.) *Diary and Correspondence of Charles Abbot, Lord Colchester.* 3 vols. 1861.
COLE, H. *Beau Brummell.* St Albans. 1977.
COLLEY, L. 'The Apotheosis of George III: Loyalty, Royalty and the British Nation 1760–1820'. *Past and Present* 102, 1984, 94–129.
—— *Britons: Forging the Nation, 1707–1837.* New Haven and London 1992.
COLLINS, LYDIA 'George Seymour Crole – A Son of King George IV' in *Genealogists' Magazine.* xxi, no. 7, Sept. 1984.
COOKSON, J.E. *Lord Liverpool's Administration 1815–1822.* Edinburgh and London 1975.
CRABB ROBINSON, HENRY *Diary, Reminiscences and Correspondence of Henry Crabb Robinson.* 2 vols. ed. T. Sadler. 1872.
—— *Correspondence . . . 1808–1866.* ed. E.J. Morley. Oxford 1927.
CREEVEY, T. *The Creevey Papers.* 2 vols. ed. Sir Herbert Maxwell. 1903.
—— *Creevey's Life and Times.* ed. J. Gore. 1934.
CROKER, J.W. *The Correspondence and Diaries of the Late Rt. Hon. John Wilson Croker . . .* 3 vols. ed. L.J. Jennings. 1884.
CROOK, J.M. and PORT, M.H. (eds) *The History of the King's Works.* vol. vi. 1973.
DARVALL, F.O. *Popular Disturbances and Public Order in Regency England.* 1934.
DAVY, J. (ed.) *Fragmentary Remains . . . of Sir Humphry Davy.* 1858.

DELVES BROUGHTON, V. *Court and Private Life in the Time of Queen Charlotte, being the Journals of Mrs Papendiek.* 2 vols. 1887.
DERRY, J. *The Regency Crisis and the Whigs, 1788–9.* Cambridge 1963.
'THE DRUID' *The Post and the Paddock.* rev. ed. 1880.
EDGCUMBE, R. (ed.) *Diary of Lady Frances Shelley.* 2 vols. 1912–13.
EDGEWORTH, MARIA *Chosen Letters.* 1931.
—— *Letters of Maria Edgeworth and Anna Letitia Barbauld.* ed. W.S. Scott. 1953.
—— *Letters from England 1813–1844.* ed. C. Colvin. Oxford 1971.
EHRMAN, J. *The Younger Pitt.* 3 vols. 1969–96.
ELLENBOROUGH, EDWARD, LORD, *A Political Diary 1828–1830.* ed. Lord Colchester. 2 vols. 1881.
ELLIOT, SIR G. *Life and Letters of Sir Gilbert Elliot.* 3 vols. ed. Countess of Minto. 1874.
FARINGTON, J. *The Farington Diary.* 8 vols. ed. J. Greig. 1922–6.
FOSTER, VERE *The Two Duchesses.* 1898.
FOX, C.J. *Memorials & Correspondence of C.J. Fox.* 4 vols. ed. Lord John Russell. 1853.
FRASER, FLORA *The Unruly Queen.* 1996.
FULFORD, R. *George the Fourth.* rev. edn. 1949.
—— *The Trial of Queen Caroline.* 1967.
FYFE, J.G. (ed.) *Scottish Diaries and Memoirs, 1746–1843.* 1942.
GARLICK, K. *Sir Thomas Lawrence.* 1954.
GASH, N. *Aristocracy and People.* 1979.
—— *Lord Liverpool.* 1984.
GIROUARD, M. *The Return to Camelot.* New Haven and London 1981.
GLOVER, M. *A Very Slippery Fellow: The Life of Sir Robert Wilson 1777–1849.* Oxford 1978.
GOLDRING, D. *Regency Portrait Painter. The Life of Sir Thomas Lawrence, P.R.A.* 1951.
GORE, J. *Creevy.* 1948.
GRANVILLE, HARRIET, COUNTESS (ed.) *Letters of Harriet, Countess Granville, 1810–1845.* 2 vols. ed. F. Leveson Gower. 1894.
—— *Private Correspondence of Granville Leveson-Gower.* 2 vols. 1916.
GREGO, J. (ed.) *Reminiscences and Recollections of Captain Gronow, 1810–1860.* 2 vols. 1890.
GRENVILLE, CHARLOTTE *Correspondence of Charlotte Grenville, Lady Williams Wynn.* ed. R. Leighton. 1920.
GREVILLE, C.C.F. *A Journal of the Reigns of King George IV and King William IV.* ed. H. Reeve. 1874. vols 1 and 2.
—— *The Greville Diary.* 2 vols. ed. P.W. Wilson. 1927.
GREVILLE, H. *Leaves from the Diary of Henry Greville.* ed. Viscountess Enfield. 1883.
GROSVENOR, C. and LORD STUART OF WORTLEY (eds) *The First Lady Wharncliffe and Her Family (1779–1856).* 2 vols. 1927.
HAMILTON, LADY ANNE *The Secret History of the Court of England from the Accession of George the Third to the Death of George the Fourth . . .* 2 vols. 1830.
HARCOURT, L.V. (ed.) *Diaries and Correspondence of George Rose.* 2 vols. 1860.

HARRIS, J., FIRST EARL OF MALMESBURY *Diaries and Correspondence.* 4 vols. ed by the 3rd Earl. 1844.
HARVEY, A.D. *Britain in the Early Nineteenth Century.* 1978.
HAYTER, J. *A Report upon the Herculaneum MSS* . . . 1811.
HIBBERT, C. *The Court at Windsor.* 1964.
—— *George IV Prince of Wales.* 1972.
—— *George IV Regent and King.* 1973.
HILLES, F.W. (ed.) *Letters of Sir Joshua Reynolds.* Cambridge 1929.
HINDE, W. *George Canning.* 1973.
—— *Castlereagh.* 1981.
HISTORICAL MSS COMMISSION *Fortescue MSS.* 10 vols. 1892–1927.
—— *Carlisle MSS.* 1897.
HODGE, JANE AIKEN *Passion & Principle: the Loves and Lives of Regency Women.* 1996.
HOLLAND, HENRY RICHARD, LORD *Memoirs of the Whig Party during My Time.* 2 vols. 1852–4.
—— *Further Memoirs of the Whig Party, 1807–21.* ed. Lord Stavordale. 1905.
HOLLAND, ELIZABETH, LADY *Journal (1791–1811).* ed. Earl of Ilchester. 1908.
HUGHES, E. (ed.) *The Diary of James Losh.* Surtees Society. vols 171, 174. 1956, 1959.
HUISH, R. *Memoirs of George IV.* 2 vols. 1831.
ILCHESTER, COUNTESS OF and LORD STAVORDALE (eds) *Life and Letters of Lady Sarah Lennox, 1745–1826.* 2 vols. 1902.
INGAMELLS, J. *Mrs Robinson and her Portraits.* 1978.
INGPEN, R. (ed.) *Letters of Percy Bysshe Shelley.* 1914.
JENKINS, ROY *Gladstone.* 1995.
JUPP, P. *Lord Grenville, 1759–1834.* Oxford 1985.
KNIGHTON, LADY (ed.) *Memoirs of Sir William Knighton.* 2 vols. 1838.
LANGDALE, G. *Memoirs of Mrs Fitzherbert.* 1856.
LAYARD, G.S. *Sir Thomas Lawrence's Letter-bag.* 1906.
LEES-MILNE, J. *The Bachelor Duke.* 1991.
LE MARCHANT, D. *Memoir of John Charles Viscount Althorp* . . . 1876.
LESLIE, ANITA *Mrs Fitzherbert.* 1960.
LESLIE, SHANE *George the Fourth.* 1926.
—— 'The Truth about Mrs Fitzherbert', *Everybody's Weekly.* 1 July 1950.
L'ESTRANGE, A.G. *The Life of Mary Russell Mitford.* 2 vols. 1870.
LEVER, T. (ed.) *The Letters of Lady Palmerston.* 1957.
LIEVEN, D. *Letters of Dorothea, Princess Lieven, during her Residence in London, 1812–1834.* ed. L.G. Robinson. 1902.
LINDSTRUM, D. *Sir Jeffry Wyatville.* Oxford 1973.
LLOYD, C. *The Queen's Pictures.* 1991.
LLOYD, H.E. *George IV, Memoirs of his Life and Reign.* 1830.
LOCKHART, J.G. *Memoirs of the Life of Sir Walter Scott.* 7 vols (Edinburgh 1837–8) or 5 vols (Edinburgh 1900).
MACALPINE, IDA and HUNTER, RICHARD *George III and the Mad Business.* 1969.
MARSHALL, A. CALDER *The Two Duchesses.* 1978.

MELVILLE, L. *The Beaux of the Regency.* 1908.

MILLAR, O. *Pictures in the Collection of HM the Queen: Tudor, Stuart and Early Georgian.* Oxford 1963.

—— *Later Georgian.* Oxford 1969.

MITCHELL, L.G. *Charles James Fox.* Oxford 1992.

MOORE, T. *Memoirs of the Life of Sheridan.* 2 vols. 1825.

MORSHEAD, O. *Windsor Castle.* 1951.

—— *George IV and the Royal Lodge.* 1965.

MUDIE, R. *Historical Account of HM's Visit to Scotland.* Edinburgh 1822.

MUIR, R.J.B. *Britain and the Defeat of Napoleon, 1807–15.* New Haven and London 1996.

MUIR, R.J.B. and ESDAILE, C.J. 'Strategic Planning in a Time of Small Government: the Wars against Revolutionary and Napoleonic France, 1793–1815'. *Wellington Studies* I, Southampton 1996.

MUNDY, H.G. (ed.) *The Journal of Mary Frampton.* 1886.

MUNK, WILLIAM *Life of Sir Henry Halford.* 1895.

MUSGRAVE, C. *The Royal Pavilion.* rev. edn. 1959.

NAMIER, L.B. *Crossroads of Power.* 1962.

NAYLER, SIR GEORGE *The Coronation of . . . George IV.* 1824.

NEW, C. *Life of Henry Brougham to 1830.* Oxford 1961.

NICOLSON, A. *Restoration. The Rebuilding of Windsor Castle.* 1997.

O'GORMAN, F. *The Whig Party and the French Revolution.* 1967.

OLIVER, J.W. *Life of William Beckford.* 1932.

PARES, R. *King George III and the Politicians.* Oxford 1953.

PARKER, C.S. *Sir Robert Peel.* 3 vols. 1891.

PATTERSON, M.W. *Sir Francis Burdett and his Times (1770–1844).* 2 vols. 1931.

PELLEW, G. *The Life and Correspondence of . . . Viscount Sidmouth.* 3 vols. 1847.

PENROSE, A.P.D. (ed.) *Autobiography and Memoirs of B.R. Haydon, 1786–1846.* 1927.

PHIPPS, E. *Memoirs of . . . Robert Plumer Ward.* 2 vols. 1850.

PLOWDEN, A. *Caroline and Charlotte.* 1989.

PLUMB, J.H. *The First Four Georges.* 1956.

POWELL, A. (ed.) *Barnard Letters, 1778–1824.* 1928.

PREBBLE, J. *The King's Jaunt.* 1988.

PRICE, C. (ed.) *The Letters of Richard Brinsley Sheridan.* 3 vols. Oxford 1966.

PRIESTLEY, J.B. *The Prince of Pleasure.* 1969.

PÜCKLER-MUSKAU, PRINCE *Tours in England, Ireland and France in the Years 1826, 1827 & 1828.* 1832.

QUENNELL, P. (ed.) *The Private Letters of Princess Lieven to Prince Metternich 1820–1826.* 1937.

RAE, W.F. *Sheridan.* 2 vols. 1896.

RAIKES, T. *A Portion of the Journal kept by Thomas Raikes Esq from 1831 to 1847.* 4 vols. 1856–7.

READ, D. *Peterloo.* Manchester 1958.

REED, M. *The Georgian Triumph, 1700–1830.* 1983.

REID, S.J. (ed.) *Life and Letters of the 1st Earl of Durham, 1792–1840.* 2 vols. 1906.

RICHARDSON, JOANNA *George IV, a Portrait.* 1966.

ROBBINS LANDON, H.C. (ed.) *The Collected Correspondence and London Notebooks of Joseph Haydn.* 1959.
ROBERTS, H.D. *A History of the Royal Pavilion, Brighton.* 1939.
ROBERTS, M. *The Whig Party 1807–12.* 1939.
ROHL, J.C.G., WARREN, M. and HUNT, D. *Purple Secret: Genes, 'Madness' and the Royal Houses of Europe.* 1998.
ROMILLY, S. *Memoirs of the Life of Sir Samuel Romilly.* 3 vols. ed. by his sons. 1840.
ROMILLY, S.H. *Letters to 'Ivy' from the First Earl of Dudley.* 1905.
ROSE, J. HOLLAND *Life of Napoleon.* 2 vols. 1934.
RUSH, RICHARD *A Residence at the Court of London.* 2nd. ser., 1845.
RUSSELL, LORD JOHN (ed.) *Memoirs, Journal and Correspondence of Thomas Moore.* 8 vols. 1853–6.
SCOTT, SIR WALTER *The Letters of Sir Walter Scott, 1787–1832.* 12 vols. ed. H.J.C. Grierson. 1932–7.
SERGEANT, P.W. *George, Prince and Regent.* 1935.
SICHEL, W. *Sheridan.* 2 vols. 1909.
SMILES, S. *A Publisher and his Friends. Memoir and Correspondence of John Murray.* 1911.
SMITH, E.A. *Whig Principles and Party Politics: Earl Fitzwilliam and the Whig Party 1748–1833.* Manchester 1975.
—— *Lord Grey, 1764–1845.* Oxford 1990.
—— *The House of Lords in British Politics and Society, 1815–1917.* 1992.
—— *A Queen on Trial.* Stroud 1993.
—— *Wellington and the Arbuthnots.* Stroud 1994.
STANHOPE, LORD *Life of William Pitt.* 4 vols. 1861–2.
STAPLETON, A.G. *Political Life of George Canning.* 2 vols. 1831.
—— *George Canning and his Times.* 1859.
STEVENSON, J. *Popular Disturbances in England, 1700–1870.* 1979.
—— 'The Queen Caroline Affair', in J. Stevenson (ed.), *London in the Age of Reform.* Oxford 1977. pp. 117–48.
STIRLING, A.M.W. *Annals of a Yorkshire House.* 2 vols. n.d.
—— *Letterbag of Lady Elizabeth Spencer-Stanhope, 1806–73.* 2 vols. 1913.
STODDARD, R.H. (ed.) *Personal Reminiscences by Cornelia Knight and Thomas Raikes.* New York 1875.
STONE, L. *The Family, Sex and Marriage in England, 1500–1800.* 1977.
STROUD, DOROTHY *Henry Holland.* 1950.
STUART, D.M. *The Daughters of George III.* 1939.
—— *Portrait of the Prince Regent.* 1953.
SUDLEY, LORD (ed.) *The Lieven–Palmerston Correspondence, 1828–1856.* 1943.
SUMMERSON, J. *Georgian London.* rev. edn. 1988.
—— *Life and Work of John Nash.* 1980.
TANNAHILL, R. *Regency England.* 1964.
TAYLOR, E. *The Taylor Papers.* 1913.
TEMPERLEY, H.W.V. 'Canning, Wellington and George IV'. *EHR.* 38, 1923.
—— *The Unpublished Diary . . . of Princess Lieven.* 1925.
—— *The Foreign Policy of Canning, 1822–27.* new edn. 1966.
THACKERAY, W.M. *The Four Georges.* 1855.
THOMPSON, N. *Wellington after Waterloo.* 1986.

THORNE, R.G. *The House of Commons, 1970–1820.* vol i. History of Parliament Trust. 1986.
TOMALIN, CLAIRE *Mrs Jordan's Profession.* 1994.
TWISS, H. *Life of Lord Eldon.* 3 vols. 1844.
VILLIERS, MARJORIE *The Grand Whiggery.* 1939.
WALPOLE, HORACE *Letters of Horace Walpole.* 16 vols. ed. P. Toynbee. 1903–5.
—— *Letters of Horace Walpole.* 9 vols. ed. P. Cunningham. 1906.
—— *Last Journals of Horace Walpole.* 2 vols. ed. A.F. Stewart. 1910.
WEBSTER, C. *The Foreign Policy of Castlereagh, 1815–1822.* 1925.
WELLESLEY, MARQUESS OF *The Wellesley Papers,* by the editor of *The Windham Papers.* 2 vols. 1914.
WELLINGTON, DUKE OF (ed.) *Despatches, Correspondence and Memoranda of . . . the Duke of Wellington 1819–32.* 8 vols. 1867–80.
WILKINS, W.M. *Mrs Fitzherbert and George IV.* 2 vols. 1905.
WILSON, HARRIETTE *Memoirs.* 4 vols. 1825.
WRAXALL, N.M. *Historical Memoirs of My Time, 1772–1784.* ed. R. Askham. 5 vols. 1904.
WRIGHT, A. and SMITH, P. *Parliament Past and Present.* 1902.
WYNDHAM, MRS HUGH (ed.) *Correspondence of Sarah Spencer, Lady Lyttelton 1787–1870.* 1912.
YONGE, C.D. *Life and Administration of . . . 2nd Earl of Liverpool.* 3 vols. 1868.
ZIEGLER, P. *Addington.* 1965.

INDEX